S0-AKB-419

China Under Mao

CHINA UNDER MAO

A Revolution Derailed

ANDREW G. WALDER

Harvard University Press

Cambridge, Massachusetts
London, England

Copyright © 2015 by the President and Fellows of Harvard College
All rights reserved
Printed in the United States of America

First Harvard University Press paperback edition, 2017
First Printing

Library of Congress Cataloging-in-Publication Data
is available from the Library of Congress

ISBN: 978-0-674-05815-6 (cloth : alk. paper)
ISBN: 978-0-674-97549-1 (pbk.)

To the memory of Richard M. Pfeffer (1937–2002)

Contents

Illustrations

Preface

The first quarter century of communist rule in China was dramatic and disastrous, the mark of a political regime whose extremism created a distinctive epoch in the history of revolution. The period bore the unmistakable imprint of Mao Zedong, who dominated his era as thoroughly as any leader in modern history. Recent publications, drawing on new sources, have clarified the shifting relationships and disagreements among China's leaders—with Mao firmly at the center—as they came to decisions that frequently proved disastrous for the Chinese people. I draw on this scholarship, but I focus on the consequences of a prior set of decisions made by these leaders, ones that were not reconsidered in the course of the Mao era. These decisions created the organization through which China's revolutionary leaders sought to enforce discipline among their subordinates and ensure that their directives were carried out. These decisions created a structure that served as the core of a new revolutionary state.

Two organizations were vitally important: the first was a Communist Party apparatus that exercised firm and at times harsh discipline over members and especially leaders—or "cadres." The second was a design for a socialist economy that was borrowed from the Soviet Union, which created problems in the many countries that adopted it. China's leaders, and especially Mao, issued directives from Beijing that reverberated through these political and economic structures, leading both to startling accomplishments that were intended, and to disastrous outcomes that were neither anticipated nor desired. This work is motivated by the conviction that to understand why leaders' decisions—especially Mao's initiatives—had the effect that they had, it is essential to understand the way that China's social structure, economy, and political system were transformed in the 1950s. These structures frustrated the designs of Mao and other leaders, leading to the dramatic and frequently disastrous outcomes of the Mao era. Although much of this book unfolds as a narrative, it is fundamentally driven by sociological concerns.

During this period, leaders' decisions were translated into action through a certain kind of political organization, in a society and economy organized in a distinctive way. Orders from the top reverberated through a large national bureaucracy and a new social structure, and in the process their intended impacts were diverted, distorted, or magnified in unanticipated ways. The centralized and disciplined nature of the party-state, which lent it such seeming strength, also bred peculiar vulnerabilities. Almost none of Mao's initiatives led to outcomes that he and his supporters fully anticipated, foresaw, or welcomed. In fact, as we shall see, most of Mao's initiatives backfired. Why?

This was a society that was organized in an unusual way, distinctive in comparison with our own, but also, by the end of the first decade of communist rule, quite distinctive compared with China's past. To understand why so many Chinese citizens participated so actively in the campaigns and conflicts of this era, we need to understand the social and organizational milieu in which people—officials and ordinary citizens alike—lived and worked. This is especially important today, after so much of that milieu has receded under the tidal force of a dynamic market economy integrated into global capitalism. My aim is to show that the events of the Mao era were an expression of distinctive institutions established during the first decade of Communist Party rule. I tell the story of the Mao era with these institutions firmly in mind.

When I took my first course on contemporary China as a college junior at Johns Hopkins in 1973, the subject matter of this book was still quite obscure, a topic for speculation about very recent events in an insular and isolated regime. When I taught my first course on this subject as a faculty member at Columbia University in 1983, I presented the material as "postrevolution Chinese society"—the new society created after the revolution of 1949 that brought the Communist Party to power. Today, after more than three decades of post-Mao history, much of the social and economic organization of that era has vanished under waves of economic reform—though much of the political organization survives.

With the benefit of hindsight, it is clear that 1949 was actually the beginning, not the end, of the Chinese revolution. The Mao era was just as surely one of revolution as the period of guerrilla insurgency and civil war that preceded it, and which served only as a prelude.

This account of Mao's China distills a perspective that has evolved over more than three decades of research and teaching. It tells the story of the period as a selective narrative, from the perspective of a sociologist deeply interested in politics and the economy—in particular, the foundations of political authority, the socialist model of development, social inequality, political conflict, and popular protest. There surely are other compelling ways to tell the story of Mao's China, but they are not my own.

My past publications about China have been for specialized academic audiences. Writings in this vein emphasize the author's conceptual framework, and new and original sources of evidence and modes of analysis, and are organized around the critical evaluation of alternative accounts. That approach unfortunately makes such work unnecessarily tedious for those outside a small community of specialists. This book draws deeply on my own research and many years of reading the work of talented colleagues, but it is not intended primarily for the specialist. Here I try to synthesize what I have learned about this phase of Chinese history in a way that speaks directly to my academic colleagues and students, while remaining accessible and clear to others.

My debts are many, both intellectual and institutional. My intellectual debts are too many to enumerate here, especially on subjects outside my own areas of research, where I have had to rely heavily on the research and writings of colleagues. I have tried to make clear in the citations to others' works where the primary debts lay; repeated citations to the same authors indicate to whom I owe my greatest debts. I am grateful to Thomas Bernstein, Jean Oi, Dwight Perkins, and Michael Schoenhals for their comments on all or part of the original draft of this book. I should also acknowledge my collaborator and coauthor, Professor Dong Guoqiang of Nanjing University's Department of History. In several of the chapters dealing with the Cultural Revolution, I draw on our coauthored publications. Nancy Hearst, at Harvard's Fairbank Center Library, helped prepare the final manuscript for the publisher. Stanford University has provided me with an ideal intellectual home for almost two decades. I would like particularly to acknowledge the generous research support provided by Stanford's Freeman-Spogli Institute for International Studies, the School of Humanities and Sciences, and the Shorenstein Asia-Pacific Research Center. The Stanford Center at Peking University provided support for the final stages of research and writing, and an inspiring physical setting where most of these chapters were drafted. I would also like to thank my editor at Harvard University Press, Michael Aronson, for his support and encouragement of a project that is so different from others that I have undertaken.

This book is the culmination of a journey that began in a Baltimore classroom in September 1973, in the course Government and Politics of China, taught by my undergraduate advisor, Richard M. Pfeffer. Ric was a committed antiwar activist and China specialist who had recently visited the People's Republic in one of the first American delegations. The unfolding Cultural Revolution fascinated him, yet he understood all too well the abuse of authority in disciplined revolutionary organizations, and the seemingly intractable problem of bureaucratic dictatorship under socialism. Ric was a passionate and demanding teacher who relentlessly forced students to examine critically all ideas, especially their own. He did this through seemingly limitless attention to student essays, ruthlessly exposing lazy rhetorical evasions and logical gaps with copious and searing marginal comments. He was also a supportive and nurturing advisor, especially after you started to get the point. My college courses did not engage me very deeply before that semester, but afterward things snapped into focus. Ric's teaching altered my life's trajectory. This was a gift that I can never hope to repay, but I dedicate this book to his memory.

China Under Mao

1

Funeral

A T 3 P.M. on September 18, 1976, Beijing's vast Tiananmen Square was filled with rows of uniformed workers and soldiers, standing silently with heads bowed. Across this nation of almost one billion people, in public squares, villages, factories, schools, and offices, Chinese citizens assembled as part of a nationwide memorial meeting for Mao Zedong, who had died nine days earlier at the age of eighty-two. All were instructed to stand in place, heads bowed, for three minutes of silence. Mao's designated successor, the relatively unknown Hua Guofeng, read a speech filled with extravagant praise for the deceased Chairman, who had led the Chinese Communist Party since the early 1930s and had thoroughly dominated the People's Republic since its establishment in 1949. The entire party leadership lined up in a solemn show of unity.

The illusion of unity was shattered on October 6, when Hua Guofeng moved against Mao's radical followers. Conspiring with other senior officials, Hua ordered his security detail to arrest Mao's key political allies. Mao's wife, Jiang Qing, was arrested in her living quarters. Three others—Wang Hongwen, Zhang Chunqiao, and Yao Wenyuan—were summoned to a leadership meeting. As they arrived, one by one, the stunned officials were taken into custody by armed guards. These individuals had done Mao's bidding during his Cultural Revolution—an assault on the party-state that crippled China's government and economy and caused the death and suffering of millions. At the time of their arrest, they represented one-quarter of China's sixteen-member Politburo, the party's top decision-making body. Wang Hongwen and Zhang Chunqiao were members of the select Politburo Standing Committee, ranked second and fourth, respectively. Soon they were reviled as a Gang of Four,

charged with counterrevolutionary subversion. In reality, their crime was
to have done Mao's bidding in the last decade of his life. Still a symbol
of the revolution's legitimacy, Mao was praised in death, but this was a
coup against the most distinctive elements of his political legacy. The unnamed ringleader of the Gang of Four was Mao himself.

Twenty-seven years before, on October 1, 1949, the fifty-five-year-old
Mao Zedong, addressing a massive assembly at the same spot, declared
the establishment of the People's Republic of China. This promised the
end of a century of economic and political decline, colonial intrusion,
foreign invasion, and civil war. For most of the previous half-century,
China was a failed state; the wreckage of an early attempt to establish a
constitutional republic.[1] For most of the half-century before that, it was
a failing multinational empire. The last imperial dynasty (the Qing, or
Manchu), established in 1644, reached its zenith in the eighteenth century, but was in deep decline in the late nineteenth century, suffering
from widespread internal rebellion and the incursions of colonial powers.[2]
The enduring historical significance of 1949 was not the triumph of the
proletariat over the bourgeoisie, nor was it the victory of communism
over capitalism. Mao's declaration of the People's Republic promised a
new, more powerful Chinese state that could withstand global political
competition and prevent the encroachment of other world powers.

    For the first time in well over a century, there would be a Chinese
state that effectively controlled its territory within secure borders, and
that was able to stamp out pockets of domestic rebellion. For the first
time in China's long history, salaried state officials, not local notables,
would administer Chinese society in rural villages and urban neighborhoods. These officials were part of a national hierarchy that connected
the apex of power in Beijing directly, and relatively effectively, with life
at the grass roots. Mao and his comrades may have viewed the victory
of the Communist Party in 1949 as part of the triumph of world socialism,
but it marked the birth of China's first modern national state.

    The past century had been brutal. The vast Taiping Rebellion of 1850
to 1864 engulfed much of the southeastern quadrant of the Qing empire for over a decade, and the epic battles that accompanied the rise and
fall of the Heavenly Kingdom of the Taiping resulted in the deaths of
more than 20 million.[3] The weakened Qing state fought against an array
of local rebellions, while at the same time losing a series of wars against
colonial powers. The antiforeign Boxer Uprising of 1900, encouraged by

the Qing court, was crushed by an alliance of foreign armies, and the empire never recovered.[4] The "revolution" of 1911 was a relatively uneventful collapse that marked the end of what had become a nearly moribund regime.[5]

The effort to establish a modern Chinese republic quickly failed. National parliamentary elections yielded a victory for the new Nationalist Party. Song Jiaoren, the party's founder and architect of its electoral victory, was assassinated shortly afterward by agents of Yuan Shikai, a former Qing official who aspired to establish his own dictatorship.[6] China quickly disintegrated into a collection of regional fiefdoms ruled by rival military overlords.[7] In the 1920s two militant revolutionary parties sought to unify the country by armed force: the Nationalist Party, led by Sun Yatsen and later by Chiang Kai-shek, and the Communist Party, eventually taken over by the Hunan radical and guerrilla commander Mao Zedong. For a brief period in the mid-1920s the two movements joined forces and enjoyed some success, but the Communist Party's commitment to social revolution repelled the propertied elites who were a core element of the nationalist movement, and the alliance split apart violently in 1927. Chiang Kai-shek purged Communists from the coalition, executing thousands in a lightning strike.[8]

The bloody struggle between these two revolutionary parties was waged for more than a decade, with the Communists driven to the edge of extinction in the mid-1930s. Then fate intervened in the form of an aggressive and militaristic imperial Japan, which initially conquered the entire northeastern region known as Manchuria (the present-day provinces of Liaoning, Jilin, and Heilongjiang) in 1931, and then in 1937 turned its attention to a massive military invasion of the Chinese homeland. The invasion and occupation crushed the Nationalist state established only a decade before, devastating the country and killing an estimated 12 million.[9]

The sudden surrender of Japanese forces in the wake of the American nuclear attacks on Hiroshima and Nagasaki in August 1945 led, after a brief respite, to the resumption of full-scale civil war. The Nationalists, who had survived the invasion in their southwestern wartime capital of Chongqing (Chungking), resumed the fight against the greatly revived Communists, who had steadily built their forces throughout northern China in a low-grade resistance movement against Japanese occupation that deliberately avoided direct combat. After a strong beginning, the civil war went badly for the Nationalists, who rapidly disintegrated as a political force after suffering a series of crucial battle-field losses in Manchuria. By the time Mao stood at Tiananmen to an-nounce the founding of the People's Republic, most of the remaining Nationalist assets had already been evacuated to the island province of Taiwan, and Mao's huge People's Liberation Army was in the final stages of conquering China's southern and western provinces.

China's citizens undoubtedly hoped that 1949 would bring an end to the devastation of the first half of the twentieth century and usher in a new era of national unity, peace, and economic progress. These hopes would soon be dashed. The era of revolution was not over; in fact it had just begun. It would bring devastation on a scale that neither Mao nor his colleagues in the leadership of the Chinese Communist Party could possibly have anticipated.

The two most famous instances of the devastation that defined Mao's legacy were the Great Leap Forward of 1958–1960 and the Great Prole-tarian Cultural Revolution, now the official name for the entire decade from 1966 to 1976, whose destructive force was felt most acutely during its first four years. The Great Leap Forward was a massive campaign to mobilize the entire population to work harder for longer hours, break production records, and catch up with the world's economic powers in a few short years. It showed off the remarkable reach of the new party-state, an organizational feat that would have been unthinkable only a decade before and that few governments could have contemplated. The result, to the surprise and dismay of the campaign's initiators, was un-imaginable disaster: a massive, man-made famine that led to the deaths of close to 30 million people, and a deep industrial depression that lasted until the mid-1960s.

The economic and demographic disaster of the Great Leap was soon followed by the political disaster of the Cultural Revolution. Mao mobi-lized student Red Guards against party officials in 1966, and after some hesitation eventually permitted workers to join in escalating attacks against local and regional party officials, who were left largely defense-less against the onslaught. By January 1967, the civilian structure of na-tional government virtually collapsed in most of the country, and it was slowly, fitfully, and violently rebuilt over the next two years. In the in-tervening period, rival rebel factions fought for power in complicated al-liances and conflicts with military units that were ordered to intervene. Many regions of China were in a state resembling civil war, with no func-tioning civilian government. Calls for warring rebels to unite under the victorious banner of Chairman Mao went unheeded, and this phase of the Cultural Revolution was ended only through the draconian application of military force.

With most of China effectively under martial law by the summer of 1968, many citizens may have hoped for a respite from strife. Unfortunately, however, military authorities and their civilian partners embarked on an escalating campaign of terror against imagined class enemies and political conspirators that unambiguously reestablished government authority, but led to the interrogation and torture of millions. The carnage ended only after the mysterious death of party vice chairman Lin Biao, the head of China's armed forces and Mao's designated successor, in September 1971. After the withdrawal of the army from civil administration, China entered an uncertain period when the former combatants of the late 1960s resumed a factional rivalry that periodically unleashed local unrest. The strife lasted until 1976, with massive protests against Mao's legacy in Beijing and other cities in April, six months before the aging dictator's death.

This was the history that hung heavily over the solemn assembly at Tiananmen Square in September 1976. Among the leaders on the rostrum were those who had supported Mao in his Cultural Revolution, attacked their colleagues with zeal, and who sought to keep China on the path of Maoist revolution, denigrating those who placed production and living standards above revolutionary principles. Also on the rostrum were those who had somehow managed to survive the tumult relatively unscathed, and others who had lost their posts, suffered humiliation and even the deaths of spouses and relatives, surviving imprisonment and banishment before being recalled to the capital in the 1970s to begin the task of rebuilding. Mao's final plans for the survival and preservation of his legacy were about to unravel in a dramatic and surprising turn only a few years after his death. This was the ultimate failure of a leader who had managed to seize one defeat after another from the jaws of an astonishing victory, consigning China to two decades of destruction and pointless conflict. Mao's destructive impulses left a China in disarray, essentially forcing his successors to start over again. Over the next three decades, they would take China in surprising new directions.

This book aims to make sense of these events and other dramatic developments of the period. Recent scholarship on Mao and his era has brought into clear focus the conflicts and motives of actors at the top of the political system, as well as the consequences of these leadership decisions for Chinese society. I draw on these works, but my account shifts attention from the question of what happened to the question of why. At the center of the narrative is Mao Zedong—what he wanted to accomplish, how he hoped to do so, and what ideas and commitments motivated his actions. The core theme is that the results of his initiatives were often unintended, unanticipated, and unwanted, not only by the broad population and the party leadership, but by Mao himself. To understand why, we need to understand the revolutionary organization that conquered the Chinese mainland by military force in 1948–1949, and the legacies of its long struggle for power. We need to understand the reconstruction of state and society in the 1950s. We need to understand how the party was organized, and how it recruited, rewarded, and disciplined its members. We need to understand the flaws inherent in the economic system imported from the Soviet Union, a system that China's leaders, especially Mao, saw as the key to China's rapid industrialization. These two organizations—the party system and Soviet command economy— were at the very core of the struggles and conflicts of the Mao era. They were the focus of Mao's dissatisfactions, and their features repeatedly frustrated his aims. The Mao that emerges from this history is in many ways an irresponsible and blundering figure, gripped by a rigid and anachronistic revolutionary ideology. Mao's personal failings, however, do not take us very far toward explaining why matters turned out the way that they did. My account begins with Mao's interventions, and follows their consequences as they coursed through the regime that he created, and ultimately throughout Chinese society.

The next five chapters of this book set the stage for the dramatic series of events that follow. They explain how China was reshaped in the decade after 1947 into a powerful and cohesive new nation-state, one with peculiar features and striking vulnerabilities. Chapter 2 is an account of the Communist Party's long road to power and the legacy of this struggle for subsequent developments. It underplays the legacy of guerrilla communism and the anti-Japanese war, so central to the founding myth of the People's Republic. The wartime base area of Yan'an was where the intense Stalinization of the Chinese party began, and where Mao absorbed the central tenets of Stalin-era communism, especially the doctrine of class struggle under socialism, long misunderstood as Mao's singular innovation. In Yan'an, the party perfected its techniques for enforcing draconian demands on its members for loyalty and conformity, and for punishing those who fell short. This would be a source of both great strength and destructive excess in future years. Long after the strategy of guerrilla war was abandoned, the massive mobilization of civilian populations to support conventional armed forces for civil war in the late 1940s was a decisive influence over the regime founded in the 1950s.

The 1950s were a period of regime building, but they were also an era of social revolution. Chapters 3 and 4 sketch the revolution's main outlines, respectively, in the countryside and cities. A system of land tenure that had existed for centuries, and much of the social structure that was built on it, was wiped out in a few short years. Landlordism and tenant farming disappeared, and the rural elites that derived power from it were eliminated. China quickly became a nation of small independent farmers. Yet within a few years the land would be taken back and farmers would be absorbed into collective farms. Urban life was similarly transformed. Shopkeepers, merchants, and wealthy capitalists who had not fled the mainland had their holdings steadily expropriated, as their firms were consolidated into government-managed collectives or nationalized as state enterprises. Urban and rural populations were registered, labeled, and tied to local communities. The organized crime and armed gangs that had plagued urban and rural China were effectively wiped out, as were the drug and sex trades and criminal protection rackets. Urban and rural society attained a new level of stability and order. In the process, the Communist Party was building a new and effective national state, and was using it to eliminate the sources of inequity and insecurity that had long plagued ordinary Chinese citizens.

As the 1950s progressed, this new national order assumed a strong Soviet flavor. Chapter 5 describes the way that China rapidly installed a version of the state socialist growth machine developed after the 1920s in Stalin's Soviet Union. In retrospect, this was an ill-fated choice, because that model of development was deeply flawed and eventually failed everywhere it was installed. But in the early 1950s this was still far from evident. The model generated rapid industrial growth in the Soviet Union, helping it to defeat Nazi Germany, and it sustained a postwar growth spurt that augmented the USSR's military might and threatened the Western powers. In the first half of the 1950s, China implemented the model with a vengeance. This was a model that dictated high rates of savings and investment, which by design ensured that consumption and living standards would not rise far above subsistence guarantees for the foreseeable future. Rationing, shortages, and substandard housing and public infrastructure prevailed in China through the end of the Mao era.

While all of these changes were fundamental, the most important change in the 1950s was the extension of the Communist Party's reach into every dimension of the country's government, social institutions, and enterprises. This trend, described in Chapter 6, is widely acknowledged but not well understood. The party did not seek to control everything. It focused its attention on organizations where key government functions were performed, where major decisions about resource allocation were made, and where China's future elite would be trained. The party organization quickly developed the capacity to allocate resources and career opportunities. This dramatically altered the incentives for individuals to join the party, inevitably changing the meaning of party membership and the motives of the people who entered into its service. Before the party's victory seemed secure, the decision to join was one that entailed considerable sacrifice, personal risk, and even danger. In the 1950s this changed completely. Party membership became a credential that boosted one's career opportunities and even the chance to receive a higher education. Party membership, especially in early adulthood, greatly multiplied the odds of attaining a position of power and privilege, and this position, once attained, created the opportunity to extend privileges to one's relatives and descendants. These advantages, however, continued only so long as party members showed unfailing loyalty and obedience.

The disciplined revolutionary organization of the 1940s inevitably evolved into an avenue of personal advancement and a structure of patronage, a trend that bothered some in the national leadership. This eventually became a singular preoccupation of Mao Zedong, perhaps the most important single plank in the Maoist political platform. Strangely, as we shall see, Mao interpreted this trend as a reversion to capitalism rather than the inevitable evolution of a bureaucratic hierarchy with monopoly control over property and career opportunities. With this fatally flawed diagnosis of the disease, Mao prescribed cures that were highly destructive and counterproductive. He flailed unsuccessfully against the problem until the end of his life.

These chapters set the stage for the tumultuous events of the last two decades of Mao's life. What is striking about these chapters is that in almost every instance, Mao's initiatives backfired, creating outcomes that were unintended, unanticipated, and unwanted, and forcing Mao to backtrack, compromise, and change course. These tumultuous two decades begin with Chapter 7, which recounts the reverberations in China of the post-Stalin upheavals in the Soviet bloc, and in particular the impact of Nikita Khrushchev's denunciation of Stalin at the Soviet Party Congress in February 1956. The criticisms stung a number of leaders in the east European satellite states, many of whom had loyally carried out policies that imitated Stalin's own. Mao was strongly associated with these policies, which he had pushed very hard, and he had consciously imitated Stalin, creating a personal cult and a regime that had many of the now-stigmatized features. Mao sought to outflank Khrushchev and initiate liberalization on his own terms. In February 1957, under the slogan "Let a hundred flowers bloom, let a hundred schools of thought contend," he confidently encouraged ordinary citizens to criticize the work of party cadres throughout the country in a campaign to "rectify" the party's behavior and head off the resentments that had undermined new regimes elsewhere in the Eastern bloc. The move backfired. In a few short weeks, initially timid criticisms led to an increasing crescendo of complaints that seemed to repudiate the party's ideology and dictatorial style of rule. Students and faculty established independent journals and clubs and held rallies and gave speeches on campuses. Workers began to agitate for wage concessions and workplace representation, and a wave of work stoppages broke out in the cities. Farmers withdrew from recently established collective farms. Young party members and Communist Youth League activists began to join the crescendo of dissent.

Mao's confident assertion that the party had nothing to fear from open criticism was a major miscalculation. In June he reversed himself and the party struck back, and it did so with a vengeance. The critics were targeted in a massive Antirightist Campaign that framed the critics as antiparty reactionaries and counterrevolutionaries. Those who had uttered virtually any kind of criticism—not just those who had offered harsh denunciations or who had engaged in organized activities—were put through harrowing denunciation meetings and isolated by colleagues and friends before sentence was pronounced. They were fired from their jobs, banished to collective farms, or sent to prison or labor camps.

Selected leaders of student protests and industrial strikes were executed. Also targeted were many thousands of young party members who had responded to Mao's call to criticize and rectify out of a sense of loyalty and idealism. The counterstrike worked and quickly quelled the agitation. This ended the last outpouring of genuinely independent political criticism of party rule until the late 1970s.

Still eager to prove that he could handle the problems of socialism in creative and daring new ways, Mao turned to a massive industrialization drive even before the end of the Antirightist Campaign. In his Great Leap Forward, described in Chapter 8, the party used its extensive new national organization to mobilize workers and farmers in a crash production campaign. Party cadres drove their subjects to work long hours to achieve ludicrously inflated targets for the production of grain, steel, and other products. The result was a fiasco of disorganization, waste, and false reporting by party bureaucrats under extreme political pressures to produce results. As signs of looming economic disaster became unmistakable, the party leadership assembled in July 1959 to decide how to scale back their policies. Mao was already aware of the problems and seemed poised to change course, but he reacted with defensive vindictiveness to a frank letter laying out the Leap's flaws from the minister of defense, Marshal Peng Dehuai. Peng was driven from his post as a traitor and Mao insisted on staying the course, launching instead a second Antirightist Campaign to target anyone who expressed criticisms or doubts. As a result, the Great Leap continued for another year, until hunger haunted even the large cities, and the famine in rural areas had led to death by starvation of tens of millions.

This was the second consecutive defeat for Mao Zedong, but compared to the Hundred Flowers gambit, this was a blunder of epic proportions. The aftermath of the Great Leap, and the political fallout that soon led to the Cultural Revolution, are described in Chapter 9. Mao permitted others to repair the damage to the economy, but he resented the blunt assessment of the Leap's failures by his second in command, Liu Shaoqi. He sensed that many of his colleagues thought little of the core ideas behind the Leap. The Soviet Union was moving in a very different direction. Khrushchev articulated a vision of advanced socialism that emphasized scientific expertise, higher education, bureaucratic planning, peaceful economic development and the raising of living standards, and a relaxation of tensions with the West. Mao saw this as an unprincipled accommodation by Soviet bureaucrats to the imperialist world system, and a reversion to a stable pattern of hierarchical privilege by an elite stratum of educated political insiders. For Mao this amounted—oddly— to a reversion to capitalism. Styling himself as a genuine revolutionary, in contrast to the post-Stalin bureaucrats leading the USSR, Mao initiated ideological polemics that led eventually to the Sino-Soviet split.

In Mao's mind, the perceived ideological wavering of his colleagues and the direction taken by the Soviet Union were intimately connected. Mao turned seventy in 1963 and had reason to be concerned about his political legacy. He had long resented Khrushchev's repudiation of Stalin only three years after his death. Mao surely recognized that even if his colleagues dared not attempt to depose him, they could simply wait until he had passed from the scene. Mao did not trust colleagues like Liu Shaoqi, Zhou Enlai, and Deng Xiaoping to continue his revolutionary legacy. In view of the path taken by Deng Xiaoping in the 1980s, his concerns appear to have been based on accurate perception, not paranoia. Chapter 9 concludes with an account of Mao's preparations for his spectacular assault on the party-state.

Mao could simply have rounded up those he considered insufficiently loyal to his vision, but this was no ordinary leadership purge. It was accompanied by a popular rebellion, initially by students, the topic of Chapter 10. Mao and the mass media openly encouraged the rebellion of college and high school students against "bourgeois" figures on their faculty and the administrators who sheltered them. As students formed Red Guard organizations and engaged in increasingly violent assaults on faculty, school administrators, and eventually government officials, their actions were celebrated in the mass media and in a series of mass rallies on Tiananmen Square during which Mao reviewed his forces. Security and military units were ordered not to interfere. The students, however, repeatedly divided into factions, and many resisted obvious efforts to manipulate and steer the movement, and launched attacks on the officials who did so at Mao's bidding.

These problems led Mao to lose faith in the student rebels, and near the end of 1966 he decided to bring industrial workers into the unfolding campaign. Chapter 11 examines the consequences of this move. Cities throughout China quickly became ungovernable. Some workers took up pay and welfare demands. Others mobilized to defend local authorities against rebel attacks. Factions began to fight one another on the streets.

By the end of 1966, most provincial governments were on the verge of collapse. In the face of this looming paralysis, Mao turned to power seizures by local rebel forces that would unite with loyal Maoist officials to overthrow local party committees and restore order. The model for this was Shanghai's January Revolution, in which a large alliance of rebel workers joined together with the Shanghai propaganda chief Zhang Chunqiao, and with Mao's blessing established a new form of government for China's largest city and proceeded to restore order with the support of the army. Zhang's coup was celebrated by Beijing as a major victory for the masses and Mao's revolutionary line, and it became a blueprint and inspiration for the victorious conclusion of the Cultural Revolution.

The imagined victory failed to materialize. Throughout China, rebel forces that attempted their own power seizures quickly fell into disagreements and split into adamantly opposed factions. The military was ordered to assist, but they either suppressed rebel forces favored by Mao and his colleagues, losing their superiors' confidence, or themselves became embroiled in local factional conflicts. Beijing's equivocations and indecision permitted local warfare to spiral out of control by the summer of 1967, leading to a situation that sometimes resembled civil war.

Mao essentially was forced to resort to martial law. The failed experiment with mass rebellion and power seizures drew to a close in 1968. Chapter 12 chronicles the army's move to enforce order, treating those who continued to resist as counterrevolutionaries and implementing a nationwide crackdown that brooked no opposition. Millions were investigated, imprisoned, and brutally interrogated in a nationwide campaign to stamp out any form of dissent, the "Cleansing of the Class Ranks." College campuses were emptied, and students sent to rural villages for reeducation for indefinite periods; faculty and administrators were dispatched for hard labor in the countryside. Government office workers were sent en masse to rural locations for reeducation through manual labor, or to factory floors as production workers. The Mao cult reached absurd heights, with citizens performing a "loyalty dance" to express their love for the Chairman, and bowing to an altar with Mao's portrait at the beginning of each workday to "ask for instructions."

These campaigns ended after September 1971, leading to an unstable period that is described in Chapter 13. Marshal Lin Biao, who had so publicly championed the Mao cult and was rewarded by promotion to the number two spot in the party hierarchy as Mao's "closest comrade in arms and successor," was dead. The official story, revealed eventually to the Chinese public, was that Lin had died in an airplane crash while fleeing to the Soviet Union after an unsuccessful military coup and attempt to assassinate Mao. The public rationale for the Cultural Revolution, which had justified the unparalleled destruction of the past five years, was in tatters.

Major changes ensued. The army was gradually withdrawn from civilian administration. Premier Zhou Enlai, who somehow survived the Cultural Revolution despite constant attacks by Mao's colleagues for attempting to blunt its destructive impact, was given authority to repair the damage. The party organization was slowly rebuilt. The Mao cult was scaled back and the public rituals curtailed. The universities began to bring back faculty members and admit small entering classes. The millions of government functionaries banished to perform manual labor were restored to office jobs. Leaders like Deng Xiaoping, who had disappeared in the tumult and were still alive (Liu Shaoqi had died in prison), were restored to positions of prominence.

This was an uneasy calm, soon broken by an upsurge of conflict rooted in the earlier period. A campaign to criticize Lin Biao gave license to many of the Cultural Revolution's victims, and some of its former activists, to criticize the movement and indirectly Chairman Mao. Former Red Guards and rebels, and students banished to the countryside, began to form pockets of critical independent thought. The jockeying among leaders in Beijing over the legacy of the Cultural Revolution encouraged their followers to resist, and factional conflicts and street protests reappeared in many large cities. The simmering conflicts found their most dramatic expression in massive demonstrations in Tiananmen Square on April 4 and 5, 1976—with counterparts in other large cities. Ostensibly a tribute to the recently deceased Zhou Enlai, these commemorations rapidly evolved into outspoken denunciations of the officials who resisted his efforts to roll back the Cultural Revolution. In retaliation, Deng Xiaoping was removed from office for a second time.

Mao left a severely damaged and backward China, and Chapter 14 reviews the state of the nation at the time of his death. The economy grew despite a sharp drop after the Great Leap and a more modest downturn in the late 1960s. But China fell far behind other socialist countries, and even farther behind Japan, South Korea, and other economies in East Asia. Average real wages for industrial workers had declined since

1957, as had housing space for urban residents, who were crowded into squalid apartments with shared facilities. Rationing and shortages of all manner of basic consumer goods were still in force, and supplies in some ways had gotten worse since the 1960s. The university system was in shambles. So was the administration of public institutions, where expertise was denigrated and where political animosities were always just below the surface. Capital equipment was obsolete and in poor repair; product designs had not been improved since the 1950s. Huge pockets of dire poverty remained in rural China, where a fifth of the population had a standard of living that by official Chinese standards was below subsistence level, and where the quality of the diet was later revealed to be among the worst in Asia.

Mao left a China that was badly broken, and it would take an enormous effort to fix it. The devastation and backwardness that he left in his wake prompted his successors to rethink the nation's trajectory— indeed, it was a historic opportunity. When they finally seized this opportunity, they rejected Mao's core ideas and even the antipathy to market mechanisms and private enterprise at the core of the Soviet economic system that had been sacrosanct in China since the 1950s. When the dust finally cleared, the new model would be the export-oriented developmental states of East Asia, whose features would be grafted onto the stock of a rebuilt and revitalized Communist Party. A reform of this magnitude could only gain traction if leaders were forced to admit that something in China had gone seriously wrong. This was not the legacy that Mao had hoped to leave. It was in fact the opposite of what he intended.

2

From Movement to Regime

Aᶠᵗᵉʳ SURVIVING two disastrous setbacks in its early years and overcoming initially long odds in the civil war with the Nationalists, the victory of the Chinese Communist Party (CCP) in 1949 was remarkable, and to many of its members must have seemed miraculous. The first setback was the ferocious purge launched by Chiang Kai-shek in the spring of 1927, which ended the early alliance with the Nationalists and decimated the Communist Party's urban networks. Party membership declined from 58,000 in April 1927 to 10,000 four months later.[1] The survivors withdrew into underground cells in the cities, but most retreated to remote rural regions and set up temporary bases. After several years the Jiangxi Soviet became the largest, after Mao and others established it in a mountainous border region that straddled three southern provinces.

The second setback was the Nationalist army's 1934 military campaign, which destroyed the Jiangxi Soviet and forced an arduous retreat by remnant Communist forces. The Red Army shrank from its 1933 peak of 150,000 to 23,000 in 1936, only half of which initially made it to the new base area in remote northern Shaanxi.[2] This left the Communists stranded in a dry and hilly border region.[3] They were spared additional attacks only by Japan's full-scale invasion of 1937, which decimated Nationalist armies and forced the government to retreat deep into China's interior.

Even after imperial Japan's sudden surrender in August 1945, victory for the Communists was still far from certain. After a forced march to Manchuria to be resupplied by Soviet occupation forces, the civil war with the Nationalists, who had much larger and better-equipped armies, initially went very badly. Communist divisions in Manchuria were pushed back against the Soviet border in the far north, and Chiang Kai-shek launched his armies into a massive assault to finish off the Communists or drive them into Siberia. Instead, the huge Nationalist armies disintegrated after several decisive defeats, and the regime's hold over northern and eastern China unraveled with stunning speed. In less than a year the Communists' situation shifted from near-defeat to an utter rout of their enemies.

The Communist Party's path to victory left a legacy that strongly shaped the regime that took power in 1949, and also the mentalities and behavior of leaders and party members in the years to come. This legacy, however, is not the one celebrated in the official myth about the years of guerrilla war, symbolized by the wartime capital of Yan'an. Nor is it the years of village reform and partisan activity in wartime base areas behind Japanese lines, an experience once emphasized in scholarly analyses and still widely celebrated in film and textbooks in China today. The CCP did not win power through guerrilla war: that was a strategy of survival during the Japanese invasion. The CCP's victory did not actually come from armed resistance against Japan: the party intentionally avoided direct confrontation with the invaders. Instead, victory came from fighting rival Chinese forces in conventional warfare. This left a legacy of a militarized party and conventional army that extracted sacrifice from subject populations in all-out mobilization for war. The mobilization for military conquest created the bureaucratic foundations for the new Chinese state and heavily shaped its future.

Explaining Communist Victory

Political revolutions can be viewed as a contest between two organizations: the established state and insurgent forces, who vie to establish a monopoly over the "legitimate" use of force in a given territory.[4] This is essentially the way that historians have understood the Communist victory in 1949. Few disagree that the Communist Party's organization and strategy were superior to the Nationalists'. There is wide agreement about the Nationalists' weaknesses, but there are different views about the Communists' strengths.

One type of explanation roots Communist success in the strategy of rural revolution pioneered by the party and associated with its leading proponent, Mao Zedong. By jettisoning Marxist dogma about proletarian revolution and shifting the revolutionary movement to the countryside, this strategy combined guerrilla military tactics with the building of grassroots political organizations that harnessed the activism of impoverished peasants.[5] There are three different versions of this argument, each of which emphasizes a different reason why the strategy appealed to China's peasantry.

The first version, and the earliest, attributes the Communists' rural support to the political impact of the Japanese invasion, which generated a wave of peasant nationalism that the Communists rode to victory. In this view, brutal Japanese counterinsurgency tactics deep in the rural interior created a strong upsurge of nationalism among farmers who previously had little sense of national identity. By focusing their efforts on rural organizing behind enemy lines, the invasion turned the Communists' guerrilla forces into champions of national salvation. Therefore the CCP rode a wave of newly awakened peasant nationalism as defenders against foreign intruders.[6]

A second view emphasizes the party's programs of rent reduction and land reform, which addressed the long-standing grievances of China's rural poor. This view stresses the impact of organizational work by the CCP in villages, especially its emphasis on attending to the perennially precarious welfare of the poorest peasants.[7] Peasant hunger for land and for relief from onerous debt and taxes was understood by the CCP to be the linchpin of rural political mobilization. By addressing the interests of landless peasants and tenant farmers, the CCP unleashed latent class conflicts that created a seemingly endless reservoir of rural support.[8]

A third view is a variant of the second. It emphasizes not class conflicts that divided villagers but a traditional peasant morality that was shared across rural social classes. According to this argument, Communist policies promoted the livelihood of the rural poor and appealed to traditional community values that enshrined a right to basic subsistence. The Communists appealed to the peasantry as the champions of a traditional culture that clashed with the market rationality of an expanding global capitalism.[9]

These are all arguments about why the guerrilla strategy earned peasant support. As explanations for Communist success, however, they take us only partway toward an answer. While there is little doubt that the CCP successfully mobilized peasants and created village-level political organizations, this strategy depended crucially on the ability to secure a region militarily. Scholars have searched in vain for correlations between regions that appeared to have social conditions that would make Communist success more likely. The only circumstance correlated with local success was the presence of armed Communist forces.[10] The party's leaders did not believe that the success of their tactics was linked to specific economic conditions. In their view, there was enough class inequality in any locality to fuel revolutionary change.[11]

The revolution carried out in areas under secure Communist control was inherently fragile. Base areas unraveled quickly if the balance of military control became unfavorable. In late 1939, after Japanese armies consolidated their gains in North China and turned their attention to the regions where the Communists had expanded their operations, the areas controlled by the CCP shrank, and their cadres found it difficult to secure cooperation from wary villagers.[12] The same thing occurred during the first six months of the civil war, when the fight with the Nationalists was going badly in North China. This led to widespread defections from local party organizations and a reversal of the changes carried out in villages. As one historian has noted about this period, "As long as the Communist armies were there, local cadres would carry out land reform and instigate political campaigns. But with military protection gone, the new adherents to the cause in the villages—those who had been recruited during the last phase of the war against Japan and during the postwar years—often switched allegiance."[13]

Another reason why guerrilla strategy falls short as an explanation for Communist success is that victory was actually attained through conventional warfare fought between large modern armies, involving massive mobilization of material and human support for each side. Guerrilla warfare permitted the CCP to survive and expand during the Japanese invasion, but this survival strategy placed minimal demands on peasants to supply Communist partisans with food, material support, and recruits. Once the civil war began, the CCP abandoned guerrilla operations. As its armies poured into Manchuria after Soviet forces occupied the territory, Mao turned to a strategy of total mobilization for revolutionary war. The Red Army, renamed the People's Liberation Army (PLA) in 1945, grew from 475,000 in 1944 to 2.8 million by 1948.[14] The resources and personnel required for this massive effort far outstripped the capacities of the older guerrilla methods. The new approach transformed Chinese society in areas under party control, as well as the party itself. The entire population was now required to take part in the military struggle against the Nationalists. Active support of the Communist war effort was compulsory, and all were expected to contribute supplies, labor, and recruits. The final years of the civil war resembled the Soviet army's conquest of Eastern Europe in the last phases of World War II. The PLA rolled south from Manchuria and adjacent regions of North China, conquering vast regions that had never before been under CCP control, and regions like Tibet and Xinjiang that had not been governed by any Chinese state since the fall of the Qing dynasty.

The organization that defeated initially superior Nationalist forces during the civil war was not made up of guerrilla partisans conducting operations in far-flung rural regions. It was a militarized party engaged in all-out mobilization to support territorial conquest by a large modern army, and it formed the kernel of a new Chinese state. If we are to understand how the Communist Party won this contest between organizations, we need to consider the reasons why the Communists' efforts in this phase of the conflict were more effective than the Nationalists'.

The Military Impact of the Japanese Invasion

Our account of this historic contest between two organizations begins on the eve of the war with Japan. In 1936, Chiang Kai-shek assembled Nationalist armies in Shaanxi Province for a final assault against the Communists' small base area in the Shaanxi-Gansu-Ningxia border region, and its capital Yan'an. At this point the Red Army had only 50,000 troops, 29,000 guns, and no air force. The Nationalists had more than 2 million soldiers and an air force with 314 warplanes.[15] Before the offensive could be launched, Chiang Kai-shek was taken into custody by troops under two of his generals who wanted him to unite with the Communists to resist Japan, which had already seized all of northeastern China and was encroaching on North China as well. The generals were not aware that Chiang's representatives had already agreed to do so in confidential negotiations. Chiang was released and the final assault against Yan'an never took place.[16]

The next year the Japanese invaded, devastating the Nationalist state and its armies, which were no match for the Japanese. Their best divisions were decimated, with 187,000 dead in the first weeks.[17] Chiang Kai-shek's elite forces were concentrated around Shanghai and the Nationalist capital, Nanjing. Over three months, 300,000 died in the defense of Shanghai, and another 100,000 died defending Nanjing. By end of 1937 the total losses were 370,000 to 450,000, one-third to one-half of the Nationalists' best divisions.[18] Their stubborn resistance inflicted unexpectedly large casualties on the enemy, for which Japanese forces retaliated with their notorious massacres of civilians when they finally reached Nanjing.[19]

The Nationalists continued their dogged resistance as they retreated to their wartime capital of Chongqing (Chungking). By late September 1939, half a million Japanese soldiers had been killed or seriously wounded in battles with the Nationalists, dashing Japanese expectations of quick victory in a lightning war. The Nationalists turned the invasion into a quagmire for the superior Japanese armies. In the winter of 1939, Chiang Kai-shek ordered a general offensive across eight war zones. From the fall of Wuhan in October 1938 to December 7, 1941, the Nationalist armies would suffer another 1.3 million casualties.[20]

The Communist forces were initially in no position to resist Japan. It was left entirely to the Nationalists to defend Chinese territory, and they bore the brunt of the onslaught. The Communists entered the war with only 30,000 troops. In September 1937 they were reorganized into the Eighth Route Army. Shortly afterward, the New Fourth Army was established to operate in central China, comprising the remnants of troops left behind in the evacuation of the Jiangxi Soviet in 1934.[21]

Mao was acutely aware of his party's strategic weakness, and he called for guerrilla warfare, the avoidance of direct confrontation with Japanese main forces, and the preservation and expansion of military resources.[22] From 1937 to 1939, during the first two years of the war, Japanese forces stayed close to railway lines and depots, leaving the countryside unguarded. When they shifted their attention to securing their hold over broader areas, the CCP had already expanded into rural areas behind their lines.[23] At this point some of Mao's commanders urged mobile warfare against the Japanese, arguing that guerrilla warfare would have little impact. They called for closer cooperation with Nationalist forces in an effort to inflict larger losses on Japanese armies, and they received support from a number of party leaders.[24] Mao, however, insisted on avoiding military confrontation and ordered the Eighth Route and New Fourth armies to disperse into small units and engage in recruitment, political work, and base area construction. Under this strategy, by design, there were to be very few clashes with Japanese troops, and even then only small ones. Japanese patrols or puppet Chinese security forces would be ambushed or raided for material and weapons. Collaborators were assassinated, rail lines torn up, mines laid on roads, telegraph poles cut down, and wire stolen.[25]

The sole exception was 1940. With growing confidence due to their expanding control of the countryside, the CCP launched its only sustained offensive of the war. Mao authorized coordinated attacks by 104 regiments against rail lines, major roads, coal mines, and other infrastructure in Japanese hands. The Eighth Route Army lost 22,000 killed and wounded, while the Japanese lost an estimated 3,000 to 4,000. The Japanese sent large reinforcements on search and destroy operations and recovered all their lost territory, leveling villages that collaborated with the CCP, massacring human populations and livestock, and building blockhouses and strategic villages. The population in the Communist-controlled areas dropped from 44 to 25 million, and the Eighth Route Army shrank from 400,000 to 300,000. By 1942, 90 percent of the former Communist base areas on the North China Plain were under enemy control or were actively contested. Having provoked a fierce reaction, Mao reverted to his previous strategy and would never launch another major offensive against the Japanese.[26]

There was a staggering imbalance in the burdens of combat. In January 1940, Zhou Enlai sent a report to Stalin, commenting on the favorable impact of the war against Japan. He stated that more than 1 million Chinese soldiers had been killed or wounded by August 1939, but only 30,000 from the Eighth Route Army and 1,000 from the New Fourth Army. Halfway into the war, the CCP had suffered only 3 percent of total Chinese military casualties.[27] Despite their devastating losses, the Nationalists continually rebuilt their armed forces and persisted in their resistance against Japan in the years to come. The last major stand was their 1944 defense of Henan, Hunan, and Guangxi against a large Japanese offensive known as the Ichigo Campaign.[28] Nationalist forces suffered another 146,000 casualties. In the words of one analyst, "Japan delivered a mortal blow to the Nationalist Chinese army from which she never had time to recover."[29] By the end of the war it was "in an advanced stage of deterioration."[30]

In the wake of the Communist victory in 1949 and the CCP's subsequent decades of lavish self-praise as heroes of the anti-Japanese resistance, the Nationalist war effort has often been overlooked and denigrated.[31] In the view of one of the most acute critics of the Nationalists' failures, their military accomplishments were considerable: "[The Nationalist army] persisted for eight years in a war against an enemy force that was decidedly superior in organization, training, and equipment. . . . Completely frustrating Japanese expectations of a quick and decisive victory, it actively fought at Shanghai, at Nanking, and on the plains of North and Central China, incurring frightful losses . . . [and] mired the Japanese army in the vastness of the Chinese nation."[32] During the entire Chinese war, Japan suffered 483,708 dead and 1.9 million wounded, and Chinese forces suffered 1.3 million dead and 1.7 million wounded.[33]

The Communists' contribution to the war effort was extremely modest. According to a December 1944 Soviet Comintern report, a total of more than 1 million Nationalist troops had been killed in battle, compared to 103,186 in the CCP's Eighth Route Army and another several thousand in the New Fourth Army. The Communists suffered only 10 percent of total Chinese military casualties.[34] One author has called Mao's famous doctrine of people's war one of the "great myths" about the period: "people's war was hardly used in the conflict against the Japanese."[35]

The Political Impact of the Japanese Invasion

The invasion's impact was not purely military. It also weakened the coherence of the Nationalist regime. The state established by Chiang Kai-shek was never a unified national organization, nor were its large armies all under central control. After the purge of the Communists in 1927, Chiang curtailed popular mobilization and negotiated a series of agreements with regional warlords, who pledged nominal allegiance to Nanjing while retaining considerable autonomy.[36] At the high point of central control in 1935, Chiang's Nationalist Party directly controlled fewer than one-third of China's provinces, primarily in eastern and central China; the rest were controlled by various warlords or the Japanese (in Manchuria).[37] Control over military forces was no different. Out of a total of 176 army divisions in 1937, Chiang Kai-shek directly controlled only 31.[38] When the Japanese invaded coastal China in 1937 and drove inland up the Yangzi River, they pushed the Nationalists out of their core homeland, and Chiang Kai-shek's elite divisions bore the brunt.[39]

Chiang's reliance on the army to unify the Nationalist regime made it, in the words of one analyst, "an extremely narrowly based militaristic regime under the guise of party leadership."[40] The army was the regime's principal foundation. The Nationalist Party and the Nanjing government never developed firm social foundations or created strong institutions. The weakening of the army during the war against Japan undermined the government and proved fatal after the Japanese surrender.[41] The invasion undercut Chiang's control over allied warlords. Government administration in areas nominally under Nationalist control deteriorated badly, undermining the ability of the central government to collect taxes and conscript soldiers. The Nationalist Party was only one of several competing political forces, and the party itself was poorly integrated and deeply factionalized.[42] Chiang Kai-shek held the entire structure together, largely through personal loyalties that tied him to top military commanders and party leaders. The party itself atrophied: "during the war, party work was nonexistent on the mass level, and the party organizations, wherever existing, were controlled and exploited by local leaders to advance their own vested interests."[43]

Chiang Kai-shek recognized the organizational weakness of his regime and admired the discipline and unity of the Communists. Liu Shaoqi codified the Communist Party's ethic of discipline and obedience in 1939: "Every Party member must completely identify his personal interests with those of the Party both in his thinking and in his actions. He must be able to yield to the interests of the Party without any hesitation or reluctance and sacrifice his personal interests whenever the two are at variance. Unhesitating readiness to sacrifice personal interests, even one's life, for the Party and the proletariat and for the emancipation of the nation. . . . "[44] In 1938 Chiang Kai-shek wrote in his diary, "Communist parties all over the world have long been working underground, thus they have a tightly organized structure and an iron discipline that defies other parties." Chiang lamented the state of his own party, which he characterized as a "special class struggling for power and selfish interests, alienating the masses."[45] After resigning from the presidency in January 1949, before his departure for Taiwan, Chiang wrote about his imminent defeat: "The chief reason, which cannot be denied, arose from the paralysis of the party: the membership, organizational structure, and method of leadership all created problems. Thus, the party became a life-less shell, the government and military also lost their soul, and as a result the troops collapsed and society disintegrated."[46] The lesson was not wasted, and as soon as Chiang landed on Taiwan he set about to create a much more centralized dictatorship, ruthlessly enforcing the discipline and coherence that his regime had always lacked on the mainland.[47]

If Chiang had long recognized the lack of unity and discipline of his forces, why was he unable to remedy the problem? Much of the answer is political geography, combined with the social composition of Nation-alist Party members. After 1927, the Nationalist Party was spread across large regions of China, concentrated in towns and large cities. Most of its members had civilian jobs and business interests, many were profes-sionals, and some were wealthy. Party life constituted only a fraction of their attention, and there were many competing family and occupational interests. Because the Nationalists were located in regions rich in re-sources, they were able to extract the revenues they needed without de-veloping strong ties to grassroots communities. Party and government posts could easily become tools of personal enrichment. The National-ists continued to rule the rural hinterland in a way similar to imperial dynasties of a past era, permitting local notables to handle the functions of government and collect taxes with relative autonomy.

Sources of Communist Party Discipline

The Communists' situation was virtually the opposite. After 1927 they were forced into isolated rural regions. As they built up their organiza-tion in resource-poor rural regions, they were forced to develop close ties with the rural populations that sustained them. Party members and cadres were not integrated into urban society; they had no competing professions, no property, and no business interests. Party work was of necessity their entire lives. And there was little option to exit if they had wanted to do so. Hemmed in first by hostile Nationalist and then by Japa-nese forces, it was difficult to defect from the movement and avoid im-prisonment, torture, or execution. Communist cadres depended on the party organization for their livelihoods.

While political geography lent the Communists an inherent advan-tage, their single-minded focus on instilling discipline and unity—in many ways an obsession—is what permitted them to capitalize on it. The party placed severe demands for discipline on its members, and its efforts to enforce it could be devastatingly harsh. In the early years, party purges were brutal and violent. The first major purge, from 1930 to 1932, was a campaign to suppress counterrevolution within the guerrilla forces in the Jiangxi Soviet.[48] Mao was convinced that resistance by local commanders was due to an underground conspiracy, and he unleashed a wave of torture and mass executions, as party inquisitors blanketed the areas involved and went after suspects.[49] A purge in another base area during the period has been described as "a near-hysterical witch-hunt, a frenzied effort by local cadres to save their own hides by coming up with expanding lists of counterrevolutionaries among their colleagues."[50] Official party histories put the death toll from that incident at 2,500, but independent historians estimate that the actual number was close to 10,000.[51] Similar purges occurred in other local bases from 1934 to 1937, involving the routine extraction of confessions under torture and the summary execution of hundreds.[52]

These terroristic and self-destructive approaches to internal discipline would be modified, refined, and expanded as the party grew during the anti-Japanese war, although charges of internal conspiracy and the extraction of confessions through psychological pressure and physical torture would recur. The new methods were developed in Yan'an and culminated in the rectification campaign of 1942–1944. The campaign was part of the intense Stalinization of the Chinese party, helped by the translation into Chinese of the *History of the Communist Party of the Soviet Union (Bolsheviks): Short Course*, which was compiled and published under Stalin's direction in 1938.[53]

The process began after the arrival in Yan'an in October 1937 of party leaders who had spent the previous years in Moscow, one of whom, Wang Ming, aspired to challenge Mao for party leadership.[54] Wang Ming had spent most of his adult life in the Soviet Union and was well known to Stalin. He was educated and articulate, far more conversant with Marxist theory than Mao, who had never been abroad and whose authority rested primarily on his abilities as a guerrilla strategist and shrewd political infighter. Wang presented himself as the true interpreter of Stalin's wishes and tried unsuccessfully to undermine Mao's authority. Shortly after arriving in Yan'an, Wang "conveyed the instruction that Mao should be strengthened 'ideologically' because of his narrow empiricism and 'ignorance of Marxism-Leninism.' "[55] Mao responded by burnishing his

Marxist credentials, solidifying his control of the party organization, and elevating his status as a leader with attributes that mimicked Stalin's in the Soviet Union.[56] Mao's budding "personality cult" was in part intended to compete with that of Chiang Kai-shek, who was the symbol of China's wartime resistance and was recognized internationally as China's leader, even by the Soviet Union.[57]

Mao was assisted in this makeover by political secretaries, especially Chen Boda, who studied at the Communist-controlled Shanghai Labor University in the mid-1920s and later at Moscow's Sun Yatsen University.[58] Chen recommended readings for Mao, instructing him in the basics and editing his drafts. Mao began with Chinese translations of two Soviet textbooks and one article published in the *Great Soviet Encyclopedia*. Easily the most influential text was the *Short Course,* available in Chinese translation in 1939.[59] The book had a major impact on Mao, and for the rest of his life it shaped his understanding of Marxism-Leninism and the building of socialism. He once said that he never read the whole book, but focused on the concluding sections of each chapter. Despite his relatively shallow engagement with the material, he adopted its interpretations uncritically and dogmatically.[60]

The *Short Course* was a schematic history of the growth and eventual triumph of the Bolshevik Party in Russia, culminating in the historic contributions of Stalin in the building of a socialist economy in the Soviet Union. Mao would later adopt this story as his blueprint for China in the 1950s. At this point in time, however, the textbook's greatest impact was in its portrayal of Stalin's struggle for dominance over his rivals for the party leadership. The *Short Course* portrayed policy disagreements as intraparty struggles that reflected "correct" and "incorrect" lines, with each line, in turn, representing a class struggle between revolutionary and reactionary forces. The book's central tenet was that class struggle continues after the establishment of socialism, and that the capitalist class always infiltrates the party with representatives who have to be rooted out and overthrown.[61] Thus policy disagreements with rivals like Bukharin and Trotsky were portrayed as struggles against conspirators who represented the capitalist class and who headed an inner-party conspiracy against socialism. The account glorified Stalin and burnished his cult as an infallible leader who unerringly supported the correct line. Mao imitated this example as he reinforced his authority with a cult of personality and demands for obedience to a new creation developed in collaboration with Chen Boda, known as Mao Zedong Thought.[62]

The Party's First Stalinist Purge

The rectification campaign of 1942–1944 completed this process.[63] As the capital of the Communists' wartime base area, Yan'an was a magnet for patriotic youth, workers, and intellectuals who fled the Japanese invasion to participate in the anti-Japanese struggle. Many were urbanites with vague leftist views. Most had not previously been party members and held liberal attitudes and idealistic views about democracy.[64] Some of them resisted the more severe forms of party discipline and were put off by the dogmatism and hierarchy of the incipient party bureaucracy. Within the party leadership, on the other hand, there was always the worry that Nationalist agents had infiltrated Yan'an during the migration touched off by the Japanese invasion.

Mao made two speeches in early February 1942 to initiate the campaign. He criticized three "mistaken tendencies" in the party: subjectivism, sectarianism, and formalism. These labels were aimed at individuals who had recently migrated to Yan'an and who still lacked revolutionary experience, and more importantly at the party officials who had recently returned from Moscow, in particular his rival, Wang Ming. The worst form of subjectivism, according to Mao, was "dogmatism"—the assertion of authority based only on the study of Marxist classics, without an understanding of specific political conditions in China. "Sectarianism" was the error of putting one's particular interests above those of the party, and by extension the higher aims of the movement. While the party needed "democracy," it needed centralism even more—subjection of one's personal interests to those of the party, as defined by its leadership. Mao declared that criticism of one's own past behavior was essential to eradicate these problems and to prevent future misbehavior. Distinguishing the current campaign from the bloody purges of the past decade (and perhaps also from Stalin's recent mass executions of party officials in the USSR), Mao described the campaign as analogous to a doctor curing the patient: the objective was to cure the symptoms and eradicate the underlying disease.[65]

Mao's call for criticism elicited an enthusiastic but unwanted response from individuals who staffed the cadre schools and party newspaper in

Yan'an. In essays published in that paper and posted as "wall newspapers," the authors interpreted "dogmatism" to mean the control of literature and art by rigid and poorly educated party bureaucrats. They argued for a greater separation of politics and literature, and greater freedom from the dictates of party propaganda. Others, like the famous novelist Ding Ling, criticized the party's shabby treatment of women and the male dominance and sexism that pervaded Yan'an. By far the most controversial and hard-hitting were a series of essays by Wang Shiwei, a translator in party organs. He charged that the officially approved literature was coarse and inferior, and called for higher artistic standards. He argued that many ranking cadres in Yan'an had become insensitive and dictatorial in dealing with their young and idealistic subordinates, alienating them from the party. He pointed out the emergence of privileges tied to rank and the creation of a stratified system of rations for food, clothing, and living quarters. He also criticized married cadres' pursuit of attractive younger women and their preferential access to them for sexual activity, and their neglect of less glamorous older wives who had been revolutionary comrades for many years. The last charge reportedly incensed Mao, who had recently abandoned his wife from the Jiangxi Soviet in favor of a young actress from Shanghai later known as Jiang Qing. Wang criticized the party leaders' habit of holding dance parties each weekend while soldiers were fighting at the front. He reported the hypocrisy with which these cadres defended their privileges and the anger they displayed when they were challenged about them.[66]

These essays hit a responsive chord with many educated individuals in the central party organs, but the critics threatened to divert the rectification campaign from its real aims. Mao wanted to strengthen party discipline and consolidate his personal authority. Independent challenges to the absolute authority he was trying to accomplish—especially the criticisms of abuses that applied especially to him—were unacceptable. The rectification campaign quickly turned into criticism and struggle sessions against the critics and those who agreed with them. While others penned abject confessions of guilt and promises to change their thinking, Wang Shiwei refused to confess and argued with his accusers. Condemned as the head of a "five-person antiparty group," denounced as a Trotskyite and a traitor, he was imprisoned along with others after a highly publicized show trial. He remained in prison until his execution in 1947.[67]

After silencing the critics, Mao unleashed the campaign on the entire party hierarchy, with an increasing emphasis on traitors and spies hidden in the party's ranks. Responsibility for organizing the rectification campaign was given to Kang Sheng, who had returned from Moscow along with Wang Ming in 1937. Kang backed Mao in his rivalry with Wang Ming and was put in charge of the CCP secret service and internal security in 1939.[68] In 1941 he was made director of a committee for "cadre screening." The counterattack against intellectuals as traitors and Trotskyites was expanded into a broad search for enemy agents in the CCP throughout all of its areas of operation, with an emphasis on "deviations in thought."[69]

The campaign to cleanse the party of suspected traitors and spies began with a screening of the files of cadres and party members. Investigators looked for those with suspicious backgrounds and affiliations—prior members of Nationalist youth organizations who had defected, and party operatives who had worked underground in enemy areas (especially if they had been arrested and later released). In the first stages of the campaign, individuals were required to "hand their hearts to the party" and report truthfully on their conversion to the Communists' cause and how they came to repudiate their previous political leanings. Inevitably, many people burnished their biographies and left out inconvenient associations or activities. When it became clear that many had been less than candid in reporting their class background and prior associations, those responsible for internal security became suspicious. Individuals who had shown too much independence of mind by questioning the authority of their superiors or expressing doubts about the wisdom of party policies were prime candidates for investigation.

As it spread, the later stages of the rectification campaign increasingly employed prolonged and psychologically coercive interrogations to extract confessions and, increasingly, physical abuse. Large numbers of false cases were built up about underground spy organizations. Confessions given under these circumstances spiraled out of control. Believing the coerced confessions, the party's inquisitors proceeded to demand names of others involved in the conspiracies. Those who confessed falsely to the charges to avoid further torment found that their ordeal was not over until they named names. As names were extracted, the new suspects were dragged in for the same treatment. The party's inquisitors generated manufactured evidence of what appeared to be a surprisingly vast number of underground conspirators within the party.[70]

The campaign terrorized the party organization and led to dissatisfaction among top leaders whose subordinates were caught up in the dragnet. In particular, Zhou Enlai was indirectly implicated in Kang's charges of a conspiracy in the underground organizations that were under Zhou's direction. Zhou denied this, and an investigation subsequently uncovered the routine use of torture to extract false confessions. Mao backtracked in October 1943, seeing how unpopular the campaign had become. Realizing that the campaign threatened to split and weaken the party, he stepped in and called a halt to summary executions and physical torture.[71]

In a March 1944 report, Kang Sheng acknowledged the abuses, but he still judged the campaign a huge success. The campaign had been very successful in "raising the consciousness of the masses" and "revealing subversive elements." However, there were some regrettable shortcomings: particularly the old problem of "applying torture, extracting a confession, and believing it." Kang attributed the recurrence of this practice to "inexperience," an unfortunate but unavoidable problem in mass movements in which "boorish attitudes" led to "oversimplified standards." Kang lamented the fact that some comrades interpreted the party's policy of leniency to mean nothing more than refraining from summary executions: "Consequently, such other punishments as beating and abuse and making arbitrary espionage accusations are considered harmless." Accepting false accusations and confessions extracted through torture "is still a mistaken idea that lingers to a serious extent among cadres."[72] Kang explained that in fact fewer than 10 percent of those who had confessed under duress were actually enemy agents.[73]

Kang Sheng bore the blame for the campaign, even though Mao was firmly behind it. Kang's influence fell and he was relegated to minor roles in the party well into the early 1960s.[74] While the campaign's excesses were officially regretted, only the use of physical torture to extract confessions was deemed to be an error. The broader aims of the campaign were not, especially the sense of fear that it provoked among both party cadres and ordinary citizens about coming under suspicion for disloyalty. The campaign essentially made it treasonous to disagree with party policies. As one analyst has noted, "the stick, a fear of implication in traitorous activities, helped maintain a level of anxiety that also induced conformity to Communist policy."[75] The discipline and conformity that resulted was an important ingredient of the CCP's success, and failure to conform was always treated harshly in the years to come.

In its isolated base area, far removed from the main theaters of the war against Japan, Mao and his colleagues molded the CCP and its armies into a disciplined fighting force. The discipline was harsh, the conformity it induced could be extreme, but despite costly abuses it achieved the intended results. During this same period the Nationalist armies confronted the final Japanese offensive and the Nationalist Party had almost ceased to function at the grass roots. Mao coercively remolded the CCP into a unified and disciplined hierarchy under his command. It was this organization that would soon face off against the fragmented and factionalized Nationalist regime that rushed to resume control over territories vacated by surrendering Japanese armies.

The Civil War

The civil war was the decisive phase of the contest between the organizations headed by Mao Zedong and Chiang Kai-shek. Although Mao prevailed in the end, the outcome was by no means predetermined. In June 1946, when full-scale civil war began, the Nationalists had 4.3 million troops and the Communists only 1.2 million, and the Nationalists had superior armaments.[76] The civil war initially went badly for the Communists, and as late as 1947 Stalin and many of Mao's colleagues called for a negotiated settlement. Mao, however, insisted that victory could be won. Chiang Kai-shek gambled everything on crushing the Communists' best divisions in Manchuria. That gamble failed, and as his armies disintegrated his state unraveled, exposing the accumulated weaknesses of the war years. The Communists abandoned guerrilla tactics, shifting to all-out mobilization for conventional warfare. In view of the Nationalist debacle in the final years of the civil war, historians have asked whether the outcome was more a reflection of Nationalist weaknesses than Communist strengths, and whether the outcome may nonetheless have been different if the leaders on each side had made different choices at crucial turning points.

Shortly after the Japanese surrender, Communist armies were merged into the renamed People's Liberation Army. The main force under General Lin Biao moved into Manchuria in late 1945 to be resupplied by the Soviet troops that had occupied the region. Lin turned his armies into strong combat units, applying military techniques he learned during his years in the USSR. He proved to be a master of the tactics of positional warfare, in particular speed of movement, surprise, and counterattack. Lin's model for the war with the Nationalists was the Soviet campaigns against Nazi Germany in Eastern Europe at the end of World War II. He argued that with the right kind of training and ample supplies of Japanese weapons (and later American weapons captured from Nationalist forces), it was possible to win this type of war.[77] Lin's confidence reinforced Mao's determination to push for a final victory.

Nationalist armies in 1946 were fragmented and still recovering from their costly battles with superior Japanese forces. Some of the remaining divisions were well trained and equipped and among the best in Chinese history, while others were poorly disciplined bands of stragglers that victimized the population for loot. Some of the commanders were deeply loyal to Chiang Kai-shek and considered him a national savior, while others were still loyal to former warlords who held positions in the Nationalist government. Because the command of armed troops was the basis for authority in the factionalized politics of the Nationalist regime, many regional commanders were reluctant to engage in combat, hoping that their rivals would bear the costs.[78]

The Nationalists also had problems reestablishing their authority in the wake of the Japanese surrender. They rushed to take control over cities in the regions long under Japanese control, pushing aside elites who had survived or who had collaborated with the occupiers. Nationalist officials often acted as if they were seizing privileges that had belonged to them in the past, enriching themselves at the population's expense.[79] They had never developed strong rural organizations. Their attempts to collect taxes during the civil war created hardships for rural populations already suffering from recent famines and wartime deprivations. Their conscription policies were onerous, coercive, and deeply resented, often taking the form of surprise nighttime raids, and they were riddled with corruption, as wealthier families could pay for draft exemptions.[80] In 1948, only 21 percent of government expenditures were met through taxation, and 68 percent were met by printing new currency, creating hyperinflation in the later stages of the civil war, and hardships that undermined morale.[81]

Chiang Kai-shek understood these structural weaknesses and lacked confidence in his ability to prevail in a prolonged conflict. He felt compelled to destroy the PLA's largest and best field armies, and he refused to contemplate negotiations or a coalition government. Late in 1946 he launched a broad attack across the entire front from Yan'an to the Pacific coast, and moved his forces deep into Manchuria. In the first months of the campaign the Communists lost one battle after another. In March 1947, Chiang's troops captured Yan'an.[82] Chiang had hoped to capture the Communists' entire leadership and destroy the army command, but a spy in Chiang's staff office warned the CCP two weeks in advance, permitting their safe evacuation.[83]

When the Communists took over large parts of Manchuria from Soviet armies, they continued to focus on the countryside, intensifying and radicalizing the rural revolution that they had earlier conducted in areas under their control. Land reform in Manchuria during 1947 and 1948 has been called "unrestricted revolutionary terror."[84] Party cadres entered villages and ensured that landlords, rich peasants, suspected enemy agents, or anyone else seen as an obstacle to Communist control were subjected to "struggle sessions" that forced victims to kneel, hear shouted accusations, wear posters or caps proclaiming their guilt, and endure interrogations that involved physical abuse and sleep deprivation. These struggle sessions were a form of political theater: individuals in these communities realized clearly that their fate under the new authorities depended on their eagerness to accuse and to condemn. The struggle sessions frequently ended in severe beatings, torture, and summary executions that were initially encouraged by the CCP before they decided later that excessive violence was counterproductive.[85]

Immediately after the liquidation of landlords and the distribution of their land and other assets, farmers were faced with demands for food, supplies, and labor. This was different from the relationship between CCP forces and the rural population in the older base areas. The earlier land reform was carried out more slowly and less coercively, and was usually less violent, and afterward much less onerous demands were placed on subject populations. This was something new: a wartime mobilization to support a large conventional army, a type of warfare that the CCP had avoided during the Japanese invasion. This new war against large Nationalist armies required huge supplies of men, weapons, war materiel, provisions, horses, and transportation equipment. Compliance was not voluntary and supplies were not purchased. A massive new army was being mobilized, needing food, support workers, shoes, uniforms, weapons, and fuel. Hundreds of thousands of soldiers and tens of thousands of Communist leaders, cadres, and local organizers also consumed requisitioned supplies.[86]

While the CCP was building its forces in the large new base area in Manchuria, Chiang Kai-shek continued his push to destroy the Communists' best armies. After more than a year of battlefield successes, the tide turned in 1948. Mao dispatched forces to a mountain range in the central plains forcing Chiang to redeploy units to defend the major cities under his control along the Yangzi River valley. The Communist counterattack ruined Chiang's strategy for victory. Their first major victory was in 1947, when PLA divisions defeated a large Nationalist offensive in the central plains. His confidence vindicated, Mao called for an offensive in all theaters of the war, assumed control of all military decisions, and confidently predicted victory within five years.[87] In April 1948, Communist forces retook Yan'an. By June the Nationalist forces had shrunk to 3.6 million, while the Communists' had grown to 2.8 million.[88]

Chiang Kai-shek redoubled his efforts to crush PLA forces in Manchuria, hoping to drive them into Siberia. He sent massive reinforcements, including his best-trained and best-equipped divisions. In a series of decisive battles during the first three months of 1948, Lin Biao's forces outmaneuvered, cut off, and destroyed Chiang's large armies in southern Manchuria, completely changing the direction of the war.[89] As the tide turned, Chiang lost confidence and began to explore a withdrawal of his best forces to Taiwan. His only strategy for victory was military and there was no backup plan. Chiang began to lose his grip on his party, and many of his subordinates began to lose faith in him. Urban support for the Nationalist war effort fell off among all groups, hyperinflation undermined the economy, and sympathy for the CCP rose among students and other urban groups. The American government, which had supported Chiang with military aid and loans, lost confidence that he could win, and their assistance slowed.[90] Chiang finally lost Manchuria in a defeat in late 1948, losing 400,000 of his best troops.[91]

In the wake of Lin Biao's decisive victories, it now looked as if Mao's unwavering confidence in victory had been prophetic. He immediately began planning for a new campaign to capture all of North China. His stature in the party assumed godlike proportions, helped by party propaganda that attributed the recent victories to his military genius. Mao had long rejected cautious advice for a slower push toward victory by 1951–1952 from the Soviet Union and other party leaders. The Soviets still officially recognized the Nationalists as the legitimate government of China. Stalin had long considered a coalition government, or separate regimes, as the most favorable possible outcome. For Mao, however, the coming offensive would finally prove that total victory was possible.[92] As the PLA pushed forward, many in the party leadership worried that their armies were overextended and needed to regroup, but Mao insisted on racing ahead to final victory. Stalin counseled caution and in January 1949 he advised Mao to negotiate a settlement, advice viewed favorably by Liu Shaoqi and Zhou Enlai. Mao took offense at Stalin's effort to stop the PLA offensive, which might have resulted in separate regimes, north and south. He ignored this advice and pushed ahead.[93]

Completing the Military Conquest

Once again Mao's confidence proved prescient. Chiang's armies collapsed and military commanders and civilian authorities began to surrender. Entire divisions defected to the Communists. The Manchurian city of Changchun had been surrounded and starved into submission by Communist forces under Lin Biao during a five-month siege that ended with the surrender of surviving Nationalist troops in October 1948. An estimated 160,000 civilians perished in the bombardment and starvation of the besieged city. The Changchun example sapped the will of remaining Nationalist commanders to sacrifice civilian populations in efforts to resist advancing communist forces.[94] Beijing was surrendered without a fight in January 1949, and Tianjin fell shortly afterward.[95] Nanjing, the Nationalist capital, fell in April, and Shanghai in May. The remnants of the Nationalist regime fled to Guangzhou, later to Chongqing, and finally to Chengdu in December 1949, before the formal transfer of the Nationalist government to Taiwan.[96]

As the PLA swept toward final victory, the CCP finally had to act on the question of where the borders of China were to be drawn. The status of Tibet, Xinjiang, and Mongolia had long been at issue. The Ming dynasty, the last period of rule by ethnic Han Chinese, was roughly one-third the size of China in 1911.[97] China's last empire, the Qing, was a multinational state ruled by ethnic Manchus who invaded Ming China in 1644 from their homeland in what is now northeastern China (or Manchuria). They greatly expanded the Ming borders through military conquest in the early 1700s, incorporating non-Han peoples in Mongolia, Xinjiang, and Tibet, who fiercely resisted the expansion of Chinese imperial rule and who rebelled periodically until the dynasty's end.[98] After the fall of the Qing in 1911, these regions reasserted their independence. The Soviet Union backed the creation of an independent Mongolia in 1921, and in 1924 the country became a communist regime and Soviet satellite.[99] This was strongly opposed by the Nationalists, who refused to recognize the new Mongolian state and continued to insist on the historical borders of the Qing empire. The Communists, heavily reliant on the Soviet Union for financial and military assistance, acquiesced to the new reality. The Nationalist regime only relinquished its claim to all of Mongolia in a treaty signed with the Soviet Union in August 1945, in return for Soviet recognition of Chiang Kai-shek as China's legitimate head of state.[100] This left only Inner Mongolia within Chinese borders.

The Communists' position on China's national borders initially supported the aspirations of large non-Han nationalities. Until the 1940s, the party's position on Xinjiang, Mongolia, and Tibet was that they would first receive "full autonomy" and then, in accord with the principle of "national self-determination," could decide whether to form a federation with China and the Han people. The CCP took pains to differentiate their own stance from that of the "reactionary forces" in China—specifically Chiang Kai-shek's Nationalists—whose policy of the "unity of five nationalities," they claimed, was nothing more than an effort to "conceal its policy of national oppression." In their 1932 statement, the CCP stated that it "acknowledged the right of national self-determination of all minority nationalities, including acknowledging their right of self-determination, even leading to their separation from China." Statements during the 1930s supported separatist movements by Tibetans as a "national liberation movement" that would release Tibet from both British (Indian) and Chinese domination.[101] This formulation equated "China" with the Han ethnicity and explicitly recognized the right of other major nationalities to determine their own political futures.

This position was reversed completely in 1949 and replaced by a plan to create a socialist state that embodied the "unity of five nationalities"— Tibetans, Xinjiang's Uighurs, and Mongolians, along with Han Chinese and Hui (ethnic Han Muslims). This was the long-standing Nationalist position that the CCP had denounced as a reactionary cover for national oppression. Mao declared this new stance in discussions with Stalin's envoy in January 1949. The new claim was that the socialist state would liberate minority peoples from feudal oppression.[102]

The conquest of Inner Mongolia and Xinjiang proceeded much as it had in China proper. These regions had already been ceded to the Nationalist regime in negotiations with Stalin in August 1945, shortly after the Japanese surrender.[103] Tibet, however, was another matter entirely. The PLA's battle to conquer Tibet was fought against Tibetan, not Nationalist, troops. Shortly after the fall of the Qing dynasty, Tibetan troops expelled the last Chinese imperial forces from their territory and the thirteenth Dalai Lama returned from exile in India to establish a new government that asserted complete independence.[104] It maintained a separate government and army in subsequent decades, and mounted a concerted diplomatic effort after the defeat of Japan to fend off Chinese claims and gain international recognition of separate statehood.[105] Tibet tried unsuccessfully to fend off the impending invasion through appeals to the United Nations, Great Britain, and the United States, and fruitless negotiations with the CCP.[106] The Chinese armies finally invaded in October 1951, overwhelming the small and poorly equipped Tibetan troops. Last-minute appeals to India and the United Nations yielded little international support.[107] The Tibetan government had little choice but to accept terms dictated by Beijing that required Tibetan acceptance of Chinese rule in return for vague and largely unenforceable promises of autonomy and noninterference in religious and social affairs. The sixteen-year-old fourteenth Dalai Lama returned to Lhasa.[108]

The CCP's new position was one of Han cultural superiority. Oppressed Tibetans were now "liberated" from their reputedly backward social arrangements. Many Tibetans found this forced settlement, and the associated claims of Han cultural superiority, difficult to accept. As the new Chinese state steadily encroached on Tibetan autonomy in religious and social affairs in the coming decades, it created for itself enduring political problems, including an armed rebellion that was crushed by the PLA in 1959.

Legacies

What lessons would Mao and other CCP leaders draw from their victory, and what legacies would the new party-state inherit from the revolutionary organization that engineered it? The first, and perhaps the most important, was confidence in Mao's judgment and leadership. At several key junctures in the party's history, Mao had taken minority positions on questions of strategy that were vindicated by subsequent events. He was one of the earliest proponents of rural revolution in a period when the party's leaders still adhered to the Soviet dogma that revolution could come only much later, after an urban proletariat had developed. In the Yan'an base area, he rebuilt the party and army into an effective force that finally presented a credible challenge to the Nationalists after the Japanese surrender. Perhaps the most decisive such instance was Mao's insistence, from the beginning of the civil war, that total victory was possible. Despite extensive battlefield losses in the first two years, Mao insisted, against the counsel of more cautious colleagues, that victory could be won and that their forces should fight on.[109] This cemented his reputation within the party as a leader of unusual ability and foresight. In the words of two leading analysts of the Mao era, "His perceived exceptional ability to solve the mysteries of revolutionary struggle in the face of overwhelming odds created a deep faith that he could chart a course others could not see . . . even when events suggested he was no longer infallible."[110]

The second important legacy was the party's emphasis on discipline and unquestioning obedience to the party line and to Mao Zedong. These features, honed during the early 1940s in Yan'an, would loom large in the subsequent history of the People's Republic. The key point, however, is not the demands that the party would make on Chinese society, but the demands that were placed on party members and especially its own cadres. The burden of undeviating loyalty and discipline is heaviest on those entrusted by the party with leadership positions. Its cadres are monitored in word and deed even more closely than subject populations and are potentially subject to harsh sanctions for deviation or dissent. The ever-present threat of sanctions for failing to thoroughly perform assigned roles accounts for the remarkable discipline and unity of purpose that the party organization so often exhibited in the struggle for power and beyond. But there was a negative, dysfunctional side as well:

overconformity and overimplementation even when conformity with directives had unintended and highly negative outcomes. This led to a recurring pattern of starts and stops to party campaigns, reversals of policy in the face of negative outcomes, or a push in one direction followed by a rapid lurch in another to correct the problems created.

The ultimate legacy that emerges from the long struggle for power was not the patient, persistent organizing characteristic of isolated guerrilla forces in base areas. In the last phase of its battle for power, the CCP generated the foundations for a vast, militarized bureaucracy that excelled at extracting sacrifice from subject populations and party cadres alike. This was a revolutionary organization determined to achieve a large objective, quickly, against seemingly impossible odds, heedless of the costs to the party and the people. In the coming decade, Mao would use his credibility to push forward policies that harked back to the revolutionary mobilization that won the civil war. In the words of one analyst, "for Mao and his followers the overriding lesson of the civil war was that whatever the adverse odds and no matter what the obstacles, revolutionary objectives could be reached by mobilizing the masses and mustering up sufficient will and determination. This proved to be a costly and fatal delusion."[111]

3

Rural Revolution

ALTHOUGH THEY OFTEN begin as insurgencies against oppressive rule, major social revolutions typically create larger, stronger, and more powerfully centralized states. They do this by transforming old social structures, destroying the power of old elites, and establishing new bureaucratic organizations that reach directly into the grass roots.[1] During its first decade in power, the Chinese Communist Party carried out this agenda with speed and thoroughness. In the countryside, this task was completed in two distinct stages. In the first stage, a revolutionary land reform, carried out as a compulsory form of staged class struggle, destroyed the economic and political foundations of the local elites who had dominated Chinese communities for centuries. In the second stage, collectivization, land was consolidated into village-wide farms, and peasants were absorbed into rural organizations in which they essentially became bonded laborers subject to the authority of leaders appointed by the new party-state.

Land Reform as Class Struggle

The tool for extending state power into China's villages was the CCP's practice of land reform conducted as class struggle. The party's conscious intent was to change the rural social structure in a way that created greater equality and promoted the interests of the poor. For this practice to succeed, however, CCP authority had to be established by securing the region militarily. By placing its cadres within militarily secured areas, having them orchestrate a campaign against groups identified as class enemies and political opponents, and creating new village governments, state power was extended directly into the grass roots.

This strategy of rural revolution was Mao Zedong's signature contribution to Marxism-Leninism and to the theory and practice of socialist revolution. Mao was one of the first and most forceful advocates of the view, contrary to Marxist-Leninist orthodoxy, that China's revolution would of necessity be a peasant revolution.[2] Mao's main responsibility from 1925 to 1927, during the United Front with the Nationalists, was the peasant movement. The leaders of the CCP considered him their leading expert on rural issues, and Mao helped to train many of the rural cadres who accompanied Nationalist armies on their march to the north. Mao argued forcefully, against opposition from both Nationalist allies and more orthodox Marxists within his own party, that China was already ripe for rural revolution, and that only a thorough transformation of its backward rural social structure would create the revolutionary energy necessary to bring China's national revolution to completion.[3]

In the months leading up to the July 1926 launch of the Northern Expedition, Mao laid out his distinctive views on the political role of the peasantry. He presented analyses of the economic structure of villages in South China, including the role of secret societies and bandits, laying out the grievances and interests of eight distinct social classes, and specifying the exploitation suffered by the majority in the form of excessive rents, indebtedness, unequal access to land, and landlord domination of local militia.[4] A resolution on the peasant movement that he helped to draft stated bluntly that in a country where 80 percent of the population lived on farms, "China's national revolution is, to put it plainly, a peasant revolution." The anticipated national revolution could not be consolidated without liberating peasants from economic and political oppression.[5] Mao wrote that the revolution could not succeed without peasant support, and that the landlord class was in fact the greatest adversary of the national revolution then under way.[6]

Mao's view of the peasant movement as a class struggle became highly controversial in the Nationalist-Communist alliance. During 1926, as the Revolutionary Army under Chiang Kai-shek moved north, it often retained village militias who were paid and controlled by landowners. Mao advocated dissolving the local militias precisely because they were controlled by landlords and would therefore block rural revolution.[7] After local militias were disarmed, new farmers' associations, created by CCP activists that followed behind the army, could operate unopposed. Led by the dispossessed of the villages, the farmers' associations conducted trials of "local bullies and evil gentry," and subjected village elites to public humiliation, beatings, and summary executions, after which they distributed the property among themselves.[8]

Soviet advisors who were assisting the Northern Expedition were alarmed by the rural violence, which in their view threatened the Nationalist-Communist alliance necessary to unite China under a new revolutionary government. In Stalin's view, the Nationalist army was needed for a "bourgeois revolution" against feudal and warlord forces in China. But if the land revolution was pushed too far it would alienate the Nationalist officer corps, many of which came from landowning families. Stalin ordered the CCP to moderate the movement, and its Central Committee tried to stop the violence. Many corps commanders in the army replaced Communist commissars with non-Communist ones, and they suppressed rural uprisings and reversed land seizures.[9]

Mao responded strongly to these criticisms and refuted the "seemingly unanimous view" that the peasant movement was deplorable, a "movement of riffraff." He argued, instead, that the peasant movement did not endanger the United Front, but promised the creation of a more unified alliance that included the majority of the Chinese people. Without the violent overthrow of the landlord class, he argued, there could be no real united front. During the revolution, "all actions of the peasants against the feudal landlord class are correct. Even if there are some excesses, they are still correct, because unless they learn to go too far . . . they will certainly not be able to overthrow the power of the feudal class built up over several thousand years."[10]

Mao had already made clear his position on revolutionary class conflict in an essay celebrating the anniversary of the Paris Commune several months before. "Only class wars can liberate humanity," he wrote. "At present, there are a considerable number of people within the country who doubt or oppose class struggle. This is because they do not understand the history of human development." The Paris Commune failed for two reasons, in his view. First, "there was no united, centralized and disciplined party to lead it," and second, "the attitude toward the enemy was too conciliatory and merciful—to be conciliatory toward the enemy is to be cruel to our comrades. . . . If we do not adopt severe measures toward the enemy, the enemy will employ cruel measures toward us." Mao argued that criticisms of "red terror" were part of a plot by imperialists to sow dissension among China's revolutionary forces. In reality, Mao wrote, "white terror" by the forces of order was always much worse.[11]

Mao's most detailed defense of the peasant revolution was the lengthy report he submitted in February 1927 to the Nationalist Party's Central Committee on the peasant movement in Hunan. The report describes a peasant rebellion against landlords and rich peasants that would become a template for subsequent communist land reform. In particular, its description became the model for the "struggle sessions" through which CCP cadres later carried out land reform, and was later applied to party rule in urban China as well. In this essay, Mao expressed views about violence as the crucible of revolution that remained at the core of his political philosophy until the end of his life.

The report praised the outburst of revolutionary violence as necessary, describing it in detail, and celebrating its liberating impact on the rural poor. He criticized those who timidly recoiled from what they called "excesses," which were in fact an inevitable by-product of revolution. Mao argued that one's attitude toward rural revolution was a test that determined whether you stood on the side of revolution or reaction. In this document, one can readily see the internal tensions that would soon split the Communists and Nationalists. Mao began with extravagant praise for the peasant rebellion:

> The present upsurge of the peasant movement is a colossal event. In a very short time, several hundred million peasants in China's central, southern, and northern provinces will rise like a fierce wind or tempest, a force so swift and violent that no power, however great, will be able to suppress it. They will break through all the trammels that bind them and rush forward along the road to liberation. They will, in the end, send all the imperialists, warlords, corrupt officials, local bullies, and bad gentry to their graves. All revolutionary parties and all revolutionary comrades will stand before them to be tested, to be accepted or rejected as they decide. To march at their head and lead them? Or to stand opposite them and oppose them?[12]

Mao described the peasants' actions with approval, and his descriptions would later become an established part of the struggle sessions conducted as part of the Communist Party's rural campaigns in future decades. "A big crowd is rallied to demonstrate against the house of a local bully or one of the bad gentry who is hostile to the association. The demonstrators eat at the offender's house, slaughtering his pigs and consuming his grain as a matter of course." Public humiliation is also an important part of the act of rebellion, and has a lasting effect:

> Parades through the villages in tall hats. This sort of thing is very common
> everywhere. One of the local bullies or bad gentry is crowned with a
> tall paper hat bearing the words "local bully so and so" or "so and so,
> one of the bad gentry." He is led by a rope and escorted with big crowds
> in front and behind. . . . This form of punishment, more than any other,
> makes the local bullies and bad gentry tremble. Anyone who has once
> been crowned with a tall paper hat loses face altogether and can never
> again hold up his head.[13]

Mao refuted the idea that this was excessive. Peasants do this only because they have been driven to it by gentry cruelty, and the gentry de-
serve whatever punishments the masses deem they should suffer: "Who
is bad and who is not, who is the worst and who deserves to be let off
lightly—the peasants keep clear accounts, and very seldom has the punishment exceeded the crime." As he argued in a famous passage:

> A revolution is not like inviting people to dinner, or writing an essay, or
> painting a picture, or doing embroidery; it cannot be so refined, so lei-
> surely and gentle, so "benign, upright, courteous, temperate and com-
> plaisant." A revolution is an uprising, an act of violence whereby one
> class overthrows the power of another. . . . If the peasants do not use
> extremely great force, they cannot possibly overthrow the deeply rooted
> power of the landlords, which has lasted for thousands of years. . . . To
> put it bluntly, it is necessary to bring about a brief reign of terror in every
> rural area; otherwise we could never suppress the activities of the coun-
> terrevolutionaries in the countryside or overthrow the authority of the
> gentry. To right a wrong, it is necessary to exceed the proper limits; the
> wrong cannot be righted without doing so.[14]

Exceeding the "proper limits," moreover, can include summary execution, and violence that reaches this level is highly effective in shaking
the old order to its foundations. "Shooting. This is confined to the worst
local bullies and bad gentry and is carried out by the peasants jointly
with other sections of the popular masses. . . . The execution of one such
big member of the bad gentry . . . reverberates throughout a whole
[county] and is very effective in eradicating the remaining evils of feudalism."[15] Mao was defiant in his attitude toward those who opposed
this revolutionary upsurge. In fact, he asserted, "Every revolutionary
comrade must support this change or he will be a counterrevolutionary."[16]
One month after Mao delivered this report, Chiang Kai-shek initiated a
violent purge of his Communist allies.

Mao always understood that revolutionary outbursts could occur only
with the backing of armed force. Left to their own devices, peasants

would be unable to break through the restraining force of gentry-led militias. A revolutionary party had to have its own armed forces to secure areas for rebellion by the dispossessed. In August 1927, four months after Chiang Kai-shek's purge of the Communists, Mao reiterated his position. "If you want to seize political power, to try to do it without the support of military forces would be sheer self-deception. Our Party's mistake in the past has been that it neglected military affairs. Now we should concentrate 60 percent of our energies on the military movement. We must carry out the principle of seizing and establishing political power on the barrel of a gun."[17] Shortly after Chiang's purge, the Communist Party organized a series of failed regional uprisings that ended with their remnant forces retreating into isolated mountain bases.[18] After consolidating their base areas, Mao and his comrades proceeded to implement the vision of rural revolution described in his reports, orchestrating them through staged struggle sessions in militarily secured villages. As described in his reports, the party mobilized the village poor in public meetings to accuse, confront, humiliate, and expropriate the property of village elites. Beatings and summary executions were a regular part of the process. From the Jiangxi Soviet to the base areas during the anti-Japanese war, to the final struggle during the civil war, to the early years after the military conquest of China, "class struggle" orchestrated as part of a set script was the primary means employed by the CCP to break the political and economic power of village elites, redistribute land, and promote new village leaders loyal to the party.

Political Impact of the Land Revolution

Revolutionary land reform had political consequences that were just as important as the economic ones. The assault on landlords and other powerful figures—expropriating their property, humiliating them in public rituals, subjecting them to beatings and summary executions, and stigmatizing the survivors and their descendants—demolished the existing foundations of both political and economic power in the countryside. Into this power vacuum was inserted a new scaffolding of party-state power. Political activists and party members, drawn primarily at this stage from the former poor, were mobilized into the land reform campaign and emerged as village leaders in a new state structure. This new state, unlike the Nationalists', would not rely on local landowning and merchant families to exercise power.

This was political revolution in the guise of land reform. It was designed to utterly destroy the wealth and influence of prior elites, and to permanently stigmatize them and their descendants. It recruited a new generation of party members and rural leaders, individuals who distinguished themselves as activists in land reform. These leaders owed their positions, and their allegiance, to the new party-state. Moreover, the process of land reform demonstrated the overwhelming power of the party to destroy its perceived opponents and remake society in a way that previously seemed unimaginable. By granting land and the promise of relative prosperity to the vast majority of the rural population, it created support for the new regime. And by mobilizing the majority of villagers to participate actively in the violent struggle sessions that so often ended in the summary execution of landlords and the seizure and division of their property, the process implicated village populations in the violence of the revolution.

William Hinton, an American communist who worked with the CCP during the late 1940s, left a detailed and memorable account of this rural revolution. Hinton reported sympathetically on the movement in central Shanxi, where the Red Army moved in shortly after the Japanese surrender in late 1945. The first step was an "antitraitor campaign." Public struggle sessions were held against the village head, the leader of the local militia, and a landlord who had collaborated with the Japanese. Communist cadres organized a struggle session and ordered the entire village to attend. The struggle targets were led to a stage, bound by hand, and forced to stand. The cadres yelled accusations at them, slapped and punched them, but despite calls for participation by the villagers, none came forward. The meeting was then postponed to the next day. That evening the cadres broke the village up into small group meetings and reviewed with them the behavior of these individuals under the Japanese. They assured the villagers that the Red Army would continue to hold the area, so they need not fear later retribution. In these meetings the cadres identified a group of activists who were instructed to stand up and begin the accusations at the mass meeting. The next day, the struggle session was more effective: more villagers participated actively, and there were more shouted accusations and more threats of violence. Several days later, some higher-ranking military and public security officials came to the village for a more extensive and emotional accusation meeting. Two of the targets were condemned to death, marched to the edge of the village, and shot. Their property was confiscated and distributed to villagers.[19]

After the collaborators were punished, the party began its campaign against wealthy village households. In 1946 they moved against landlords, who were accused of hoarding grain during a recent famine. Village cadres led struggle sessions, forced the landlords to kneel, and beat them to make them reveal where they had stored their money and gold. They were not executed, but several of them fled.[20] This was the opening wedge of a broader campaign against landlords and the local Catholic Church. The heads of prominent local families were subjected to struggle sessions. Shouted accusations, beatings, forced confessions, and torture were used to extract information about hidden wealth. This was more violent than the previous campaigns, and quite a few individuals were beaten to death or committed suicide. The property of these individuals and of the local Catholic parish was seized and distributed to the village poor.[21]

By mid-1946, a new village government was in place, and there were enough party members to form a party branch committee. But there were problems: the new leaders, who exercised unchallengeable authority with the backing of the Red Army and party organization, immediately began to abuse their power. Hinton details the way that the new village cadres and militia heads engaged in corruption, coercion, beatings, sexual harassment of women, and even rape, with little recourse by powerless villagers.[22] These problems were apparently widespread in the "liberated areas" during the civil war in North China, and the party leadership decided to send a "work team" of fifteen people, including officials from the county seat, along with teachers and political activists from a local university (including Hinton) to investigate and rectify the problems. The work team took over the leadership of the village and investigated the behavior of the village leaders and party branch. They set up a peasants' association, elected new leaders, and set up a new village government. They documented landholding patterns prior to the land seizures through interviews with villagers and small group meetings, and classified households as poor, middle, rich peasants, and landlords.[23] In these interviews and small group meetings they also solicited reports of abuse by the village leaders.[24]

As Hinton's detailed account makes clear, revolutionary land reform was above all an act of state building: it destroyed the foundation of the previous order, cleared the ground for new political organizations, recruited new leaders from among formerly marginal social groups, and granted benefits to the vast majority of farmers that would create widespread support for the new party-state.[25] It created state machinery that for the first time in Chinese history could directly collect taxes from individual households.

In Chinese imperial dynasties, the state structure extended no lower than the county seat. This was the lowest level at which there existed salaried officials that were part of the imperial bureaucracy. County magistrates were responsible for collecting taxes and keeping local order; they hired their own staff and established networks of influence with other local notables, often those who were property owners and had passed lower levels of the imperial examinations. Villages were essentially governed autonomously by local propertied elites, who maintained temples and schools, led kinship organizations, maintained local militia, and donated resources for poor relief.[26]

By the 1940s, local society and politics had changed greatly, but the pattern of rule by local elites continued in altered form. The traditional gentry—degree holders in imperial examinations—no longer played the role in local governance that they once did. The imperial examinations were abolished in 1905, and few of the degree holders were still around. They were replaced by other local notables—merchants, big landlords, and local political actors—who served as intermediaries with the district government. In some respects they were more autonomous than the traditional gentry, who owed their status to performance on the imperial examinations.[27]

C. K. Yang described the Guangdong village of Nanching in 1948 in terms that had changed little from the imperial era: "In the Republican period, political order within the county functioned mainly through the informal local community leadership, with the county government as the supervising agent; and the village stood as a highly autonomous self-governing unit." Since the fall of the last imperial dynasty, "the national government failed to substantially alter the traditional decentralized pattern of local government in which the village political life operated largely by its own local power structure and was but weakly integrated into the system of central authority."[28] Yang described a village where clan organizations were responsible for maintaining roads, dykes, and canals, funding village schools, and arming local militia for protection against bandits. Crop protection teams were also established by groups of poorer and middle-class farmers to protect against bandits and theft, and they established connections with the local underworld, sometimes forming alliances with gangs of racketeers.[29] Informally constituted local power groups coexisted with one another in the village.[30]

Yang followed the transformation of the village though the first years after the consolidation of Communist rule, and chronicled the building of the new state at the grassroots level. Class struggle and land reform occurred in ways described elsewhere in China, and coincided with the suppression of "local bullies," although no public trials or executions were initially held within the village. Households were given class labels. Land, household items, farm tools, and draft animals were seized and redistributed to poorer households, as was clan property devoted to the funding of schools and temples.[31]

The political changes were equally radical. The party established a new power structure backed by armed force. The crop protection association was disarmed and disbanded. Soldiers confiscated firearms. The power of prominent families melted away, and many fled to Hong Kong; the clan organization was stripped of its property and former social functions. The first agents of the new state to appear in the village were fully armed soldiers and officers. After land reform was completed, in the 1951 campaign to "suppress counterrevolutionaries," sixteen individuals were executed without trial or public explanation, spreading fear among villagers who were uncertain what made these individuals "enemies of the people." The new subdistrict government appointed a village head and vice head, and a new people's militia directly under the subdistrict government was formed.[32] Yang concluded, "in an amazingly short time the Communists abolished the old system of formal government in Nanching and completely disintegrated the informal local structure of power and authority . . . a development which moved China perceptibly closer to the structural reality of a modern state and immensely increased the collective strength of the nation's central political power."[33]

Economic Impact of the Land Revolution

The economic consequences of the land revolution were just as dramatic. In short order, land expropriated from prosperous families was transferred to poor peasants, creating a remarkably equal distribution of land. Poor and lower-middle-class peasants comprised more than 57 percent of the rural population, but owned only 24 percent of the land in the 1930s. After land reform, their share of the nation's farmland almost doubled, to 47 percent. Rich peasants and landlords suffered drastic losses. Rich peasants, who comprised 3.5 percent of the population, owned more than 18 percent in the 1930s, but were left with 6.4 percent after land reform. Landlords bore the brunt of the campaign, just as they had borne the brunt of the violent struggle sessions and executions. Only 2.5 percent of the population, they owned almost 40 percent of the land in the 1930s, but were reduced to barely more than 2 percent after land reform.[34] Figure 3.1 illustrates the impact of this radical land redistribution on landholdings. Poor peasants more than doubled their average farm size, and middle-class peasants improved their holdings slightly, while the farms of rich peasants shrank by roughly a third—though their farms were still much larger than all other groups'. Landlords were devastated by land reform, which clearly focused its political animus on them. Their average farm size shrank by 90 percent, and after land reform their holdings were the same as those of the village poor.[35]

By design, violence was integral to the process. It was entirely possible, however, to redistribute land and break landlord power without violent struggle sessions, executions, and political stigma attached to elite families. Moderate but effective land reforms were carried out in postwar

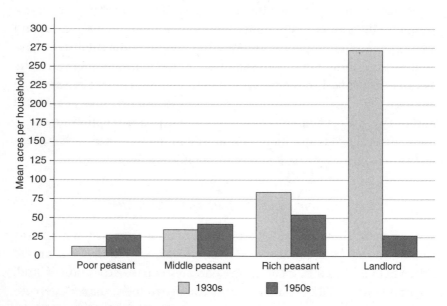

Figure 3.1. Average farm size, by class category, before and after land reform. *Source:* Riskin (1987, 51).

Japan, South Korea, and Taiwan in the 1950s, leading to a more equal distribution of land and creating the foundation for a prosperous small-holding agriculture and rapid rural development. This nonviolent approach to land reform stripped landlords of their traditional sources of income and undercut their dominance of the rural economy, but they received partial compensation and were not denied all other forms of wealth or treated subsequently as political outcasts.

The land reform belatedly carried out by Chiang Kai-shek's Nationalists shortly after their retreat to Taiwan illustrates this point. Land reform was discussed constantly without action in Nationalist legislatures during their long years on the mainland, but after consolidating a much more centralized and oppressive dictatorship on Taiwan, Chiang Kai-shek finally forced it to completion. From 1949 to 1953, rents for tenant farmers were reduced by law to no more than 37.5 percent of the annual crop yield; public land and land expropriated from Japanese owners was sold to landless farmers at a deep discount; upper limits were placed on landholdings; and private land in excess of these limits was sold cheaply to small farmers. Landlords were compensated for the expropriated land in the form of stock in government-owned corporations. The percentage of families that owned their own farms rose from 36 to 65 percent, and the percentage that rented land dropped from 39 to 11 percent. This did not level property ownership to the extent that it did on the Chinese mainland, nor did it punish landlords economically or physically liquidate them as a class. Nonetheless, landlord power was essentially broken in rural Taiwan, as independent farmers organized rural credit and savings associations and transport services, and promoted rural industry.[36]

Consolidating Rural Control

The process of change was not smooth, nor was state building without its complications. In the early 1950s, party organizations in rural counties were forced to take measures against party members and rural cadres who failed to perform their duties in desired ways. One problem was a tendency of rural party leaders to become focused on the prosperity of their new family farms. Some rural cadres expressed satisfaction that the land revolution had achieved its goals, and now that they had a workable family farm, they concentrated on economic rather than political activities. The demands of political leadership conflicted with the time necessary to farm successfully, especially because village leadership positions were poorly compensated. Significant numbers of village party members employed hired labor on their farms, which was viewed as a form of economic exploitation, raising concerns that the party organization was losing its proletarian character. This led to a 1951 campaign against "rightist tendencies" in village party organizations. Ten percent of village officials and party members were expelled and many more subjected to withering criticism and minor forms of punishment.[37]

A second problem that emerged early on was abusive behavior by new village leaders of the kind documented by Hinton in base areas during the civil war. This included the suppression of criticism, the use of coercion and intimidation to achieve compliance with party policy, and the routine use of physical intimidation and even severe beatings. This kind of behavior was officially attributed to excessive bureaucratic pressures placed on village cadres by their superiors to comply with party-mandated targets. A 1953 campaign targeted these abuses of power. Once again, those who occupied the lower rungs of the new party-state were subjected to investigation, criticism, expulsion, and in some cases imprisonment.[38]

In many rural regions, especially those where the People's Liberation Army rolled through quickly on its campaign of military conquest, new rural governments were established on shaky foundations. Guizhou Province, conquered in November 1949, is one such example. Land reform was conducted quickly and new village governments were set up. But organized resistance to the new regime soon appeared in reaction to demands for large grain deliveries to the new military government. Leadership posts were handed out to individuals who initially seemed cooperative with PLA forces when they passed through, but many later led popular resistance. After the PLA moved on to Tibet and Yunnan in January 1950, anti-Communist guerrillas gained strength and the CCP was soon forced to withdraw from twenty-eight besieged counties. The battle to bring all of Guizhou fully under control continued well into 1951. The PLA returned and employed violently coercive methods described as "terroristic." There were similar problems elsewhere in southwestern China, requiring intensified suppression by the PLA.[39]

After China entered the Korean War in October 1950, the new regime became increasingly concerned about internal security and launched a nationwide campaign to "suppress counterrevolution." The sweeps in Guizhou were only one part of this nationwide effort. Like land reform, the campaign aimed at eliminating groups that the regime considered to be political and social rivals. This included former Nationalist soldiers and party members, bandits, local strongmen, leaders of religious sects and secret societies, Catholic priests and Protestant ministers, and ordinary criminals. The campaign was reminiscent of land reform, with public trials, denunciation meetings, imprisonments, and executions.[40] Although there are no agreed figures for the total numbers executed and imprisoned during land reform and the campaign to suppress counterrevolution, the number easily ran into the millions. An estimated 1.5 to 2 million people died during land reform from 1947 to 1952.[41] Internal party reports suggest a minimum number of 710,000 executions during the campaign to suppress counterrevolution, with another 1.2 million imprisoned. Unofficial estimates are frequently much higher.[42]

Toward Collective Farms

The rural economy recovered quickly from the civil war, and there were signs that China's new system of small family farms would raise rural living standards. Rural markets revived, household incomes rose, and the first years of the People's Republic were a welcome respite from previous years of foreign invasion and civil war.[43] But the new regime's goal was not to create a system of smallholding private agriculture. This was made clear in Mao's 1953 "General Line for the Transition period." Land reform was designed to break landlord power, generate peasant support, and create the foundation for a new socialist state. The next stage was a socialist economy on the Soviet model, and this meant the end of private ownership and the formation of collective farms.

In 1953, shortly after land reform was completed, rural officials pushed farm households to pool labor, share draft animals, and engage in other forms of mutual aid and cooperative activity. A new policy for "unified sales and purchase" of grain meant that private grain markets were banned and all crops had to be sold to state grain procurement stations in villages at prices fixed by the state.[44] In 1954, grain sales became compulsory and all "surplus" grain—defined as a fixed per capita household ration—had to be sold to the state. Despite the fact that farming required more strenuous physical exertion than most urban jobs, the rural grain ration was set lower than in the cities.[45]

This was the first step toward a system that would permit the state to extract grain from villages in amounts and at prices that it alone determined. Rural China started down the road to Soviet-style collective agriculture, and the only question was how long the process would take. The first step in what originally was to have been a gradual process of collectivization was the formation of mutual aid teams among independent farmers. Mutual aid teams pooled the labor of a number of households during the busiest periods of planting and harvesting. Families still owned their own draft animals and agricultural implements, but shared them with team members during peak seasons when they worked together to put the crop in the ground or bring in the harvest. The next step was the formation of agricultural cooperatives. In the cooperatives, families continued to own their land, but the cooperative owned draft animals, tools, and any machinery, and families contributed funds to the cooperative for the purchase of seed and fertilizer in bulk, fodder for draft animals, and fuel for machinery. Members of the cooperative also assisted one another during the peak planting and harvesting seasons, like the mutual aid teams.[46]

The final stage was the collective farm—land was no longer owned and cultivated by families, but was consolidated into large farms that were under collective ownership and run by village leaders appointed by the party. A collective farm was managed like a factory, with collective members in the role of employees. The managers of collective farms organized all agricultural operations, assigned jobs to individuals, stored and marketed the harvest, and kept the proceeds in collective bank accounts.[47]

Mao consistently pushed for more rapid transformation of China's economy toward a Soviet model than the Soviet Union and other Chinese leaders thought wise. Stalin counseled Mao to move slowly, keeping existing economic structures in place for the foreseeable future, and to adopt a long timetable for the collectivization of agriculture and socialist transformation of industry. Mao, however, was determined to move China rapidly along the path to socialism as laid out in the *Short Course*, which described a radical process of collectivization early in the history of the Soviet Union.[48] But Stalin, in his 1951 book *Economic Problems of Socialism in the USSR*, ignored his own signature contribution to socialist development (or perhaps belatedly acknowledged the damage it caused the Soviet economy) and asserted that rapid economic transformation could not be obtained through the mere application of political will. In that work he argued that there were "laws of development" that applied equally to socialism and capitalism.[49] Stalin also believed that China was more backward economically, unprepared to move directly to socialism, and that to make this attempt would set back economic development. Many other Chinese leaders—especially Zhou Enlai, Liu Shaoqi, and Deng Zihui—shared this view. They had more contact with the Soviet Union and were better versed in current ideas about socialist economics, and argued for a more cautious approach.

Mao implicitly rejected this position in the early 1950s, and by the early 1960s, in his unpublished "reading notes" on Soviet political economy, he explicitly criticized this shift by Stalin.[50] Essentially, Mao rejected the late Stalin in favor of the early "revolutionary" Stalin, and continued to believe that China could replicate the Soviet pattern described in the *Short Course*. Mao was characteristically in a hurry to push revolution forward as quickly as possible, and did not believe that China was as backward as Stalin thought. While Stalin was alive, Mao did not contradict him, but he quietly ignored his advice. After Stalin's death in March 1953, Mao immediately pushed on with mutual aid teams and cooperatives, and began a collectivization drive that initially was to be completed in the early 1960s.[51] After clashes with other leaders in 1957 about the pace of collectivization, Mao denounced several of them for "rightism," and called for the immediate completion of collectivization by 1958.[52]

Village cadres began organizing mutual aid teams in 1951. By 1953 half of all households were members, and by 1954, 85 percent. After Mao forced the pace of collectivization in the "high tide" of 1955 and 1956, cooperatives were formed very rapidly: 62 percent of households joined them by the end of 1955, and a reported 100 percent by the end of 1956. The decision to forge ahead even faster to full-scale collective farms was made near the end of 1957 and, in a massive mobilization that began near the end of that year, 100 percent of households were reportedly absorbed into collective farms by the end of 1958.[53] The apparent speed of completion suggested a process that was relatively smooth and successful, especially in comparison with the extensive violence employed in the Soviet Union, and the catastrophic famine in Russia and

Ukraine that was a direct result.[54] Nonetheless, there was widespread local resistance, even isolated rebellions, and considerable hardship and local hunger created by rural cadres who felt compelled to complete the process rapidly and at any cost.[55]

The Village as a Collective Farm

The result of the collectivization drive was a radically new form of social and economic organization. For farm households, the fruits of land reform lasted for a remarkably short period of time. The land gained by poorer households was no longer theirs, and the ability of farmers to decide what to produce and how to allocate their labor to enhance family incomes was completely lost. Household farming was pushed almost to extinction, relegated to marginal family sidelines that were only partially tolerated in subsequent years. The rural markets that depended on family production of eggs, chickens, hogs, handicrafts, and other products largely disappeared, replaced by state purchasing stations for staple and cash crops. Now all land, tools, and draft animals were under collective ownership and control.[56]

By the late 1950s, collective farms doubled as units of government and as economic enterprises. Collective farms fluctuated in size during the late 1950s—in the Great Leap Forward they were expanded to enormous scale, but by the early 1960s they settled into a pattern that survived into the early 1980s. The farm population in a county was organized into communes, the name for the collective farm. The commune headquarters was the lowest branch of the state bureaucracy, with a party secretary and party committee at its head, and a staff of officials on the state payroll. Communes had an average population of around 15,000 and usually spanned a number of separate villages. Each commune contained an average of fifteen production brigades of around 220 households and 980 people. A production brigade was roughly equivalent to a village, although larger villages might be divided into two or more brigades, and in more sparsely populated regions a brigade might span two or more small settlements. Each brigade, in turn, was divided into an average of seven production teams. The production team, the basic unit of agricultural organization, was relatively small. They averaged just over thirty households and around 145 people by the early 1970s.[57] The production brigades and teams had their own heads, accountants, and other officials, whose salaries were part of brigade and team budgets. They were not part of the state civil service system, which reached only so far as the commune headquarters, and they were also considered farm households and resided in the community.

Commune leaders made production decisions based on targets sent down from the county, which were passed down to the brigades and teams. The leaders of brigades and teams were in charge of fulfilling the plans. They assigned jobs to individual farmers and organized planting, harvesting, processing, storage, and transport. Farmers received "work points" for their assigned labor, which were recorded in team accounts and accumulated over the year. Any cash surpluses in the collective accounts were divided among households according to the number of work points that individuals in the family accumulated over the year. Each member of the team also received basic grain rations, set according to age and gender, that came out of the grain stores that the brigade retained after meeting state sales targets. Because rural residents could only procure grain from their production teams, farmers were effectively blocked from spending significant periods of time away from the village. Migratory labor of the type that was common before collectivization, and that became widespread in China after the 1970s, was effectively ended. Farmers were also subject to involuntary and uncompensated "service labor" on road building and water conservation projects during the agricultural slack season that was mandated by county officials and organized by communes. Farmers were essentially tied to the land in a form of bonded labor.

Collective agriculture fully consolidated the state procurement system that was put into place beginning in 1953. Staple grains (rice, wheat, barley, maize, and sorghum), oil-bearing crops (peanuts, rapeseed, sesame), and cash crops (cotton, tobacco, sugar, hemp) could be sold only to state purchasing stations, at state-set prices. The system was easy to enforce, because commune and brigade officials—not households—were in control of the crop and were evaluated and rewarded (or punished) according to their fulfillment of production plans, and alternative market outlets were unavailable. The system permitted state planning agencies to control the terms of trade with the farm sector, and to directly influence the mix of crops that were grown.[58]

Soviet-style collective agriculture was designed to extract grain in large volumes and at low prices in order to fuel rapid industrial development in cities. Low food prices permitted lower wages for urban workers, which left more funds for capital investment in the industrial economy. Over time, cropping decisions became increasingly focused on staple crops. The prohibition of independent off-farm employment and nonagricultural sidelines by households forced China's peasants into subsistence agriculture. The demands for high production and sales targets by the state, and the setting of deliberately low procurement prices, meant that many residents on collective farms found their grain rations to be increasingly tight and their cash incomes depressed. By the 1970s, with the exception only of "economic" crops like tobacco and hemp, procurement prices barely covered production costs for most products governed by the state purchasing system.[59]

Household production was frowned upon, and in some periods punished severely, because devotion to household production directly conflicted with commitment to collective activities. For most of the next two decades, household sidelines of any significant volume were effectively banned. Chickens, ducks, hogs, and fishponds were maintained by production teams and brigades, and the labor devoted to them was compensated with work points. The products were marketed by the collective in the same way as crops. Some brigades and communes organized off-farm enterprises—construction teams, handicraft workshops, or small industrial enterprises like brick kilns. Commune and brigade officials managed these enterprises, assigned workers to jobs, and collected and banked the proceeds. Workers were paid in work points and at times partially in cash.[60]

The periodic rural markets that had characterized village life in China for centuries went into deep decline, and they survived only in the form of illicit black markets.[61] In their place a state procurement system appropriated agricultural products from collective farms in volumes and at prices set by state planning agencies. Planners tried to ensure that they left enough food in collectives to permit farmers a basic standard of living—but not much more. The emphasis on staple grain production reduced the variety of crops and sideline products that was typical under household agriculture, effectively pushing Chinese farmers into grain-centered subsistence agriculture. This kept cash incomes low relative to urban areas. Differences in living standards within brigades and teams were reduced even further than was the case after land reform. Certain jobs in a collective were less arduous but had a higher work point valuation—leadership positions, tractor drivers, and carpentry, for example—while unskilled field labor earned fewer work points. Yet the differences in income were limited, and the result was a leveling of living standards within villages.

These changes gave rural cadres considerably more power than they had before collectivization. "One of the major consequences" of this change, according to Huaiyin Li, "was the creation of co-op cadres as a privileged group in the village society." Previously these individuals had been veterans of the revolution or activists in land reform and the creation of cooperatives, and in many cases "they had won villagers' respect for their hard work, austerity, and intimacy with the masses." After the creation of collective structures, however, "they alienated themselves from the rest of the community because of their privileges; they received plenty of workpoint subsidies and, without doing much work, they earned more income than most strong laborers did." These developments were in many ways inherent in the new structures themselves: "They controlled all aspects of the co-op economy, including the assignment of work opportunities, the awarding of workpoints, the distribution of agricultural products, and management of co-op finance." The shift was marked by an increasing reliance on administrative orders, coercion, and in some cases the abuse of farmers in the form of shouting and beatings. This also gave rural cadres the opportunity, for the first time, to engage in "various forms of corruption and malpractice."[62] This imported Soviet system bureaucratized rural life: "Agricultural collectivization not only enabled the state to extend its reach down to each household but also resulted in the creation of millions of grassroots cadres; so huge were the ranks of the cadres that they were practically out of the government's direct control."[63]

Rural China Transformed

In ten years, the CCP radically transformed rural China. In earlier times Chinese villages were governed by local elites whose authority was based on some combination of private wealth, education, and armed force. Chinese states had always been distant from village life, collecting taxes through local elites but otherwise leaving rural communities largely to themselves. Land tenure patterns varied enormously across China, from large-scale landlordism run on behalf of wealthy lineages to widespread share tenancy, hired agricultural labor, and self-sufficient, independently owned small farms. Secret societies and religious sects were widespread.

Christian missionaries made converts deep into the countryside in the nineteenth and early twentieth centuries. Banditry was common, private militias hovered between protection and predation, and life was insecure in many rural regions.

The extension of state power into rural China began with the Communist Party's establishment of a monopoly on the use of armed force. Bandits, private militias, secret societies, organized religion, and religious sects were suppressed. It was ultimately armed force that backed the revolutionary land reform that eliminated prior village elites. The first step in the extension of state power was to destroy social groups that exercised authority, and to obliterate the economic foundation for their elite status. As they destroyed previous structures of wealth and power, the party drew poor peasants into political involvement as land reform activists and, after training and indoctrination, elevated them to new positions of village leadership. Redistributing land and other forms of wealth among villagers, the party created a reservoir of support, while at the same time demonstrating beyond all doubt the reach and capacity of the new state.

Having already extended state power far more deeply into villages than any prior Chinese state, the CCP quickly moved to extend its control into the operation of agriculture itself. The land and draft animals distributed to families during land reform were rapidly merged into collective farms. The state and its village representatives now controlled decisions about production; they controlled the crops after harvesting; they controlled the sales and distribution of the products; and they controlled the cash proceeds and distributed incomes to farmers. They also controlled the labor of farmers, and could prohibit their departure from collective farms. The land reform represented an initial rural revolution that radically transformed the economic structure of rural China and greatly extended the reach of the state into village life. Collectivization represented a second rural revolution that radically transformed the economy in a very different direction, and extended the reach of the state even more deeply into activities that had for millennia been the province of kinship groups and farm households.

4

Urban Revolution

FROM THE LATE 1920S, the Communist Party's strategy for revolution focused on rural China. Mao's early doctrine about class struggle was applied in regions that the party controlled, and as the PLA rolled south and west in its military conquest of China after 1947, CCP cadres orchestrated revolution in villages according to a well-practiced script. The cities, however, were another matter entirely. Not until April 1946 did the party take control of a major city, when they took over Harbin from departing Soviet forces. The first major city that the PLA occupied outside of Manchuria was Zhangjiakou, in northern Hebei, which they held from August 1945 to October 1946 before losing it once again to advancing Nationalist forces.[1] Initially, their strategy was to implement military control and leave existing ownership of industry and commerce intact, with the exception of state enterprises controlled by the Nationalists. In the cities, the main emphasis was to stabilize the economy and promote industrial development, not to obliterate the economic foundations of the old society. The policy was to move slowly, preserve the industrial foundations for national economic strength, and only gradually shift toward a socialist planned economy.[2]

Although there were underground party operatives in trade unions, schools, police forces, and government offices, the CCP had only a small fraction of the cadres necessary to run the cities. Moreover, unlike the countryside, in cities the party lacked an obvious constituency that made up the majority of the population, and that would immediately benefit from its presence in the same way as poor peasants. In the cities were concentrated former members and officials of the Nationalist Party, industrial capitalists and trade unions, middle classes and intellectuals.

These groups had uncertain loyalties at best, and had few reasons to welcome the CCP and its programs.

In some of the first cities to be captured in Manchuria and North China, PLA occupation forces, unprepared for their new tasks, failed to follow orders. Troops and party personnel seized private firms and handicraft workshops, dismantled factory equipment, and confiscated citizens' personal possessions, declaring them "enemy property" for "military use." These actions disrupted urban economies and created an atmosphere of fear among groups whose cooperation the party would need. Mao did not want these errors repeated, and he directed the PLA to avoid similar abuses and respect property and citizens as they assumed urban control.[3] The party had no choice initially but to rely on existing office personnel and police forces to keep order.

Eventually the CCP did adapt some of its approach to rural revolution in the cities. There was no obvious counterpart to the land revolution, but the techniques of mass mobilization translated well. The party pursued urban state building through a series of mobilization campaigns that combined coercion with attempts at popular persuasion. As in the countryside, the process was at times violent and could rely on brute force, open intimidation, and even terror. But coercion and terror alone could not accomplish the party's aims: the party built grassroots organizations that permitted them to monitor the population, reward and punish, and extend their control.

In the years from 1949 to 1956, the CCP extended its reach in the cities through three distinct types of mobilization campaigns. The most dramatic were mass campaigns designed to enhance their political control. This included the urban version of the "campaign to suppress counterrevolution," and the subsequent Three Anti and Five Anti campaigns against corruption and tax evasion, which expropriated private business assets. A second type of campaign was designed to change behavior and attitudes in targeted populations. This included campaigns against crime, drugs, and the sex trade, and the "thought reform" campaign designed to remold the thinking of "bourgeois intellectuals." A third type was to mobilize the urban bureaucracy to complete specific tasks, like the registration of the urban population, the vetting of politically reliable police forces, the collectivization of services and handicrafts, and the nationalization of industry.[4]

By the mid-1950s, as the initial push to eliminate enemies and silence potential critics took hold, the party began to extend its control over the population through bureaucratic means. A household registration system fixed the population in place, preventing permanent moves and unauthorized travel. A supply system and urban rationing allocated food, housing, and material goods according to status and rank. Government-appointed officials monitored activities in neighborhoods and coordinated their work with neighborhood police stations. Private handicrafts, services, and manufacturing were placed under government ownership and control, and a new employment system assigned jobs bureaucratically rather than through voluntary choice. The urban population was registered according to social class and political history, and a system of political dossiers was established to keep track of individual behavior and political leanings. In the second half of the 1950s, the mass meetings, public trials, and executions relied upon so heavily in the early years were replaced by bureaucratic routines within state-organized work units and neighborhoods.

Establishing Order

When the PLA entered a city, its first act was to replace all the top municipal officials with cadres and officers who had traveled south with the conquering armies: a "military control committee."[5] Most of the cadres who came south with the army were veterans of northern base areas, were natives of that region, and were unable to speak or understand southern dialects.[6] The party faced a severe shortage of reliable cadres with urban experience. There were too few party members in the local underground, and regional guerrilla forces lacked urban experience. Student activists who joined CCP-led organizations and who traveled south with the troops helped to fill the gap, but there was little choice initially but to rely extensively on existing urban administrators and even existing police forces.[7]

More than 60 percent of the Nationalist police forces in Shanghai kept their posts during 1949 and 1950 after "reeducation classes." They were supervised by a staff of newly trained police officers from the PLA and by underground party members who had infiltrated the police force in earlier years.[8] In Shanghai, the CCP utilized the existing organizational structure of neighborhoods established under the Japanese occupation and kept by the Nationalists after their return. The party built on the existing system of household registration, but updated and expanded it, adding food ration cards. Unlike the Nationalists, the new regime used basic-level neighborhood organizations to mobilize participation in mass meetings and political campaigns.[9]

The reeducated police forces' first task in Shanghai was to strengthen social order. They shut down small peddlers and kiosks on the streets, cutting their number in half. All publications were required to register with the police in order to operate legally. Currency exchanges were shut down. Beggars, pickpockets, and other vagrants were arrested, registered, and sent for reeducation. Scams run by urban gangs in collaboration with pedicab drivers were stopped. Counterfeiters were executed. Former Nationalist soldiers and officials were ordered to register. If they came forward voluntarily they were promised leniency; if they failed to register, they were threatened with harsh punishment. Harsh measures against crime were based on the principle that those arrested were guilty, and that only those who confessed would be granted leniency. Major offensives were mounted against armed robbers and underground Nationalist operatives left behind to engage in sabotage, subversion, and assassination. These initial moves were intensified after the onset of the Korean War in 1950, in the campaign to suppress counterrevolution, when the new regime pushed much harder, and more violently, to consolidate its hold.[10]

The new regime made clear that members of the large expatriate community, many of whom had long been resident in China, were no longer welcomed. Police harassment, expropriation of homes and property, and imprisonment of foreign businessmen, consular staff, teachers, missionaries, and even students were common even before the onset of the Korean War, when the persecutions intensified, leading to a wave of imprisonments, expulsions, and occasional murders. China's foreign community was largely expunged by 1951. Particularly hard hit were the Catholic and Protestant churches and their networks of orphanages, charity organizations, and convents. In a few years they would be replaced by a wave of advisors from the Soviet Union and its newly conquered satellite states.[11]

Eliminating Opposition

The campaign to suppress counterrevolution of 1950 and 1951 tightened control after the initial period, when public order was the primary objective. As in the countryside, the initial conquest by PLA forces left behind widespread pockets of resistance. In the cities, the primary concern was active Nationalist underground operatives who engaged in sabotage and assassination. However, the campaign also targeted secret societies, underground criminal gangs, and religious sects, which had been a major feature of Chinese urban life and had the capacity to organize resistance to the new regime. The campaign was carried out in cities through mass rallies, public struggle sessions, the broadcast of public trials over loudspeaker systems and radio stations, and a large wave of highly publicized arrests and executions.[12] The denunciation meetings were well staged, emotional, and often ended with the crowd's demand for immediate execution, which was frequently carried out summarily. Those targeted in the campaign but who managed to escape imprisonment were placed under "control" by public security forces, essentially a form of probation, and were kept under surveillance in the years to come.[13] As the campaign intensified, struggle sessions and mass trials were a ubiquitous feature of the urban scene: in Hangzhou, more than 450,000 residents attended 1,545 mass rallies to denounce counterrevolutionaries.[14]

According to official figures, more than 1.2 million people were arrested, ultimately being sent to labor camps, and no fewer than 710,000 executed.[15] There is evidence that the number of executions went far beyond what the party leaders initially intended. Mao Zedong tried to regulate the rate of executions during the course of the campaign, sometimes encouraging greater vigilance, other times trying to moderate the campaign's ferocity. He intervened repeatedly through comments on reports, and at one point suggested a rate of 0.1 percent of the population as the proper level of executions.[16] Local officials, not wanting to be viewed as soft on counterrevolution, tried to comply with this number, treating it as a quota. The campaign's original documents specified spies, saboteurs, and members of underground resistance organizations as the targets for arrest and execution. But many localities could not find enough individuals in these categories to fill the quota. Members of criminal gangs and leaders of religious sects were often thrown into the mix, as were individuals arrested on vague charges of being "local bullies"—without being charged with specific acts. In the course of the campaign, former Nationalist soldiers and officials who had registered after being promised leniency were nonetheless arrested and executed as well. In Guizhou, all eighty-one county magistrates in power during the last days of the Nationalists were executed, as were almost all of the township heads near the city of Chengdu.[17]

The campaign virtually wiped out organized resistance, and it decimated the Nationalists' remaining underground networks. Acts of assassination and sabotage dropped drastically. But by the party's own standards, the number of executions was far too high. Internal party investigations in 1953 revealed that large percentages of those executed were innocent and were hastily executed on fabricated charges. Loyal party members were executed in some of these cases. Especially hard hit were Nationalist officials and soldiers who had voluntarily defected to the CCP in the final stages of the civil war. Promises of leniency made to those who did not defect, but who registered voluntarily after the Nationalists' defeat, were ignored. As signs of runaway indiscriminate killings became apparent to the party's leaders, escalating even after orders to stop, Mao intervened to call a halt to the campaign.[18]

The numbers arrested during these suppression campaigns quickly outstripped the capacity of conventional prisons to house detainees.[19] The prison system inherited from the Nationalists proved woefully inadequate, and the new regime augmented its holding capacity with a massive new system of labor reform camps. By the end of 1951, more than 2 million individuals were imprisoned, 670,000 of which were in the new labor camps, where they were required to contribute through labor to their own upkeep. By 1955, more than 1.3 million were in the labor camps. Conditions were brutal, hunger and physical abuse rampant. The growth rate of the camp and prison populations was suppressed by high death rates.[20]

Suppressing Religious Sects, Secret Societies, and Urban Gangs

In January 1949 the CCP banned secret societies and religious sects. The directive that did so denounced them for their ties to the Nationalist Party, for collaborating with the Japanese, gathering intelligence, spreading rumors, and staging local uprisings.[21] Religious sects drew their primary membership from among the first generation of rural migrants to cities like Tianjin. They were strong in northern China, where the most important was known as the Unity Sect *(yiguandao)*. A specific order targeting this sect was issued in 1950. It had a philosophy that was a mixture of Buddhism, Taoism, Confucianism, Christianity, and Islam, with borrowings from other native sects. The sect was viewed as a major threat to the new government. In the city of Tianjin, which had an adult population of 1 million in 1951, there were over 200,000 members, concentrated heavily among men who worked in small handicraft and commercial establishments, and women in the first generation of urban families.[22] It included an estimated 11 percent of the population of Suiyuan Province, and 15 percent of the population of Beijing, and its membership was growing. An estimated 1,100 officers in the Beijing Bureau of Public Security were members, and local party cadres and members of the Communist Youth League were also found to have joined. In one Beijing district, 23 percent of all the police officers were members of the sect.[23]

The group obviously had the capacity to subvert the new regime. The Unity Sect was openly opposed to communism and had earlier agitated against land redistribution. Before the triumph of the CCP, it spread rumors that the party would enforce the sharing of property and wives. During the Korean War, it proclaimed the coming of a third world war that would destroy the new regime. Before the onset of the campaign to suppress counterrevolution, the CCP criticized the sect and urged members to withdraw from the organization and come forward to register voluntarily. Afterward, however, moves against the Unity Sect were folded into the campaign against counterrevolution. Sect members began to inform on one another; its leaders were subjected to mass denunciation meetings and executed; and the trials and executions were given wide publicity. The campaign effectively broke the back of the organization.[24]

A similar fate befell the secret societies and criminal gangs that had long flourished in Chinese cities. The secret societies were large and relatively well organized, drawing members overwhelmingly from second or later generations of urban dwellers, especially among workers in the transport industry. In coastal cities like Tianjin and Shanghai, they were a major political and economic force under the Nationalists, engaged in smuggling opium, running brothels, controlling the docks and freight delivery, and running many of the trade unions in these sectors. They were heavily represented among coolies, dockworkers, pedicab drivers, and freight haulers. Criminal gangs were smaller and more concentrated in local neighborhoods. They were typically composed of rural toughs who practiced extortion and ran protection rackets. In many parts of cities under Nationalist rule, they had been the sole organization that could guarantee the security of small merchants in return for payoffs.[25]

Both groups had ties to Nationalist officials that were part of the pervasive corruption that plagued that party during its years on the mainland. The Green Gang, in particular, was well integrated with the urban Nationalist administration. Chiang Kai-shek reportedly joined the organization in the 1920s and relied heavily on Green Gang members in his violent purge of Communists in Shanghai in 1927. The head of Shanghai's Green Gang, Du Yuesheng, had close ties with the Shanghai municipal government, and had extensive relationships with the Nationalist Party organization there.[26] The CCP had good reason to treat the secret societies as subversive.

When the CCP took over the cities, there was always the possibility that they could obtain Nationalist Party membership lists, so when they warned members to register voluntarily or face severe consequences, the threat had real force. But secret societies and criminal gangs did not keep written records, and it was much harder to compel them to come forward. When the CCP took over Tianjin in January 1949, they immediately attacked Green Gang control over the transport industry. They established a new freight company and service stations in different neighborhoods, and they organized coolies into brigades that marched in the streets, chanting denunciations of coolie bosses. They also established new trade unions to provide the protections that gang bosses and secret societies had formerly provided. Coolie bosses who cooperated and informed on others were permitted to join the new union, while the more violent or stubborn ones were denounced and excluded. Public security operatives were sent to meetings of the new union, and they warned the coolie bosses to desist. Study classes were organized to promote loyalty to the party and new union and to criticize the "reactionary feudal secret societies."[27]

The gang bosses were more difficult to eradicate than initially anticipated. They continued to use intimidation against those who sided with the new union, and they were able to infiltrate their loyal followers into positions of leadership. Party cadres were dismayed to find that the secret societies had infiltrated the new freight company and transport union. This led to a wave of arrests in the last half of 1950 as the campaign against the urban gangs was folded into the campaign to suppress counterrevolution. Harsher methods ensued, and all identified coolie bosses were arrested. Denunciation meetings were organized once again, but now criminal sentences were passed. In the spring of 1951, the denunciation meetings led to a wave of highly publicized executions of coolie bosses, which finally dismembered the urban gangs.[28]

The Campaign against Vice

The harsh campaign against secret societies and criminal gangs curtailed the rampant drug trade and organized crime of the Nationalist era. The approach to the sex trade proceeded differently, but was equally effective. The CCP issued directives abolishing sex work as soon as it began to take over cities from 1948 to 1950. As it consolidated urban control, the party closed brothels and sent women back to their native places in the countryside or provided jobs for them in the cities.[29]

Women engaged in the sex trade were considered by the CCP to be part of the working class, not criminals. The party viewed sex workers as being exploited by others; the criminals were those who profited from their activities. The new authorities closed down the nightclubs, bars, and brothels where they worked. They enforced a strict ban on street solicitation. They opened reeducation centers that also hosted drug addicts and beggars. The reeducation centers were not voluntary. The inmates were not free to leave. They were given medical treatment and subjected to propaganda, discipline, and retraining. They engaged in study, mutual criticism, and manual labor. When they were considered to have sufficiently reformed, they were released, assigned to new jobs, and in some cases introduced to marriage partners. Many, however, were removed from the city and sent permanently to distant regions.[30]

More punitive measures were reserved for brothel keepers and pimps who persisted in the trade. In Shanghai in 1950 the authorities publicized the execution of two brothel keepers who were still recruiting women. In 1951, during the campaign to suppress counterrevolution, all remaining brothels were closed, and several of their operators were executed after public trials. The trade persisted on a small scale after 1952, and the authorities increasingly treated sex workers who resisted the early drive against the trade as criminals. By the mid-1950s, as the private economy was close to elimination, the trade had largely disappeared.[31]

Curbing Organized Labor

Labor unions had always been active under the Nationalists, and they quickly revived after the Japanese surrender. Gang bosses controlled only a fraction of them, in trades like the transport sector. Major industries in Shanghai and other cities had long been organized by labor unions, and many of them had long histories of labor militancy.[32] Some were affiliated with the Nationalists; others were independent but had long been infiltrated by communist operatives. Many of these unions saw the advent of Communist Party control as an opportunity to advance their interests at the expense of employers. The hyperinflation of the final years of Nationalist control had eaten deeply into their living wage, and many unions acted to recoup their losses.

As China's large cities fell under CCP control in the latter half of 1949, they experienced a massive upsurge of labor activism by existing union organizations, some of them with Nationalist affiliations—in fact, the largest wave of labor activism in modern Chinese history.[33] Many of the unions organized workers' militias to enforce their strike activity, and these militias were under unions, not under the public security bureau or military occupation forces. Some party cadres, who had long been involved in underground labor organizing, viewed these union activities with sympathy.

Given their ideological affinity for the industrial proletariat, one might expect the Communist Party to be sympathetic to the upsurge in strikes, but this was by no means the case. The CCP was now in charge of administering the cities, and it was intent on maintaining order and reviving the economy. Labor strikes undermined this stability and threatened to set back industrial recovery. Moreover, many of the unions had nationalist affiliations in the past, leading to suspicions about their motives.

In early 1952, China's minister of labor and head of the All-China Federation of Trade Unions, the veteran communist leader Li Lisan, was removed from both posts. He was denounced for encouraging trade union "syndicalism" that was divorced from party leadership, and accused of promoting "economism"—an unprincipled concern for workers' material welfare—and for advancing the interests of "backward workers." As was the case in the coolie trades, new trade unions were formed and the former members of the old unions absorbed into new structures with new leaders. The union-organized workers' militias were shut down.[34] The new official trade unions discouraged strikes and other forms of labor militancy, especially when state-owned enterprises were involved. After the mid-1950s, strikes by industrial workers were considered to be subversive criminal acts, subject to swift retribution.

Intellectuals and Universities

China's urban intellectuals were also brought to heel. Many had been educated in the West, relatively few were Marxist-Leninists, and most were liberals committed to principles of democracy and free intellectual inquiry.[35] These attitudes needed to be changed. The party conducted a "thought reform" campaign among educated elites to correct these mistaken views, which had no place in socialist China. The objectives of the campaign were stated in a *People's Daily* editorial in October 1951: "College teachers in the new era must boldly criticize their erroneous and incorrect thoughts. On the one hand they must examine themselves and oppose the attitude of self-complacency and self-delusion, and, on the other hand, they must boldly criticize each other."[36] The campaign intensified in September 1951 with the isolation of more than 3,000 faculty in twenty universities and colleges in Beijing and Tianjin for four months of "remolding and study." The purpose was to combat "worship of the so-called 'American way of life,'" and a preference for "teaching the old stuff they learned in England and America ten, twenty, or thirty years ago." This was wrong, and academics had to learn the "revolutionary standpoint," the "standpoint of serving the people, the viewpoint of materialism, and the method of dialectics." The students in these months-long classes read party documents, the works of Marx, Lenin, Stalin, and Mao, and speeches by CCP leaders. They engaged in criticism and self-criticism designed to eradicate their erroneous thoughts.[37] The campaign at Zhejiang National University was carried out in typical fashion. Faculty were subjected to lectures, criticized for their bourgeois political standpoint, and compelled to criticize one another in small groups and to write elaborate biographies that confessed to backward worldviews. Those who were unable to produce convincing self-criticisms were forced to do so until they were sufficiently thorough, and they were subjected to denunciation meetings if they failed to make the grade.[38] Those unable to withstand the pressures to confess and reform their thoughts sometimes found a way to flee to Hong Kong or, on rare occasion, committed suicide.[39]

Most confessions contained formulaic pledges of allegiance to the new regime and its ideology, coupled with self-criticism for the harm done previously as bourgeois intellectuals. One faculty member stated in May 1952, "I feel extremely grieved to realize how much harm has been done to the people because of my failure to use faithfully the ideology of the proletariat as a yard-stick in my work. . . . Henceforth I will redouble my efforts to study Marxism-Leninism and the thought of Chairman Mao, with the hope of reforming fundamentally. I will steadfastly hold to my position with the working class in order to serve the people better."[40]

Particular pressure was brought to bear on scholars who had studied with or who were otherwise connected to prominent Chinese intellectuals. For example, former students of China's famous liberal philosopher Hu Shi were required to denounce him for his "decadent and reactionary" standpoint. Hu Shi's own son, for example, concluded a long denunciation of his father with this statement: "I boldly use the scales of historical materialism to weigh his worth to the people. From the standpoint of class analysis, I clearly see him as a faithful minister of the reactionary class and an enemy of the people." Hu Shi was just one of a long list of prominent intellectuals whose influence the new regime felt necessary to diminish in this fashion.[41]

The primary objective of the campaign was to reorient China's intellectuals to the Soviet Union and away from the influence of scholarship that emanated from the leading research institutions and liberal arts universities in capitalist countries. The core doctrine was that all scholarship, from the natural sciences to the liberal arts, ultimately expressed the interests of the ruling class. In addition, the vast majority of China's intellectuals, from prosperous households, were assumed to be sympathetic to the class interests of landlords and capitalists. Moreover, the vast majority of faculty members in China's universities had studied abroad, had studied in Chinese universities with foreign-educated scholars, or had been exposed to curricula that were developed in the

United States, England, or Germany, in some cases in institutions modeled after foreign universities or directly founded and sponsored by Christian missionaries or Catholic orders. Soviet scholarship was the new revolutionary model. It reflected the interests of the proletariat and advanced the cause of revolution.

If faculty members were to keep their positions in the new China, it was essential that they repudiate their associations with bourgeois educational standards and pledge loyalty to Soviet standards. The pressures became particularly intense after China entered the Korean War. One foreign-educated editor stated in a July 1952 confession, "I had blindly worshipped the 'material civilization' of European and American imperialism and especially the 'science' and 'culture' of American imperialism. . . . Not until the 'Resist-America, Aid-Korea' campaign was underway did I awaken . . . to realize the decadent nature of American imperialism and the ugliness of American cultural aggression. . . . The American imperialists are the deadly enemy of the Chinese and of all the peace-loving peoples of the world."[42] Another stated, "I now understand that to hate America and to love the Soviet Union are two sides of the same coin. After I began to hate America, I naturally came to see that the Soviet Union is lovable and worthy of respect and admiration. . . . Soviet specialists are selflessly helping us, and the Soviet Union is unconditionally lending us support in world affairs. I feel ashamed that I have in the past stood on the same ground with the reactionary elements."[43]

The more prominent the scholar, and the more detailed the denunciation of the West, the more valuable and widely publicized were these statements. The published self-criticism of the prominent Tsinghua University physicist Zhou Peiyuan, who was educated at Chicago and Cal Tech, included the following passages about his several stays in the United States:

> During the four years of my first sojourn in the United States I saw only the skyscrapers, automobiles and the licentious and shamelessly free-spending life of the exploiting classes, but I did not see the tragic exploitation of the toiling masses by the monopolistic capitalists. . . . I erroneously thought that American "democracy" was good and that the people had freedom of speech. . . . I did not realize that the American President and the so-called government officials were slaves of the monopolistic capitalists, and the bickerings reported in the newspapers

were merely the ravings of one ruling clique against another. . . . My second trip to the United States in 1943 was the most shameful chapter of my life. I went in the name of a scientific worker from a democratic country engaged in opposing fascism, but actually, in early 1945, during my stay in America, the glorious victories of the Soviet Union in Eastern Europe had already spelled the ultimate doom for Fascist Germany. . . . I became an instrument of American imperialism and yet felt it was my "honor."[44]

A professor of biology from Wuhan University excoriated himself for his years of study and research in the laboratories of Harvard University, ashamed of his "blind admiration of America in all phases of his work." He had used American laboratory equipment and followed American teaching methods. He taught Darwin's theory of evolution instead of the more advanced theories of the Soviet scientist Michurin, which were consistent with the scientific Marxist doctrine of dialectical materialism. He committed the "extreme error" of exchanging laboratory specimens with American scholars. He confessed to the mistake of accepting financial aid from Harvard and collecting specimens for the U.S. Department of Agriculture: "I failed to realize that botanical resources were a matter of great value to the imperialists in their exploitation of colonial and semi-colonial countries." After sincere reflection and hard study, the scholar concluded that "only by applying Marxism-Leninism—the thought of Mao Zedong and the theories of Michurin—is it possible to have a Chinese botanical science dedicated to service for the people."[45]

This last confession of a reformed intellectual points to a source of tension that was to fester in Chinese universities throughout the early 1950s infatuation with the Soviet Union. Michurin was a geneticist who championed the idea that acquired characteristics could be inherited genetically—a variant of an old idea attributed to the eighteenth-century French naturalist Lamarck, which had long been rejected in favor of the Mendelian understanding of genetics and Darwinian theories of natural selection.[46] Because Michurin's theories were superficially consistent with Stalin's understanding of dialectical materialism, they were promoted as official Soviet science in opposition to "bourgeois" genetics.[47] His ideas were developed after his death by the Soviet biologist Lysenko, who, writing retrospectively about his celebrated discoveries in 1953, stated that "Stalin's teaching about gradual, concealed, unnoticeable quantitative changes leading to rapid, radical qualitative changes permitted Soviet biologists to discover in plants the realization of such qualitative transitions, the transformation of one species into another."[48] In the early postwar period, widespread questioning of the scientific basis for Lysenko's claims within the Soviet scientific community was silenced by accusations of "idealism," "complicity with imperialism and the bourgeoisie," "groveling before the West," "metaphysics," "racism," and "alienation from practice." Lysenko and his followers branded the "bourgeois science" of genetics as "attempting to justify the class struggle and the oppression, by white Americans, of Negroes." "Rotting capitalism, at the imperialist stage of development, gave birth to a still-born bastard of biological science, the thoroughly metaphysical and antihistorical doctrine of formalist genetics."

A Soviet scientist writing in the 1960s noted, "This stupid and vulgar demagoguery could not, of course, have scored a serious success; it only increased the opposition of the scientists." It is doubtful that many of China's best scientists were persuaded either. Within a decade Michurin and Lysenko were widely acknowledged as scientific quacks in the Soviet Union, the entire episode an embarrassing symbol of the subservience of science to ideology and ignorant politicians.[49]

In many fields of study—including biology, physics, economics, and history—Chinese academics were forced to conform to similar doctrinal claims that they knew to be nonsense, and to comply with academic standards they considered laughably ignorant. Some Soviet scientists, on arriving in Chinese universities, were impressed with the quality of the scientific laboratories, which was often superior to what was available in the Soviet Union at the time. Some of them were quietly appalled by the way in which well-trained scientists schooled in the world's finest research institutions were bullied and denigrated by dogmatic and ignorant party hacks, whose behavior and attitudes reminded them of the Soviet Union in the final years of Stalin's life, and whose main function appeared to be the prevention of useful scientific work.[50] The thought reform of the early 1950s and the political authority of party secretaries was deeply resented, and in the Hundred Flowers period of 1957, critics in universities and research institutes lacerated the party for the dogmatism and ignorance that it fostered.

Expropriating Private Assets

The urban private sector declined immediately after 1949, even before the party leadership announced its decision to move toward socialism in 1953. Government agencies began to take over banks and wholesale suppliers, making it more difficult for businesses to obtain credit and financing, supplies, and customers. These changes deprived the private sector of the means to compete and grow. Between 1949 and 1952, private firms' percentage of output sold on open markets declined from 88 to 44 percent. Increasingly, private firms depended on state contracts for their business: the output sold by private firms on state contracts rose from 12 to 56 percent during the same period.[51] In these early years, the share of industrial output in the private sector shrank from 63 to 39 percent, rapidly losing ground to state, cooperative, and joint public-private enterprises.[52] Without any explicit attacks on the private sector, it was gradually being squeezed by state policy and made dependent on state agencies.

The gradual squeezing of the private sector turned into a frontal attack in 1952. The party launched the Three-Anti movement to combat "corruption, waste, and bureaucratism," and the abuse of power by cadres in urban administrations.[53] The campaign struck civil servants who had stayed in their posts and pledged loyalty to the new regime. Coercive interrogations and physical torture of those who "refused to confess" led to a wave of executions and suicides, and soon paralyzed the party's administrative hierarchy, causing Mao to call off the campaign.[54] Of the estimated 4 million individuals who were investigated and 1.2 million who were convicted on vague charges of corruption, fewer than 200,000 were party members.[55]

The campaign then pivoted to an attack on private businesses. The Three Anti campaign was merged into a Three Anti, Five Anti campaign. The new claim was that corruption among cadres was caused by the business practices of private entrepreneurs. The new Five Anti targeted "tax evasion, bribery, cheating on government contracts, theft of economic intelligence, and stealing state assets." Work teams moved into private businesses, demanded to see their accounts, and conducted all-night interrogations that pressured business owners to confess to corruption and tax evasion, reveal the source of their "illegal profits," and divulge hidden assets. Large fines were levied that bankrupted many businesses, which subsequently closed. Many business owners "voluntarily" turned their firms over to the government as payment for their alleged back taxes and criminal fines.[56] By the end of the campaign, the urban private sector had shrunk to the point where it produced barely 37 percent of industrial output value—roughly half of the percentage it produced in 1949.[57]

The campaign was an assault not only on private business activity, but also on all independently organized activities that involved resources not controlled by the new government. A case in point was the assault on private charities, the main means of welfare relief in Chinese cities before 1949. There were close to 1,300 nongovernmental organizations in Shanghai in 1949, many of them private or religion-based charities. Wealthy citizens were permitted to continue operating them after 1949, and in the first years they were helpful to the CCP in restoring social order. Some of the philanthropists were welcomed into municipal associations run by the new city governments, and their philanthropy was welcomed in a period when the new regime still lacked the capacity to deliver welfare to deprived citizens.

This began to change in 1951. The first step in the eventual closure of private charities was the campaign to suppress counterrevolution, which brought attacks on charities with funding from the United States, staff who were U.S. citizens, or ties to overseas religious organizations. These organizations were denounced as subversive and forcibly closed. Charities that had close ties to the Nationalist regime were also treated with increasing suspicion. The end came with the Three Anti, Five Anti campaign, which was applied to the private charities with equal force. Essentially an attack on the social elite that funded and directed the charities, the same allegations of bribery, tax evasion, and hiding of assets were applied to those who operated charities. Large fines and orders to close or merge with government agencies followed. By 1954 the private charity sector in Shanghai was no more.[58]

Registering Households

During these years, a system of household registration was set up in urban areas, which eventually locked urban residents in place and kept rural residents out of the cities. By the end of the 1950s, without a valid urban household registration, one could not establish identity and citizenship, prove official status, qualify for rations of food and clothing, find shelter and employment, attend school, marry, or join the army.[59] The foundations were laid from 1953 to 1956, with the completed collectivization of agriculture and the nationalization or collectivization of urban services, handicrafts, and industry. The authorities set up the system to prevent unauthorized migration from the countryside to the city, and also to send "excess" urban populations back to villages or to interior cities scheduled for industrial development.[60]

Regulations issued at the end of 1954 established police substations in urban neighborhoods, and they began to take over population registration and enforcement of residence status. At same time, urban street offices were established along with state funding for their operations, which authorized ten to fifteen salaried staff by the 1960s.[61] A June 1955 regulation established a permanent system of household registration: prior permission was required to move one's residence, and hotels required travel documents authorized by work units or local governments. In August 1955, the first regulations on grain rationing in cities were issued, consolidating control over population movements.[62] Except for its temporary collapse during the chaotic Great Leap Forward in 1958 and 1959, the system effectively kept rural migrants out of cities and prevented unauthorized travel until the late 1970s.[63]

Organizing Neighborhoods

The household registration system was the linchpin for administering urban neighborhoods during the 1950s. Each city was divided into urban districts, which typically contained several hundred thousand people. The districts, in turn, were divided into subdistricts operated by Street Committees, which in turn were divided into an average of roughly eight neighborhoods, which were run by Residents' Committees composed of several hundred households. The Residents' Committees, in turn, were divided into Residents' Small Groups that contained anywhere from fifteen to forty households living in a single building or along a single lane.[64]

The party appointed all of the officials that staffed these urban organizations. Salaried state officials staffed the district and street committees, but workers in the neighborhood committees were mostly volunteers. They patrolled the area, checking to see whether there were overnight guests or other unregistered individuals living in local homes. They put up propaganda posters, operated public address systems that made political announcements and read news reports, and convened political meetings to transmit government messages. They also carried out sanitation campaigns, helped to administer grain and other rations, and mediated disputes between households or within families, including marriage counseling. They patrolled the neighborhood, investigating anything out of the ordinary, and checked the identity of individuals not known to them. Because households almost never had private telephones, the committee's telephone doubled as a public phone, and one of the members of the committee staff monitored it, logged telephone calls, and notified residents when they had received one.[65]

The socialist transformation of industry, which was completed in a rapid campaign conducted in 1955 and 1956, was the final step in the consolidation of the new regime's control over the urban economy and city residents. In a highly publicized mobilization campaign, the owners of the remaining private businesses were pressured to "donate" their firms to the state, or to convert them to "joint state-private" ownership, which was essentially a halfway house toward full state ownership. The former owners received shares in the resulting state enterprises, in many cases continuing to work as managers. The state sector produced 80 percent of all industrial output in 1957, and the "joint" category soon disappeared from government statistics.[66]

As the urban economy was brought under state control, the outlines of a new type of work organization took shape. This was the "work unit" that would play such a central role in the lives of urban citizens, and it became the second pillar of urban social organization that worked alongside neighborhood organizations and household registers to monitor urban citizens and fix them in one place. After household registration was in place and after industry and commerce were transferred to state control, jobs were allocated by state agencies and the allocation became virtually permanent.[67] The work unit increasingly assumed the role of providing housing and many of the goods and services formerly provided by private service establishments. Pensions were funded through work organizations, as were state medical insurance and disability coverage.[68] Work units also became organs of political and social control that were in many ways more effective than neighborhood committees. They organized political study and convened political meetings, both during and after working hours. They organized birth control campaigns, approved applications for marriage and divorce, and provided authorization to travel between cities. Their party organizations were responsible for carrying out political campaigns and implementing state policies, and their security departments carried out both political and criminal investigations and turned over violators to the judicial authorities.[69]

The City Revolutionized

These urban transformations, coupled with the revolutions in the countryside, gave the new Chinese state an unprecedented ability to extend its power into communities, workplaces, and families. This new state had capacities similar to those built up over a more prolonged period in the Soviet Union, and it paralleled those being built in the satellite states of Eastern Europe. For China this was historically unprecedented. In China's traditional empires, state structures reached no lower than county seats. The situation did not change fundamentally under the Nationalists, whose state-building efforts were crippled by factionalism inherited from the warlord past and by a devastating foreign invasion. The CCP, a far more disciplined and unitary force, followed up its military conquest of China with a characteristically disciplined and focused attack on impediments to the extension of central state control. The CCP was on a mission to build a strong modern state, one that was based on a completely foreign, indeed Western, model.

During the 1950s the CCP decisively ended a centuries-old pattern of indirect state rule by local elites. The power of propertied elites who had ruled their communities through the end of the Nationalist era was utterly destroyed. Rural banditry, organized crime, and governmental corruption, rampant during the Nationalist era, were all steadily brought under control. Secret societies and heterodox religious sects were suppressed; the ubiquitous sex and drug trades were effectively ended. These were all signs that China's new rulers were different, and that the nation had truly entered a new era. China was no longer subject to foreign military occupation and colonial control of its major coastal cities. The new state mobilized millions of soldiers that fought to a standstill with superior Western armies on the Korean peninsula.

The changes wrought during the first eight years of revolutionary state building, however, were symptoms of a deeper transformation. The CCP embarked on building a powerful modern state, but one that was patterned after a distinctive new form of twentieth-century civilization—

Soviet state socialism. This new civilization was founded on two pillars: a bureaucratically administered economy that utterly rejected market mechanisms, and a disciplined and unitary party organization that extended its reach deep into society and economy. Each of these two pillars had striking flaws, ones that would soon become increasingly apparent to Mao and other leaders. The struggle against inevitable bureaucratic tendencies in the economy and the party would preoccupy Mao for the rest of his life, spurring destructive impulses that marred the last two decades of his rule. In order to understand the next twenty years of Chinese history, it is essential to examine the bureaucratic features of the economy and the growing party organization that made China's new dictatorship, and the next twenty years, so distinctive. These are the subjects of the Chapters 5 and 6.

5

The Socialist Economy

AFTER THE SPLIT with the Soviet Union in the 1960s, China became famous for deviating from the Soviet model of development. As the primary architect of the Great Leap Forward and the Cultural Revolution, Mao became a symbol of China's quest to forge a unique road to socialism. Mao's later reputation, however, obscured his earlier enthusiasm for the full-blown Soviet model. From the outset of the People's Republic, Mao was one of China's most enthusiastic supporters of Soviet economic practice, and pushed to impose central planning faster and more thoroughly than many of his colleagues were inclined.[1] Mao's ideas about socialist economics were decisively shaped by reading the Stalinist *Short Course,* a history of the USSR that sketched out the stages of Soviet development.[2] Mao decided to move rapidly to the full Soviet model as early as 1950, but did not publicly declare his intention to do so until the end of the Korean War in 1953. His "General Line for the Transition Period" of 1953 was a thinly disguised copy of Stalin's own statement on the subject in 1929.[3] China, along with other members of the postwar socialist bloc, proceeded to implement the core elements of the mature Stalinist system: absolute single-party rule by a disciplined and hierarchical party organization, massively expanded internal security organs, and a dominant figure glorified as the supreme leader. The political system was paired with an economic model that mandated complete state ownership and control over the economy and a strong emphasis on heavy industry and armaments.[4]

During the 1950s, China developed deep and extensive ties with the Soviet Union, and faithfully adopted the USSR's organizational model in the design of party and state organs, the educational system, research institutions, and the management of state enterprises. More than 200 industrial plants were built by the Soviets, forming the core of China's new industrial system. As many as 10,000 Soviet and East European advisors spent time in China, working on more than 300 major industrial projects, and almost 40,000 Chinese were trained in the USSR and Eastern Europe.[5] In many areas, the Chinese implemented the Soviet blueprint so thoroughly that their own arrangements exemplified textbook ideals more fully than actual Soviet practice.[6]

In light of the worldwide collapse of the Soviet model some forty years later, Mao's enthusiasm might seem to have been driven primarily by political dogma. At the time, however, there was every reason for confidence in the Soviet model. Czarist Russia was easily defeated in World War I, but thirty years later the Soviet Union, the least economically developed of the major combatants in World War II, absorbed the full brunt of an even more formidable German attack and turned back the enemy while fighting alone in Europe. The Soviet industrialization drive of the 1930s was widely credited with making the difference. The Soviet system outperformed the German economy in the production of munitions by more than twofold, and it proved superior at extracting human and material resources from its population, supporting a fighting force far disproportionate to the size of its economy and initial level of economic development.[7] This was the model for the intense war mobilization in Manchuria that later secured Mao's final victory over the Nationalists.

Even before it proved to be a superior war economy, the Soviet Union experienced rapid economic growth throughout the 1930s, while the capitalist West remained mired in the Great Depression. From the beginning of its First Five-Year Plan in 1928 to the eve of its war with Germany, the per capita gross domestic product of the Soviet Union grew by an annual average of 3.8 percent—compared with the depression-wracked U.S. economy, which stagnated during the same period.[8] From 1928 to 1949, the Soviet economy sustained growth at an annual rate of 3.2 percent, double that of the United States.[9] This was a remarkable record, especially because much of Soviet territory west of the Ural Mountains was devastated by warfare from 1941 to 1944. This rapid growth continued well into the 1960s. The Soviet economy continued to grow from 1950 to 1965 at an annual rate of 3.4 percent, compared to 2.3 percent in the United States.[10] The vitality of the Soviet economic system, and in the eyes of some its superiority, was demonstrated by the USSR's launch of the world's first orbiting satellite in 1957. This economic model turned the Soviet Union into a major world power, and it had obvious appeal to the leaders of revolutionary China. The appeal of the Stalinist model was twofold: it laid out a clear map of what was to be done, and it provided a model of how to develop unity of thought and action around that plan. One observer of this period has noted, "particularly after a revolution, countries seize on preexisting ideas to guide them through times of high uncertainty and to allow them to legitimate and coordinate their actions. This solution can often produce a more slavish imitation of another country's experience than might seem merited on grounds of pure efficiency."[11]

State Socialism as a Growth Machine

What made this socialist growth machine so successful? The most important foundation for rapid and sustained growth was the fact that market demand and financial markets were not the drivers of the economy. Fluctuations in aggregate demand and the instability of financial markets had generated periodic economic crises and depressions throughout the relatively short history of the capitalist system, and the crises seemed to become more severe and prolonged, culminating in the Great Depression of the 1930s. Market demand did not drive economic activity in the Soviet system, and financial markets did not exist. State planners ensured effective demand by providing enterprises with mandatory production plans that were increased annually. Financing was provided by the state, which allocated investment and operating capital through the state banking system in line with the requirements of state-mandated production plans. The instability characteristic of capitalism was therefore entirely absent from the Soviet model.

The Soviet system was designed to promote capital formation at an accelerated pace. Instead of permitting growth rates to be determined by the vagaries of the consumption and savings decisions of households and the investment and production decisions of private firms, the state itself regulated levels of consumption and investment. Soviet planning set priorities based on their distinction between two types of investment: productive and unproductive. Productive investment increases the output of producers' goods—used by factories to make other products. This category includes all of the sectors symbolic of modern industrial strength:

mining, metallurgy, chemicals, petroleum, machine building, motor vehicles, aviation, armaments, and the physical infrastructure upon which these industries rely. Unproductive investment is essentially anything that is consumed by end users and not subsequently employed in manufacturing. This includes all consumer goods: clothing, household furnishings, bicycles, private telephones, and civilian automobiles. It also includes the retail and service sectors that cater to private consumption. This also includes housing: apartments depreciate as soon as they are occupied and do not themselves contribute directly to material production.[12]

The Soviet model achieved rapid growth by pouring investments into sectors defined as productive at the expense of sectors defined as unproductive. This is why mature socialist economies became famous for massive heavy industrial sectors alongside woefully undeveloped consumer goods sectors and overcrowded, substandard housing. Consumer sacrifice was considered an acceptable cost in order to build the heavy industrial base on which a modern economy and strong national defense are based.

From the perspective of socialist economics, unproductive investments are wasteful, and a major flaw of capitalism as a development model. The wasteful consumer sectors of modern capitalist economies were viewed as socially and economically irrational. Capitalist economies expend huge resources for no other purpose than to encourage consumer demand. Examples are legion. Television sets, audio equipment, or private automobiles are redesigned every year to attract buyers. Huge budgets are allocated to marketing and advertising to convince consumers to purchase. Scores of nearly identical products vie for consumer attention with expensive packaging designed to draw the shopper's eye on store shelves. Entire sectors of the economy are devoted to the completely unproductive task of urging people to buy things of questionable value: marketing, retail sales, advertising. And after new consumer products are purchased, perfectly usable but no longer fashionable items are discarded.[13] To an orthodox economist in the Soviet mold, capitalism is an empire of waste—resources that could be devoted to socially rational purposes are instead squandered on unproductive activities that only serve the circulation of goods and to promote unnecessary household expenditures. This kind of argument appealed to leaders searching for an economic model that would generate rapid industrialization.

In order to maintain maximum levels of investment in productive
sectors, the state owned all productive assets and the financial sector.
There could be no significant private enterprise, no private finance. State
planners made all production and investment decisions. The financial
sector, no longer a dangerous source of economic instability, simply allocated capital as part of the state production plan. This also required
that state planners set the prices for virtually all products. With prices
set by the state, planners could ensure that resources flowed to favored
sectors.[14]

The most important example of this control of pricing was the agricultural sector, which served the function of providing inexpensive foodstuffs for a rapidly growing urban workforce. Collective farms were an
integral part of this system, because the state's agents administered these
farms and controlled the production of the harvest and its allocation.
Collective farms were required to sell quotas of grain and other foodstuffs to the state at low prices—essentially extracting surpluses out of
the countryside to promote urban industry. Inexpensive food was an essential part of the growth engine: low prices for food staples meant a
lower cost of living for urban workers, which in turn permitted the state
to pay urban workers lower wages. Coupled with limited investment in
consumer goods and housing for urban workers, this permitted state industries to accumulate greater surpluses that could be reinvested at higher
rates in the further expansion of (productive) industries. This, in a nut-
shell, is the relatively simple design of the Soviet economic model: the
state limits improvements in living standards in order to promote savings and industrial investment. Consumer prosperity would have to wait
until a later stage of economic development.

The Industrial System

The Soviet development model created a world of management that was
remarkable in its simplicity.[15] Each year a factory would receive two plans:
a production plan and a supply plan. The production plan would be laid
out in a grid: the rows specified the planners' annual quotas for the various products of the enterprise; the columns specified the end users to
whom the products were to be sold. The supply plan was the flip side of
the production plan: the rows specified the quotas for the various supplies that the planners estimated were necessary for the factory to meet
its production quotas; the columns specified the factories from which

the enterprise was permitted to purchase a certain quantity of an input within the plan. The entire industrial system was essentially an interlocking network of production and supply plans that created elaborate connections among enterprises and state purchasing agencies.

Negotiations among enterprises proceeded largely in accord with the production and supply plans. Customers included in your production plans would arrive early in the year to settle product specifications and delivery dates. Your purchasing agents would travel to the enterprises named in your supply plan to do the same. If the plan was fulfilled, the transactions among producers and suppliers would be completed at fixed state prices, and funds would be transferred among accounts kept at state banks. A factory's financial plan advanced to the firm a set amount of working capital needed for completion of the plan. Completion of the plan meant that a factory would make a preplanned level of profit, almost all of which would be remitted to the state's financial arm to fund further industrial investment. Small percentages of factory profits could be retained for production bonuses for managers and workers.

On the surface it might appear that there was virtually no room for entrepreneurship in an economy organized in this fashion. Such appearances would be deceiving. There were always gaps in the production and supply plans. Planners wanted to encourage efficiency in the use of resources, but they could not do so by using price mechanisms, which were simply an accounting device that shadowed planned transactions. Instead, they encouraged efficiency by devising tight plans: not all of the supplies needed for production quotas were specified in purchasing plans. Planners assumed that managers stockpiled inputs in their storerooms or, if not, they would have to find ways to economize on the use of materials: reduce scrap and waste in the production process or economize on fuel and energy.

An additional problem with the supply plan was built into the structure of the planned economy: inputs that were delivered "within the plan" were frequently not of the specifications needed by the purchasing enterprise. Supply plans did not designate precise specifications of the goods to be supplied. Product quality—for example, thickness or tensile strength of steel, or spare parts of a specific size or design—had to be negotiated by procuring agents with the supplying firm. Sometimes the supplier claimed an inability to produce to the needed specifications. More commonly, after the supplier agreed to the indicated specifications, the goods that were eventually delivered were not what the contract specified. There was little recourse for the aggrieved firm: contract law was virtually nonexistent, and the supplier had little incentive to satisfy customers' precise needs—there was no prospect of losing customers in this planning system. Unless the manager of the aggrieved enterprise had considerable rank and influence, and could pull strings within the party hierarchy, there was little for the supplier to fear. Managers had little choice but to try to rework the supplies into usable form, or put them in storerooms, hoping to exchange them for supplies with the proper specifications.

In practice, managers responded to tight supplies through a flourishing barter trade. This was the realm of entrepreneurship in the planned economy. Socialist factories maintained only a minimal sales force: all they had to do was sit in their offices and accept appointments with the end users specified in production plans. Supply departments, on the other hand, were much larger operations, and were most important for the fulfillment of production plans. Supply departments sent procuring agents around the country in search of inputs that another factory might be willing to trade for an item that they in turn needed for their own production process. Often the procuring agent would travel to a familiar firm used to solve supply problems in the past. At other times they would attend large "goods ordering meetings," essentially conventions organized by regional planners for enterprises to solve their supply problems.

It is here that human ingenuity defeated the bureaucrats' best-laid plans. Managers, recognizing that the only constraint on their ability to complete production plans was a supply shortfall, stockpiled supplies in storerooms to guard against future shortfalls. In many years it was possible to overfulfill production targets, not report the output, and stockpile these products in storerooms. These in turn could be bartered with other enterprises to secure supplies for future production. This created a pervasive hoarding mentality at the level of the enterprise that actually went beyond the supplies that a factory needed for its own production. Procuring agents often found it impossible to arrange a straight trade that provided production inputs needed by both sides of the transaction. In these cases, one party to the trade might accept products that they did not need for their own production process, but which were nonetheless in short supply and could readily be traded with another firm for inputs that were actually needed. Factory storerooms therefore stockpiled finished products that were not sold to customers and were of no direct use to the factory, but were held on the chance that they could be traded for supplies that the factory needed. In short, planners were engaged in an elaborate game with the managers of state firms. They tried to estimate slack resources and force managers to use them by devising tight plans. Managers, in turn, responded by stockpiling supplies and other items for a pervasive barter trade that served to exacerbate supply shortages and tie up huge inventories in warehouses.[16]

To those familiar with the workings of a market economy, this elaborate barter trade would seem counterproductive and unnecessary. A simpler solution would be to permit a market in scarce "outside the plan" supplies, with prices to be set according to their scarcity. Factories could then buy and sell scarce supplies, allocating them for more efficient uses. Motivated by the incentive to turn stockpiled goods into cash, they would release their stockpiled inventories, reducing supply shortages and promoting greater resource efficiency in the economy as a whole.

This obvious solution was ruled out by several hard realities. The first was that enterprise managers were not permitted to conduct money transactions with enterprises that were not in their production or supply plans. State banks administered enterprise funds and allowed transfers among enterprises only for officially approved uses. The second is that so long as enterprise managers were evaluated solely by the fulfillment of production plans, and so long as almost all of their firms' profits were remitted to the state, they would have no economic incentive to sell their stockpiles for cash. The financial gain from these transactions would simply be appropriated by the state, and the manager would still face an uncertain supply of scarce inputs on unpredictable markets and at prices that could not be anticipated. The ultimate constraint, of course, was political. Permitting a free supplementary market in scarce materials would potentially subvert the planned economy, as managers diverted supplies "within the plan" to profitable uses outside the plan. This was a concession to capitalism that Soviet planners were unwilling to make almost until the very end of the Soviet Union, and the idea was anathema to Mao and most of the party leadership during his lifetime.

The Shortage Economy

The Hungarian economist János Kornai has done more than anyone to characterize the flaws in this economic model, which ultimately proved its undoing. He aptly described this economic system as "resource constrained," in contrast with a market economy, which is "demand constrained."[17] At the level of the firm, production in a demand-constrained economy will continue to the point where buyers for the products can no longer be found. To continue to produce in the absence of customers would raise costs and lower profits, potentially threatening the survival of the firm. In a socialist economy, these considerations are irrelevant. Demand is guaranteed in state plans; firms are not only given production quotas, they are also given lists of buyers who are designated to purchase specific amounts of the firm's output for the year. The socialist economy is "resource constrained" because production will continue until the plan is met—or until the firm exhausts its supplies of inputs.

The result of this resource constraint is the prevalence of the hoarding that we have just described, and which was characteristic of industrial management in every country where this model was implemented.[18] The unfortunate result is a very inefficient use of capital. An economic system that is designed to funnel maximum amounts of investment into heavy industrial sectors to spur rapid growth has the unintended consequence of enshrining an extremely wasteful use of resources in the favored industrial sectors. Market capitalism may produce large numbers of "socially wasteful" products very efficiently, but state socialism churned out large volumes of heavy industrial goods, often substandard, and very inefficiently.

Firms that operated at a deficit were subsidized. It was almost unheard of in this system for a state enterprise to be closed, for several reasons. Even if the firm operated at an accounting loss, it still provided employment for local workers. In addition, the firm put pension and medical costs for its labor force, both active and retired, into its costs of production. Firms that were large and old had significant pension obligations that made their operations inherently less profitable, but they were still funding the state's welfare system. Moreover, socialist firms built and maintained housing and services for employees that could not be readily obtained elsewhere. Finally, the firm's products were needed as inputs in the supply plans of other enterprises, part of the interlocking network of input and output plans.

For these reasons, closing a socialist enterprise entailed costs for the government that might far outweigh the expense of subsidizing its continued operations. Closing a firm would create unemployment, undermine the supply and maintenance of housing and services, offload pension costs onto the government, and force planners to find alternate sources of supply for the products of the closing firm. Needless to say, the larger the firm, and the more important it was as an employer and supplier, the greater the inherent cost of closing operations simply because of accounting deficits. The government, as owner, was dependent on the firm just as surely as the firm was dependent on the government.[19]

The result of the investment bias toward heavy industry, and the inherently soft budget constraint on firms, was an industrial sector in the Soviet bloc that lagged far behind international standards in its use of inputs. Industry received a much higher share of total investment in state socialist than in capitalist economies, even in their mature phase after 1965. Industrial investment in socialist economies averaged 40 percent of total national investment; in capitalist economies, 25 percent.[20] As these figures suggest, and as the earlier discussion makes clear, economic growth was achieved in socialist economies by pouring resources into industry rather than developing more efficient ways to use these resources. In one study, improved factory productivity in mature socialist economies contributed an average of only 27 percent to economic growth from 1960 to 1988, while the comparable figure for capitalist economies was 65 percent.[21] This was the system that Mao was in a hurry to implement in the 1950s, and Mao would struggle in the years to come to devise ways of resolving these inherent flaws without violating core tenets of socialism that he had absorbed from Soviet doctrines of the 1930s. This proved to be an impossible task.

Enterprise Welfare Provision

Socialist economies were designed to achieve full employment. In addition to the absence of layoffs due to the characteristic business cycles of market capitalism, there was no incentive for managers to cut the labor force to reduce costs. The wage bill was budgeted as part of the annual plan, and was a fixed cost of production in an economy that did not evaluate firms by their profitability. But the role of the socialist enterprise in promoting social welfare was not limited to providing full employment. Throughout the Soviet bloc, and to a pronounced degree in China, the workplace became the focal point for the delivery of the entire range of state insurance and benefits, and the provision of housing and a wide range of other services. By the end of the 1950s, China's version had evolved into its urban "work unit system" that continued to develop throughout the Mao era. The work unit, in the larger and better-endowed workplaces, became an intense focus of social and political life for urban Chinese.[22]

The first notable feature of the work unit in China was that employment was permanent: employees could not be fired except for criminal or political offenses that involved imprisonment. By the same token, workers could not leave to take up employment elsewhere. Upon the completion of schooling, urban residents were assigned jobs by labor bureaus (or by personnel departments that handled university graduates). Except for management and party personnel who had career lines that led out of state organizations into higher posts in the bureaucracy, all employees could therefore expect to remain in the same work unit for the duration of their careers. Whether they remained within the same workplace or were promoted higher in the party or government hierarchy, administrative decisions governed job assignments.[23]

In addition to providing secure lifetime employment, the work unit delivered and in fact funded health and accident insurance and pensions.[24] Employees received basic coverage with employment, and the costs were covered directly in the work unit's budget, itemized as a cost of production in an enterprise or as part of the budget of a state agency or institution. Pensions were paid in cash, at the workplace, and retirees lined up at the cashier's office to collect their pension payments at the end of each month. If the work unit was large enough, or had the resources to do so, it also directly provided health clinics and in-patient hospital services. The largest state enterprises frequently provided hospitals, nurseries, and kindergartens for preschool children of employees, and sometimes even primary schools on site.

The work unit was also a major provider of housing. By the end of the Mao era, roughly one-third of urban residents lived in apartments that were built, maintained, and allocated to them by their work units, very often on site.[25] There was no private market in housing, and the only alternative was through the city government. As a result, many large and important work units—state enterprises, government agencies, and institutions like major universities—became integrated communities with employees living together on site throughout their adult lives, raising families together in housing complexes, and remaining after retirement.

As the private service sector was closed down in the 1950s, work units picked up services formerly supplied by the market. Work units developed meal halls and food stalls for employees and their family members. They built shower and bath facilities for employees, whose apartments rarely had these luxuries. They opened up retail shops and grocery stores. They organized barber shops and hair salons. They built auditoriums that could be used to stage concerts or plays, or show feature films. They built gymnasiums or laid out sports fields for athletic teams, and if they did not have sufficient resources to do this, they would organize teams to compete in municipal leagues. Some even provided transportation for commuters who did not live on site, and others organized and paid for periodic vacation tours for employees and family members.[26]

Those who worked for large state enterprises also might receive periodic benefits from the flourishing barter trade between firms. Procuring agents at times would obtain large batches of scarce consumer items: radios, wristwatches, famous-brand bicycles, and in later years even black-and-white television sets. These goods would be distributed to favored employees and their families. Some work units established regular relationships with collective farms, and traded manufactured items for supplies of scarce foodstuffs. Many tried to provide these rare food items—smoked hams, chickens, melons—at major holidays to build employee morale.

The extent to which urban work units developed into self-contained communities was documented by a mid-1980s survey of China's third largest city. Just over 85 percent of the surveyed individuals had meal services, medical clinics, and shower facilities in their work units; two-thirds had infant day care centers and reading libraries; half of them had auditoriums that doubled as cinemas and organized vacation tours; more than one-third had organized sports teams; one-quarter had barber shops and on-site sports facilities; and one-fifth offered bus services for commuters.[27] But not all work units were equal; they varied considerably in the resources at their disposal, which translated into differences in standard of living. Large state enterprises and higher-ranking government offices were favored over other work units. In a market economy, income differences across occupations determine the lifestyle and living standards of different social groups. In China, wages were low and wage differences modest, so a major component of inequality was the capacity of the work unit to supply goods and services, virtually all of which were provided either free or for a nominal charge. Surveys conducted in the early post-Mao era revealed large differences in the services and benefits available to employees in enterprises of different size and rank.[28]

Work units also became the locus of an individual's identity. The standard means of personal identification was the work unit identity card, issued by the unit's personnel department. Every employee also had a personal dossier that recorded family background, class status, educational history, and political demeanor. A combination of employment record and police file, the dossier was kept at the place of employment. No one could transfer to a new work unit without transfer of the dossier.[29] In order to travel to another city, work unit permission was required. If travel was on official business, the work unit would procure the train, bus, and on rare occasion air tickets. If travel was for personal reasons, the employee needed an official document from the work unit certifying the individual's permission to travel. Work unit permission was required to officially register a marriage; divorce required similar work unit consent.[30]

Consumer Austerity

The decline in the role of money and markets meant that different means had to be devised to handle the inevitable consumer shortages. Consumer austerity was central to the design of the Soviet growth model: investment in consumer goods, and all manner of unproductive investments, were neglected in favor of productive investments in heavy industry. There are three ways to deal with pervasive consumer shortages. The first, largely rejected in all socialist economies, is rationing by price. Prices of scarce goods rise to levels that are affordable to only a small portion of the population. In a socialist system, where production is not oriented to market demand, shortages will persist, and scarce goods will become permanently accessible only to a minority that can afford high prices. The second method is rationing by queue: prices remain fixed, and consumers exercise vigilance to find items that are in stock. They stand in line to make a purchase, hoping that supplies last until they get to the front of the line. This requires large expenditures of time and effort by consumers to find retail outlets that stock the items they need. The third approach is administrative rationing: prices are fixed, and coupons are issued to individuals or families that permit them to purchase a rationed item. In the case of a major item like an apartment or the purchase of a private automobile, individuals or families put their names on waiting lists and are called when their turn comes up. The administrative approach saves time and effort over the second, and in theory provides broader and more equal access to scarce goods at low prices, although rank will still have its privileges.

Administrative rationing was prevalent in the Soviet Union during wartime and in the immediate postwar period in the Soviet bloc. It was also used selectively during World War II in the market economies of the United States and England, whose governments mobilized for all-out warfare against the Axis powers; rationing was more comprehensive in England than in the United States, and lasted for a number of years after the end of the war. As the economies of the postwar Soviet bloc recovered, and the supply of food and basic consumer goods improved, administrative rationing was gradually abandoned and rationing by queue became common (though housing and private autos continued to be allocated administratively). Vigilant shopping and long waits in line at retail shops became the norm, and they were a prominent feature of social life in the Soviet bloc.[31]

With a much larger and poorer population, China had to manage its food supplies very carefully, and with a much lower initial level of economic development, consumer goods were in shorter supply and much more basic than in the more prosperous economies of the Soviet bloc (no motorcycles, televisions, or private autos). After the appearance of long lines for basic foodstuffs in large cities in 1953 and 1954, the gathering of large numbers of disgruntled shoppers in major cities presented an obvious threat to public order. China moved quickly in 1955 to put in place a comprehensive system of administrative rationing for a wide range of goods, from staple foods to major consumer items (and housing).[32] The system remained in force throughout the Mao era.

The bottom rung of the rationing system was for basic requirements: food and clothing. Staple grains (either rice or wheat flour), meat, cooking oil, and cloth were available only with ration coupons. This was a national system, and coupons were issued separately by province and could be redeemed only where issued. The coupons were distributed by place of residence: if a family lived in work unit housing, they would receive rations through the work unit; if they lived outside, they would receive them through the residents' committees. The importance of these coupons is indicated by their appearance: they were printed in color, with a design as elaborate as the regular national currency.

The most highly valued consumer durables were also rationed, but the supply was more irregular. Individuals working in resource-rich work units were favored in these distributions, as were individuals of higher rank. Ordinarily, workplaces and neighborhoods organized waiting lists for the "industrial coupons" that permitted one to purchase an item at a state retail outlet. The most valued coupons were for three famous-brand bicycles that were manufactured in Shanghai and Tianjin (Phoenix, Eternal, and Flying Pigeon). Bicycles were the primary means of urban transportation; the main streets of major cities during rush hour were broad rivers of bicycles, slowly moving in unison. Many bicycles of lesser quality were widely available, although they were markedly inferior: tires punctured easily, spokes broke with regularity, frames cracked unpredictably, and parts rusted out quickly. The famous brands were known for using the best-quality steel and rubber; durable, reliable, and safe.

Other highly valued consumer durables were rationed in a similar fashion. Foot-powered sewing machines were essential. They were copies of 1950s Soviet models that were in turn copied from the product marketed by Singer in the United States until the 1920s. They were needed to make the most efficient use of cloth rations: premade clothing was a less efficient use of the ration coupons. The most valued item of all was living space. Housing conditions were very cramped in urban China in the 1950s, and as the population grew, families became crowded into ever-smaller spaces. Young couples that registered to marry faced long waits at work units or city neighborhoods for an apartment; they could not file an application and be placed on the waiting list until the marriage was officially registered. Separation and divorce did not constitute valid grounds for making a housing application (not surprisingly, divorce rates were very low but grew rapidly with increased housing supply in the 1980s). Growing families expanded, often living in a single room, and filed their own applications for larger quarters. Ordinary citizens rarely had private kitchens and almost never had fully functional private bathrooms. Apartments had running water, perhaps a sink, but kitchen facilities and bathrooms were in the hall (or in outdoor courtyards or on the street) and shared with neighbors. In work units and neighborhoods, citizens used every means at their disposal to influence authorities to move them up on lists and convince them of the urgency of their need. Allocations of new apartments to neighbors or coworkers could stimulate loud complaining among those passed over. By the end of the Mao era, this led to an urban culture that was seemingly obsessed with influencing decision makers to make allocations in one's favor, and cultivating networks of connections with others to exchange favors and prosper under these conditions of scarcity.[33]

Political Implications of Economic Problems

This is the economic system that Mao pushed to impose rapidly in the 1950s. It is important to understand how the system worked, and its inherent flaws, because proposed solutions had political implications that would contribute heavily to a split between China and the Soviet Union, and eventually to the Great Leap Forward and the Cultural Revolution. The split in world socialism, and the raging political conflicts within China in the 1960s and 1970s, originated in disagreements about how to solve the problems just described.

The flaws of this institutional design became visible in China as soon as the system was implemented. They had long been known in the Soviet Union. The new satellite states in Eastern Europe were struggling with them for the first time. In the Soviet bloc, the 1950s were a time of active discussion about how to improve the design of the system.[34] It had mobilized capital for the early stages of heavy industrial growth and had promoted national defense. But now, many thought, it was time to look more closely at the system's obvious flaws. Improvements in living standards would be impossible so long as the industrial system continued to waste investment and resources. Somehow, greater efficiency had to be wrung out of this hopelessly bureaucratic mode of economic organization.

There were three basic approaches, each of which had political implications. The first, and the one that was increasingly favored in the Soviet Union, was the application of modern scientific management techniques to the planning process.[35] Modern statistical techniques and mathematical models would be employed by highly trained experts to perfect input-output planning. This set of solutions relied heavily on trained scientific personnel in elite bureaucratic departments. It did not threaten the dominance of the party or its control over the economy, but it implied that party officials had to cede considerable authority to technical specialists. It also meant that politicians with grandiose and unrealistic ambitions would confront expert advice that placed limits on their politically inspired plans. This was a vision of a socialist economy run according to scientific principles, implemented by elite experts in a large bureaucracy.

The second approach was to rely on market mechanisms to supplement the planned economy. This was pioneered in Yugoslavia in the 1950s and Hungary after the late 1960s, and was under wide discussion in the Soviet bloc at the time.[36] This approach called for an end to input-output planning and granting enterprise managers greater discretion over their production lines and greater responsibility for finding customers. Enterprises in this scheme would become "responsible for their own profits and losses." Goods would circulate increasingly based on market prices that reflected relative scarcities. The state's monopoly over ownership would be maintained, but enterprise performance would be based on profit criteria rather than simply meeting output quotas. In theory, as managers became more sensitive to price and cost, they would become more efficient in their use of inputs and capital. Firms that made greater profits could pay higher wages and bonuses, and provide better housing and services. This approach relied on profit incentives and market mechanisms to coordinate the socialist economy. Chinese economists were among the first to champion this approach; the most famous was Sun Yefang, who began advancing these ideas in the mid-1950s.[37]

The third approach was the one favored by Mao Zedong. This was essentially a form of political fundamentalism that idealized the principles of a wartime economy. Mao favored the kind of political mobilization that had worked in Manchuria during the last years of the civil war: "politics in command" in the form of party secretaries who pushed employees and enterprises to display greater commitment to the socialist cause and sacrifice for the common good. In Mao's view, only political mobilization could unleash the creativity of the masses of workers and dig out slack resources that lay fallow in conventional methods—as increasingly seen by the problems of hoarding and inefficiency in the bureaucratic Soviet model. This approach put party secretaries in command of an enterprise and drastically reduced the authority of educated experts. It refused to be bound by bureaucratic rules and regulations that tied up organizations in red tape. It did nothing, however, to change the underlying reality that the entire economy was organized as a massive bureaucratic machine—it simply put the economy in the hands of political bosses.

Mao's approach, by the 1960s, also came with a strident political critique of the first two approaches.[38] The scientific management solution empowered experts in a massive bureaucracy who were, in his view, inevitably "bourgeois" in their outlooks and orientations. Mao had no intention of permitting his revolutionary party to yield power to bureaucratic experts, and he did not want to empower highly educated elites who rose to their positions through a stable bureaucratic career. He would eventually charge that this would lead inevitably to the rebirth of a class-stratified capitalism. It is odd that Mao identified this vision of scientific management by a massive bureaucracy as "capitalism"—it would seem to be the very antithesis of an economy organized along the lines of market competition. Yet in rejecting this model and labeling it as capitalism, Mao would make very clear that he utterly rejected this answer.

Reliance on market mechanisms to improve incentives and cost efficiency was, in Mao's mind, even worse. For him, this was the very definition of capitalism, and market approaches to the problems of socialism were completely beyond the pale. Mao identified socialism with the system inherited from the Stalin-era Soviet Union. If it no longer worked the way that it had in its glory years, this was because party cadres no longer played the animating role that made the system work. It was the role of the party to mobilize enterprises and their personnel to greater accomplishments, greater efficiencies, greater commitment to the socialist cause. Party leadership and an emphasis on hard work as a political obligation was the remedy to the inefficiencies and contradictions that plagued the socialist model. Failing to recognize this would inevitably lead to rule by a narrow bureaucratic elite and class rule, and perhaps the full-blown restoration of capitalism. This was the vision that Mao tried to enact during his Great Leap Forward of 1958–1960. In the wake of the Leap's humiliating failure, one of the primary motives of the Cultural Revolution was to ensure that China would never resort to either the bureaucratic or the market solutions after he had left the scene.

6

The Evolving Party System

SINCE THE LATE 1920S, the CCP had been a revolutionary organization, governing far-flung and isolated rural base areas, organizing villages behind Japanese lines, operating underground in cities controlled by the Japanese or the Nationalists, and mobilizing forces to fight a civil war. We have already seen that the party transformed both city and countryside during the 1950s as it consolidated its new regime. However, the party itself was changing inexorably as it established a new state. Before 1949 it was an organization designed for political and military combat. To administer China it expanded drastically in size, recruited new kinds of members with new skills, and administered cities as well as villages.[1] The Soviet model that the CCP adopted so faithfully in the 1950s made the growth of a massive and complex bureaucracy a foregone conclusion.

At the time of the Japanese surrender in August 1945, the party had 1.2 million members and an army of 910,000.[2] The mobilization in Manchuria in the late 1940s greatly expanded the size of both. During the military conquest of the mainland, large numbers of new members flocked to the winning side. By the time the new regime was established in October 1949, there were 4.5 million party members, the core of a new regime that was to rule a nation of 541 million.[3] The party was about to undergo a profound and largely unforeseen transformation.

From Political Movement to Ruling Party

To join the party before its victory was a different matter than joining it afterward. The CCP referred to those who joined prior to its victory as "revolutionary cadres"—an official status that recognized contributions in an era of risk and sacrifice. In subsequent decades, these party members filled the top spots in the new administration, and their families carried the most favored household status. Inheriting this favored status, their offspring would receive special preference in admission to the party and to schools, and in job assignments. Those who had served in the Red Army before its victory had a similar status—"revolutionary soldier"—and their offspring received similar preferences in later years.[4]

Revolutionary cadre status acknowledged the fact that joining the party before its victory represented commitment to a cause, one that entailed considerable risk, hardship, even loss of life or limb. One could not say the same about those who joined after the party's victory. As the years went by, and as the party consolidated its control over the economy and the educational system, joining it was an act of loyalty to established authority, one likely to be rewarded with status and career advancement. To be sure, party members were still expected to sacrifice time and effort, perform unpopular tasks, and set aside their personal beliefs under party discipline that could be harsh. Whatever an individual's motivation, the personal risks and sacrifice involved in this decision paled in comparison with those of the earlier era, and the potential rewards were large.[5] As the party grew in the 1950s, new members were recruited in universities, offices, and factories. They had different skills and life experiences than the revolutionary generation. The party quadrupled in size by 1965, by which point post-1949 recruits outnumbered revolutionary cadres by a ratio of more than three to one.[6]

The Party's Reach

The party organization was at the core of the new state, and as the Soviet system was put into place, it exercised control over job assignments, the allocation of material goods, school admissions, and appointments to leadership positions in government and enterprises. Its reach extended into all social institutions and economic enterprises, right down to the village, the factory floor, and the staff office. Essentially an interlocking chain of committees that replicated itself from the top leadership in Beijing down to the grass roots, the party maintained a separate administrative system that supervised and controlled government and administration at every level. At the top was the CCP Politburo, composed of twenty full members and six alternates in 1956; the seven most influential of these individuals served on the smaller Politburo Standing Committee, which met more regularly. Mao Zedong, as party chairman, was at the apex of this structure. The Politburo was a subset of a much larger and largely ceremonial Central Committee, which included some 197 full and alternate members in 1956. It met irregularly and had little direct influence on decision making.[7]

Directly subordinate to the national organization in Beijing were party committees that were in charge of each of twenty-nine province-level jurisdictions. Party secretaries, the top officials in each province, chaired these provincial committees and met regularly with the smaller standing committee. This structure was replicated down each level of government all the way to the grass roots. Below the provincial committees were municipal and prefectural party committees; below these were county and city district party committees; and below them party committees in every rural commune, every university, all but the smallest factories, and any other organization of significance.

This national network of party committees exercised control over administrative decisions at each level. Provincial governors, for example, were themselves party members and members of the standing committee—if the party secretary was not in fact also the governor. The same was true for mayors, county magistrates, factory executives, and university presidents. If the top administrators at each level were not also party secretaries, they were almost always members of its standing committee and held the post of party vice secretary. In this fashion the party's national organization paralleled, and was intertwined with, the administration of government, economic enterprises, and public institutions at every level.

At the bottom of the hierarchy were the party branches. This is where ordinary party members were integrated into the national organization. Party branches supervised an average of fifteen members in an office, workshop, academic department, or collective farm. Party members attended separate meetings that were closed to others, and they were subject to party discipline exercised by a party branch secretary. The branch secretary, in turn, was subordinate to the general branch secretary, and selected branch secretaries were members of the general branch committee. General branch secretaries, in turn, were subordinate to the party secretary, and were themselves often members of the party committee.

This was the power structure of the new party-state. Several implications of this structure should be immediately apparent. The first is that this was a single hierarchy that was directly subordinate to the top leadership in Beijing and was expected to faithfully carry out directives from the top. No important decisions could be made at any of these levels without the consent of party secretaries and the support of the party organization. The second is that this hierarchy was extraordinarily large. By 1955 there were already 9.4 million party members, and this number doubled again by 1965, to 18.7 million.[8] By the latter date there were more than 80,000 party committees organized throughout the country, 42,000 general branches, and 1.2 million grassroots party branches.[9] The third is that there were millions of party positions to be staffed: each party committee had a party secretary and vice secretaries, along with administrative staff; each general branch and branch also had a secretary and vice secretary. The party organization, therefore, defined career opportunities for hundreds of thousands of party cadres, a separate career path for individuals that in theory could lead to promotion up the hierarchy to the apex of power in Beijing. There was no other path to the top.

Despite its massive size, the party organization was not distributed evenly across regions and organizations. Aggregate membership figures are misleading: workers and farmers consistently comprised more than 80 percent of all members, with the vast majority in the latter group.[10] Aggregate figures mask the concentration of party members in specific organizations and occupations. The party concentrated its influence in settings where decisions were made, capital was invested, resources were allocated, and power exercised. This meant that rates of party membership were much higher in cities than in the countryside; much higher in large and important organizations than in small and unimportant ones; and much higher among top decision makers than among ordinary staff and workers.

Surveys conducted in the early post-Mao era reveal the enduring legacy of the party's concentration on important organizations and occupations.[11] By the 1990s, 17 percent of adults in urban areas were party members, but only 5.8 percent in the countryside. In cities, rates of party membership varied directly with the importance of the organization. Employees of state enterprises were twice as likely to be members of the party than employees of smaller collective enterprises (19 versus 9 percent), and employees of government offices were twice as likely to be party members than those who worked in schools, hospitals, and research institutes (64 versus 33 percent). In both city and countryside, rates of party membership rose sharply by occupational rank. In the countryside, only 4.6 percent of adult farmers were party members; 22 percent of those who were village (or production brigade) cadres of any rank; and 78 percent of those who were top officials in a village (or production brigade). In cities, rates of party membership rose by rank in a similar fashion: 8 percent of manual workers were party members, 15 percent of white-collar workers, 49 percent of lower-ranking cadres, and 85 percent of high-ranking cadres.[12]

These figures illustrate an important feature of the party in power: it was strategic and selective in focusing its efforts. Ruling communist parties are highly elitist. Because their goal was to control both government and economy, party organizations were concentrated where power was exercised and resources allocated, and in those occupations that exercise power over people and resources. Accordingly, the intensity of pressures to conform, and the pervasiveness of politics in the lives of citizens, varied with the party's coverage of different social settings. Peasants on collective farms were least subject to the party's daily demands; blue-collar industrial workers somewhat more so. But in settings where power and resources were concentrated, the intensity of political discipline and intrusion of politics into lives rose.[13]

Political Surveillance

The party's growing network was the public, overt side of political power. It grew alongside a covert network of political surveillance—a new state security network under the Ministry of Public Security. The agency's purpose was not to safeguard public order, but to consolidate the new regime's control and afterward to safeguard the party's power. The public face of order maintenance—household registration, neighborhood organization, school and workplace dossiers, and work units—might make it appear that an extensive covert network of state security agents played little role. But this was not the case. The public security organs were an ever-present backdrop to the public face of political power, and operated in ways that paralleled the Soviet KGB and the East German Stasi.

The ministry built a hierarchy of regional and local bureaus beginning in 1949, modeled after the Soviet KGB. Its network of covert officers and agents focused heavily on urban areas and border regions populated by non-Han nationalities. It conducted counterintelligence operations against foreign agents, monitored the population for signs of political subversion, and guarded critical economic infrastructure against sabotage.[14] To perform these tasks, the ministry and its regional bureaus placed covert case officers (salaried professional employees) and agent-informers (nonemployee civilians) in government offices, universities, factories, and other institutions. During the 1950s, ministry regulations mandated that roughly one-third of the staff in university personnel departments were to be covert state security officers who developed networks of agents in the school and compiled case files—separate from the personnel dossiers kept by these departments—that monitored the political leanings of faculty and students.[15] Officers with similar functions were placed in factories, banks, hospitals, and other urban organizations. Security officers in the national railway system maintained networks of agents that numbered 10,000 by the mid-1950s.[16]

The ministry recruited and ran three kinds of agent-informers. The first, "secret investigation agents," were tasked with monitoring potential sites of subversion in society at large. These agents reported on what they observed in schools, factories, inns, restaurants, movie houses, and especially foreign-related organizations. "Case agents," a second category, were employed not for general information gathering and monitoring but to penetrate targeted groups and organizations as part of sustained investigations—especially churches or other organizations with foreign ties. The third category, "critical asset guardians," were stationed in or near strategic installations and factories—the railway network, major manufacturing complexes, the postal and telecommunication systems, and installations related to military weapons programs. Their task was to assist case officers in guarding against sabotage and leaks of sensitive information.[17]

Agents were recruited from all walks of life. Political activists and party members could be relied upon to cooperate when asked, but their public political leanings were unlikely to be trusted by the kinds of people targeted for investigations. At the opposite extreme were "bad elements," recruited precisely because they had access to other suspect groups. Their cooperation could be secured by exempting them from imprisonment on the condition that they inform on their associates. Individuals targeted during the 1950s campaigns to eliminate counterrevolutionaries were occasionally offered immunity in return for their assistance in providing information about others.[18] A third category was neither loyal political activists nor politically suspect individuals, but individuals who were persuaded to report on what they observed in staff offices, churches, foreign trade organizations, and banks.[19] Recruitment appeals ranged from blackmail, to appeals to patriotism and political loyalty, to a more subtle mixture of implied reward or threat.[20] The surveillance networks could be effective only so long as they remained covert. The ministry had elaborate procedures for confidential communications between agents and officers at permanent safe houses or temporarily borrowed sites, coded communications, and special telephone exchanges.[21] This surveillance network was based primarily on human intelligence, verbal communication, and written paper files. Not until long after the Mao era would China's state security agencies develop more pervasive and technologically sophisticated forms of surveillance.

Party Recruitment

In a society where the party organization selects individuals for leadership positions in a national hierarchy, party membership becomes a very important avenue of personal advancement and social mobility. If only 17 percent of adults in cities are party members, and fewer than 6 percent in the countryside, party membership is clearly not something that is open to all. Those who joined the party after its triumph typically did so after establishing a sustained record of political activism and commitment to party policy and their work unit superiors. They joined the Communist Youth League in schools or workplaces, likely rising to leadership positions in these organizations. While on the job, they were typically the first to come to work, the last to leave, the first to speak out in meetings where party policies were being discussed, and the first to express support for them. If the party organization demanded that they report on their coworkers' words and deeds, they did so. If a campaign required that a targeted individual be denounced for an alleged political error, they would do so. After establishing a record of activism and loyalty, they put themselves forward as candidates to the party branch—or were invited to apply. After checking family background and other materials in the individual's dossier, the successful applicant would be accepted as a candidate member and placed under the tutelage of a designated sponsor, who was charged with "developing" him or her. After a period of close observation as a candidate member, full membership followed.[22]

Individuals were most likely to join the party when they were young. Data from life history surveys reveal that after 1949, individuals' likelihood of joining the party rose to its maximum at ages twenty-two and twenty-three and dropped off rapidly thereafter.[23] If one had not joined the party by age thirty-five, it was highly unlikely that one would ever join. For individuals in manual occupations, party membership was the primary way to attain promotion out of jobs in the fields or on the shop floor. Once one completed schooling and was given a first job assignment, attaining party membership was the most important single factor in improving one's odds of career advancement. Decisions made early in one's career therefore affected the extent to which one's subsequent career would be shaped by active participation in party-directed activities.[24]

What do we know about the characteristics of those who were recruited into the party during this period? A clear picture emerges from the analysis of life history surveys, which allow us to estimate how the odds of joining were affected by one individual characteristic, holding other characteristics constant.[25] The first is that men were almost twice as likely to join the party as women—other things being equal. This could be due to traditional discrimination against women in male-dominated party organizations, and it could also be due to lower rates of application among women due to cultural expectations or additional household responsibilities that fall disproportionately on married women, making them less available for the activities that establish a record of political activism in the work unit. The second is that parentage matters: individuals whose fathers were already party members were twice as likely to become party members. This could be due to higher parental pressures on offspring to become politically active and apply, and also to favoritism shown by party branches to sons and daughters of party members. The third is that position mattered greatly. Individuals who were already in a low-level leadership post were almost three times more likely than others to become party members—suggesting that they first proved themselves in entry-level leadership tasks and that the party wanted to ensure that leaders were under party discipline.

The interesting feature of these estimates is that these odds were multiplied, not just added together, when an individual had more than one characteristic. So, for example, a man whose father was a party member and who was in an entry-level leadership post was around twelve times more likely to be recruited into the party than a woman whose father was not in the party and who was not in a leadership position ($2 \times 2 \times 3$). At the other extreme, highly skilled professionals were far less likely to become party members than anyone else—only 16 percent as likely as nonprofessionals. This indicated the party's suspicion of the educated elite, which became pronounced after 1957; it probably also indicates unwillingness on the part of educated professionals to put themselves under party discipline. Education was valued—just not too much of it. Those who completed high school were 70 percent more likely to become party members than those without a high school education, but a college degree did not improve the odds of membership over those with a high school education.[26]

Class Categories and Family Origin

The CCP adopted the late 1920s Soviet practice of sorting its population into class categories. As in the Soviet Union, these categories were inspired by Marxist class analysis, but they were in fact political statuses that became characteristics of entire families, passed down through generations and enforced by bureaucratic rules. The Soviet Communist Party classified its population during the 1920s to distinguish "proletarian" elements from "exploiters" and "class enemies." Once identified, those in the proletarian categories enjoyed certain privileges and opportunities, while those in the exploiter categories faced certain forms of discrimination and restricted opportunities.[27] The system of bureaucratic class identities served several purposes: social justice, social engineering, and regime consolidation. Proletarian categories were to be favored in admission to the party, promotion at work, and advancement into higher education, because these groups were denied opportunity in the old society. Individuals from exploiter households, who previously enjoyed huge advantages in opportunities, were henceforth to face certain forms of discrimination. By favoring households that benefited from the revolution, new elites would form through the process of higher education, replacing the old elites who had lost status and power in the revolution. These new elites would presumably be more loyal than those from former exploiting households, who were understood to be hostile to proletarian power. They were designated as class enemies and periodically abused as "enemies of the people."[28]

These categories were strongly emphasized in the Soviet Union in the late 1920s. They became a tool in the "class war" waged in the Soviet "Cultural Revolution" of 1928–1931, when those from "bourgeois" backgrounds, especially trained professionals and members of the old intelligentsia, were targeted by party activists as subversive representatives of an alien class culture and faced demotion, and in some cases firing and banishment from cities. This campaign expressed Stalin's novel claim that class struggle actually intensified even after the expropriation of former exploiting classes' assets eliminated the material basis for class differences. Class enemies, he asserted, would scheme to prevent the final victory of socialism.[29] The Soviet party backed away from class discrimination in the early 1930s, and by 1937 Stalin's new constitution ended class discrimination. This, however, did not prevent individuals from exploiter backgrounds from being targeted as class enemies in Stalin's massive purges of 1937–1938.[30]

China affixed class categories to its population long after the practice had fallen out of favor in the Soviet Union. As in the Soviet Union, these class categories were "file identities" that were fixed by the classification of the male household head at the time of the CCP's "liberation" of a locality.[31] Cadres assigned these identities to rural households during the course of land reform, on the basis of their investigation of landholding and individual political histories garnered during the visits of work teams to villages. Class categories were affixed to households based on some combination of their economic status and the political activities of the male household head. In the cities, they were assigned on the basis of written individual autobiographies that were placed in permanent dossiers. Individuals were told to report fully on their entire work histories, describing the positions they held and the occupations of their parents. They were also instructed to report fully on their own and their parents' political histories. It was impossible to complete detailed background checks on everyone; cadres who compiled the dossiers and decided on classifications would often check with coworkers and other family members to ensure consistency and the veracity of self-reports. The most thorough background checks were done on those who were already in positions of some authority, or who were applying for party membership.

As in the Soviet Union, the effort to classify households into loyal (proletarian) and enemy (exploiter) categories was plagued with ambiguity and contradictions. The ambiguity came in two forms. First, in many cases individuals worked in a variety of occupations during their lives. Individuals could rise from humble backgrounds to establish a business and accumulate some wealth; or they could lose privileged positions through bankruptcy or unemployment in the course of their careers. These kinds of disruptions were common during the Japanese invasion and civil war, which could lead to drastic changes in a family's fate. Upward and downward mobility could make class designations an arbitrary judgment call. Second, large segments of the population could not readily be assigned to either proletarian or exploiter categories. In the countryside, the CCP adapted the Soviet categories of "poor," "middle-class," and "rich" peasant and added two more: "poor and lower-middle" and "landlord." This was necessary to cover the common situation of self-sufficient households who ran their own farm or small business entirely with household labor. The same was true of urban professionals, white-collar workers, teachers, and intellectuals. Because they were not engaged in material production, they were not exploited in Marxist terms, and they did not hire others or possess capital that made them exploiters. Like middle-class peasants, urban middle classes were assigned politically ambiguous labels.

The system was also rife with contradictions. The first was the conflation of "class" with political affiliation. In the Soviet Union, membership in the Communist Party before the classification of the population in the 1920s made one proletarian, regardless of family background or personal occupation before joining. This practice was adopted in China. People who joined the party or the Red Army before their victory were considered revolutionary even if they had come from prosperous exploiter households. The Communist Party attracted many patriotic students during the anti-Japanese war, during a period when high school and university education was limited to individuals from prosperous households. The party itself was founded and led by the sons of prosperous rural families, and it attracted many individuals from similar backgrounds in the long course of its movement. Life history surveys conducted in the 1990s have shown that the class status and educational level of the male founders of revolutionary households were surprisingly high, surpassed only by those designated as exploiting classes.[32]

The reverse relationship also holds: no matter how humble one's origins, to have joined the Nationalist Party or army would have erased one's proletarian origins and would make one a class enemy. This was especially egregious in the case of Nationalist army veterans who fought against the Japanese while Communist armies deliberately avoided combat. The same ambiguities evident in classifying occupations apply also to these political categories. This was pronounced in cases where individuals defected from the Nationalist cause to join the Communists. This occurred on a large scale late in the civil war.

Another contradictory feature of these classifications is that they are inherited. This means that individuals who grew up in households classified as landlord or capitalist would still be considered as such, even if their families' assets had been expropriated before they were born and they grew up in dire poverty. The same applied to individuals whose fathers or grandfathers had been officials in the Nationalist Party or officers in Nationalist armies—even if they had no prior contact with these forebears because they had been executed or fled to Taiwan. On the other hand, revolutionary cadres and soldiers were assigned to leadership positions after the party's victory and rose at high rates into important positions. This meant that their offspring were considered revolutionary, even if they were raised in privileged households, with spacious apartments and household servants.

Although these labels were intended to be permanent, in practice they could be altered due to political investigations or individual behavior. Individuals who had successfully hidden aspects of their past from the new regime might find their prior histories exposed and their political labels altered. Individuals who fell afoul of authorities in subsequent campaigns might find that their family origins were reclassified in a less favored category. The flexibility, indeed malleability, of these labels—a product of their fundamental ambiguity—meant that many individuals could never be assured that favorable status in the eyes of the regime would be permanent. These bureaucratic identities could always be revised due to individual behavior or reinvestigation.[33]

A final ambiguity is the way that class categories overlapped with gender. Household categories were fixed by the status of male household heads, and they were inherited through the male line. This meant that a woman from an exploiting class could marry a man from a revolutionary or proletarian background and enjoy the security and privileges that accrued to the male's status. Such a woman would have offspring who would inherit the advantages of the more favorable household classification. The obvious gender dimension of these categories had a major effect on marital choice in China, in both rural and urban areas.[34] The practice had no foundation whatsoever in Marxist theory, but was instead an expression of the patriarchal attitudes of a traditional society that the party officially dismissed as "feudal."[35]

The class labels were divided into three broad categories. "Red" classes included revolutionary and proletarian households. They were presumed to be loyal to the party and the revolution, and were to be shown preference. "Ordinary" classes included the old middle classes. They were presumed to be neutral, or wavering, in their loyalties to the revolution, and were to receive neither preferences nor penalties. The "black" or "bad" classes were households classified as either "exploiting class" or "reactionary" (see Table 6.1).

These labels were an important criterion in determining party membership, and special preference was shown to individuals from revolutionary households.[36] Those with a revolutionary class label were roughly twice as likely to become party members in the Mao era than individuals from ordinary proletarian categories, controlling for gender, age, and years of education. By the same token, those from non-red categories—former middle classes, exploiting classes, and political reactionary origins—were much less likely to become party members than others. Those from proletarian households were twice as likely as professionals to join the party, and those from revolutionary households were almost four times more likely.

Political Loyalty and Career Advancement

Just as the party screened for loyalty in deciding whom to admit, party organizations also screened individuals for political loyalty—real or presumed—in decisions about college admissions, first job assignment, and promotion to higher rank. Party membership itself was an impor-

Table 6.1.   Political classifications of households

(1) Categories	(2) Labels	(3) Percentage of Urban Population
"Red" category		
Revolutionary classes	Revolutionary cadre, revolutionary soldier, revolutionary martyr	4.4
Proletarian classes	Poor and lower-middle-class peasant, worker, urban poor	77.8
"Ordinary" category	Middle-class peasant, white- collar staff, intellectuals, teachers, professionals	14.4
"Black" category		3.4
Exploiting classes	Capitalist, landlord, rich peasant	
Reactionary classes	Nationalist Party member, official, or soldier; "counterrevolutionary," "bad element," "rightist"	

Sources: Columns 1 and 2, Kraus (1981); column 3, Walder and Hu (2009, 1405).

tant credential, especially among working adults, but other criteria were important, especially among the young. Two of these criteria were inherently political: one's record of political activism and one's family background as designated by the inherited class label.

Advancement in China's school system was highly competitive, and the odds of reaching the top of the educational ladder were very steep. Of the 32.9 million children who entered primary school in 1965, only 9 percent could expect to enter junior high school. Only 15 percent of junior high school entrants, in turn, could expect to graduate and enter high school. Among the highly selected group that graduated from academic high schools, only 36 percent could expect to enroll in a university. Of those who entered primary school in 1965, only 1.3 percent could expect to attend an academic high school, and only one-half of 1 percent could expect to attend university.[37]

Through the mid-1960s, the most important criterion for admission to academic high schools, and for university admission, was a standardized entrance examination—city or county-wide for high school, nationwide for university. This highly competitive and meritocratic system, however, could be influenced at the margin by political criteria that were built into the admissions process.

The first criterion was the family's class label. Applicants from revolutionary and proletarian households were to be shown preference if their exam performance was near the threshold score for admission; applicants from exploiting or reactionary households had to score well above the threshold level to gain admittance.[38] College admissions were an openly political form of "affirmative action" designed to promote "red" classes at the expense of all others. The stated preference for proletarian households opened up educational opportunities that were virtually unattainable for individuals from these backgrounds before 1949. As late as the 1930s, most of the students in China's universities were from wealthy families, and in the elite colleges almost every student was.[39] Despite the intentions of the policy, however, students from revolutionary backgrounds benefited from the preference for red classes far more than the proletarian students, while students from the former middle classes and even former exploiting classes still entered university at much higher rates.

Table 6.2 illustrates the impact of class labels on school admissions in two of Beijing's elite schools in the mid-1960s: Tsinghua High School and Tsinghua University. In both of them, the non-red classes did far better than the policy might suggest. Tsinghua High School was an elite

Table 6.2.   Admission rates to elite schools by class background, mid-1960s

Class Label	(1) Percentage of Enrollment, Tsinghua High School	(2) (Col. 1)/ (Col. 5)	(3) Percentage of Enrollment, Tsinghua University	(4) (Col. 3)/ (Col. 5)	(5) Percentage of Urban Population
Proletarian classes	11	0.14	38	0.49	77.8
Revolutionary classes	25	5.7	9	2.0	4.4
Middle classes	55	3.8	42	2.9	14.4
"Exploiting" classes	11	3.2	11	3.2	3.4

Sources: Columns 1 and 3, Andreas (2009, 70) (percentages are rounded averages of two estimates when they differ); column 5, Walder and Hu (2009, 1405).

boarding school in the far suburbs of the capital and drew its body of applicants from Beijing. It is striking (column 1) that students from revolutionary households are represented far out of proportion to their size in the urban population of China (column 5). This is surely due to the concentration of revolutionary cadres in the nation's capital, where they occupied high-ranking posts. Equally striking is the fact that students from middle and even exploiting classes are represented at far higher levels than their weight in the population, as indicated by the ratios in column 2 (ratios above 1.0 indicate overrepresentation, while ratios below 1.0 indicate underrepresentation). Students from proletarian households were a small minority at the high school and they were vastly underrepresented relative to their share of the urban population.

Class representation at Tsinghua University was different, because it attracted applicants from the entire nation and not just the nation's capital. This is why revolutionary classes occupied a much lower percentage of the student body than in the high school, although they were still overrepresented relative to their population size, as indicated by the ratios in column 4. Proletarian classes occupied a much higher percentage of the student body than in the high school, but still less than half their share of the urban population. Remarkably, both the middle classes and "black" classes—the elite of the old society—occupied a proportionally much greater share of college slots than students from all other backgrounds. The highly meritocratic test-based system worked against the intentions of the class line policy.[40]

The reason for this lingering overrepresentation of old elites is no mystery. In any society, children who grow up in households with educated parents have advantages: due to greater educational resources in the home; due to their parents' ability to help them with schoolwork; and especially due to the high expectations that they place upon their offspring. China's former elites found ways to succeed in this educational system despite the discrimination against them enshrined in the class label policy. This became a major political issue in the mid-1960s and was the primary reason why entrance examinations were abolished during the Cultural Revolution.

Political activism was the second criterion used by the party to influence opportunity, and in theory individuals from all family backgrounds could strive to compile a strong political record. These were the same attitudes and behaviors that were important in admission to the party. Because high school students and all but a small number of university students were too young to be eligible for party membership, activism in the school setting was demonstrated by participation in the Communist Youth League, especially by taking up leadership posts in the organization. High schools and universities maintained active youth leagues that were directly subordinate to party committees, and they contained a full complement of league branches and leadership posts that mirrored those of the party organization itself. Students who had a history of work as "student cadres" in these organizations compiled a strong record, recorded in their personal dossiers, that was explicitly taken into consideration and could be decisive in cases where one's standardized tests scores were marginal, or in deciding to which school or program of study an individual would be assigned.[41]

The same two political criteria—class background and political activism—were employed in assigning students to jobs after graduation, although party membership at this stage became an emblem of political loyalty for the university students who had joined while still in college. In 1965, for example, 7.8 percent of Peking University students were already party members, and 13 percent of Tsinghua University students.[42] These students had the best possible records of political activism. Combined with class origin, college transcripts, and advisors' recommendations, college graduates were selected by ministries, research institutes, state enterprises, or graduate programs. Those who were already party members had a wider range of opportunities.

There was an obvious tension between political and meritocratic criteria for advancement. Surveys conducted in later years yielded a clear picture of how this potential conflict was handled. Essentially, the party created two separate career paths that required different credentials.[43] Not surprisingly, to attain an important leadership position in government, industry, or public institutions, it was essential to have attained party membership long beforehand, but a college degree was not essential.[44] Party members were more than eight times more likely to be promoted into a decision-making position than nonmembers, controlling for a range of other individual characteristics. The role of prior education was similar to what we saw earlier for the attainment of party membership: graduation from high school increased one's odds of promotion 2.5-fold, while having a college degree did not provide any additional advantage.

Given the emphasis on political criteria for college admissions and job assignments, it is remarkable how little party membership mattered for those who became scientists, engineers, doctors, economic analysts, government planners, or university instructors. Through the mid-1960s, these were well-compensated positions with high prestige, but prior party membership played no role in attaining this kind of elite occupation. Education, however, was overwhelmingly important. A high school diploma increased the odds of becoming an elite professional almost ninefold, and a college degree increased the odds almost an additional fivefold. Prior party membership had no net impact. The professional career was based on formal education, period.

While it might appear that the regime was relatively indifferent to the educational qualifications of its party, government, and enterprise officials, this was far from the case. We noted earlier that party members were most frequently recruited while very young, especially those who showed early signs of both political loyalty and leadership ability. Although these individuals rarely obtained a college degree before joining, the party maintained a large system of adult education and selected young party members with leadership potential for further education. Party members could be admitted into regular universities as adults based on recommendation and sponsorship by work unit party organizations. The most visible example of this program was the practice by work unit party organizations of recommending individuals for admission to a university. These were known as "cadre-transfer students." Regional governments also organized part-time adult education programs on a massive scale, all designed to upgrade the quality of leaders. Party members were more than five times more likely to receive higher education through these sponsored adult programs, and after completing adult education at the college level, they were more than four times more likely than those who graduated from college before working to be promoted into a senior leadership position.[45]

Power and Privilege

Joining the party had no immediate impact on one's standard of living. It simply opened up the possibility of future career advancement, either as a party cadre if one was a party secretary at some level, or an administrative cadre if one held a management position in an enterprise or government agency. China had a single nationwide cadre ranking system, ranging from the lowest, grade 26, to the highest, grade 1. Ministers and higher-level cadres generally occupied ranks 6 and above, while middle-level cadres, beginning with division chiefs, occupied ranks 15 and above.[46] Differences in standard of living were not the product of differences in income. Money incomes could vary considerably, but purchasing power did not directly translate into different levels of material prosperity. Privilege came directly from the rules that governed the entitlements for officials who had achieved a certain rank, and were entitlements for which the cadres either did not have to pay, or for which only a nominal fee was charged.

Privilege came in virtually all dimensions of one's professional and personal life. Officials above a certain rank did not ride a bicycle, but had access to an automobile (with driver) provided by the work unit. They found it easier to travel domestically, and for long-distance travel, higher-ranking cadres had the right to sit in soft-seat or soft sleeper compartments of trains, avoiding the badly overcrowded and uncomfortable hard-seat cars for the masses. Ranking cadres had access to larger and better apartments and were more likely to have private bathrooms and kitchens. At the highest levels, officials might live in a single-family bungalow, be served by maids and nannies, and have round-the-clock access to a car and driver. Ranking cadres also had better access to foods and consumer items that were rationed in the general population. When they traveled, they had access to better-quality hotels and guesthouses, and when they ate in restaurants, they did so in separate cadre sections that had better service and better-quality food.

Rank also affected access to information. Official party and government documents were issued with a range of security classifications that were keyed to an official's rank. Only officials above a certain grade could read designated documents and reports. The party published several internal newspapers and bulletins that had a far greater range of information than what was published in the official mass media. *Reference Materials (cankao ziliao)*, a restricted-circulation bulletin published by New China News Agency, contained translations from foreign news outlets that contained material considered more sensitive than what was available in a similar publication, *Reference News (cankao xiaoxi)*, which was available to all cadres during the Mao era. *Internal Reference (neibu cankao)*, published twice daily by the New China News Agency, contained domestic news reports intended specifically for China's political elite. It contained reports on problems encountered in implementing national policies, natural disasters, regional protests, and a range of other news items deemed inappropriate for wider circulation.[47] Ranking officials were also able to gain access to foreign books and movies that were banned to the general public.

Although living standards and privileges were carefully calibrated to bureaucratic rank, the privileges were relatively modest, and standards of living were not strikingly different from ordinary people until one reached the top ranks. Even the highest officials in China throughout the Mao period had material lifestyles that paled in comparison with those of wealthy individuals in market economies. Compared with later years, there was virtually no conspicuous consumption. Corruption was rare and petty in scale where it did occur. Nonetheless, the privileges that came with rank were highly valued in an economy that enshrined seemingly permanent consumer austerity. A cadre career permitted one to escape the privations of rationing and shortages and live with a level of comfort and convenience that few citizens in China would be able to experience.

A Closed Hierarchy

In a state socialist economy with a single party hierarchy, power and privilege were inevitably intertwined. This, however, was not cost free. There were distinctive features of life as a party bureaucrat that were fundamentally different from those of civil servants in market economies with liberal political systems. The first distinctive feature is that officials did not have any personal wealth or any means of support other than their government positions. To be sure, they had savings accounts, and they owned certain household items, but they did not have any significant property or independent means of support. The homes they occupied were allocated to them at a nominal rent, but they did not own them. The automobiles belonged to their organization. Their expenses were covered by the organization. They did not accumulate significant wealth, even if their careers were long and they rose high in rank. Their privileges were a direct expression of their rank, and they enjoyed them so long as they were in good political standing.

The second distinctive feature is related to the first: cadres had no alternative to working for the party-state. They could not withdraw from an official career to go into consulting or private business. They could not emigrate. They could not choose to retire and live off of their accumulated savings. They could not transfer to another organization or province to start anew. If they tried to quit the system, or withdraw from active party life, this would be interpreted as a sign of political wavering, a decline in commitment, a breach of party discipline. The only exit option in this career path was essentially involuntary and unappealing: a demotion or expulsion that brought with it immediate loss of the privileges accorded to that rank.[48]

These implications are often missed in discussions of cadre privilege. These privileges came at a cost. Cadres were entirely dependent on the party organization for their livelihoods and the privileges that they enjoyed, and they continued to enjoy them only so long as they remained in good standing. The party's demands for conformity and loyalty did not end with the conferral of party membership, or with appointment as an official. Cadres were pressured to carry out policies, some of which made little sense, to reach targets, and to identify and punish allegedly disloyal individuals in their work units. More than any other social group—except perhaps career military officers—they were subject to the discipline of the regime. They could not openly resist extreme demands from above, and always lived under the knowledge that failure to perform, or failure to comply with party policy, could seriously jeopardize their current standing and future opportunities. A negative evaluation for substandard performance or wavering loyalty could have lifelong repercussions in a system where there was only one employer. The worst possible experience was a rectification campaign or a search for hidden enemies similar to that carried out in the party rectification of 1942–1944 in Yan'an. That could lead to a loss of position and status, and even to prison or a labor camp. These pressures affected China's cadres more than any other social group.

Dilemmas of a Changing Party

The transition from revolutionary party to a political bureaucracy was a fundamental change, inevitable once the decision to follow the Soviet model was made. The incentives for individuals to join the party, the rewards in careers opened up by party membership, and the qualities and motivations of the individuals attracted to the party, were all fundamentally different from those of the long years of revolutionary struggle. Controlling all economic resources and access to career advancement, the party became the route to power and privilege. It became a massive bureaucracy, operating like a political machine, with all of the problems of bureaucratic organizations throughout the world.

Not long after the new state was consolidated at the end of the 1950s, Mao began to have misgivings about these developments and saw them as a threat to the ideals of revolutionary sacrifice and struggle. A bureaucratic system staffed by individuals motivated by career advancement and special privileges threatened to replace one form of oppression with another. Many of Mao's colleagues in the national leadership did not see this as a negative development. Instead, it was part of the evolution toward a modern form of scientific socialism, a system that relied on advanced science and technology, and modern forms of industrial organization to create a modern and prosperous nation. This model assumed the party's monopoly of power, but it also involved a major role for the highly educated professionals upon which this vision depended.

This was the vision of a socialist future that became the hallmark of Soviet socialism as it emerged from the Stalin era. To be sure, this was no path toward democracy, and certainly was not a path toward market-based capitalism. But the system was far more stable and predictable than its earlier incarnation in the Stalin era. Massive campaigns against hidden enemies were to be discontinued; claims of continuing class struggle and underground conspiracies were declared a regrettable error of the past; victims would be released from labor camps and their convictions overturned. If they avoided signs of dissent, citizens could lead secure lives, unworried that they might be accused of an imaginary political crime. Public adulation of a great leader as a national hero and genius was a sign of ignorance and national backwardness, a manifestation of feudalism and a regrettable deviation from the socialist path that led to unimaginable suffering and destruction under Stalin's iron rule.

By the mid-1960s, Mao had decided that this post-Stalin Soviet view of a socialist future was a deviation from the correct revolutionary path. His vision was very different, and he was unwilling to permit his party-state to evolve into a stable bureaucracy ruled by bureaucrats who lorded over subordinates and paid lip service to revolutionary ideals, but were motivated by career advancement and material comfort. Mao's answer was essentially to revive what he saw as the spirit of struggle and sacrifice that had led to improbable victories in the past—not careful planning and reliance on scientific and technical experts, but the mobilization of party and society to achieve victories over nature and over enemies that were attempting to subvert the revolution from within. Mao eventually decided to smash the machine and start over, relying on his prestige and status as a Stalin-like genius to mobilize the masses against the party establishment, and members of the establishment against one another. It would take several more years, and several more political episodes beginning in 1957, for him to come to this conclusion. The result, eventually, was the Cultural Revolution.

7

Thaw and Backlash

BY 1956 CHINA had almost completed a series of revolutionary changes. Land reform was followed by the rapid formation of collective farms. Private industry and commerce disappeared as productive assets were nationalized. The foundations for a bureaucratic economy along Soviet lines were laid. The party's networks of power spread across the country, working their way into factories, offices, and villages. Status no longer came from ownership of property, and wealth could no longer be passed across generations. Instead, people were granted access to public property and services based on their rank in a bureaucratic hierarchy, access to which came through the party system. Educational institutions and intellectual life were remolded, and previously strong influences from the West were repudiated in favor of "advanced" Soviet doctrines. China's historic links with the world's market economies were severed. While China was not subject to dictates from Moscow, it was drawn firmly into the orbit of the world communist system.

This was China's first coherent national state since the fall of the Qing empire, integrating almost all of the former imperial territories. It was also China's first unified modern state, one with a salaried bureaucracy that reached from Beijing into rural and urban communities. In 1956 China's leaders could look back with satisfaction and view the near future with confidence. From their perspective, they consolidated control over China after an unexpected victory in the civil war; their armies had fought to a standstill with the United States and other nations on the Korean peninsula; and they had made unexpectedly rapid strides toward socialism. In particular, collective agriculture was put in place without the violent coercion and devastating famine that had marred Soviet collectivization in the early 1930s.

To be sure, coercion and terror propelled these changes forward. The land reform and campaigns against "counterrevolution" in the early 1950s led to the execution of more than a million and the imprisonment of many more. The Three Anti, Five Anti campaign coercively expropriated the assets of urban shopkeepers and business owners. The Thought Reform campaigns forced educated Chinese to publicly repudiate their beliefs, promise to remold their reactionary views, and pledge loyalty to the new regime. Campaigns against a series of "deviations" from correct socialist doctrine repeatedly targeted authors and academics, even the party's own leading intellectuals, for their erroneous and subversive thoughts, which sometimes were treated as counterrevolutionary conspiracies.

These changes were rapid, more rapid than originally planned. Mao had been the most forceful advocate of an immediate transition to Soviet-style socialism. He pushed this forward after he unveiled his "General Line" of 1953, criticizing and on occasion bullying other leaders who argued for a more measured pace of change. Mao identified socialism with the model created by the Soviet Union under Stalin, and he was impatient with arguments that change should be gradual. Above all, Mao pushed for rapid industrialization, and he saw the transformation of the economy along Soviet lines as the surest way for China to succeed. Against those who counseled a more cautious and balanced approach, he pushed hard for larger grain deliveries from the new collective farms and for increased investment and output in heavy industry. Mao's identification with Stalin-era Soviet socialism was symbolized by the growing cult that surrounded his leadership of the party. His collected works were published; his portrait hung in offices and factories throughout the country; and Mao Zedong Thought was still enshrined in the 1945 party constitution as the guide to all of the party's work. By his own standards, Mao had been remarkably successful.

Developments in the Soviet bloc after Stalin's death in March 1953, however, took a very different direction than in China during the same period. In 1956 their implications hit China hard, generating deep disagreements within the leadership and the new regime's first real political crisis. From this time forward, almost continuously until Mao's death, this sense of success and optimism would be absent, replaced by a series of disruptive crises.

Instability in the Post-Stalin Soviet Bloc

The changes in China during these early years had also taken place in the Eastern European nations occupied by the Soviet army at the end of World War II. By 1953 they had reached roughly the same point as China in 1956. The results, however, were much less favorable, coming to a crisis in mid-1953. The impetus for China's political crisis of 1957 is typically attributed to Khrushchev's denunciation of Stalin at the Soviet party's Twentieth Congress of February 1956, but that speech was the culmination of changes in the Soviet bloc that began soon after Stalin's death three years earlier.

The "Moscow Communists" who had taken control of puppet regimes in the Soviet sphere of control in Eastern Europe all implemented policies of rapid socialist transformation, repression of political enemies, purges of political opponents, and ambitious industrialization programs similar to those implemented in China. Like Mao, their leaders imitated the standard Soviet playbook, mimicking the revolutionary changes in the Soviet Union of the late 1930s. Dominant leaders in these countries modeled themselves after Stalin, frequently adopting the trappings of a leadership cult.

The intense "construction of socialism" in these regimes created severe disruptions. They were most obvious in the German Democratic Republic, which was established in 1949 as a separate state. The new regime had previously attempted to establish political control through the application of coercive force, but in 1952 an intensified campaign to build socialism began. It featured a crackdown on private enterprise, attacks on Protestant churches, a shift to heavy industrial investment that led to lower wages, rationing and food shortages, and "class struggle" conducted against those who resisted.[1] Close to half a million people fled for the Western zone in the early 1950s, with a sharp increase in the first months of 1952, when hundreds of police and border guards also joined the widening flow to the West. The exodus threatened the regime's economic plans, depleting its skilled workforce, and was solved only by the construction of the Berlin Wall in 1961.[2] Early signs of strain also appeared in Bulgaria, where rapid collectivization and severe repression created economic hardships from 1948 to 1950, generating a series of regional rebellions.[3]

After Stalin's death, the new Soviet leadership signaled its intention to moderate the repressions of the Stalin era and to back away from some of the policies that created widespread dissatisfaction in the satellite states. This signaled an opportunity for change, and unrest followed as people took to the streets in protest. Strikes and demonstrations broke out across Bulgaria in May 1953.[4] The announcement of new economic policies in Czechoslovakia that devalued the currency and reduced purchasing power led to sporadic strikes and demonstrations during the first three months of 1953. As news of the rumored devaluation spread, more than 32,000 workers joined strikes and protest marches during April and May. When the devaluation was finally implemented on June 1, thousands of workers walked out of the large Škoda auto factory in the Bohemian city of Pilzeň, and other citizens joined them. Violent confrontations with militia and security police ensued, with injuries on both sides. After army units refused to fire, demonstrators stormed and trashed government buildings, beat up unpopular officials, and threw busts of Stalin and the Czech communist leader Gottwald out of windows. The revolt was crushed only after special units from the Ministry of Interior were sent from the capital in Prague.[5]

The Pilzeň rebellion was quickly overshadowed by a much larger one that spread across East Germany two weeks later, one so extensive that it threatened the survival of the new regime. Economic policies similar to those in Czechoslovakia touched off a wave of protest: under the new industrial system, the pace of work would increase, but wages would be "readjusted" downward. Strikes began immediately after the smaller paychecks were issued. In mid-June, massive street demonstrations began in Berlin, and over half a million citizens joined the striking workers. They assembled at party and government headquarters, and their demands escalated to calls for free elections. After initial economic concessions, the government appeared paralyzed, and the unrest spread to all of the industrial cities in the Eastern zone, leading to a general insurrection on June 17. As the crisis spread, with the regime on the verge of collapse, only the declaration of martial law and massive intervention by armored Soviet troops and tanks restored order. Dozens were killed, many more were arrested, and a wave of executions followed.[6] The German rebellion, so close on the heels of the Czech unrest, shook the confidence of communist leaders throughout the region and caused the new post-Stalin leadership in Moscow to rethink its policies.

The Soviet response was to initiate a thaw, a relaxation of levels of overt repression and a pullback from the rush to build socialism at an accelerated pace. The basic policies were correct, they concluded, but they were implemented in a heavy-handed fashion. Stalin's onetime secret police chief, Beria, was purged and executed early in the post-Stalin power struggle, and the repressions of the recent past were blamed on him.[7] The process of de-Stalinization began in Moscow, with the systematic release of political prisoners and the partial relaxation of its repressive political atmosphere. As criticism of the USSR's Stalinist past gained momentum, communist leaders in the satellite states were criticized for relying too heavily on repression to implement change, for forcing a too-rapid transition to socialism, and for pushing to accelerate industrialization at the expense of citizens' living standards. Moscow dictated a "new course" for Eastern Europe: de-emphasis of "class struggle," a new emphasis on elevating living standards, and a less dogmatic and more open approach to intellectual life.

Now openly critical of leaders who engaged in "waves of repression," "economic adventurism," and the "personality cult," Moscow forced changes throughout the region, in some cases ordering entrenched leaders to step down. The hard-line Hungarian party secretary Rákosi, for example, was forced to yield the post of prime minister to the reform-minded Imre Nagy, who initiated a new course in economic policy and intellectual life.[8] Crash drives to nationalize industry and raise output, mass purges and political terror, and exaggerated praise for great leaders were now out of favor, blamed for disrupting economies and generating discontent that created political instability. As Khrushchev consolidated his power in the Soviet Union, he ordered the creation of special commissions to reinvestigate charges against Stalin's victims and release thousands of prisoners from labor camps.[9]

Yugoslavia under Tito had been the first to denounce Stalinism. After its expulsion from the Soviet bloc in 1950, its leaders developed an elaborate critique of the bureaucratic degeneration of the Soviet Union.[10] Within the Soviet bloc, no country went further in criticizing the Stalinist legacy than Poland. In January 1955 the party issued a harsh assessment of Stalinism's impact. Unofficial critics were more outspoken and over the rest of the year the boundaries of permissible criticism widened. Much of the dissatisfaction came from within the party, among committed communists who strongly objected to the party's recent direction. Heavy-handed repression and censorship were part of what repelled them, but they also objected to the bureaucratic centralism inherent in Soviet economic planning. Party economists in Poland and Hungary, following ideas developed earlier in Yugoslavia, devised plans for decentralizing the bureaucratic economy, borrowing techniques from market economies to generate greater efficiency and higher living standards.[11]

These trends contrasted sharply with China's direction during the same period. Mao was still pushing China along the path blazed by Stalin, seemingly oblivious to the liberalization and relaxation in the Soviet bloc. He began his own push for rapid collectivization and nationalization in 1953, just as Moscow was condemning these policies as "adventurism" in the satellite states. The nationwide campaign against the editor and essayist Hu Feng and "Hu Feng elements" in 1954, and the return to mass arrests and executions in the new "elimination of counterrevolutionaries" campaign of 1955, contrasted sharply with the widening thaw in Eastern Europe. And the Stalinist personality cult Mao had cultivated since the late 1930s remained undiminished. Mao was finally forced to confront these contradictions in February 1956, after Nikita Khrushchev's hard-hitting and emotional denunciation of Stalin.

Khrushchev Denounces Stalin

Although de-Stalinization had been gathering steam for almost three years in the Soviet bloc, Khrushchev's speech to the Twentieth Congress of the Soviet Communist Party on February 25, 1956, came as something of a shock. Indeed, the content of his speech went far beyond the expectations of many in the Soviet leadership, and quite a few of them felt that he had gone too far. The ostensible topic was the "personality cult," but Khrushchev went on to detail the murderous purges that devastated the party leadership in the late 1930s. This broke new ground and had more profound implications. The Soviet leadership had heretofore blamed Stalin's deputy, the former security chief Beria, for the mass executions of loyal communists. Now Khrushchev made clear that Stalin himself was the villain. In a four-hour speech, Khrushchev portrayed Stalin as a sadistic mass murderer, and the cult of praise he deliberately built for himself was a grotesque manifestation of tyranny in its most evil form.[12]

Observers from all of the fraternal communist states were in attendance, including many of their top leaders. There were hints earlier in the congress that Stalin's standing had been diminished, but delegates all leaped to their feet and cheered loudly when words of praise for Stalin in a letter from Mao Zedong were read to the audience.[13] Khrushchev's "secret speech" was given on the last day of the congress, at an unscheduled closed session for Soviet delegates. It was a devastating attack on Stalin. Khrushchev called him guilty of "a grave abuse of power." Under his direction, "mass arrests and deportation of thousands and thousands of people, and executions without trial or normal investigation, created insecurity, fear, and even desperation." The escalating charges of massive underground conspiracies to engage in counterrevolution had been "absurd, wild, and contrary to common sense." Innocent people confessed in the face of bizarre accusations "because of physical methods of pressure, torture, reducing them to unconsciousness, depriving them of judgment, taking away their human dignity." Perhaps the most stunning passages in this long speech were the statistics that Khrushchev cited on the extent of the purges of the 1930s, based on recent investigations. Of the 139 full and candidate members of the 1934 Central Committee, 98, or 70 percent, had been arrested and executed. Of the 1,966 delegates to the Seventeenth Party Congress of 1934, 1,108 were arrested for alleged counterrevolutionary crimes. The shock that this registered in the audience is recorded in the transcript ("indignation in the hall").[14] Khrushchev attacked Stalin's "mania for greatness" and the "nauseatingly false" adulation that he demanded for himself. Khrushchev portrayed him in reality as an incompetent leader and a weak wartime commander. His purges of the Soviet military command immediately prior to the war had fatally weakened Soviet defenses, and his collectivization campaign had ruined Soviet agriculture.[15]

In the words of his biographer, Khrushchev's speech "was the bravest and most reckless thing he ever did."[16] There had been a long debate about its contents in the weeks leading up to the congress, and most of his colleagues argued strongly that his criticism of Stalin should be restrained. The final draft of the speech was revised repeatedly until the day it was delivered. Khrushchev's text went much further than his colleagues expected, and in the surge of emotion during its delivery, he added even more colorful flourishes. In early March an edited copy of the transcript was printed in a small red-covered booklet with the label "top secret," and distributed to party committees and nonparty activists around the country.[17]

Foreign delegates to the congress were given oral briefings on the speech late at night on February 25. Many of them, especially leaders of satellite states who were Stalinists of the old school, were stunned. The Polish leader Bierut was in the Kremlin hospital with pneumonia when a copy of the speech was given to him. He had a heart attack while reading it and died on March 12.[18] The Polish party, which was already gripped by de-Stalinization, made an unauthorized official translation, published 18,000 copies, and distributed them to all party groups in the country. Distributed so widely in a party already in ferment, it was inevitable that copies would find their way outside the country. The *New York Times* published passages from the speech in mid-March and a full translation on June 5, 1956, ensuring worldwide circulation.[19] China's leaders received a full text of the speech shortly after excerpts appeared in the Western press in mid-March.[20]

Khrushchev's speech had repercussions throughout the Soviet bloc, even in North Korea, where Kim Il Sung had worked hard since the end of the Korean War in 1953 to consolidate his personal dictatorship and isolate his increasingly reclusive regime from Soviet and Chinese influences. The cornerstone of Kim's personal power was a new ideology known as *juche,* a nationalistic concept of self-reliance, an effort to assert national independence in the face of the regime's obviously heavy dependence on its two powerful sponsors, the Soviet Union and China. When Kim visited the Soviet Union and several East European countries in June 1956, Khrushchev and other Soviet leaders criticized him for his economic policies and especially for his effort to create a cult of personality around himself. These developments encouraged individuals within the Korean party leadership who were critical of Kim. At the end of August, several leaders associated with a pro-China faction sided with a pro-Soviet faction and directly challenged Kim over his economic policies and his growing personality cult. Kim initiated a purge, and several top officials fled and sought asylum in Beijing and Moscow. Shortly afterward, Mao and Soviet leaders criticized Kim's use of arrests and executions to deal with inner-party disagreements, and his practice of labeling critics as foreign agents and class enemies. A joint Sino-Soviet delegation to Pyongyang to help Kim "correct his errors" was able to extract only temporary and limited concessions.[21]

Upheaval in Poland and Hungary

The impact of Khrushchev's revelations was far more dramatic in Poland and Hungary, where it destabilized both regimes in crises that reached a climax in October 1956. Poland barely averted a Soviet invasion; the Hungarian regime collapsed in the face of a national insurrection, and communist rule was restored only after a massive invasion by Soviet and other Warsaw Pact troops.

Even before Khrushchev's speech, the Polish party was a hotbed of ferment against the abuses of the Stalin era. After General Secretary Bierut's sudden death in mid-March, he was succeeded by Edward Ochab, who initiated a liberalization from above that was matched by a radicalization from below. Young intellectuals formed independent discussion groups around the country; tens of thousands of prisoners were released; and critical articles were published in official outlets. The Catholic Church recovered; workers began to agitate about pay and working conditions; farmers complained about compulsory sales at state-set prices and demanded a rollback of collectivization; and party cadres and security police became demoralized.[22]

Ochab tried to steer a middle course between hard-liners and those who wanted a distinctively Polish road to socialism. One of his first acts was to restore the party membership of Władysław Gomułka, a moderate leader who had been pushed aside by Bierut as general secretary in 1948 and subsequently arrested and expelled from the party in 1951. Bierut did not release Gomułka until 1954, forced to do so in the face of the de-Stalinization initiated in Moscow. Gomułka became a symbol of reform and Polish independence, and the situation soon spun out of control. In June, factory workers in the industrial center of Poznan held demonstrations to demand higher wages, which quickly escalated into a full-scale uprising involving more than half the city's population. Communist Party offices were set on fire, and demonstrators led by factory workers clashed with security forces and the Polish army, leading to at least seventy-four deaths and hundreds wounded.[23]

After the suppression of Poznan, ferment continued in the party, creating a groundswell of support for Gomułka, who returned to the Politburo and soon replaced Ochab as the top leader.[24] The selection of a new Polish leader without Moscow's consent alarmed the Soviets: worse, the Poles were also demanding the dismissal of the Soviet marshal imposed on Poland as minister of defense. Soviet troops in Poland moved toward Warsaw, and additional troops moved to the Polish border. Khrushchev demanded a meeting in Warsaw but was refused. On October 22 a series of massive rallies took place in a number of Polish cities. In Warsaw half a million filled the streets to demonstrate against Soviet interference. The rebellion spread to rural areas: by the end of 1957, 85 percent of the cooperatives had been disbanded, a complete rollback of the regime's collectivization drive. Khrushchev flew into Warsaw uninvited, accompanied by several other Politburo members, and after angry exchanges was convinced to call off the threatened invasion and let Gomułka stabilize Poland, which he did successfully until the next round of Polish unrest in 1970.[25]

Khrushchev's compromise on Poland was dictated by even larger problems in Hungary. In July the Soviets insisted that Mátyás Rákosi, the hard-line Stalinist party secretary who was responsible for a series of purges and executions of party leaders during his reign, step down from his post. He had recently deposed the reform-minded Prime Minister Imre Nagy and expelled him from the party at the end of 1955 for "rightist deviations." In the wake of Khrushchev's February speech, Rákosi was forced to backpedal, and he rehabilitated a number of communists that he had imprisoned or executed in earlier show trials against alleged "Titoist" spies. The most important of these was László Rajk, who was minister of the interior before Rákosi had him executed in 1949. The move deeply undercut Rákosi's credibility, because he had used the charges against Rajk to justify a much larger wave of arrests of party leaders.[26] Intellectual ferment in Budapest was centered on the Petőfi Circle, an intellectual forum that Rákosi set up in March 1956 in response to Khrushchev's speech. The group became increasingly radicalized and turned into a center of opposition to Rákosi himself. Moscow became alarmed and lost confidence in Rákosi's ability to keep order, and in mid-July removed him in favor of Ernő Gerő.[27]

The situation turned critical in October. At an officially approved public reburial of Rajk, now a martyr to Stalinism, Imre Nagy assured those present that soon Stalinism would finally be buried. One day later he was readmitted to the party, and he became the most credible candidate to stabilize Hungary under a course of reform. Street protests soon took a more radical turn. On October 22, 5,000 students gathered at Budapest University of Technology and issued a manifesto that called for the withdrawal of Soviet troops, inner-party elections, the removal of all Stalinists in the leadership, and the formation of a new government under Nagy. They declared solidarity with the Polish "movement for national independence" and demanded "freedom of opinion and expression" and "freedom of the press and radio." The next day, October 23, the students gathered at the Budapest radio station to demand that their manifesto be read to the entire nation. The director of the station agreed and staged a fake broadcast over local loudspeakers. When the students learned of the subterfuge, they laid siege to the building. Elsewhere in Budapest that same day, the gigantic statue of Stalin in the central square was toppled to the cheers of tens of thousands of citizens. Khrushchev instructed Gerő to reappoint Nagy as prime minister late that evening. Nagy, however, refused Soviet instructions to sign a formal request for Soviet troops to restore order. Instead, he declared martial law and ordered Hungarian troops to enforce it. Soviet troops already stationed in Hungary nonetheless moved into Budapest in the early morning hours of October 24—6,000 soldiers and 700 tanks. They were overwhelmed by crowds who fought them in the streets with firebombs and small arms, and by Hungarian troops that fought on the side of the insurgents.[28]

In the midst of the insurrection, Nagy replaced Gerő as party leader, and he formed a coalition government that included the leaders of other political parties that were forced to disband in the 1940s. As fighting continued in the streets, Khrushchev initially decided to withdraw his troops. Mao agreed, and counseled him to let the "Hungarian working class" decide the fate of the country. They both changed their minds after two incidents. In the first, a crowd besieged the Budapest party headquarters, grabbed security police, and lynched them from lampposts (along with Budapest's first party secretary) in retaliation for a mass shooting of protesters. Shortly afterward, Nagy declared Hungary's intention to withdraw from the Warsaw Pact and called for the permanent withdrawal of all Soviet troops. Khrushchev then organized a massive Soviet invasion, which killed more than 2,500 Hungarians and wounded more than 20,000. Seven hundred Soviet troops were killed in the fighting. In the postinvasion crackdown, more than 100,000 were arrested for counterrevolution and more than 200,000 fled across the border into Austria. Nagy was imprisoned and eventually executed along with his minister of defense in 1958, after receiving promises of safe passage out of the Yugoslav embassy, where he had sought refuge. The Hungarian party-state had to be rebuilt from scratch.[29]

Out of Step: Chinese Political Trends after 1953

These developments shocked China's leadership, and they were a major challenge for Mao. Although Mao had not carried out massive leadership purges of the kind attributed to Stalin, China had seen repeated persecutions of "antiparty groups" and "counterrevolutionaries" in a series of campaigns after 1953 that smacked of the final years of the Stalin era. Prominently targeted during this period were left-wing writers who had opposed the Nationalists and supported the Communists, but who had from the beginning chafed at the rigid dictates of bureaucrats who demanded strict conformity with the doctrines of socialist realism.[30] These authors pushed for a more nuanced and less stereotypical portrayal of characters and plots, and proved to be thorns in the side of propaganda bureaucrats. In 1954 and 1955 a series of them were subjected to denunciations for "bourgeois idealism" and lost their editorial posts: among the more prominent were Feng Xuefeng and Ding Ling. Essentially, this was a renewal of the campaign to remold the thinking of intellectuals and to expunge independent thought.[31] In the summer of 1955, the charges against the famous author Ding Ling escalated into an accusation that she had formed a conspiratorial antiparty group. She and her subordinates were removed from their posts and detained for investigation.[32]

These figures typically confessed to the charges against them in an effort to lighten their punishment, but one individual refused to acknowledge error and argued against his accusers. This was the prominent writer Hu Feng, who was a member of the National People's Congress, the editorial board of *People's Literature,* and the executive board of the Chinese Writers Association. He submitted a long report to the Central Committee in July 1954 that criticized the rigid and dogmatic censorship of literature and poetry and repudiated specific propaganda officials by name. The response was harsh, seemingly all out of proportion to the issues at stake. There followed a 1955 campaign against the Hu Feng Counterrevolutionary Clique.[33] Hu and his close associates were imprisoned as counterrevolutionaries, and a nationwide campaign against Hu Feng elements targeted those with similar viewpoints. More than 2,100 authors and editors were investigated as members of the counterrevolutionary clique; ninety-two were imprisoned and scores removed from their posts.[34]

The literary persecutions were limited in scope, but they were part of a broader wave of repression that culminated in the campaign to eliminate counterrevolutionaries, launched in July 1955. This was an intense nationwide scrutiny of individual dossiers, a reexamination of political histories, interrogations of suspects, and the solicitation of secret denunciations. The campaign continued under various guises through 1957, by which point more than 18.6 million individuals were investigated, and more than 257,551 were found to be counterrevolutionaries or "bad elements." Most of them were sent to labor camps or relocated to villages to work "under supervision." During its course, 1,717 targets of the campaign committed suicide.[35]

In short, political trends in China since the death of Stalin had more closely resembled the persecutions of the last few years of the Stalin era than the thaw and partial liberalization in the post-Stalin Soviet bloc. They had not, however, even begun to approach the level of repression during Stalin's great purges of the late 1930s. Nonetheless, Khrushchev's denunciation of Stalin placed the CCP, and especially Mao, in a politically awkward position. China was out of step, staying the Stalinist course.

The Hundred Flowers

Developments in the Soviet bloc affected China after some delay, in two phases. In response to Khrushchev's February 1956 speech, China scaled back the praise of Mao, began to emphasize collective leadership of the party, and initiated a belated thaw of its own. In response to the October upheavals in Europe, Mao went further, staking out a new position as an advocate of openness and criticism. He pushed hard, against strong resistance from his colleagues, for a rectification campaign that brought ordinary citizens into the process as critics of dogmatism and abuse of power. This was a politically adroit and unexpected move, uncharacteristic of Mao's political mentality up to that point in time. As a potential target of de-Stalinization, Mao tried to outflank criticisms by posturing as an advocate of openness and popular restraint on party power.

Mao's pivot away from his identity as a loyal follower of Stalin was perhaps not the utterly cynical ploy that it seemed. True, Mao created a personality cult in Yan'an in the early 1940s. His party had used extensive coercion and terror in consolidating control over China, and he was an advocate of rapid socialist transformation in both agriculture and industry. However, many of the faults for which Khrushchev excoriated Stalin, and many of the errors of Moscow communists in the satellite states, could not (yet) be laid at Mao's doorstep. Mao had not conducted extensive purges of China's leadership, complete with Stalinist show trials. He had not carried out mass executions of party officials. True, he had pushed for an overly rapid "transition to socialism," but the disruptions and violence that accompanied this in the Soviet bloc were largely absent in China, and there were no rebellions of the kind seen in Eastern Europe. Mao could legitimately claim that the initial phases of socialist transformation in China had been handled relatively well.

Nonetheless, China's reaction to Khrushchev's February 1956 revelations was guarded and defensive, and the initial steps toward de-Stalinization were measured. The speech had surprised and alarmed China's leaders, who, like other fraternal communist parties (and indeed Khrushchev's own colleagues), had not been warned in advance of its content. Mao and others in the leadership concluded that Khrushchev had gone much too far, failing to recognize Stalin's accomplishments. They worried, as did many of Khrushchev's colleagues, that the harsh repudiation of Stalin undermined the credibility of the socialist bloc and strengthened the imperialist enemies of socialism. Especially galling to them was the personal nature of Khrushchev's attack, which in Mao's view failed to provide a theoretical rationale for distinguishing Stalin's errors from his accomplishments. China's leaders became preoccupied with how to distinguish their recent history from the Stalin era, and how to distinguish Mao from Stalin.[36]

The result was a *People's Daily* editorial on April 5, 1956, titled "On the Historical Experience of the Proletarian Dictatorship." Its main thrust was that excessive denigration of Stalin was mistaken: his accomplishments far outweighed his errors. Implicitly, it also deflected criticism of Mao for developing a personality cult of his own. Mao then gave two speeches, the first on April 25, titled "On the Ten Great Relationships," which called for "long-term coexistence and mutual supervision" with the small noncommunist parties that were permitted to survive, symbolizing a "united front" of all patriotic Chinese, and in particular with the professional and managerial classes that made up the bulk of the "democratic" parties' membership. More notable was Mao's famous speech of May 2, 1956, which called for the policy symbolized by the slogan "let a hundred flowers bloom, let a hundred schools of thought contend"—signaling a relaxation in the fields of culture and scholarship, and an openness to non-Marxist ideas that might serve the task of national development. Conflicts "among the people" were not always tantamount to conflicts "between the people and the enemy." These speeches, along with the April 5 editorial, criticized excessively harsh repression, neglect of collective leadership, turning legitimate differences of opinion into political errors or crimes, and excessive haste in economic policy.[37] This was a relatively moderate and, in the minds of China's leaders, a properly balanced approach to de-Stalinization.

The speeches initially did little to encourage open debate, for obvious reasons. The campaign against the Hu Feng Counterrevolutionary Clique and especially the campaign to eliminate counterrevolutionaries were still fresh in everyone's minds. But Mao's speeches were followed by both concrete and symbolic changes. Liu Shaoqi and Peng Zhen called on the security agencies to arrest fewer people, give lighter sentences, and use less harsh methods.[38] At the party's Eighth Congress in September 1956, Mao Zedong Thought was removed from the party's constitution.[39] Moreover, the political report issued at the congress stated that the socialist transformation of industry and agriculture had resolved class conflicts based on previous modes of production, and that now the primary task was the creation of a modern industrial base.[40] Also significant was the drastic demotion of Kang Sheng, one of the primary architects of the terroristic party rectification campaign of 1943, a movement that had solidified Mao's hold over the party during the period when his personality cult began. Kang was demoted from the sixth-ranked member of the Politburo to the fifth alternate member, which put him twenty-third in the national leadership rankings, a drop of seventeen places.[41] The party congress gave clear signs that the CCP was backing away from some of its more pronounced Stalinist tendencies.[42]

Disagreements about Rectification

Mao wanted to go further, but there was resistance. His call for ordinary citizens to criticize the party's errors—expressed in the April 5 editorial

"On the Historical Experience"—were not included in Liu Shaoqi's political report to the Eighth Party Congress.[43] The party leadership had agreed that a rectification campaign was essential, but there were disagreements about how to proceed. Mao advocated "open-door rectification"—encouraging ordinary citizens to criticize party officials. The alternative was "closed-door rectification"—having party members criticize one another for their shortcomings. To his credit, Mao did not believe that preaching correct behavior within the party was sufficient to prevent abuses that generated dissatisfaction with party rule. He argued that outsiders should also express their frustrations. Permitting their free airing, he felt, would lead to greater social and political harmony. Opponents of open-door rectification, on the other hand, argued that open criticism of the party from outside could demoralize party cadres and lead to political instability.[44]

This disagreement reportedly pitted Mao and Deng Xiaoping on one side against Liu Shaoqi and Peng Zhen on the other. The Hungarian revolution deepened the disagreements, with some arguing that openness could lead to chaos, while Mao argued that only open-door rectification could have prevented the Hungarian upheaval. Mao ultimately won the argument.[45] China's official response to the Hungarian uprising was expressed in a second *People's Daily* editorial, "More on the Historical Experience of the Proletarian Dictatorship," published on December 29, 1956. The editorial refuted the claim, expressed by Yugoslavia's Tito, that the Hungarian revolt was a reaction against Stalinism, which in turn was an inevitable outgrowth of the Soviet system. The Chinese argued that the problem was not the system, but leadership errors that created "contradictions between the government and the people." In other words, the Hungarian uprising was due to erroneous leadership practices, not the Soviet system. Party officials tended to be "dogmatic, bureaucratic, and sectarian," behaviors that could be corrected. Calls to change the system were wrong, a revision of Marxism-Leninism.[46]

This was a limited and conservative doctrine. There could be no change in China's new political and economic institutions. The system was not the problem, and reforms in governance and economic organization were therefore out of bounds. The problem was incorrect behavior of individual cadres. The institutions that China copied from the Soviet Union were to be maintained.

Mao elaborated this idea in his speech of February 27, 1957, "On the Correct Handling of Contradictions among the People."[47] This was his case for open-door rectification, and it was Mao's attempt to establish himself as an innovative leader of world communism. His essential point, expressed in a long and rambling speech of almost four hours, was that contradictions between the party and the people are normal and need not be viewed as class struggle. Contradictions between the party and the people should be sharply distinguished from contradictions between the party and class enemies, and criticism of the party does not necessarily represent counterrevolution waged by hostile social classes. A party that cannot accept criticism and that treats all critics as class enemies will commit the errors that led to the Hungarian uprising.[48]

Mao's speech was an effort to push harder to carry out rectification. He referred repeatedly to resistance by party cadres to open-door rectification.[49] Mao followed up with similar speeches to a variety of smaller audiences, traveling outside Beijing throughout the month of March.[50] After his earlier "Hundred Flowers" speech, the party's propaganda apparatus had essentially sabotaged that call by organizing a campaign of denunciation against an author of a short story that portrayed a young communist demoralized by the cynicism and incompetence in his party organization.[51] Mao was especially angry with the *People's Daily*, which did not publicize his new ideas on "contradictions" until after he called its editor, Deng Tuo, to his living quarters and angrily dressed him down, along with several other propaganda officials.[52] Mao's attack broke the logjam. Prominent opponents of the policy, in particular Peng Zhen, finally gave in, and the newspaper published a series of five editorials in mid-April that criticized those who opposed opening up and "letting a hundred flowers bloom."[53] The rectification campaign was finally launched on May 1, 1957. The Hundred Flowers would last only five weeks, but would be as dramatic as it was short.

The Popular Response

Party organizations throughout urban China held forums that welcomed criticism of the attitudes and conduct of party cadres.[54] Once it became clear that retaliation against critics did not immediately occur, critics became more numerous and outspoken. Party officials were exposed to unrestrained comments from those subject to their authority. These were thoughts that subordinates had previously not dared to express. The result, for party cadres, was often humiliating and demoralizing. As critics found their voice, and as their colleagues and even selected party members voiced agreement, the criticisms became more severe. The demands for redress quickly moved beyond the boundaries of the campaign and into the inherent defects of Soviet-style institutions.

The new system of party control in urban workplaces came in for particularly harsh criticism. Speakers lamented the requirement that party members exercise authority in every organization: party cadres overruled decisions made by experts and dismissed the advice of those with far more extensive experience and better education; party cadres lacked ability, bungled their jobs, and showed open disrespect for those under their authority; they took privileges for themselves, appointing their spouses to well-paid jobs in their own organizations; and party members were always shown favoritism in promotions, even when they were totally unqualified for their jobs, and in some cases barely able to read.[55]

Journalists complained about their inability to do their jobs and about the way that censorship demeaned their profession. They decried the lack of real access to the decisions of government and demanded greater freedom to report truthfully. They complained that newspapers had become organs that simply repeated exactly what government officials said, and that journalists and editors were forbidden to think for themselves. The more outspoken critics declared that the party's objective in the field of journalism was simply to keep people in ignorance.[56]

Academics were particularly bitter about the impact of the party system. They decried controls by the party that placed severe restrictions on the natural sciences and virtually destroyed the humanities and social sciences, forcing adherence to outdated Marxist dogma. They denounced rigid conformity to Soviet doctrines and scholarship: the worship of things Russian and the knee-jerk rejection of anything from America. Critical thinking was forbidden and punished when exercised; unqualified party secretaries oversaw research and teaching in subjects where they lacked even minimal qualifications; faculty and researchers were so intimidated by past political campaigns that they dared not express opinions. Research in some fields had ground to a halt because of the doctrinaire attitudes of ignorant party secretaries. Economists decried the decline of their discipline: statistics and survey sampling were denounced as "bourgeois science" and scholars were forced to repeat ritualistic quotations from Marxist classics, with "proofs" based on simple arithmetic.[57]

Authors and editors who had endured recent campaigns against liberal thinking in their fields spoke out in defense of their earlier views and penned satirical essays that skewered the dogmatism of communist bureaucrats. One essay published in *People's Literature* lampooned the unthinking dogmatism of party officials and the constantly shifting party line:

> Certain of our high-ranking cadres . . . have such remarkable talents that they, however ill-read seem extremely capable of directing others in their studies, and of criticizing those who obtain their ideas from books. . . . It is characteristic of this sort of Marxist leader that, although his theories may change time and time again, he never admits a mistake. Each time his views undergo a reversal he considers them to be correct. . . . This is to say that he never thinks for himself. . . . He is, however, a leader. Therefore, it is unfortunate for those who must follow him.[58]

These criticisms may well have stung party cadres who were used to agreement from intimidated subordinates, but in many organizations the critics strayed into statements that were clearly critical of the system itself, not just the behavior and attitudes of individuals. A professor at Chinese People's University asserted that the current situation was worse than under the Nationalists, and the party had completely separated itself from the people: "the masses want to overthrow the Communist Party and to kill the Communists." If the party did not fundamentally reform itself, this critic argued, it would be swept away and collapse.[59] A professor at Shenyang Normal University painted a painful picture of party rule:

> Since the founding of the Republic, particularly in the last one or two years, the Party has become superior to the people and has assumed privileges, praising itself for its "greatness, glory and correctness." . . . For this reason, Party prestige is falling day by day. More and more persons with impure motives join the Party. They join the Party because they can win glory and acquire power, influence, and money. Imbued with despicable individualism . . . they flatter the Party, bow to the Party and obey the Party on everything. . . . The absolute leadership of the Party must be done away with. . . . The Constitution is a scrap of paper and the Party has no need to observe it. . . . As to freedom of assembly, association and publication, this is just something written in the Constitution; actually, citizens can only become obedient subjects or, to use a harsh word, slaves. . . . A system of general election campaigns should be put into effect alongside the abolition of the absolute leadership of the

Party. The people should be allowed freely to organize new political parties and social bodies, and to put out publications so as to open the channels of public opinion, supervise the government, combat cheap praises and encourage them to oppose an undesirable status quo even if it meant opposition to the Communist Party.[60]

Another charged that in the past, the party had stood up for the people, but now it ruled them like an oppressive master: "instead of standing among the masses, it stood on the back of the masses and ruled the masses." Political activists volunteered in public but informed on people in private; they pretended to be selfless and self-sacrificing but in fact were scheming to better themselves at the expense of others.[61] Another complained about the self-censorship and alienation involved in surviving as a party member in an oppressive environment: "to be a Party member one had to regard oneself as either a lunatic or a corpse. One could speak one's own mind only in the privacy of one's own bedroom."[62]

These were indictments of the system, not the shortcomings of individual cadres. The complaints of professionals and academics, however, were not the developments that most alarmed party leaders. What ultimately led to the abrupt end of the Hundred Flowers was the independent mobilization of students, especially university students, and an even more troubling rise of unrest among industrial workers.

Student activism in the capital was centered at Peking University, which historically had been the initiator of student movements earlier in the twentieth century. The first wall posters appeared in mid-May and the campaign grew quickly. A "democracy wall" was established near the center of campus, attracting huge throngs of people to read and paste up essays. The wall became a site for public debates and speeches. Independent political clubs and discussion groups were formed, and they issued their own mimeographed newsletters and journals.[63] A translation of long excerpts from Khrushchev's speech was posted at the university in May.[64] Among the most common complaints were the injustices committed during the campaign to suppress counterrevolution, the negative impact of party rule in educational institutions, the obviously false charges against the "Hu Feng Clique," the narrow adherence to the Soviet educational model, the excessive politicization of academic courses, and the dogmatic and "sectarian" attitudes of party officials toward nonparty teachers and students. Other critics challenged the party's claims that living standards had been improved, and complained of the growing gap between a dictatorial party and the people.[65]

Of the speeches made at Peking University, the most famous and controversial were those of a bluntly outspoken law student from nearby People's University, Lin Xiling.[66] In a May 23 speech, Lin openly challenged the party's verdict against Hu Feng and his associates, pointing out the obvious fact that his suggestions to the Central Committee were fully in line with the current Hundred Flowers policy. His suggestions about art and literature were "correct"; his purge as a counterrevolutionary was based on Mao's old and outdated talks from the early 1940s. Lin was dismissive of the charge that Hu Feng formed an "antiparty group" because he "communicated secretly" with others: "Well, who doesn't communicate privately? This makes people not dare to tell the truth to one another." Why, despite the obvious, had the party not reversed this perversion of justice? "I think that the Communist Party is in an embarrassing position and doesn't know how to get out of it. It knows it has made a mistake, but refuses to admit it."[67]

Lin then moved on to draw parallels between the crimes of Stalin, as outlined in Khrushchev's "secret report," and the same errors in China: "Our country also expanded the scale of suppression of counterrevolution." She knew this because of her internship in a district court, where they spent almost all of their time reviewing cases brought against alleged counterrevolutionaries that were obviously false. These problems, she asserted, were rooted in the institutions themselves: "I heartily agree with the Yugoslav opinion that the cult of personality is a product of the social system. . . . The problem of Stalin is not the problem of Stalin the individual; the problem of Stalin could only arise in a country like the Soviet Union. . . . Genuine socialism should be very democratic, but ours is undemocratic."[68]

Lin bluntly stated her view that the problems with China's Soviet system were too severe to be corrected by superficial measures like Mao's rectification campaign:

> We don't think it sufficient for the Party merely to employ methods of rectification . . . and make minor concessions. . . . During the tempest of the revolution, Party members stayed together with the people; but after the victory of the revolution, they climbed up into the ruling position and ideological limits were imposed. They want to suppress the people; they adopt policies aimed at deceiving the people. . . . I am not

optimistic about the rectification, because there are still too many guardians of the rules. These guardians want to use the fruits of socialism, bought with the blood of the martyrs, as a ladder to climb to higher positions.

Lin closed her rousing speech by referring to students who were mobilizing in Wuhan, Nanjing, and elsewhere in China, and called for a nationwide struggle to establish "genuine socialism," which she saw as part of the same agenda that inspired the Hungarian upheaval: "The blood of the Hungarian people was not shed in vain!"[69]

In a second speech at Peking University one week later, Lin elaborated on her claim that the abuses typical of Stalinism were rooted in the organizational structures of Soviet-type regimes. She made clear the source of her inspiration: "The problem of Yugoslavia: I am very interested in this. Here is socialist democracy." In China's bureaucratic personnel system, "A man is judged not by his virtues and abilities, but by whether or not he is a party member. . . . Some party members rushed to join the party in order to enjoy the resultant privileges; those who do not join the party have no future."[70] These tendencies were rooted firmly in the new organizational structure of China's economy and political system, which in turn had its roots in "feudalism and fascism"—also "toadying to foreigners": "The compradors toadied to foreigners and worshipped America; our learning from the Soviet Union is just like that."[71]

Lin Xiling was able to read a translation of Khrushchev's speech, and it had a deep impact on her thinking: "I used to have a very good impression of Stalin, and I was very angry about the criticism of him at the Twentieth Congress. But after I read this secret report, I began to see through Stalin. An appraisal of Stalin cannot be based on the cult of personality; it must be based on the system itself." The excessive persecution of alleged counterrevolutionaries was Mao's idea, which "was influenced by Stalin's erroneous theory that class contradictions will become more and more acute after socialism is established."[72]

Lin's position was one of democratic socialism; she admired efforts by Polish, Hungarian, and especially Yugoslav thinkers to step away from the Stalinist past and generate a new form of socialism. This was far beyond the boundaries of Mao's conception of party rectification. Lin was not alone, nor was she the most extreme. Others went much further. At

Peking University a Hundred Flowers Society pushed for "democracy and freedom," declared that Marxism and the proletarian dictatorship were out of date, and called for the formation of new political parties and genuine multiparty competition.[73] Wall posters likened the classification of households according to their political status to a kind of caste system, and in the hands of personnel departments, it had become the foundation for a new ruling class.[74]

The idea that China had already created a new privileged class was stated repeatedly in the dissident posters during this period. One of the most extreme statements was by an anonymous writer who appears to have been a middle-aged party functionary, and it expressed the viewpoint of a deeply alienated insider:

> I am weak, with neither courage nor a fighting spirit. I only know how to live at the beck and call of the leaders. I eat well every day and draw a high salary. . . . A great many leading cadres are enjoying a luxurious life of banquets and villas. Why should I live so frugally? How many people have learned to fake obedience, bow to the leadership, turn their backs on the masses, and thus become high-ranking officials and dignitaries? . . . For twenty years I've seen through the imperialists. Facing the enemy, my eyes were red with anger and I would risk losing my head and shedding my blood; but facing the dictatorship of the Communist Party I am cowardly and powerless. . . . We have given our blood, sweat, toil, and precious lives to defend not the people but the bureaucratic organs and bureaucrats who oppress the people and live off the fat of the land. They are a group of fascists who employ foul means, twist the truth, band together in evil ventures.[75]

This writer went on to pour contempt on Mao, portraying him as a hypocritical tyrant. "I protest against Chairman Mao's recent statement to the Youth League Central Committee that 'the Party is the leading core in all work, and any deviation from socialism is erroneous.' This statement should be translated as follows: 'It is necessary to accept Party dictatorship; anyone who opposes the words of the super-emperor is wrong and should be killed forthwith.'" The writer compared Mao with the first emperor of the Qin dynasty, a famous tyrant known for treachery and his massacre of scholars during a violent and brief reign: "Your majesty! How many people have had their ideals and hopes destroyed by just one word from you! Your majesty! Emperor Qin Shi Huang was nothing but an obscure dwarf compared to you. . . . Since 1949 you have killed more than 700,000 people (this doesn't include those who committed suicide). Kill if you like! Kill off all the Chinese!"[76]

The writer also ridiculed the myth of Yan'an communism. "Dictator, you've turned into a brute. In Yan'an . . . how many so-called suspects did you kill? You called this 'internal purification.' . . . In the so-called holy land of Yan'an, Wang Shiwei was rectified simply because he mentioned the large kitchen, the medium kitchen, and the small kitchen. . . . Where is he now? Nobody knows. When the students of Resist-Japan University were fighting desperately at the front, you were 'drinking and whoring it up' in Yan'an. What a hard life you had in the caves!"[77]

For obvious reasons, the mass media did not publicize sentiments like these, and there was no public reporting on the student activism. Party officials were kept informed, however, by confidential reports published in the bulletin *Internal Reference* and other classified materials.[78] The open expression of sentiments like these indicated that the rectification campaign was going off the rails, just as the opponents of open-door rectification had feared. Mao had been wrong, and he began to have serious misgivings. He had mistaken intimidated obedience for consent and had underestimated the resentment that the repressions of the 1950s had created, especially among educated Chinese. He had assumed incorrectly that the relative quiet in China throughout 1956 had meant that there was firm popular trust in the regime.

The formation of independent clubs and publications went far beyond the original conception of the campaign, as did calls for the end of party dictatorship. Even more alarming was the rapid mobilization of students across the country, which many likened to the famous May Fourth Movement of 1919 that touched off the modern era of revolution. Student activists at Peking University traveled to Tianjin to organize and mobilize students there.[79] "Democracy walls" and "freedom forums" spread to campuses across the country. By the end of May similar levels of campus ferment were reported at all thirty-one college campuses in Beijing, and at universities in Wuhan, Shanghai, Nanjing, Jilin, Tianjin, and Lanzhou.[80] High school students who failed to gain admission to university staged strikes and demonstrations, in some cases attacking school buildings and destroying equipment; college students dissatisfied with their job assignments and other issues staged strikes and demonstrations on their own campuses in Wuhan, Xi'an, Guangzhou, and Shenyang.[81] Students went out onto the streets to stage demonstrations and protests in

Wuhan, Nanjing, Chengdu, Qingdao, and Guilin.[82] Youth league organizations in many schools were turning into centers for dissent.

An even greater potential threat, given the earlier rebellions in East
Germany, Poland, and Czechoslovakia, was labor protest. Workers mobilized to protest working conditions that were imposed under the new
planned economy. The industrial city of Shanghai was a microcosm of
a wave of worker protest that began in 1956, reaching a peak during the
Hundred Flowers. There were labor disputes at 587 enterprises in
Shanghai in the spring of 1957, involving close to 30,000 workers. More
than 200 of them were factory walkouts. An additional 700 enterprises
experienced less serious forms of industrial conflict. This was the largest
wave of labor unrest experienced at any point in Shanghai's long history of labor activism, with the sole exception of the six months after
the communist takeover of Shanghai in 1949. An internal party bulletin
in 1957 estimated that more than 10,000 strikes had erupted in China
in the spring of 1957, and it described widespread student boycotts, mass
petitions, and demonstrations. In Shanghai, the majority of the disputes
were in factories that had recently converted from private to joint state
ownership, and they were a reaction to the reduced wage levels and elimination of former rights to bonuses and other perquisites that were won
through bargaining with private employers in the past. When the state
took over the firms, wages and privileges were "readjusted" downward—
much as they had been in Berlin and Pilzeň a few years before. Workers
spoke out against the bureaucratic and authoritarian character of labor
relations, and they openly denigrated party secretaries and "puppet"
trade unions.[83]

Rural protests were also widespread, coming on the heels of the rapid
and involuntary formation of collective farms in the previous year.
During these weeks, farmers openly expressed dissatisfactions that came
to a head near the end of 1956. They were later detailed in an internal
party report. Villagers complained about the new restrictions on the use
of their time, cadre mismanagement and arbitrariness in job assignments
and income distribution, loss of income and a drop in the quantity and
quality of food allocations, and "rudeness" and "oppression and bullying"
by the new village cadres. They also complained about embezzlement
by cadres, squandering of public funds, and their habit of cursing at,
beating, and tying up villagers who openly complained. The report
quoted some farmers as claiming that "to join the co-op is no better than

staying in a labor camp" and that the new collective structures caused "increases in suffering rather than income."[84]

The protests in villages are less well documented, but there are indications that unrest was widespread, and where it did occur the consequences were severe. Across Jiangsu Province, farmers forcibly seized harvested grain, angrily confronted rural cadres, and withdrew from collective farms.[85] In one county in Zhejiang Province, there were major protests in twenty-nine out of thirty-three townships from mid-April 1957 to the end of May, and farmers withdrew from collective farms in droves. Participation in collective farms in the county fell from 91 percent to 19 percent of households; rural cadres were beaten and their homes were invaded and ransacked. Similarly large outbreaks were reported in Shanxi and Guangdong.[86] In border areas, radical collectivization bred stubborn and well-organized regional rebellions.[87]

China's leaders had ample cause for alarm. Initially, Mao persisted in defending his vision of open-door rectification, making light of student protests and strikes, arguing that they were nothing to get overly alarmed about. He was unable to calm his colleagues' fears, and there was a clear sense that the situation was about to spiral out of control. Most disturbing was the fact that young party members were expressing some of the most pointed criticisms, and that Communist Youth League organizations were becoming a focal point for dissent. The multiple threats of a national student movement, mass protests by workers, and the defection of young party members—all symptoms of earlier mobilizations in Eastern Europe—finally closed the debate. Developments vindicated leaders who had feared that open-door rectification was potentially destabilizing. Mao backtracked, reversed himself, and ordered a harsh crackdown.[88]

Backlash: The Antirightist Campaign

The campaign's reversal was signaled in a front-page *People's Daily* editorial on June 7. The central thrust was that open-door rectification had been turned into merciless attacks on the party and on socialism. These were attacks on socialism by "rightists" whose words and actions expressed the interests of former exploiting classes. Essentially, this new stance reversed the party line enunciated at the Eighth Party Congress that the socialist transformation of the economy had eliminated the basis of class conflict. In effect, the open-door rectification of the Communist Party turned into a rectification of the people by the Communist Party. Those who had expressed criticisms during the Hundred Flowers were now targeted in a nationwide Antirightist Campaign. The democracy walls were shut down; students and workers who persisted were arrested; the independent clubs and newsletters were forcibly closed.

The forums that previously encouraged the free airing of criticisms were now turned into forums for denouncing those who had made the mistake of offering criticisms in the preceding weeks. The Antirightist Campaign lasted far longer than the Hundred Flowers and continued into early 1958. The entire party apparatus was mobilized to document the critical utterances and activities of people during the Hundred Flowers. Accused rightists were denounced angrily in workplace meetings. They were held in isolation and made to write full confessions. Individuals deemed to have made the most outrageous criticisms were put on a stage and denounced at mass rallies. Local party committees were given percentage guidelines that dictated the scope of the movement. This had the effect of sweeping even those who had made the most superficial and well-intentioned criticisms onto the list of victims.[89] While the campaign was prosecuted with particular intensity in universities and other organizations with high percentages of educated personnel, it reached into factories and deep into the countryside as well. In rural counties it focused on middle school teachers, former landlord and rich peasant households, and those who had complained about corrupt and abusive village cadres.[90]

As the campaign got under way, Mao's February speech "On the Correct Handling of Contradictions among the People" was finally published. It was not the same speech that Mao gave in February, which had been replayed to many audiences by a tape recording. The revised version of the speech contained several warnings that "excessive" criticism would not be tolerated, which were not in the original speech. The new version mentioned class struggle, also absent in the original. The original had a long passage criticizing Stalin for failing to distinguish between two kinds of criticism, and for treating all criticism as a contradiction with the enemy, thereby "making a mess of things." That passage was deleted, as was another: "Whoever said anything critical was suspected of being an enemy and risked landing in jail or having his head chopped off." Also deleted was Mao's paraphrase of Khrushchev's claim that "90 percent" of the delegates to the 1930s Soviet Party Congress were shot, and 80 percent of the Central Committee. Mao's casual mention in his original speech that "small numbers" had been killed earlier because it was "absolutely necessary" in China—700,000 from 1951 to 1953, and 80,000 since 1955—also disappeared. Mao's discussion of widespread student disturbances over the past year as representing "contradictions among the people" was also deleted.[91]

The revisions in the published version of the speech were cover for Mao's obvious political miscalculation. He had pushed hard, with great confidence, for open-door rectification, and he had been proven dead wrong about its outcome. The revisions, along with Mao's later disingenuous claims that he had all along been preparing to "lure the snakes out of their holes," were designed to save his face with party members. Of deeper long-term significance, however, is the fact that the prosecution of class struggle was revived as one of the party's central tasks. The bland statements about peacefully building the economy from the 1956 party congress were set aside.[92] The effort to recruit intellectuals and experts in the task of economic development was abandoned, and intellectuals were increasingly treated as potentially subversive. China's brief flirtation with de-Stalinization was now at an end.

The campaign to punish rightists involved tens of millions of citizens who participated in denunciation meetings and rallies, and hundreds of thousands of activists who denounced the victims or served as informers. By the time the campaign concluded in early 1958, a total of 550,000 people were designated as rightists.[93] They were sorted into categories based on the severity of their crimes. A small number whose actions and utterances were deemed to be openly counterrevolutionary were executed. This included some of the leaders of violent student protests and some of the workers who organized strikes.[94] Large numbers received an indeterminate sentence in a labor camp. Many of the most notorious rightists ended up serving sentences of more than twenty years and were not released until after Mao's death. Those whose crimes were deemed somewhat less severe were sent to collective farms, and some of them were pardoned in the early 1960s. Others suffered demotions and loss of pay but remained in their schools and workplaces under a form of supervised probation. All of them suffered under the burden of the rightist label until after Mao's death. Their family members suffered as well, because the rightist label, like "landlord" or "Nationalist," was one that affected all members of a household. The end result of Mao's Hundred Flowers initiative, which had the objective of cementing close ties between the party and educated urbanites, was to destroy this link.

There were subtle signs during this period that Mao's credibility and judgment were questioned publicly, if indirectly.[95] Mao disagreed with Liu Shaoqi about the conduct of the Antirightist Campaign for most of 1957—the more the dangers of class enemies were emphasized, the worse Mao's judgment looked. Eventually the two sides reached a compromise after several months of jousting over the nature and scope of the campaign.[96] In June 1957, just as Mao was forced to retreat from the Hundred Flowers, Khrushchev barely averted being thrown out of office for the upheavals his "secret speech" had created in Eastern Europe. The charge against Khrushchev was that his reckless actions and headstrong leadership had led him to commit a series of errors. He faced withering criticism from a majority of Politburo members, but he was later able to turn the tables on his opponents and purge them from the Politburo as an "antiparty group."[97] The efforts by Mao and Khrushchev to push liberalization backfired on both of them, although the challenge to Khrushchev was far more severe. While Khrushchev was able to extend his limited de-Stalinization in the years to come, Mao snapped back to his earlier persona as a proponent of militant class struggle under socialism. From this point on, China and the Soviet Union moved in opposite ideological directions.[98]

Defeated in his brief initiative as a proponent of limited de-Stalinization, Mao turned his energies to the struggle for rapid economic development. His instrument for waging this struggle was the Communist Party, and the methods would resemble the mass mobilization of the last stages of the civil war. The outcome, as we shall see, was far more disastrous for China, and damaging to Mao's credibility, than the events of 1957.

8

Great Leap

T HE ANTIRIGHTIST CAMPAIGN merged seamlessly into the Great Leap Forward, a gigantic production drive that failed disastrously. The Leap's failure was inevitable, but disaster was not. The economic reasoning behind the Great Leap Forward was flawed and would not have achieved its lofty goals under any circumstances. Disaster, however, was created by the politics of the Leap: it was launched and sustained through two massive campaigns to root out disloyalty within the party. The Antirightist Campaign was not directed solely against those who had criticized the party from the outside in the spring of 1957; it also victimized many thousands of party members and young cadres who had responded to Mao's call to correct the party's flaws through open criticism. These criticisms were now treated as political disloyalty, taking a "bourgeois" and "liberal" standpoint against a "proletarian" and "socialist" one. Mao asserted that these differences reflected an ongoing class struggle in China that was expressed within the party itself. Party members were punished as rightists for voicing ideas that allegedly expressed the ideology of the former exploiting classes. Their antisocialist stances, it was said, were designed to weaken the party politically and halt China's transition to socialism.

As the Antirightist Campaign merged with the Great Leap Forward, enthusiastic support for the production drive and faith in its success became the primary mark of political loyalty. Skepticism about its measures or the claims made on its behalf, or factual reporting of problems created by the policy, became a mark of political disloyalty. After severe problems emerged and evidence mounted that the Leap's policies were creating a disaster, a second loyalty campaign, against "right-wing opportunism," was launched against those who reported failures or who advocated slowing down. This prevented a course correction that could have avoided the Leap's most spectacular failures, saving tens of millions of lives.

Origins of the Great Leap Forward

During the 1950s Mao consistently pushed for a more rapid transformation of China's economy into the Soviet mold. The collectivization of agriculture and socialization of industry were both completed much more rapidly than originally planned, largely due to his intervention. This created problems in agriculture in 1955 and 1956, and leaders who were in charge of economic planning warned against excessively high targets for grain production and other quotas. Pushing for a "rash advance," they argued, would create imbalances and harm long-term economic growth, creating problems for farmers' own livelihoods. During 1956 and 1957 they were able to curb Mao's urge to push output targets to unsustainably high levels—but not for long.[1]

Mao pushed back hard at party meetings in September–October 1957, in the midst of the Antirightist Campaign. He called for much more ambitious production targets. He turned questions of economic policy into questions of political loyalty. He declared that the main contradiction in China, as demonstrated in the criticisms voiced by rightists, was a class conflict between the bourgeoisie and proletariat. Party leaders who had recently opposed a "rash advance," he declared, committed a "rightist deviation." This erroneous political line, he charged, led to a soft line on class struggle that encouraged attacks by the "bourgeoisie" and "rich peasants" in 1957.[2]

Mao's aspirations for the Great Leap Forward originated during his November 1957 visit to Moscow for the fortieth anniversary of the Russian Revolution. At the previous year's party congress, Khrushchev claimed that the new Soviet five-year plan would be a "big step forward" in the building of communism, and in May 1957 he declared that the USSR would overtake the United States in the output of "important products" within fifteen years. In private conversations, Khrushchev likely told Mao that their Seventh Five-Year Plan was projected to overtake the United States in per capita industrial output by 1970.[3] Mao, like Khrushchev, was an optimist about socialist development, and he shared Khrushchev's disdain for experts and planners who insisted that such grand plans were impractical. His confidence was reinforced by Khrushchev's grandiose claims. While still in Moscow, he phoned his colleagues in Beijing and declared that opposition to rash advance was wrong, and that a socialist economy could advance much more rapidly than his cautious colleagues thought.[4]

Khrushchev's boasts inspired Mao to pledge publicly in Moscow that China would overtake Great Britain in fifteen years. This became party policy two weeks after his return from Moscow.[5] Mao planned to achieve a sudden economic breakthrough with political mobilization. The Chinese economy grew rapidly during the First Five-Year Plan from 1953 to 1957, but typically for the Soviet model, growth was highly imbalanced. Industry grew five times faster than agriculture. Per capita grain output grew slowly, with no net increase in the grain that could be extracted for the industrial workforce.[6]

Mao was impatient with officials in planning ministries who counseled caution and balance, and he believed that collectivization and mass mobilization would overcome all barriers.[7] He rejected the balanced approach to industrial development advocated by officials like Chen Yun and Deng Zihui, whose ideas were supported by Premier Zhou Enlai. Chen Yun wanted higher incomes for peasants and increased investment in light industry that would provide them with consumer goods to buy. The accumulation of profits from light industry, in turn, would provide the investment funds for heavy industry. Chen Yun's approach was similar to that advocated by Nikolai Bukharin in the Soviet Union during the 1920s—an approach rejected by Stalin and declared a right-wing deviation in his struggle for dominance over his rivals (as described in the *Short Course* on Soviet history, which defined Mao's understanding of Marxism-Leninism).[8] Although Chen Yun's approach ran counter to Soviet orthodoxy of the early Stalin era, it was very much in line with retrospective critical thinking about the Soviet development model that was widespread in the Soviet Union and Eastern Europe in the 1950s. Mao's views on the subject were distinctly old-fashioned and, to those steeped in socialist economics, they were dogmatically narrow minded and twenty years out of date.

Mao's answer was to achieve a rapid breakthrough in grain supplies through organizational changes and political mobilization. More grain would be extracted from the countryside to support higher investment in heavy industry. Mao believed that larger and more "socialist" farm units would bring economies of scale, and that intensive mobilization of existing resources, particularly labor, would lead to a breakthrough in output. As in the traditional Soviet model, capital investment would be lavished directly on heavy industry, especially on sectors like steel.[9]

Mao's uninformed ideas about economic growth were not sufficient by themselves to generate the disasters of the Great Leap. The Leap's outcomes were the product of welding these ideas onto a political campaign that cast economic policy in terms of political loyalty, equating it with class struggle. The Leap would have failed to spur economic growth; the politics of the Leap turned it into a disaster.

Mao went on the offensive in a party conference in January 1958, blasting Zhou Enlai and other leaders who had criticized rash advance. He asserted that this erroneous line gave courage to rightists. In party meetings over the next several months, he continued to criticize the emphasis on balance, planning, and economic laws. He charged that these principles were based on mere "superstition" and "dogmatism." Mao proclaimed that China henceforth would "put politics in command" and emphasize the human factor and mass enthusiasm. Professional experts would no longer dominate decision making. Their belief in rational planning and scientific standards were "bourgeois superstition." Instead, party cadres and the masses would take over from the experts, who wielded their rules and regulations merely to buttress their status and authority.[10] Mao pushed for "going all out," launching "technological revolution," criticizing "rightist ideology," and "smashing superstitious belief in both experts and Soviet practice."[11]

This was the first time that Mao asserted his view about the economy so forcefully, essentially moving toward a personal dictatorship that tolerated no opposition. Those with different policy views were severely criticized. During 1958 he took direct control of the economy, bypassing economic planners in the industrial ministries in Beijing and turning to provincial party secretaries and the national party apparatus to carry out his directives. He ratcheted up political pressure to increase production targets by warnings about class struggle within the party. He called "opposition to rash advance" anti-Marxist, and asserted that rash advance was the Marxist view. He warned of the danger of splits in the party. He alleged that "antiparty cliques" appeared in several provinces, leading in May 1958 to highly publicized purges of provincial leaders associated with the earlier criticism of rash advance. Zhou Enlai and other officials were forced to make humiliating self-criticisms, and several were removed from their posts. For a period it seemed that Zhou Enlai might even be removed as premier.[12]

These threats pressured leaders at all levels to display unquestioning enthusiasm for the Leap. Meetings held to set production targets turned into criticism sessions against the incorrect line of opposing rash advance. As the continuing Antirightist Campaign spread into the countryside during 1958, it targeted those who had objected to rapid collectivization or who had pointed out the problems it created.[13] It silenced any objections and made enthusiasm for Mao's line the definition of political loyalty.

The strategy of economic development that Mao rejected—the one devised by Chen Yun and supported by Zhou Enlai—presumed that ministries and bureaus, and the planners, professional managers, and technical experts who staffed them, would be in charge of setting economic targets and investment priorities. This was the modernized Soviet practice of the postwar era, a bureaucratic procedure where plans were transmitted to provincial and regional governments from above. During 1958 Mao took the planning process out of their hands and turned it over to party secretaries of provinces, who were compelled to respond enthusiastically in such a tense political atmosphere. Planning for the Great Leap became a politically charged pledge campaign, conducted in a cascading series of party conferences in which party secretaries at each level vied with one another to promise large increases in the output of grain, steel, and other key products. This put enormous power back into the hands of the party organization itself, which took over economic decision making at all levels of government. It also put enormous pressure on party officials at all levels to conform to expectations of wholehearted support and, subsequently, to fulfill their pledges.

As party secretaries promised implausibly large increases in output, Mao was greatly encouraged. In May 1958 he proclaimed that he had previously been too conservative: it would now take only seven years to surpass Great Britain, and fifteen to catch the United States.[14] Steel targets escalated wildly. National output in 1957 had been 5 million tons, and the planners' original target for 1958 was an ambitious 5.8 million. By September 1958, pledges by provincial party secretaries had inflated the year's target to 11 million tons, and the plan for 1959 to an absurd

39 million.[15] Capital investment in heavy industry soared to support these pledges. New plant capacity had to be built, primarily through the importation of equipment from the Soviet bloc (paid for by the increased export of grain). The initial capital investment target for 1958 was 14.5 billion yuan, but this was quickly raised to 38.6 billion.[16]

Party secretaries pledged equally fantastic increases in agriculture. Grain output in 1957 was 195 million tons. During the course of 1958, targets rapidly escalated to more than 350 million tons.[17] Unlike those of heavy industry, these massive increases were to be accompanied by only small increases in capital investment. In their frenetic attempts to meet grossly unrealistic new output quotas, party officials in rural regions made radical organizational changes and placed draconian demands on peasants.

The Rural Great Leap Forward

The strategy for increasing grain output relied heavily on expanding irrigation and bringing new land into cultivation. Dams and canals served areas that were larger than the boundaries of collective farms, so the first step in the campaign was to amalgamate existing collectives into much larger units. In 1957 there were roughly 70,000 communes, which contained an average of approximately fifteen production brigades (roughly equal to villages). During 1958 these collective farms were combined into roughly 23,000 gigantic communes, containing an average of more than fifty villages. This permitted party cadres to mobilize massive labor armies for major construction projects.[18]

Internal changes were also made in collective farms. Agricultural production was to be organized in a military fashion. Families were ordered to turn over personal possessions—cookware, tables, chairs, and cabinets—for communal mess halls. Families were no longer to store and prepare their own food; this would be done collectively. The recording of work points would be suspended, because massive new demands were to be made on farmers' time and effort. Families would eat what they needed in the mess halls, no longer limited by the calculation of household rations. Nurseries and child care centers were established, releasing women and the elderly for labor. When the meal halls, child care centers, and other official buildings were to be constructed, farmers were assigned to these projects as construction laborers. In some cases, private homes were pulled down as sources of building materials. Farmers were organized into large brigades along military lines, often segregated by gender. This work was largely uncompensated and was in no way voluntary. If you refused to work, you had no right to eat in the collective mess hall, the only source of food.[19]

The production drive was organized like a military campaign. A model commune in Henan province set up twenty-eight production corps, which were in turn divided into regiments, companies, platoons, and squads. Farmers were expected to obey strict rules of discipline: obey the leader and follow orders; work actively; do not arrive late or depart early; wage a constant struggle against capitalist thinking; and cooperate. Farmers were required to work at least twenty-eight days each month. All were required to rise with the morning bugle call, take meals together, and go to sleep at the same time. This model commune replaced private housing with communal barracks, segregated by gender, with children housed in a separate building.[20]

Prior to the Great Leap, labor on collective farms had a rhythm that was determined by the seasons. Planting and harvesting were the busiest periods, and winter was slack time. The Great Leap obliterated this rhythm with constant and seemingly ceaseless demands for hard labor, not only in the fields but also on massive irrigation projects, road building, and terracing of hillsides. To help provincial leaders meet their inflated targets for increased industrial output, communes established small factories. To contribute to the province's inflated quotas for producing steel, villages set up primitive makeshift steel furnaces, which had to be fueled and maintained around the clock. The diversion of labor away from agriculture frequently left too few farmers on the land to tend crops or bring in the harvest. Farmers whose lives were previously governed by agricultural seasons now found that virtually all of their time and effort was subject to the seemingly insatiable demands of commune officials for unrelenting labor.[21]

The new people's communes intensified communal life far beyond that of the recently established collective farms. They also greatly expanded the rural bureaucracy. The centralized direction of all aspects of rural production required larger salaried staffs at each level of the hierarchy. Communes typically had at least thirty cadres, production brigades around ten, and a production team around five. This was a massive increase in the administrative overhead from only two years before.

Prior to collectivization, typically one salaried cadre was responsible for several villages. Now each village was required to support the salaries of a team of roughly five, and full-time salaried cadres were added at the commune level.[22] Nationwide, this represented a new rural bureaucracy of millions of full-time officials, a further drain on rural incomes. Moreover, this new bureaucratic stratum exercised centralized control over resources that previously had been in the hands of households or village governments. They controlled larger budgets, made decisions about expenditures, and they controlled villagers' time, labor, and even food supply. This opened up opportunities for small-scale corruption and privilege, in addition to the abuse of power.

The Cycle of Bureaucratic Self-Deception

The Great Leap Forward generated disaster through mutual deception and ultimately self-deception within a massive bureaucracy whose agents at all levels were placed under immense political pressure to agree and conform. In the first wave, after seeing purges of colleagues for "opposing rash advance," party officials at each level in the national hierarchy pledged impossibly high increases in grain output, displaying full confidence and enthusiasm over the prospect. Self-deception also meant agreeing that obviously counterproductive measures would have positive results and violating common sense by implementing them. It then took the form of reporting extravagant successes to superiors, which were duly publicized and celebrated, putting greater pressures on other party leaders to implement the same misguided practices and report the same successes. As failures multiplied, it took the form of hiding the evidence, blocking negative reports, and insisting that all was well even as crops failed and starvation spread. Next, rural cadres in the midst of a growing famine were trapped by their earlier false reports of massive grain harvests, forcing them to come up with even larger deliveries of grain to the state, exacerbating famine conditions that were already under way. The final act of deception was the claim that peasants were hiding grain, eating too much, and that rural leaders who reported that there was simply no grain left to deliver were submitting false reports and hoarding grain for their own use. This led to a tragic campaign to strip farmers of their dwindling food stores even as the famine was already well advanced.

The first step in the cycle was the new planning process, which consisted of group meetings of party secretaries of provinces, cities, counties, and at each level down the hierarchy, to pledge production targets for the coming year. The first rounds of such meetings were held just as the Antirightist Campaign was nearing its end and as Mao was openly linking opposition to rash advance to a rightist deviation within the party leadership. These pledge meetings resembled an auction, with undue influence being exercised by the highest bids. High bids pulled the others along, because no one wanted to be seen as lagging behind.[23] When provincial officials held planning meetings at the district and city level, they put immense political pressure on their subordinates to pledge output targets that would permit them to fulfill their provincial pledges. As a margin of safety, they routinely pushed subordinates to pledge targets whose sum was higher than the initial provincial pledge, guarding against possible shortfalls. This led to increasingly unrealistic targets as the process moved down the hierarchy.

One problem with these escalating demands was that they conflicted with one another. Demands for immediate increases in grain output conflicted with the reality that this would be possible only after improvements in irrigation and water control brought more land under cultivation. Rural officials diverted massive amounts of labor away from farming for crash construction projects to build dams, reservoirs, and canals, and to terrace hillsides for cultivation. This diverted labor from planting, cultivation, and harvesting, leading to smaller yields than would otherwise have been the case. Similar problems were created by the diversion of labor for the smelting of homemade steel from local scrap metals, and transferring farm laborers to new factories that were established by commune and county governments. Rural cadres could only respond to these conflicting objectives by driving farmers to work harder and faster.

The next step in the cycle of mutual deception was a series of model practices that were said to contribute greatly to the attainment of seemingly impossible objectives. Two such methods were close planting and deep plowing. These were prescribed by party authorities and accompanied by press reports that celebrated their value. Close planting was ostensibly designed to bring higher yields on limited cropland simply by planting seeds closer together, and applying much larger amounts of fertilizer. This had two negative results. It led to the use of much higher amounts of seed grain during the planting season, and the sprouts competed with one another for sunlight, water, and nutrients in the soil, leading to stunting and crop failure. This depressed agricultural output wherever it was tried, and also caused enormous waste of seed grain and fertilizer. Successes using this technique were nonetheless enthusiastically reported in the mass media. Deep plowing was similarly destructive. It turned fertile topsoil, already thin and depleted in much of China, deep underground, and pulled nutrient-poor subsoil to the surface.[24]

Desperate to make good on impossible pledges, local cadres made decisions that were self-defeating and ultimately harmful. One common example was the destruction of valuable crops, like orchards, in order to bring more land under grain cultivation. Another was the extension of grain planting onto land that was poorly suited to wheat or other grains, leading to lost output of nonstaple products. One of the more surprising and harmful was a common response to shortages of fertilizer. Peasant homes made out of mud brick and straw were torn down to fertilize the fields, leaving surprisingly large percentages of farmers in some regions without shelter for an extended period.[25] Carried out in haste and without consulting civil engineers and other experts, irrigation projects could create severe environmental damage. In one region they led to waterlogging that drew salt into the topsoil, sharply reducing crop yields. Dams built hastily were prone to collapse during rainy seasons, leading to disastrous floods. Hillsides that were terraced or cleared of trees for planting grain led to severe soil erosion and the clogging of streams and rivers with silt.[26]

Failure was not an option. Officials who reported that these politically lauded practices were unwise risked political censure for lack of faith in the party and the Great Leap. Cadres at all levels were aware of the problems but hesitated to speak, and they actively suppressed the spread of information that would expose them for submitting false reports. Years later they would explain their failure to report the spreading famine to their superiors as resulting from "fear of being labeled a right deviationist." In other cases, when they reported starvation conditions to their commune superiors, they were explicitly warned that they were expressing "right deviationist thinking" and were "viewing the problem in too simplistic a manner." In one production brigade, cadres were expected to report increased grain output, but "those who failed had to go through group training, criticism, struggle, and beating."[27] Visiting official delegations were taken on carefully planned tours designed to prevent them from discovering local problems. Party investigators who nonetheless found evidence of unreported famines were threatened by local officials and in some cases prevented from leaving the area.[28] Local officials underreported deaths and devised elaborate strategies for falsifying statistics, often with the connivance of superiors who were equally anxious to avoid negative reports.[29]

The statistical system was completely politicized. Party committees at all levels had to approve the statistics submitted to higher levels. During the first year of the Leap, statistical agencies were told, "Our statistical work is carried out in service to others, not to ourselves. Whether something is wanted or not, or what is wanted, is up to others. The calculation methods and specifications are likewise applied according to the requirements of whomever we serve."[30] When provincial statisticians complained that their party committees were reporting false numbers, they were told, "The Great Leap Forward is an irresistible trend; all you can do is obey the provincial party committee. Some day the central government will ask you for the actual figures, so you must make sure to have all the real numbers ready to present them at any time."[31] In 1959, as problems caused by the Leap were becoming too large to ignore, the State Statistical Bureau insisted on submitting accurate reports. Their leaders were compelled to make a self-criticism for their "inadequate political consciousness" and for trying to "blow a cold wind on the Great Leap Forward." The Statistical Bureau was instructed to "resolutely defend the party's General Line and launch a counterattack in the struggle against right opportunism."[32]

The Cycle of Bureaucratic Oppression

Farmers did not always comply voluntarily with the demands placed upon them, and not all local officials complied enthusiastically with orders from above, agreed with obviously wrongheaded directives, submitted false reports, and covered up disastrous failures. As time wore on, the cycle of bureaucratic self-deception became unsustainable without the application of coercion, through intimidation and surprising levels of violence, of individuals who failed to fall into line or who tried to report the truth. This would give the rural Great Leap many of the violently oppressive features that were later observed on an even wider scale during the Cultural Revolution. In this sense the mutual deception was enforced by a party bureaucracy that did not want to hear bad news and willfully misinterpreted it when delivered.

The Great Leap in rural areas was destructive from the beginning. Despite widespread self-censorship and false reporting, some accurate reports did reach central authorities as early as April 1958 that food shortages and food riots were disturbingly widespread. By the last half of 1958 there were unmistakable signs of impending famine. By early 1959 famine was spreading nationwide.[33]

As problems multiplied, Mao stated a point of view from which he never wavered: the General Line represented by the Great Leap was absolutely correct, and its accomplishments far outweighed its shortcomings. Criticism of the Leap reflected class struggle, attacks by enemies of the party and socialism, as his speech to a February 1959 party conference asserted:

> The relationship between our achievements and our shortcomings is, as we usually say, the relationship between nine fingers and one finger out of ten fingers. Some people suspect or deny the 1958 Great Leap Forward, and suspect or deny the advantages of the people's communes, and this viewpoint is obviously completely wrong. . . . Extra large communes are the best means for us to achieve the transition from the rural socialist collective system to the socialist system of full public ownership, and are also the best means of accomplishing the transition from socialism to communism. If suspicions develop regarding this basic issue, this is completely wrong, and it is right deviation. It is necessary to anticipate . . . [that] factions will come out jeering at us, and . . . that those landlords, rich peasants, counter-revolutionaries, and bad elements will carry out acts of sabotage.[34]

Instead, Mao blamed local officials for pushing policies too far and too fast, for incompetence, and for setting excessively ambitious targets. He acknowledged reports of hunger, but insisted that the problems were not that severe, and were due to implementation at lower levels and not the principles behind the Leap.[35]

The primary cause of famine was excessive procurement of grain based on wildly inflated harvest figures.[36] When provincial officials falsely reported massive increases in grain harvests the previous year, their quotas for delivery of grain were raised accordingly. The actual grain harvest in 1958 was 200 million tons, a mere 2.5 percent increase over the previous year. Yet the official figure for the grain harvest was a ludicrously inflated 375 million tons.[37] For obvious reasons, provincial officials were finding it impossible to meet the higher procurement quotas. Due to spreading hunger and the disruption of collective farms in 1958, crops were already failing, and the grain harvest would drop 15 percent in 1959. Provincial officials were placed in a very difficult situation, and Mao was already talking as if the problems with the Leap were their fault.

How could provincial officials extract themselves from this dilemma? They could admit that the previous year's grain harvest figures were a fantasy—for which political retribution was sure to follow—or they could blame their subordinates. And this is what many of them did. In January 1959 Guangdong Province reported that in fact the grain was there, but was being hidden by peasant households with the connivance of local cadres. They reported great success in a campaign to scour the villages to dig out the hidden grain. Anhui Province submitted a report that stated, "The issue of so-called grain shortages in the countryside has nothing to do with lack of grain, nor is it linked to excessive state procurements: it is an ideological problem, in particular among local cadres." The report explained that the hoarding was due to local worries that communes would not let them retain enough grain, or that they were holding some back to avoid much higher quotas the next year, or that they suspected other leaders were withholding grain to shift the burden onto them.[38]

Mao, who was already forced to acknowledge serious problems with the Leap but was unwilling to acknowledge flaws in its overall design, jumped at the idea. He declared that the problem of "hiding grain" was "very serious," and called for an intensified effort to procure more.[39] Thus began the nationwide campaign to combat "false reporting and grain hoarding." Officials at any level who insisted that in fact there was no more grain, and that peasants were already starving, were treated as if they were part of the conspiracy against the Great Leap Forward and, by implication, Chairman Mao.

The campaign was conducted as a form of political warfare. Village leaders and ordinary farmers who denied that there was any hidden grain were subjected to verbal abuse and threats that frequently escalated into beatings and even torture. One elderly rural cadre reported years later, "If you didn't beat others, you would be beaten. The more harshly you beat someone, the more firmly you established your position and your loyalty to the Communist Party. If you didn't beat others, you were a right deviationist and would soon be beaten by others."[40] In one commune, the county party committee ordered an investigation that began at the top of the local party hierarchy. At the meeting where the order was relayed, seven commune cadres were strung up and beaten, one of whom died at the scene.[41] Violent struggle sessions and beatings were administered to rural cadres who insisted that there was no grain left. Many escaped with demotions or expulsions from party posts, but some committed suicide.[42]

The campaign was even more devastating when it reached farm households. Homes were ransacked for hidden grain, and household heads detained and interrogated, threatened with imprisonment, beaten, and even tortured.[43] When hidden grain could not be found, furniture and other family property was looted, leaving many rural families already suffering from hunger utterly destitute. Sometimes homes were pulled down as punishment for refusing to reveal hidden grain and further grain rations were denied, condemning the victims to death through starvation. Many localities formed "labor reform brigades" where suspected hoarders were forced to perform hard labor on starvation rations. No matter how violent local officials became in their frenetic efforts to uncover more grain, there was very little left. The campaign simply accelerated the deepening famine.[44]

As the campaign against hoarding was under way, the party leadership met in July and August 1959—the Lushan Plenum—to consider "readjustments" in the Great Leap and alleviate some of the severe problems that Mao had been forced to acknowledge. Many leaders were now acutely aware of the spreading famine, in part by visiting their home villages and talking to relatives. Top military officers were aware of the problem through reports submitted by junior officers and enlisted men, most from rural areas, about the plight of their families. These officials clearly recognized the disastrous outcomes of many of the core policies of the Leap, and they were hopeful that Mao could be convinced to change course and avoid further damage.

Unfortunately, this did not happen. Mao reacted violently to criticisms of the Leap that clearly implied that there were few accomplishments to brag about, and that the problems were not due to poor implementation by local cadres.[45] He heard reports that some members of the Central Committee had spoken privately in blunt terms about the failures of the Leap, calling backyard steel furnaces "useless," the entire policy a wrongheaded result of "hubris," and questioning Mao's repeated claim that the "shortcomings" were equivalent to only "one finger" and the "accomplishments" equivalent to "nine fingers." He was especially bothered by reports that some of these same officials compared his imperious behavior toward others in the leadership with "Stalin in his later years."[46]

Mao decided to strike back after receiving a note from the minister of defense, Marshal Peng Dehuai, that detailed the shortcomings of the Leap. Mao's response was emotional and vindictive, destroying any possibility of adjusting Leap policies to prevent disaster from growing even larger.[47] He immediately called together the Politburo Standing Committee and demanded severe criticism of Peng Dehuai and several other top leaders for forming an "antiparty clique" that engaged in a "savage assault of right-wing opportunism." Escalating his claims about class struggle within the party, he denounced the critics in personal terms as careerists and plotters who lacked loyalty to the party and the cause of socialism.[48] Other top officials, even those who inwardly shared the critics' views, fell into line and denounced their errant colleagues in equally vicious language.[49]

In his speech to the gathering on August 2, Mao referred to a fundamental "line struggle" within the party:

> Is our line actually correct or not? Some of our comrades are expressing doubts. . . . Soon after arriving at Lushan, some comrades called for democracy, saying we're not democratic now, we can't speak freely, there's a kind of pressure that prevents us from daring to speak. . . . Only later did it become clear that they wanted to attack this General Line, that they wanted to sabotage the General Line. When they say they want freedom of expression, what they want is freedom to destroy the General Line with their speech, and freedom to criticize the General Line. . . . The Lushan Conference is not a matter of opposing the Left, but of opposing the Right, because [right] opportunism is a vicious attack on the party and the party's leading organs, and an attack against the people's undertakings.[50]

Mao followed up these charges with two memos in mid-August that were even more defensive and emotional. "To those splittists within the Communist Party, those friends at the most extreme right. . . . You're unwilling to listen to me; I'm already in 'Stalin's last years,' and have become 'arbitrary and rampaging,' not giving you 'freedom' or 'democracy,' while 'subordinates magnify the actions of their superiors.' . . . No one is able to speak frankly to my face, only your leader is qualified to do so. It's just too deplorable, and apparently only your emergence can save the day."[51] Mao would have none of this. "The struggle that emerged at Lushan was a class struggle, and a continuation of the life-and-death struggle that has been going on between the bourgeois class and the proletarian class in the course of the socialist revolution for more than ten years now."[52]

This, finally, was Mao's full application of the Stalinist playbook that he absorbed from the Soviet *Short Course* back in Yan'an. Policy disagreements express class struggle, and the leader is the only fount of truth and wisdom. Doubters are traitors who express the interests of capitalists and imperialists. The official resolution on Peng Dehuai defined the problem as "a right-deviating opportunist anti-party clique led by Comrade Peng Dehuai," which engaged in a "savage attack against the Party's General Line, against the Great Leap Forward, and against the people's communes." The resolution called for the entire party to expose "the true face of this hypocrite, careerist, and conspirator." Everyone was called upon to proclaim the correctness of the Great Leap Forward and repudiate all doubters: "Insistently crushing the activities of the right-deviating opportunistic anti-party clique led by Comrade Peng Dehuai is absolutely essential, not only for defending the party's General Line, but also for defending the central leadership of the party headed by Comrade Mao Zedong, defending the unity of the party, and defending the socialist undertaking of the party and the people."[53]

Thus began a second "antirightist" campaign—against "right-wing opportunism"—that ensured the death through starvation of tens of millions. This second political campaign diverted the party from a midcourse correction that could have moderated the disaster that the Great Leap was rapidly becoming. China was teetering on the edge of a famine of historic proportions, Mao's reaction at Lushan was the final push over the cliff. It reinforced the ongoing campaign against the imaginary phenomenon of "false reporting and grain hoarding" by launching a campaign against equally fictitious local antiparty cliques of right-wing opportunists. The campaign punished more than 10 million people nationwide as right opportunists.[54]

Any sensible view would have recognized that the root cause of the disaster was mass mobilization within a coercive bureaucracy that

threatened cadres at all levels for failing to respond enthusiastically to
unrealistic demands of the party center, and which punished cadres,
sometimes with brutal violence, for pointing out obvious problems with
these demands. Mao, however, concluded illogically and self-servingly
that the problems were due to a "fierce countercurrent in opposition to
the socialist road." He attributed the origins to sabotage by antiparty
cliques and class enemies.[55]

Instead of blaming rural violence and starvation on the "class struggle"
that he had himself ordered to combat "false reporting and grain
hoarding" and "right-wing opportunism," Mao asserted that "alien class
elements" had usurped power in the Chinese countryside. Rural cadres
who had acted as Mao's most loyal and politically zealous agents in pros-
ecuting his misguided campaign were blamed for the disasters that ensued. A Central Committee report issued at the end of 1960 stated that
the problems were "absolutely a matter of counterrevolutionary restoration, and a ruthless class retaliation against the working people by landlords and by the Kuomintang [Nationalists] in the garb of the Communist Party."[56] The Central Committee charged that "counterrevolutionaries
and bad elements usurped party and administrative leadership, and using
the campaign against right deviation as a cover, they . . . adopted the tactics of landlords and the Kuomintang, such as arbitrary beatings, arrests,
and killings to implement wide-scale class retaliation. . . . Leaders and
cadres at all levels became organizers and leaders in the domination and
oppression of the people, and cold-blooded killers as well."[57]

In short, these problems were not the result of a coercive bureaucratic system that demanded unquestioning loyalty from agents that were
mobilized to engage in a relentless class struggle against imaginary enemies. The real problem was subversion by class enemies who infiltrated
the ranks. It simply could not be true that loyal party cadres committed
atrocities under pressure to conform to wrongheaded policies emanating
from Beijing. In discussing the case at a meeting of the Henan Provincial Party Committee in December 1960, one official stated his resolve
to carry out the struggle against the enemy:

> What is at issue is our inadequate understanding of the very evident con-
> tradictions between the enemy and us, and our inability to clearly per-
> ceive the Kuomintang implementing a bourgeois class retaliation in the
> guise of Communist Party members. . . . To see the masses dying, yet
> keep the grain locked in storerooms and refuse to distribute it; to watch

the communal kitchens close down and yet not allow the masses to light stoves in their own homes; to refuse to let the masses harvest wild herbs or flee the famine . . . to treat people worse than oxen or horses, arbitrarily beating people and even killing them, lacking even a shred of human feeling—if these people were not the enemy, who were they? . . . These people, for the sake of their own self-preservation, slaughtered our class brothers, and we must kill them with equal ruthlessness.[58]

In the Henan prefecture where the abuses were particularly severe, thousands of rural officials were removed from their posts, more than 10,000 subjected to struggle sessions, and quotas for executions of erring cadres were issued by the hundreds for each county.[59] Because the culprits were alleged to be the landlords and rich peasants who had survived land reform and the earlier campaigns against counterrevolutionaries, these "bad class" groups were singled out for victimization as well.[60]

The Magnitude of the Famine and Its Causes

The famine was not officially acknowledged until several years after Mao's death. Data on famine-related deaths were a closely guarded secret even at the highest levels. When presented with a detailed report that put the death toll in the tens of millions, Zhou Enlai reportedly instructed the officials responsible to destroy all copies of the report and the original data on which it was based.[61] No population figures were published for two decades. When the post-Mao government began to release population and agricultural statistics, demographers immediately noticed unmistakable evidence of a famine of surprising magnitude.[62]

Not until the 1982 national census and the release of data from the 1953 and 1964 censuses could the demographic impact of the Great Leap Forward be calculated with precision and confidence. The national averages, for a country with more than 600 million people, were staggering in their implications. The crude death rate increased 2.5-fold from 1957 to 1960, life expectancy at birth fell from 49.5 to 24.6 years, and infant mortality more than doubled. China's population declined by more than 10 million in the four years after 1958 (Table 8.1). The census data yield estimates of close to 30 million "premature deaths."[63]

Although the famine is now officially acknowledged, the Chinese authorities still find it difficult to admit its magnitude and true causes. The

Table 8.1.   Demographic impact of the Great Leap Forward

Year	Crude Birth Rate (Births per Thousand)	Crude Death Rate (Deaths per Thousand)	Life Expectancy at Birth (Years)	Infant Mortality Rate (Deaths per Thousand)	Population (Millions)
1956	39.9	20.1	47.0	143	619.1
1957	43.3	18.1	49.5	132	633.2
1958	37.8	20.7	45.8	146	646.7
1959	28.5	22.1	42.5	160	654.3
1960	26.8	44.6	24.6	284	650.7
1961	22.4	23.0	38.4	183	644.8
1962	41.0	14.0	53.0	89	653.3
1963	49.8	13.8	54.9	87	674.2

Source: Banister (1984, 254).

famine is referred to as "three years of natural disasters"—floods, droughts, and storm damage.[64] This explanation is contradicted by regional data on weather damage and crop output. Only 9.6 percent of sown areas were affected by natural disasters in 1959, when the famine reached its height; 16.6 percent in 1960, and 20.1 percent in 1961. Only 9.6 percent of sown areas were in designated disaster areas two years running. Weather damage in 1959 was no worse than in 1956 and 1957, when grain harvests increased.[65] Less than 13 percent of the decline in grain output was attributable to weather, and this would not have led to famine if Great Leap politics had not prohibited the delivery of grain back to villages.[66]

Accurate agricultural statistics for these years are sobering. Real grain output actually increased by only 2.5 percent in 1958 (Table 8.2). The harvest decreased drastically after that, falling by almost 30 percent through 1960 before gradually increasing once again. China's agriculture was so damaged by the Great Leap Forward that grain output did not return to 1958 levels until 1966. The emphasis on grain output led to even larger declines in other food products. The output of oil-bearing crops in 1960 was less than half of output in 1957, and lower than any year since 1949. Output of sugarcane and sugar beets in 1962 was one-third less than in 1957, and output of meat less than half.[67]

Beijing, however, was initially working with a very different set of figures on grain output. The initially reported 1958 harvest was 375 mil-

Table 8.2. Grain output and procurements during the Great Leap Forward

Year	Grain Output (Million Tons)	Grain Procurement (Million Tons)	Retained Grain per Capita (Kg/Person)
1956	193	40	284
1957	195	46	273
1958	200	52	268
1959	170	64	193
1960	143	47	182
1961	148	37	209
1962	160	32	229
1963	170	37	231
1964	188	40	256
1965	195	39	261
1966	214	41	282

Source: Li and Yang (2005, 846).

lion tons; in 1980 it was reported that the actual number was 200 million tons.[68] In 1959 reported output was 270 million—not the actual 170 million. Not until 1960, when the famine had grown to historic proportions, did Beijing report a more realistic harvest figure of 150 million tons (against an actual 143).[69] In the meantime, for two years larger grain deliveries were demanded from collective farms. In 1959, after grain output fell by 30 million tons, procurements increased by 12 million tons. In 1960, when the famine could no longer be ignored, procurements fell to 47 million tons, still far too high: this was the same procurement levy as in 1957, when output was 52 million tons higher (Table 8.2). Grain procurements as a percentage of the harvest reached an all-time high at exactly the point when harvests began to fail, edging close to 40 percent in 1959, which was almost double the percentage of the harvest claimed by the state in 1956 (Figure 8.1).

The available food grain left in collective farms dropped drastically: from 284 kilograms per person in 1958 to 182 in 1960 (Table 8.2). The damage wrought by Great Leap policies was so deep and prolonged that the per capita grain supply in collective farms did not return to 1956 levels until a decade later (Figure 8.2). This was due to the continued bias shown to cities in the allocation of food supplies. The cities experienced severe disruptions in food supplies, which were further stressed

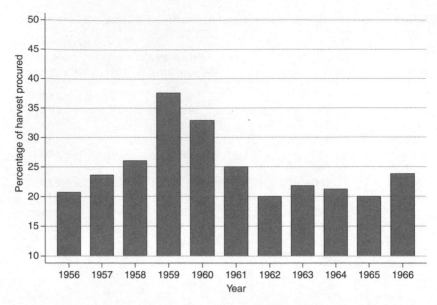

Figure 8.1. State grain procurements, as percentage of harvest, 1956–1966.
Source: Calculated from Li and Yang (2005, 846).

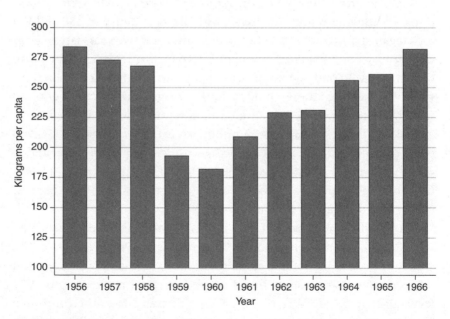

Figure 8.2. Grain retained by collective farms, 1956–1966. *Source:* Li and Yang
(2005, 846).

by starving refugees from suburban communes. Beggars roamed the streets, fights broke out at grain shops, and petty theft and armed robbery became more common.[70] Supplies of pork to Shanghai fell by almost 90 percent from 1957 to 1961, and low supplies of other foodstuffs led to widespread diseases of malnutrition. Beijing's 1961 death rate was double the 1957 figure.[71] Nonetheless, cities received enough supplies of grain to avoid famine.

The regime worked hard to conceal these problems from their urban populations and especially from the outside world. Refugees fleeing the famine caused the International Red Cross to offer food aid, which the regime flatly refused.[72] Grain exports to the Soviet Union and elsewhere in the Eastern bloc as loan repayments continued.[73] Net grain exports in 1959 actually increased by more than 50 percent. They continued at reduced levels in 1960, even after the extent of the famine could no longer be ignored. Not until 1961 did China become a net importer of grain.[74] This two-year delay in purchasing grain on international markets led to net grain exports of almost 7 million tons. This amount of grain could have supplied 16 million people a survival diet of 2,000 calories per day for almost two years.[75] International trade policy, motivated by a concern to save face for China's leaders, made the famine much worse.

The Great Leap in Industry

The Great Leap Forward had an impact on manufacturing industries that was just as devastating in statistical terms as it was in agriculture. Given the magnitude of the famine generated by the destruction of agriculture, it is understandable that industry has received much less attention. When industries fail, output falls, and workers are laid off. The Great Leap's destruction of the industrial system did not generate millions of deaths, but it created an industrial depression that lasted for years.

The reasons why are easy to understand. As noted in Chapter 5, the Soviet industrial system was "resource constrained" rather than "demand constrained." In this resource-constrained economy, production stops when the supply of inputs—fuel, raw materials, spare parts—falls short. The vision behind the Great Leap was to expand the entire industrial system by transcending in one fell swoop the resource constraints that held back production. This was to be accomplished by massive inputs of both labor and capital. Existing workers were mobilized (involuntarily) to work harder, faster, and longer hours. New plant capacity was built. Local governments established large numbers of new factories and mobilized labor from rural communes to operate them. Output targets were raised across the board. Party secretaries at all levels were pressured to pledge greatly inflated targets for steel, coal, chemicals, petroleum, machinery, and motorized vehicles. By pushing everyone to work harder and faster, and to squeeze every ounce of slack resources out of the industrial system, a virtuous circle of increasing supplies would lift the resource constraints on industry and accelerate China's industrialization.

This idea made sense to Mao and was an appealing notion to party cadres. By commandeering industry for a massive political campaign, the lumbering bureaucratic system borrowed from the Soviet Union would spring to life, as party leadership would unleash human potential to previously unimagined heights. Seemingly impossible goals could be achieved—as in the last phase of the civil war—only if the party relentlessly mobilized people and material resources and focused them single-mindedly on the task. Overnight, the shortage economy would become a thing of the past.

In the short run, factories could meet demands for vastly increased output only by speeding up existing operations. This could be accomplished by altering or abandoning procedures designed to ensure product quality, worker safety, or the maintenance of capital equipment; by mandating involuntary overtime work; or by hiring large numbers of new workers. Local officials in less industrialized regions responded to calls for increased output by rapidly establishing new factories or expanding the few that already existed. They did this by hiring large numbers of new workers from nearby collective farms, part of the diversion of labor from agriculture to industry that eventually harmed grain output. County seats and rural towns throughout China reported massive increases in industrial employment in 1958 and 1959. Almost all of this increase was in simple, labor-intensive operations that could increase output with little capital investment.

The demand to speed up existing operations ran roughshod over procedures established by engineering and technical staff to ensure product quality, worker safety, and the maintenance of capital equipment. This frequently pitted party secretaries and party activists against white-collar staff and skilled veteran workers. Party secretaries who insisted on smelting steel at faster rates, finding substitutes for scarce alloys, or reducing chemical checks for quality overrode concerns by technical staff and skilled workers who pointed out that heating batches faster would waste scarce fuel and that altering the chemical composition or skipping quality inspections would result in products that did not meet technical specifications for the steel needed by downstream users. In machine tool or production line operations, party secretaries found it expedient to speed up operations by cutting back on quality inspections, increasing the pace of work, or lengthening the working day.

Technical staff, veteran workers, and trade union officials understood that these proposals would lead to breakdowns of capital equipment, industrial accidents that imperiled worker health and safety, and flawed products that did not meet quality specifications and that therefore represented a waste of scarce resources. Party secretaries silenced such objections. In meetings designed to "unleash the creativity of the masses," political activists proposed shortcuts and innovations of the type described above that were celebrated within the factory (and the press). Engineers and technical staff that raised objections about waste, quality, or safety were subjected to criticism as "bourgeois experts" whose reactionary views were allegedly based on "superstition." In the wake of the Antirightist Campaign, few were so foolish as to persist in their objections that the party's celebrated production drive would likely backfire.

These predictions soon came to pass. Factories experienced a wave of industrial accidents and equipment breakdowns. Workers pushed to endure long shifts made mistakes due to fatigue; safety regulations ignored in the push for speed led to fatal accidents.[76] Equipment that was pushed faster or longer than it was designed for, or that was used beyond scheduled inspections and maintenance broke down, and even when the breakdown did not involve injuries or fatalities, production would be shut down while time-consuming repairs were made.

Despite these setbacks, production was increased, at least at first. Predictably, however, the increased quantity of output led to a sharp decline in quality. Producers therefore faced a choice, but one that in the context of the times was by no means difficult. They could acknowledge the substandard quality of their products, declare them unusable, not include them in their production quotas, and rework them into usable products. This meant that they would not fulfill their quotas, and that the labor, materials, and fuel expended to produce the substandard products had been wasted.

Party secretaries overwhelmingly chose to declare all the output up to standard and ship it to end users, silencing managers, workers, and engineers who suggested otherwise. This meant that they simply passed the problem on to the factories that used their products. Factories throughout the industrial system received shipments of steel that was too brittle or too soft to be used in their products; parts that could not be used for their assembly processes; machine tools that broke down or failed to operate; trucks that broke down constantly. Despite the increase in the quantity of available inputs, there suddenly developed, throughout the industrial system, a severe shortage of inputs of sufficient quality to sustain manufacturing operations.

A production drive designed to overcome resource constraints led instead to a resource crisis. Factories throughout China were receiving inputs that they could not use. They expended additional energy and labor simply to rework the inputs into usable form (if possible), or they tried to barter the useless materials to other factories that had the capacity to do so (and that were themselves desperate for usable inputs).

This was an industrial depression in the making, with fundamentally different causes than the financial panics and downturns in demand that create depressions in market economies. China's Soviet-style industrial system, constrained by resources, systematically wasted resources on a monumental scale, creating a cascading shortage crisis. Electricity, gasoline, fuel oil, and coal were expended in vast quantities in order to generate products that could not be used.[77]

By 1960 all of the slack in the industrial system was exhausted. In 1961 industrial output simply collapsed. Net industrial output dropped by almost 50 percent through 1962 (Figure 8.3). The damage to the industrial system was so severe that output did not recover until 1964. Workers added during the upsurge of 1958 and 1959 were laid off, and part of the pre-1958 labor force was laid off as well.[78] Total nonagricultural employment dropped from just under 60 million in 1960 to 42 million in 1962, and employment in state industry dropped from 21.3 million in 1960 to 11.2 million in 1963 (Figure 8.4).[79] Many of these workers had migrated from nearby collective farms early in the Great Leap Forward. Now they were forcibly returned to collective farms on a massive scale. China's urban population, 99.5 million at the end of 1957, ballooned to 130.7 million in 1960. By 1962 it was reduced to 116.7 million.[80] The number of industrial enterprises in China, which had more

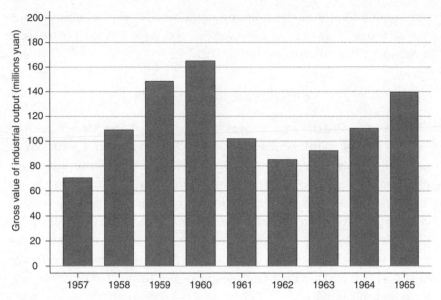

Figure 8.3. Gross value of industrial output, 1957–1965 (constant yuan).
Source: State Statistical Bureau (1983, 214).

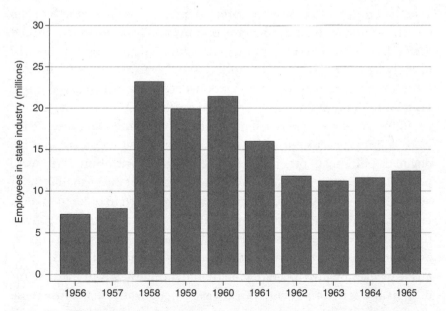

Figure 8.4. Employees in state industry, 1956–1965. *Source:* State Statistical
Bureau (1983, 126).

than doubled early in the Leap, dropped precipitously as many of the new factories set up in rural areas were closed. As late as 1965 there were fewer industrial enterprises than in 1957.[81]

A Centrally Planned Depression

The Soviet industrial system was designed to ensure steady growth without the instabilities due to business cycles and financial panics characteristic of market capitalism. Mao sought to make an innovative contribution to world socialism with his Great Leap Forward. His was an innovation of dubious distinction: he inadvertently figured out how to create a massive depression in an industrial system that was designed precisely to avoid one. The famine of 1960–1962 was less of an innovation. It was an unfortunate repeat of the disastrous Soviet experience of 1932–1934, which China had been fortunate to avoid in its earlier collectivization campaign.[82]

The collapse of the Chinese economy in the early 1960s was as severe as the United States' Great Depression. Per capita income dropped 32 percent in the United States between 1929 and 1933; in China it dropped 35 percent between 1959 and 1962. The two depressions, however, had different causes. The Great Depression was created by deep structural problems in a market economy, and as a result the United States did not fully recover until 1940. China's depression was created entirely by faulty government policy, and the economy revived more quickly after those policies were abandoned. China returned to pre–Great Leap levels of output by 1964, only two years after the low point.[83]

China's economic crisis had political and organizational causes. They were political because of Mao's extraordinarily bad judgment and his dogmatic bullying of other leaders who disagreed with him. They were political also because of Mao's reaction to criticisms at the Lushan Plenum and the fierce Antirightist Campaign that he launched in order to squelch criticism. That campaign prevented a timely correction to Leap policies that could have saved tens of millions of lives. The causes were organizational because of the way that pressures from the top induced unrealistic pledges by provincial, regional, and local officials to increase industrial and agricultural output. They were organizational because these officials, faced with a choice between reporting actual failure or imaginary success, chose the latter. Mao's intervention had caused both his economic system and his mobilization-based political organization to break down. In Manchuria in 1948–1949, Mao had seized victory from the jaws of defeat by pushing his army and party organization far beyond ordinary limits. Ten years later he used the same methods and seized defeat from the jaws of victory. Mao could not have undermined his credibility as a leader and thinker in a more spectacular fashion. The political fallout from the Great Leap disaster would take several years to become manifest, but when it did so in the form of the Cultural Revolution, it hit China very hard.

9

Toward the Cultural Revolution

A DISASTER OF THE MAGNITUDE of the Great Leap, attributable directly to Mao's bullying and erratic leadership, was bound to create serious political fallout. Surprisingly, it did not lead to efforts to remove him from office, nor did it seriously weaken him politically. But Mao was forced to retreat from his unrealistic views about the speed of economic development. Other leaders, even those who had initially supported the Leap and who acquiesced in Mao's attack on Marshal Peng Dehuai and his "antiparty clique," took this opportunity to rein in the political excesses of the period. They subtly tried to steer economic policy away from Mao's obsession with class struggle as a way to speed industrial development and took strong measures to repair a badly damaged economy.

Mao initially agreed to backtrack on Great Leap policies. In agriculture this meant dividing the massively enlarged communes into more manageable units, closing the communal meal halls, ending military-style mobilization of labor, and restoring production teams and in many places household farming, with clearer incentives and rewards for production. In industry, it meant returning authority to managers and technical specialists, respecting their advice, ending crash production drives organized by party branches, and providing incentives for workers in the form of wage raises and bonuses. Throughout China, it meant a relaxation of the shrill insistence that economic policy reflected a class struggle between the proletariat and the bourgeoisie. Ideas prevalent in the modern socialist bloc about how to remedy the flaws of Soviet-style economies were given a broader hearing. Intellectuals and scientists were to be given greater autonomy to consider ideas and express viewpoints that were suppressed by the party's ideologues. Class origins and political loyalty were to be de-emphasized in university admissions.

Mao tolerated these changes only to a point. He viewed them as temporary concessions to repair problems inadvertently created by the Leap. Even in the depths of China's depression and famine, he bridled at frank assessments that portrayed the Leap as the disaster that it was. And he reasserted his insistence on class struggle as soon as the worst of the economic crisis had passed. Though Mao did criticize himself for excessive optimism, he never admitted that the core ideas behind the Great Leap were at fault. He continued to assert, despite all evidence to the contrary, that the positive accomplishments of the Leap far outweighed its shortcomings.[1]

More disturbing to him was the fact that some leaders, led by a stubborn Liu Shaoqi, frankly challenged his claim that the Leap had many accomplishments to commend it. Also troubling to Mao was the call to rehabilitate those wrongly accused of "right-wing opportunism" in 1959 and also those purged for "opposing rash advance" in 1957–1958. All of these subtly implied that Mao had committed a fundamental "error of line." The limited thaw in intellectual life, moreover, bred the airing of views that were clearly opposed to Mao's most cherished commitments and suggested a different path toward building socialism that reflected negatively on Mao himself. Mao soon turned to loyal subordinates to push back against these trends, reviving his insistence on the centrality of class struggle under socialism.

Rescuing China from Mao's Leap

In November 1960 the party finally issued an "urgent bulletin," drafted by Zhou Enlai, calling for the restoration of smaller collective farms, the end to commandeering the resources of teams and households, the restoration of private plots for rural families and their right to engage in small-scale household production, the restoration of the work point system, increased rural incomes, the revival of rural markets, and "a genuine balance between work and rest."[2] A few weeks later Mao made a limited self-criticism at a party conference, admitting that he had erred in expecting an overly rapid transition to communal ownership and in pushing too many large public works projects. He conceded that changes in ownership and agricultural organization would take more time to complete.[3] These moves finally permitted the long-delayed correction that brought the Great Leap Forward to a halt.

By this time it was clear that the Leap had led to mass starvation, and Mao could no longer maintain his fantasy that the problem was due to "false reporting and grain hoarding." He sent out investigation teams to rural areas led by his political secretaries and other top officials. Liu Shaoqi, Deng Xiaoping, Zhou Enlai, and other leaders went to rural areas themselves to investigate in the aftermath of the famine.[4] What they learned shocked them: not until the policies were clearly reversed, and they went to the countryside themselves, did they grasp the full measure of the brutality and suffering to which China's peasants were subjected by local officials during the Great Leap Forward.[5]

Assigning Responsibility

Once the famine was acknowledged within the higher reaches of the party, it became increasingly difficult to assert that the positive accomplishments of the Leap greatly outweighed its shortcomings, and that problems were attributable to the schemes of alien class elements. In January 1961 the party proceeded to make concessions to household farming, rural markets, technical expertise and material incentives in industry, and greater autonomy in scientific research and intellectual life.[6] But there were widely varied understandings within the party about what had gone wrong. The Central Committee convened an unusually large party conference in January 1962 designed to talk through the experience and "unify thinking" about the economic crisis. Officials in charge of party committees at five levels of the national hierarchy were invited to Beijing for a session known as the Seven Thousand Cadres Conference.[7]

The conference began with small-group breakout sessions to discuss a report drafted by Liu Shaoqi and Deng Xiaoping. It was a contradictory mix of wholehearted affirmation of the correctness of the General Line that inspired the Leap while pointing out a series of errors committed by the "party center."[8] This led to an unexpected level of questioning about whether the policies themselves, rather than local implementation, were the real cause. This in turn provoked a reaction by staunch defenders of the Leap's core policies, prompting Mao to order Liu to have his drafting committee revise the report. The committee itself split over assigning responsibility to the party's top leadership. Some members argued strongly that the entire party leadership shared responsibility, including Mao. This led others to strenuously defend Mao's leadership as indispensible and unerring, and to affirm the absolute correctness of his vision.[9]

When Liu Shaoqi read his report to the conference, he carefully prefaced his remarks with praise for Mao, but he also said several things that flew in the face of Mao's claims. Liu said that agricultural production had drastically decreased from 1959 to 1961, and that industrial output dropped 40 percent. The Great Leap Forward, he concluded, had actually been a great leap backward. He pointed out that when he visited villages in Hunan, the farmers told him that the problems were "three parts natural disaster and seven parts man-made disaster"—a counterpoint to Mao's repeated insistence that it was "nine fingers" good to "one finger" bad. Liu was equally blunt about attributing responsibility: "If we fundamentally refuse to acknowledge that there have been shortcomings and errors, or claim they're just on minor issues and try to beat around the bush or cover things up, and don't practically, realistically, and thoroughly acknowledge our past and existing failings, then no summing up of the experience can be carried out, and bad cannot be turned to good." Liu called the core policies behind the Leap an "experiment," and said that the ultimate verdict would become clear only as a result of practical experience.[10]

Liu's assessment was far more negative than Mao's, and his statement about acknowledging errors, whether or not intended as a challenge to Mao, caused the conference to be extended for several days while a number of delegates felt compelled to defend the correctness of the Leap and pledge loyalty to Mao, blaming the Leap's problems on natural disasters that were "exceptionally serious and long-lasting." Perhaps the most vocal and enthusiastic support came from Lin Biao, head of China's military and member of the Politburo Standing Committee, who stood strongly on Mao's side on this occasion as he had at the Lushan Plenum of 1959 in the attacks on Peng Dehuai.[11]

After the conference, Mao departed Beijing for Wuhan, and Liu Shaoqi convened a series of meetings to plan measures to rescue the economy. These meetings gave a much more dire assessment of China's economy than the one painted at the Seven Thousand Cadres Conference. Liu stated that the party had not yet sufficiently faced up to facts, and he argued that China was facing a deep crisis, requiring not routine readjustments but "emergency measures." When Liu, Deng Xiaoping, and Zhou Enlai flew to Wuhan to present this dire assessment to Mao, he agreed to the emergency measures but objected that the report still painted too bleak a picture.[12]

Despite Mao's objections, Liu forged ahead with recovery measures. In May he developed a plan to restructure the economy, and he stated that the economic foundation of China was unsound, a situation that could lead to political instability. Under his direction a series of measures were designed to put the economy on a firmer footing. The urban population was drastically reduced, with 10 million shipped back to the countryside by the end of 1962. Capital construction projects were curtailed. Experiments with household agriculture were expanded, and party members who were criticized and disciplined for right-wing opportunism would have their cases reexamined, potentially leading to reversal of their verdicts.[13]

Mao surely sensed a political drift in the party leadership that was flowing against him. He was particularly alarmed by reports that individual farming was proving popular with regional officials and farmers, and that it was being implemented more extensively than he had anticipated. He began to push back hard against the practice by harshly criticizing provincial officials who promoted it.[14] In July, shortly after returning to Beijing, Mao summoned Liu Shaoqi to his living quarters. Mao confronted him, expressing anger at his negative reports and the rush to backtrack on so many Leap policies. Liu responded with bluntness that virtually no one in the top leadership circle had dared with Mao for years: "History will record the role you and I played in the starvation of so many people, and the cannibalism will also be memorialized!" Mao reportedly shot back, "The Three Red Banners have been refuted, the land has been divided up, and you did nothing? What will happen after I die?"[15]

Mao must have sensed that Liu's stubborn insistence on the seriousness of China's economic crisis, and his measures to reverse the failures of the Leap, signaled that his commitment to Mao's most cherished objectives was uncertain, along with that of other top leaders. Particularly telling in this exchange is Mao's query, "What will happen after I die?" He was already acutely aware of how Khrushchev had repudiated Stalin in 1956, and his comments after the Lushan Plenum of

1959 suggested that he was already aware of talk in the top reaches of the party that his behavior resembled Stalin's in his "later years." Mao's concerns, in hindsight, have to be viewed as realistic. Even if Mao did not need to worry that his control over the party was in danger, he had every reason to be concerned that after his death his core ideas would be repudiated.

A Temporary Thaw

The Great Leap Forward was launched as a general attack on intellectuals and a denigration of their claims to authority. Beginning with the Antirightist Campaign and throughout the Leap there were attacks on bourgeois science, social science, and traditional humanistic fields. Class struggle had to be reflected in scholarship. Foreign bourgeois ideas and "revisionist" views from the socialist bloc were criticized and suppressed, along with traditional humanistic learning and any scholarship or art that did not express a "Marxist worldview" and active support of the party's General Line. Older intellectuals were sent to perform manual labor and lost their leadership positions in universities and academies in favor of younger, party-oriented individuals. Engineers were told to learn from peasants and workers; fields like mathematics and scientific theory were slighted in favor of the teaching of practical technical skills.[16]

As the party backed away from the Great Leap, it also retracted these counterproductive policies and began to court academics and educated specialists as part of the strategy of economic recovery. This led to a brief period of intellectual relaxation, a "thaw" similar in some respects to that initiated by Mao during the Hundred Flowers. This time, however, it was Liu Shaoqi who initiated the thaw, and the purpose was not to promote criticism of the party bureaucracy, but instead to reengage China's educated elite in the urgent task of economic construction. In mid-1961 the party signaled that it was not necessary for intellectuals to constantly profess ideological devotion to the party. They could show their patriotism simply by contributing to China's development.[17] This was followed by the rehabilitation of many of those condemned as rightists in 1957. Many were permitted to return to their former jobs.[18] The party's new professed attitude was one of respect for the skills and learning of intellectuals, which were no longer denigrated as "superstition" rooted in bourgeois ideology.[19]

The new policy permitted greater latitude for the use of scientific theories, even social science theories, from bourgeois sources. Economists began to offer arguments about economic reform that paralleled ideas being widely discussed in Eastern Europe and the Soviet Union. These ideas were rooted in critiques of the Soviet model of economic development that began in the late Stalin era and that developed further after his death in 1953.[20] China's leading journals of economics soon published articles that echoed Soviet bloc discussions about profit and efficiency under socialism, the role of prices and market mechanisms, the promise of mathematical modeling in the planning process, and the utility of charging interest on capital.[21] All of these ideas had been previously condemned as applications of capitalist economic principles as reflected in bourgeois social science. Among those who led these discussions was Sun Yefang, who had first advanced these ideas in 1956, and who resumed his advocacy from 1961 to 1963.[22]

The period also saw a brief cultural renaissance. Banned books were republished. Literary styles other than orthodox socialist realism—the unfailing celebration of proletarian heroes—were openly encouraged. The intrinsic value of art for art's sake—independent of class or political content—was more widely appreciated. Official journals and newspapers criticized cultural bureaucrats who acted like oppressive overlords, ignorant about literature and art and interested only in asserting their power and privilege.[23] During this period a major literary conference convened by the deputy director of the CCP Propaganda Department criticized the doctrines of socialist realism, and encouraged writers to denounce mass campaigns and crash programs, to portray the Great Leap in fiction not as a utopia in the making but as an unfortunate tragedy, and to depict accurately the suffering of peasants.[24]

Despite the new latitude for discussion of formerly proscribed ideas, intellectuals, especially in universities, were understandably much more hesitant than they had been in 1957. There were no independent journals or clubs as in the Hundred Flowers. The most critical expressions actually came from educated officials who were relatively high in the party hierarchy, principally in the CCP Propaganda Department and Beijing Party Committee. The criticisms that emanated from intellectuals in these institutions were not aimed at the party as in the Hundred Flowers, but at the kinds of policies recently pushed by Mao and the political mentality that they expressed.

One center for this activity was the Beijing Municipal Party Committee, under the city's first party secretary, Peng Zhen. During breakout discussion sessions at the Seven Thousand Cadres Conference, Peng had been one of the few who dared to suggest that Mao himself shared responsibility for the Great Leap's disasters.[25] Beijing's newspapers and journals published a series of essays and fictional works that appeared on the surface to be mild social and historical commentaries, but could also be interpreted as subtle criticisms of Mao's leadership and his recent policies, although they were not widely understood as such at the time. The essays of Deng Tuo are one example. Reflecting Mao's displeasure at the paper's delayed and reluctant support for his Hundred Flowers policy in 1957, Deng was removed as editor of *People's Daily* and was kicked upstairs as director of ideology and culture for the Beijing Party Committee.[26] His regular column in the *Beijing Evening News*, "Evening Chats at Yanshan," which totaled 152 installments from March 1961 to September 1962, contained a number of essays that could be read as indirect criticisms of the Mao cult, arbitrary leadership, irrational behavior and arrogance of officials, the denigration of science, the ignorantly wishful thinking behind the Great Leap, and the punishment of honest officials who bring bad news.[27] Many of these themes were elaborated in the short column "Notes from Three Family Village," which appeared in each issue of the journal *Frontline*, edited by Deng Tuo, at about the same period of time. The pieces spanned a range of topics and were written under a pseudonym, primarily by Deng Tuo, Wu Han, and Liao Mosha, a former journalist and historical novelist who was now a senior official in the Beijing Municipal Party Committee, responsible for propaganda and education.[28]

Wu Han, a distinguished historian of the Ming dynasty and one of several deputy mayors of Beijing, wrote a series of plays about a courageous and upright Ming dynasty official named Hai Rui, who insisted on offering criticism to an isolated and out-of-touch emperor, telling him that if the peasants' plight was not alleviated by returning the land to them, the dynasty would be lost. In June 1959, shortly before the Lushan Plenum, he had published in *People's Daily* a vernacular translation of Hai Rui's 1566 memorial to the Ming emperor, under the title "Hai Rui Scolds the Emperor." The translation included the passage, "In earlier years, you did quite a few good things, but . . . all officials in and out of the capital know that your mind is not right, that you are too arbitrary, too perverse.

You think you alone are right, you refuse to accept criticism and your mistakes are many."[29] After the Great Leap, Wu Han wrote these plays at the urging of one of Mao's secretaries, who heard Mao complain in 1959 that no one dared speak up in front of him. Mao responded positively, praised the work, had several friendly encounters with the historian, and gave him a signed copy of the fourth volume of his *Selected Works.*[30]

Reasserting the Radical Vision

This period of relaxation was brief. Mao soon pushed back to reassert his vision and reaffirm his control over the political agenda. At party meetings in August 1962 he criticized excessively gloomy assessments of the Leap, enthusiasm for individual farming, and the trend of "reversing verdicts" on right-wing opportunists.[31] Warning against class polarization due to individual farming, he asked, "Have we arrived at socialism or at capitalism? Do we want agricultural collectivization? Are we going to divide up the fields and assign production quotas to households or have collectivization?" He blamed the increasing trend toward private farming on a "certain petty bourgeois component" in the party, individuals with only a quasi-Marxist outlook: "There are quite a few comrades within our party who lack adequate psychological preparation for socialist revolution." Mao asserted that the verdict against Peng Dehuai's "antiparty clique" was correct.[32]

Mao reasserted the core of his political beliefs in a speech to a party plenum in September 1962. It proved to be the ideological inspiration for the Cultural Revolution.[33]

> In the entire historical period of the transition from capitalism to communism . . . there exists a class struggle between the two roads of socialism and capitalism. The overthrown reactionary ruling class has not resigned itself to its demise; they're still scheming for a restoration to power. At the same time, society retains some bourgeois influence and the force of custom from the old society, as well as a tendency toward spontaneous capitalism among a portion of small producers. . . . It's unavoidable that this class struggle should be reflected within the party. The influence of foreign imperialism and domestic bourgeoisie are the social roots of revisionist thinking within the party. While carrying out struggle against class enemies at home and abroad, we must be at all times on guard and resolute in our opposition to all types of opportunistic ideological tendencies within the party.[34]

The Socialist Education Movement

Mao's renewed assertion of the ubiquity of class struggle under socialism soon led to the Socialist Education Movement, launched tentatively in late 1962, initially in order to target corruption and abuse of power in the countryside. Mao had asserted that the problems of the Great Leap were the work of class enemies who had seized control of the party at the grass roots. Mao asserted that the fate of socialism rested in China's countryside, and this new campaign pursued the issue further.[35] The campaign took another year to take shape. The basic approach was to send work teams of party officials to rural areas to investigate local abuses. But there were fundamental questions to be resolved. How large should the effort be, and how many work teams should be mobilized? How harshly should the targets of the campaign be treated, and how many officials should be removed from office? Should the work teams be under the authority of county-level party committees who might cover up misbehavior by their direct subordinates, or should the campaign be run from the prefecture or province, taking it completely out of the hands of local party officials? The campaign proceeded in fits and starts, without a clear animating focus, for well over a year.[36]

Although Mao and Liu Shaoqi had previously clashed about the Great Leap, Liu wholeheartedly embraced the notion that rural problems were a manifestation of class struggle. He accepted Mao's premise that class enemies had taken over communes and had infected their party branches. Liu took over the campaign in 1964 and made it his own, and expanded it to include urban institutions as well. He ordered the formation of much larger work teams, made up of officials of higher rank and controlled from higher reaches of the party hierarchy. He dictated a more militant stance, a more dire definition of the severity of the problem, and the adoption of harsh methods against rural leaders who had engaged in corruption and abuse of power. Liu's militant stance and energetic mobilization to prosecute this class struggle initially met with Mao's wholehearted approval, because it pursued with a ruthless thoroughness Mao's vision of class struggle under socialism. With Mao's approval, large work teams were dispatched throughout the country. They launched extensive investigations and purges of large percentages of local cadres. The campaign unfolded through mass meetings, struggle sessions, and on occasion beatings and suicides of targeted officials.[37]

This was the largest assault on the national party organization since 1949. It wrought havoc on local party organizations in the countryside, which readily collapsed under the assault of militant work teams, requiring that authority be taken over by the work teams themselves.[38] It had a similarly disruptive effect on urban institutions, throwing party committee authority into question in enterprises and universities. A newly assertive Liu Shaoqi showed determination to exert his authority over the national party machine, and he dressed down provincial party secretaries who dragged their feet.[39]

One would have thought that Liu's stance would please Mao, but by the end of 1964 Mao expressed strong objections to the way that Liu was running the campaign, and in particular with the way in which he was asserting his authority as a proponent of a radical political line. Mao's concerns may have been touched off by news of Khrushchev's ouster by his Politburo colleagues in October 1964, and the subsequent perception in Beijing that Moscow's new leaders were carrying out "Khrushchevism without Khrushchev."[40] Now that Liu was taking over Mao's signature obsession with class struggle and pursuing it aggressively, this raised the specter of "Maoism without Mao." More significantly, the new Soviet leadership denounced Khrushchev for "harebrained schemes" in the economy, and for an erratic and moody style of leadership that led to bullying his colleagues and treating them with disrespect.[41] Mao's transgressions in both areas evidently were far worse. By directing this Maoist campaign with such intensity, Liu appeared to be asserting his own claims to leadership.

Mao provoked a disagreement with Liu Shaoqi over the aims and methods of the Socialist Education Movement at the end of 1964. At a December party conference he openly criticized Liu's running of the campaign.[42] He complained that it was too broad and focused on too low a level in the party hierarchy. Mao insisted that the campaign should focus on party cadres, and instead of focusing on corruption, it should "attack the faction of capitalist roaders in the party." At a later session, when Mao went on the attack again, Liu refused to be walked on, an unusual stance for members of the top leadership. Liu questioned Mao openly at the meeting, claiming that he did not understand the concept of "capitalist roaders in the party," asking Mao to explain what he meant. The next day Mao surprised everyone with a long monologue on the Socialist Education Movement that ended with accusations against unnamed officials for trying to revoke his right to attend meetings and to express his own views.[43] Mao took over the conference and ordered the retraction of a document issued about the Socialist Education Movement the previous day and had a new document issued in its place, which emphasized that the campaign should focus on "people in positions of authority taking the capitalist road" even in prefectural, provincial, and central party organs.[44] With this document, Mao seized back the class struggle agenda from Liu Shaoqi.

By shaking up party organizations at the grass roots, the Socialist Education Movement created deep divisions that would surface once the Cultural Revolution got under way. This impact was most obvious in urban areas. In the fall of 1964 the campaign was extended into the cities and targeted 1,800 large state enterprises and a number of universities and research institutes. The focus in these organizations was less on corruption and abuse of power than on "peaceful evolution" toward revisionism.[45]

The way that the campaign divided urban enterprises is illustrated by the Yangzi River Machine Works, a large state enterprise in Nanjing.[46] This large manufacturing complex was under the dual leadership of the Fourth Ministry of Machine Building in Beijing and the Nanjing Municipal Party Committee. The ministry was in charge of business operations while the Nanjing Party Committee directed party affairs. The enterprise was founded in 1945 by the Nationalist government, and had many workers and staff from that era. These "old personnel" had an identity distinct from the younger workers, technicians, and demobilized People's Liberation Army soldiers who came later.

In September 1964, the Fourth Ministry of Machine Building sent a work team of more than 600 cadres to investigate the enterprise, headed by the ministry's party vice secretary and director of its Political Department, who had a military background. The work team head, representing the ministry, concluded that the factory's party leadership, under the direction of the Nanjing Party Committee, had become thoroughly revisionist. The work team conducted a deep purge of the party apparatus. The party secretary lost his post, and close to half of the middle-level and higher cadres were labeled members of his clique. Almost all of them were subjected to struggle sessions along with a number of workers and technicians who were criticized as their loyal followers. The conduct of the campaign was an implicit rebuke of the Nanjing party authorities.

In January 1965, after Mao's criticism of Liu Shaoqi's version of the campaign, the ministry's work team was ordered to engage in self-criticism and moderate and narrow its purge. Many of the factory leaders targeted in the earlier phase were restored to their posts. The work team withdrew in July 1965 and a few months later the ministry sent a veteran army officer to serve as the new party secretary. The previous factory director and some of the other top managers and party secretaries survived the purge and kept their posts. This was a compromise between the Beijing ministry and the Nanjing party authorities. The purge was halted in midcourse, but the work team remained in charge and appointed new leaders. The Socialist Education Movement opened up severe conflicts within this large state enterprise without ultimately resolving them, creating deep cleavages that would break out into open warfare in the fall of 1966.

A second example traces the same process at a leading university—one that would soon have momentous national implications. The cleavages created by the Socialist Education Movement at Peking University would provide the spark that initiated the Cultural Revolution in June 1966. In July 1964 Kang Sheng ordered a small team of ten cadres, led by the vice head of the CCP Propaganda Department, to investigate the university's leadership. They interviewed a number of disgruntled cadres and instructors, the most outspoken of which were Philosophy Department political instructors and veteran party members who had been involved in a series of conflicts with the university's party leadership since the late 1950s.[47] Joining these instructors was Nie Yuanzi, a party committee member who had become general branch secretary of the Philosophy Department only months before. The investigation team submitted its report at the end of August. It asserted that there were many politically impure elements and foreign spies in the university and that school's party committee did nothing about it. Kang Sheng accepted the report and its conclusion that "bad elements" had wormed their way into the school's party apparatus.

A large Socialist Education Movement work team went to the campus in October 1964 to begin a full-scale investigation. Led again by the same vice head of the CCP Propaganda Department, it was composed of over 200 cadres from propaganda, cultural, and educational units nationwide. At the end of November the work team concluded that the school's party organization had indeed taken the capitalist road. In January 1965 they began to stage struggle sessions against alleged class enemies; large numbers of party secretaries and standing committee members found themselves accused of antiparty activity. The school's party leadership, and in particular Party Secretary Lu Ping, was charged with permitting open subversion.

The campaign seemed excessive to many members of the work team and to officials in the Beijing Municipal Party Committee, the CCP Propaganda Department, and the Central Party Secretariat. In January 1965, the university's party secretary, Lu Ping, and a deputy party secretary, Peng Peiyun, made self-criticisms at a meeting of the Beijing Municipal Party Committee, but they also protested the campaign's methods. A heated debate ensued, but Beijing Party Secretary Peng Zhen sided with Lu Ping. Deng Xiaoping agreed, criticized Kang Sheng for instigating the episode, and cleared the university's party leadership of wrongdoing. In March 1965 Deng Xiaoping ordered the CCP Propaganda Department to conduct a rectification campaign of the university and work team, and correct the problems that had made the campaign so disruptive.

The tables were then turned on militant work team members and their supporters in the university. In three conferences held between March and July 1965, the work team was criticized for "leftist" errors. Members of the university's party apparatus who had supported the work team's accusations were forced to make self-criticisms—most notably Nie Yuanzi, the Philosophy Department's party branch secretary, and a number of instructors in the department who had supported her. Those who had stood up to denounce the school's party secretary now had to serve under him. The cleavages opened up during the campaign would come back with a vengeance one year later.[48]

The Break with the Soviet Union

China's relationship with the Soviet Union had been strained since Khrushchev's denunciation of Stalin in 1956 and had deteriorated further during the Great Leap Forward, a campaign that the Soviets viewed with open skepticism. Mao bristled at the USSR's leadership of the world communist movement, especially over their assessment of the world situation and the desirability of relaxing superpower tensions. The relationship worsened in the early 1960s and led effectively to a final break in 1963. The final exchanges between the two sides dramatically illustrate the doctrinal differences that divided the two main communist powers at that time and led the Chinese side to articulate a vision that was pursued with a vengeance during the Cultural Revolution.

The Chinese view was presented in a lengthy statement about the world communist movement in July 1963. The core of the Chinese position was essentially about confrontation with imperialism and de-Stalinization.[49] The Chinese asserted that American imperialism was pursuing worldwide aggression and must be confronted. World peace could be achieved only through armed struggle, not appeasement and naive calls for universal disarmament. Nuclear weapons did not alter the necessity for struggle and revolution; the Soviets could not use the threat of nuclear war to back away from support for revolutionary struggles in the Third World. Socialism would not triumph simply through a peaceful competition with the capitalist world system. Class struggle and the dictatorship of the proletariat inevitably persist for a long time after the establishment of a socialist state, and efforts to scale back the vigilant hunt for internal class enemies and spies that implied that former social classes no longer existed were bourgeois concepts. Attacks on the "personality cult" were nothing more than an excuse for the Soviet Union to force other communist states to change their leaders.[50]

The Soviets responded with an open letter to the world communist movement. They expressed surprise that any communist party would express support for the personality cult, which had long been exposed as a petty bourgeois notion. The clear implication was that the Chinese were simply defending Mao's anachronistic cult of personality, a symptom of the worst features of Stalinism. They also insisted that nuclear weapons did lead to a "radical, qualitative" change in the nature of struggle against capitalism, because a nuclear exchange would wipe out the proletariat of a country just as certainly as the small number of capitalists. The Soviets charged that China's position lacked any class content because it treated with utter insensitivity the lives of hundreds of millions of individuals in the working class who would perish in nuclear war. The Soviets signed a partial test ban treaty with the United States immediately afterward on July 20, guaranteeing a final split between the two communist powers.[51]

The relationship broken, China geared up for a massive propaganda campaign against the Soviet Union. The task was led by Kang Sheng, who presided over more than one hundred writers divided into eight working groups housed in the Diaoyutai state guest compound. They produced a stream of polemical statements about Soviet policy, the most important of which was the last, the "Ninth Polemic" of July 1964.[52] The essay expressed what was to be the ideological justification for Mao's Cultural Revolution.

The document portrayed a Soviet Union that was the scene of repeated attacks by the bourgeoisie on the proletariat. The "revisionist Khrushchev clique" promoted material incentives, widened income differences by permitting high salaries, defamed the dictatorship of the proletariat by attacking the personality cult, and substituted capitalist for socialist methods of management. "The revisionist Khrushchev clique are the political representatives of the Soviet bourgeoisie, and particularly of its privileged stratum," and they had taken control of the party and government after purging genuine communists. As a result, "the first socialist country in the world . . . is now facing an unprecedented danger of capitalist restoration." Khrushchev adhered to the American policy of "peaceful evolution," which promoted the rollback of socialism.[53]

The essay then turned to the implications for China. The crucial question for China was how to train a generation of revolutionary successors who would carry on the true Marxist-Leninist tradition, whether the party and state would remain in the hands of genuine proletarian revolutionaries, and whether their successors would continue to "march along the correct road laid down by Marxism-Leninism." The central question was how to prevent the emergence of Khrushchev-style revisionism in China. This was "a matter of life and death for our Party and our country. . . . It is a question of fundamental importance to the proletarian revolutionary cause for a hundred, a thousand, nay ten thousand years."[54] The essay did not say how this should be accomplished. This would be the objective of the Cultural Revolution, launched two years later.

Preparing Mao's Assault on the Party

Mao prepared carefully for the coming upheaval. Although his colleagues were almost always deferential to him personally, he could not be certain that there would be no coordinated resistance if his intentions were known in advance. Not until his loyalists were in place would he be ready to launch his assault on the party. Mao intended not merely to remove from the party leadership prominent communists from the revolutionary generation—starting with the second-ranking official, his designated successor Liu Shaoqi—he also intended to mobilize a massive purge of the entire party apparatus, to root out all officials at all levels who in word or deed showed a tendency toward "revisionist" thought and behavior. Mao's charge—it would soon become clear—was that there was a massive nationwide conspiracy of revisionist officials, influenced by remnants of former exploiting classes and their ideas. He planned to wipe them out in a massive upheaval of as-yet undetermined form and duration.

Mao could not do this without the services of individuals whose personal loyalty to him transcended their loyalty to the party organization. These individuals had proven themselves utterly loyal to him in past conflicts and could be relied upon to do his bidding without question. Mao's actions were the very definition of an antiparty conspiracy. His moves from late 1964 to mid-1966 laid the groundwork for seizing control of the party apparatus, the government, and the army and security services, cementing his unquestioned personal control as his attack on the party began.

The two most important individuals in this respect were his wife, Jiang Qing, and Lin Biao. Jiang Qing had not previously been active in Chinese politics, held no government or party post, and had not appeared in public for many years. In the early 1960s she became active in artistic circles, promoting operas and plays with revolutionary content and becoming a leading critic of traditional themes from the prerevolution era. With Mao's backing, she prompted the publication of harshly critical essays of playwrights and productions that lacked revolutionary messages. In the course of her activities she formed an alliance with sympathetic ideologues in the Shanghai propaganda apparatus, in particular Zhang Chunqiao, who was a member of the Shanghai Municipal Party Committee and head of its Propaganda Department, and Yao Wenyuan, who was Zhang's subordinate as deputy propaganda chief and editor of *Liberation Daily*.[55] When Jiang was unable to have her attacks on authors published in the Beijing media, she found ready cooperation in Shanghai. As she became more active in suppressing alleged subversion in artistic fields, she received help from the armed forces and its publications, which Lin Biao put at her disposal. Jiang organized forums on literature and art under the auspices of the PLA as well as the Shanghai

Party Committee, during which she expressed harsh criticisms of the laxity of Beijing cultural and propaganda officials while praising individuals like Lin Biao and Kang Sheng.[56]

Lin Biao had shown unswerving loyalty to Mao, and his leadership of the PLA during the final phases of the civil war had vindicated Mao's view that victory could be won. He supported Mao during the Lushan Plenum in 1959 and the Seven Thousand Cadres Conference of 1962, when he strongly backed Mao's charges against the "Peng Dehuai antiparty clique" and heaped extravagant praise on the Great Leap Forward. After Lin replaced Peng Dehuai as minister of defense, he turned the PLA into a totally Maoist institution, a model of upholding guerrilla traditions and the idea that human motivation is more important than modern weaponry. He argued in conferences of senior military officers that Mao was a genius, and his Thought was the "apex of Marxism-Leninism." He organized a highly publicized campaign to propagate Mao Zedong Thought throughout the armed forces. In 1961 he ordered the compilation and publication of a small handbook of Mao's aphorisms, which later achieved fame as the "little red book," *Quotations from Chairman Mao Zedong.*[57]

Another important Mao loyalist was Kang Sheng. Kang directed the later phases of the party's ferocious rectification campaign in Yan'an in the early 1940s. He suffered from the backlash against the use of torture to extract false confessions and for the wide scope of the campaign, essentially taking the blame for a policy that Mao had initiated. Once a member of the party's top leadership, he was sidelined afterward and served in provincial posts in the 1950s. At the Eighth Party Congress in 1956 he was drastically demoted, apparently as part of the general revulsion against widespread repression by security services in the wave of de-Stalinization in the communist bloc.[58] In the early 1960s, Mao brought Kang back to Beijing to assist him in fighting revisionism and ideological backsliding and developing the polemics against the Soviet Union. Kang's elevation was completely due to Mao's patronage, and he was entirely dependent on Mao's support for his position.[59]

Chen Boda was in a similar position. As Mao's political secretary in Yan'an, he played a key role in developing the Mao cult and Mao Zedong Thought, and along with Kang Sheng he was responsible for the rectification campaign of the early 1940s. Chen had unfailingly supported Mao's position in the Great Leap Forward and in the post-Leap disagreements about its causes. The party's theoretical journal, *Red Flag*, founded under his editorship in 1958, became the home of a number of leftist authors who could be counted upon to provide ideological cover for Mao's initiatives, and *Red Flag* effectively became Mao's unofficial mouthpiece during the 1960s. Chen, like Kang Sheng, owed his position entirely to Mao's support and patronage.[60]

Another crucial loyalist was Premier Zhou Enlai, although his relationship with Mao was very different. Zhou had a long history of prominent positions in the party, and in the 1920s and early 1930s had outranked Mao. As premier, he headed China's State Council and the national government and had a reputation as a skilled, tireless, and honest administrator. He had a well-deserved reputation for pragmatism and loyalty to the party line. Above all, he had unfailingly proven himself loyal to Mao since the 1930s, taking his side each time that Mao chose to attack colleagues for alleged errors, including the purge of Peng Dehuai. Whenever he was criticized for deviation from Mao's thinking, he unfailingly engaged in long and abject self-criticism and pledges of loyalty. Mao valued Zhou for his loyalty and administrative ability, but he was not a loyalist motivated by belief in—or even approval of—Mao's ideas.[61]

Mao proceeded with moves to ensure that his loyalists were in control of the levers of national power. In a series of coordinated moves beginning in November 1965, he removed potential sources of resistance to his plans to upend China's political order. He had Peng Dehuai moved out of Beijing to the far southwest and abruptly removed Yang Shangkun from his position as head of the CCP's General Office, which controlled the flow of documents at the top of the party apparatus. Mao replaced Yang with Wang Dongxing, a Mao loyalist who headed the central guard unit charged with Mao's security and who accompanied Mao everywhere.[62] In January, he ordered an investigation of Luo Ruiqing, chief of staff of the Military Affairs Commission, who was in charge of day-to-day operations of the PLA. Luo had a history of conflict with Lin Biao over the politicization of the army and the denigration of modern weaponry and training. After a series of harsh denunciation meetings, Luo Ruiqing attempted suicide in March. This ensured that the PLA command was entirely under Lin Biao's—and Mao's—control.[63]

Peng Zhen and Lu Dingyi were the final two barriers to be removed. Peng, Beijing party secretary, also headed a party group in charge of the national propaganda apparatus. A longtime friend and associate of Liu Shaoqi, he had openly resisted Mao's rectification campaign of 1956–1957.[64] At the Seven Thousand Cadres Conference in 1962, he suggested that Mao shared responsibility for the Great Leap disasters. In response to escalating denunciations of literary and intellectual figures in 1964 and 1965, Peng had tried to blunt politicized attacks and insisted on distinguishing artistic from political issues.[65] In these efforts Peng had worked closely with Lu Dingyi, head of the CCP Propaganda Department.

Mao struck after Liu Shaoqi left for an extended trip abroad in late March. During Liu's absence, Mao summoned Kang Sheng, Jiang Qing, and Chen Boda to Hangzhou, and he condemned Peng Zhen and the CCP Propaganda Department, headed by Lu Dingyi, for protecting "antiparty elements" and resisting his directives. He ordered the disbanding of the CCP Propaganda Department, the Beijing Party Committee, and Peng Zhen's five-man group in charge of culture.[66] On April 2, *People's Daily* denounced a "black line" in the Beijing propaganda establishment. Peng Zhen, Luo Ruiqing, Lu Dingyi, and Yang Shangkun were denounced as an "antiparty group." Their subordinates were arrested. The Beijing party apparatus was decimated by purges, and several prominent figures committed suicide.[67]

Through these rapid and coordinated moves, Mao secured his personal control over the national propaganda apparatus, the armed forces, and the communication flow to the national party apparatus. Security arrangements in the capital were reorganized. Armed troops and public security forces were placed under the unified command of a newly appointed commander of the Beijing Garrison.[68] Liu Shaoqi was far from the capital when Mao openly revealed his hand. The first moves in Mao's antiparty conspiracy now complete, his Great Proletarian Cultural Revolution was about to begin.

10

Fractured Rebellion

Mao's cultural revolution began with the leadership purges of May 1966. But what was the Cultural Revolution? In answering this question, we can only refer to what the Cultural Revolution eventually became. Mao appears not to have had a clear plan in mind at the outset, and he was repeatedly forced to improvise and change course. At crucial junctures he was frustrated by events and by the behavior of his loyal subordinates. The struggles that he set in motion repeatedly moved in directions that he had not anticipated, forcing him to react and reconsider. Other than the destruction of the national bureaucracy and the purge of alleged revisionists, it is hard to decide whether the outcome of the Cultural Revolution was what Mao had in mind. In fact, it is very hard to say what Mao did have in mind. What the Cultural Revolution eventually became was probably not anticipated by Mao himself, or by anyone else in the party leadership.

From one perspective the Cultural Revolution was a massive purge. Its explicit purpose was to remove "people in authority taking the capitalist road," Maoist code for revisionists. Starting with Liu Shaoqi and Deng Xiaoping at the top, and eventually down to the level of party secretaries of rural communes and state factories, cadres lost their positions on an enormous scale. As in the Soviet Union in the late 1930s, vast numbers were ejected from their posts. In the Soviet Union, those purged were unfailingly sent to labor camps or executed. In China they might be imprisoned for a period, sometimes dying in custody or committing suicide, but the standard treatment was public humiliation and beatings at the hands of rebel groups, brief imprisonment in makeshift cells, and later long stints of manual labor in factories or the countryside. Unlike

Stalin's victims, the vast majority survived and eventually returned to office.

But the Cultural Revolution was much more than a leadership purge. A purge removes individuals from office while leaving the structure of offices intact. The Cultural Revolution aimed at the destruction of the bureaucratic system that China copied from the Soviet Union. In its place would be a much simpler network of committees that merged civilian and military cadres with rebel representatives, working with office staffs that were only a fraction of the size of the former bureaucratic departments. These were intended to be disciplined political hierarchies, led by individuals vetted for absolute loyalty to Mao's vision, and they were to administer China in ways that resembled the wartime mobilization against the Nationalists. Eventually, between 70 and 90 percent of the employees of central ministries were sent to rural reeducation centers known as May 7 Cadre Schools, where they performed manual labor.[1]

The destruction and rebuilding of China's party-state was to be accomplished from both above and below. Mao began with a rapid restructuring of power at the apex of the political system, the first stage of which was complete by late summer of 1966. The Central Committee's established structures were gutted by purges and paralyzed, making resistance nearly impossible. Its bureaucratic departments were downsized and merged, while decision-making authority was shifted to informal committees staffed by Mao loyalists who reported directly to him alone. These informal bodies grew in scope and power as the Cultural Revolution continued. As the formal bureaucratic structures of the party-state were further weakened via purge and dismemberment, they eventually collapsed and ceased operating. Committees of Mao loyalists at the apex of the party-state carried out the destruction and dismemberment of the national bureaucracy, on Mao's authority, even though they had no foundation in the party or state constitution.

The other distinctive feature of the Cultural Revolution was the simultaneous mobilization of a mass insurgency from below. The insurgency targeted officials at all levels that were deemed insufficiently loyal to Mao Zedong Thought. One of the primary reasons for the initial restructuring of the organs of national power was to facilitate this popular insurgency and to steer its activities in directions desired by Mao. On the surface, the student Red Guard movement that burst onto the scene so dramatically in August 1966 appeared to be chaotic and disorganized. In fact, it was monitored and guided by full-time "liaison personnel" stationed on campuses who reported on local developments while relaying advice, encouragement, and instructions to student rebels. These networks of influence steered the student movement in the summer and fall of 1966, but as the manipulation became increasingly obvious it fostered backlash and divisions.

Restructuring the Apex of National Power

The May 1966 denunciation of the Beijing "antiparty clique" began a rolling series of purges that decimated the administrative structures of the Central Committee and the city of Beijing. By July, all ten Beijing vice mayors had been removed from office, along with all but two members of the Beijing Party Secretariat. In October these two were also purged, and eighty-one department directors or vice directors were imprisoned.[2] Departments under the Central Committee Secretariat were dismembered: 234 cadres in the CCP Propaganda Department were removed from office, and the department was downsized into an Office for the Propagation of Mao Zedong Thought. The CCP Organization Department was also gutted: its entire leadership was removed in August and the vast majority of more than 200 staff placed under investigation.[3]

These changes marked a drastic shift in the structure of national power. The CCP Politburo, its Standing Committee, and the party's bureaucratic departments in the capital steadily lost power and eventually ceased to function. A new ad hoc committee, composed of those who had proven themselves personally loyal to Mao, took over their leading roles. The Central Cultural Revolution Group (CCRG) was formally established at the end of May. Its membership evolved rapidly over the next year. The key players were familiar figures whose loyalty to Mao was beyond question, and whose positions depended entirely on Mao's patronage. They were experienced almost exclusively in the field of propaganda or security, and had distinguished themselves in earlier struggles against liberalization and "bourgeois" tendencies. None of them were full members of the Politburo at the time; none of them held positions that made them responsible for government departments or the economy.[4]

Initially the CCRG was formally headed by Chen Boda, Mao's tutor in Marxism-Leninism back in the Yan'an era and editor of the party journal *Red Flag*, which became the mouthpiece of the CCRG and the authoritative voice of Mao's political line. Kang Sheng, who had driven the party's 1943 rectification campaign to violent excesses and who recently had directed the large writing group that wrote polemics against Soviet "revisionism," was a key "advisor." Two important vice heads were Jiang Qing, Mao's wife since 1938, who held no formal party or government position, and Zhang Chunqiao, the director of the Shanghai Propaganda Department, who had assisted Jiang Qing in her earlier forays against liberalization in the arts and culture. The other key members were all ideologues who had distinguished themselves as polemicists or "theorists." This included Yao Wenyuan, Zhang Chunqiao's subordinate in the Shanghai Propaganda Department, and a series of relatively young figures with histories of collaboration with Chen Boda, Kang Sheng, or both: Wang Li, Guan Feng, Qi Benyu, and Mu Xin.[5]

The CCRG became Mao's headquarters for conducting a campaign to attack, downsize, and dismantle the existing party-state. As we shall see, it was far more effective at destruction than at building new organs of power. The CCRG's authority depended entirely on Mao, and its actions were based on their understanding of Mao's intentions, which often shifted and were left vague and undefined for long periods of time. Beginning as a writing group of roughly ten individuals, over the next year it grew rapidly into a small bureaucracy that occupied seven villas in the Diaoyutai state guest compound on the western edge of Beijing. It replaced the CCP Secretariat, recently headed by Deng Xiaoping, which handled the Central Committee's day-to-day operations. As the central bureaucracy of the party-state was decimated by purges and drastically downsized, the CCRG grew in scale and power.

Unfortunately for Mao, by all accounts the CCRG was a chaotic and poorly organized entity that was beset by internal conflicts and an obvious lack of coordination. Its membership was constantly in flux, and by January 1967 more than half of the original nineteen members and advisors had been either purged or otherwise sidelined. Many of the members were openly antagonistic toward one another, and there were few clear lines of authority and no division of labor. Moreover, the reporting lines to Mao were never formalized. There were no regular written reports, and Mao received different oral versions of the same events from different individuals. It did not help that Mao kept himself aloof, rarely attending meetings, often living in provincial villas far from Beijing. To make matters even more confusing, neither Chen Boda nor

Jiang Qing convened meetings of the group. Neither were capable or experienced administrators, and both had erratic and difficult personalities. This responsibility fell to Premier Zhou Enlai, who was not formally a member of the group. Zhou set the agenda for meetings and could speak publicly in the name of the CCRG.[6] Zhou, however, had very different political leanings from the radical members, and throughout this period he tried subtly to blunt the impact of their more destructive initiatives. The CCRG radicals understood this, viewed Zhou with considerable distrust, and frequently tried to undermine and block him.

In August 1966 Mao reshuffled the party leadership, drastically reducing the role and formal rank of Liu Shaoqi and Deng Xiaoping, promoting more senior members of the CCRG, and elevating Lin Biao to the position of first party vice chairman and Mao's designated successor. Lin, however, had no taste for civilian administration, and limited himself to military matters. Instead, duties formerly handled by Liu Shaoqi and Deng Xiaoping were handled by Zhou Enlai, who convened an informal "central caucus" on an irregular basis that assumed the functions formerly handled by the Politburo Standing Committee and Party Secretariat. Mao and Lin almost never attended.[7] These changes evidently placed Zhou Enlai at the very center of the new structure of power, in many ways an indispensable cog in the Cultural Revolution power machine. Zhou had little independent authority, but because virtually all decisions and their implementation went through his hands, he influenced the course of events.

Also founded during this period and taking on an increasingly important role was the Central Case Examination Group. It grew out of the committee set up to investigate the Beijing "antiparty group" in late May 1966. Its members included virtually all of the members of the CCRG and Kang Sheng, along with Minister of Public Security Xie Fuzhi and Lin Biao's representative, his wife Ye Qun. The group's purpose was to investigate, unmask, arrest, and imprison "revisionists" and "traitors" in the CCP. As the purges of the Cultural Revolution expanded, the group's activities and size also grew.[8]

The Central Case Examination Group eventually employed thousands of staff members who were in charge of scores of investigations into suspected underground traitor groups. They coordinated their work with quasi-independent mass organizations across China that did local investigations on their behalf.[9] By 1968, a total of eighty-eight members of the Central Committee were under investigation for suspected "treachery," "spying," or "collusion with the enemy." The group's activities spread through a nationwide network of "case groups" and took on enormous scope by 1968. In gathering their evidence, the case groups, especially those at the grass roots, relied heavily on coercive interrogations, employing threats and both mental and physical torture. Seemingly a throwback to the Soviet purges of the 1930s, the key charges brought against revisionists had little to do with policy positions they had taken or their public activities. Instead, the victims of these investigations faced implausible charges of treachery: underground antiparty activity, spying on behalf of the Nationalists or foreign intelligence services, or betraying the revolutionary movement before 1949.

Mobilizing Mass Insurgency

The Cultural Revolution also mobilized a mass insurgency that targeted bureaucratic structures from below. For almost two years, students and eventually industrial workers were given nearly free rein to form organizations to criticize and "drag out" officials who, in their view, exhibited tendencies that marked them as revisionists. This aspect of the Cultural Revolution bore a certain resemblance to Mao's insistence on "open-door rectification" of the party in 1956 and 1957. But in 1957 Mao did not sanction independent organizations, or even the removal of individual officials by "the masses." Mao's assessment of the party was fundamentally different than in 1957, when he believed that well-meaning criticism by ordinary citizens of individual cadres was sufficient to rectify the party's problems. The threat of evolution toward revisionism was now so serious, in his view, that only a massive mobilization that cleansed the party of revisionists, smashed the bureaucratic machinery, and trained a new generation of revolutionary successors could prevent China from taking the Soviet road.

The popular insurgency, however, was not left to its own devices. One of the primary functions of the CCRG was to monitor activities on campuses, instigate and support rebellion, and actively undermine serving officials through back-channel communication and encouragement. The CCRG attempted to run the mass movement to subvert the established order in ways reminiscent of the underground communist movement in areas controlled by the Nationalists before 1949. Its activities in 1966 and 1967, however, were much more public and open, even though they maintained private, even clandestine, links with the more influential Red Guard leaders.

These efforts, like the CCRG itself, started out small but grew rapidly. They began in June and July 1966 with a small number of junior CCRG members and related staff, along with a handful of investigative reporters, who traveled to Beijing's college campuses to establish links with student activists, providing back-channel information and advice. As the Red Guard movement grew rapidly in August, hundreds of reporters from *Liberation Army Daily* and the New China News Agency were drafted into roles as liaison personnel and stationed on college campuses throughout the country; their numbers eventually approached 1,000. They established relationships with Red Guard leaders, submitted regular reports to their superiors in Beijing, and in many cases provided information and advice to student activists about imminent shifts in Cultural Revolution politics. The reports that they submitted to the CCRG were distilled into the *Cultural Revolution Bulletin*, of which fewer than twenty copies were printed and distributed to Mao and a selected group of other leaders. This served as an alternative source of information to the more established and widely distributed classified bulletins for the party elite provided by the New China News Agency, *Internal Reference*, which began publishing a supplement titled *Cultural Revolution Trends* in August 1966. By November two were issued every day.[10]

Mao and the CCRG utilized this intelligence network to monitor trends in the student movement, steer it in desired directions, identify and promote promising and cooperative student leaders, and warn off those who were saying and doing things that were not approved. Near the end of 1966 the network was crucial in identifying dissident Red Guards who were critical of the CCRG, and in orchestrating their arrest and denunciation. Some of the liaison personnel became permanent fixtures on campuses, inserting themselves into the deliberations of the leading rebel groups, and were treated by them as authoritative sources of intelligence and advice and as a direct link with the CCRG. As the CCRG consolidated its links with favored student factions in the nation's capital, the Beijing students in turn established "liaison stations" in provincial capitals throughout China, providing advice and direction to local Red Guards. This added another, more public layer to the CCRG's national network of influence. By the fall of 1966 the CCRG regularly invited favored Red Guard leaders for consultations and strategy sessions held at their Diaoyutai headquarters, and eventually even at the leadership compound of Zhongnanhai or the Great Hall of the People.[11]

Mao and the CCRG also took a series of highly visible as well as less obvious, even mundane, measures to facilitate student rebellion. The mass media consistently encouraged the student rebels, praising them in an unrestrained fashion. Beginning on August 18, Mao and other leaders held a series of appearances at gigantic mass rallies held on Tiananmen Square, all of which were lavishly covered in the national media. By the time the last one was held in November of that year, some 12 million people had attended them.[12] If students were to devote themselves full time to this political campaign, they would obviously have to set aside their studies. The barriers to political activism evaporated in mid-June, when all classes were suspended along with final exams, the conferral of degrees, job assignments, and college entrance examinations. Students now had nothing to do except remain on campus and participate in the campaign. Equally important was an order to keep dormitories and meal services in operation into the summer vacation and beyond. In late August two decrees ordered the Public Security Bureau and armed forces not to interfere in Red Guard activities. These orders were strictly observed until December 1966, when the security forces were ordered to move against students who were critical of the CCRG itself.[13]

Despite all of these measures, the CCRG found the Red Guard movement difficult to control. It repeatedly generated splits and controversies that required their intervention. Through increasingly overt and heavy-handed manipulation, the CCRG was able to steer the movement in its desired direction, but its manipulations provoked a backlash. The opposition became so widespread and troublesome that it provoked a harsh year-end crackdown by the security forces and a wave of arrests of dissident Red Guards.

The University Red Guards

Emblematic of the behind-the-scenes manipulation of the Red Guard movement was the appearance of the "first Marxist-Leninist wall poster" at Peking University, which became famous nationwide as the opening salvo of the Cultural Revolution. On May 25, 1966, seven instructors of Marxism-Leninism in Peking University's Philosophy Department put up a wall poster that denounced the university's president (who was also party secretary) and two other officials as revisionists who were linked to the Beijing antiparty clique. Their alleged crime was to conspire to block the free mobilization of the masses and to divert the campaign into small forums that permitted them to exercise "sinister" control. Their behavior showed that they were "a bunch of Khrushchev-type revisionist elements."[14]

Although this wall poster took on mythical status as the precursor of the Red Guard movement and made its reputed author a political celebrity, none of the authors were students, and most were senior party members. Nie Yuanzi, who became known as the primary author, was in fact a member of the university's party committee and general branch secretary of the Department of Philosophy. In 1966 she was already forty-five years old, a revolutionary cadre who left high school during the Japanese invasion to become a party activist in Yan'an, and her long history in the party afforded her extensive elite connections. She was nonetheless a likely candidate to denounce her school's party leadership. She and her allies were among those who attacked the university's leadership during the Socialist Education Movement two years before, and they suffered criticism after the campaign reversed direction. She and her colleagues were under a political cloud, serving under a party leader they had tried to overthrow, and many of them were in the midst of arranging transfers elsewhere.[15]

The famous wall poster appeared after back-channel encouragement arranged by Kang Sheng, who sent confidential emissaries to Peking University to arrange the denunciation of the university's leaders. Kang's emissaries assured them that there would be no repercussions this time around. The wall poster had its intended effects on the campus community, creating an uproar. Kang provided Mao with a copy of the wall poster, and Mao saw his opportunity: he ordered that it be broadcast nationwide and published in party newspapers throughout the country along with lavish editorial praise. This sealed the fate of the university's leadership. The next day they were publicly denounced and removed from power and a work team of scores of ranking party officials moved onto the campus to take over from the now-defunct party committee. The impact was immediate. The work team cooperated with Nie and her colleagues in a massive purge of the campus hierarchy that essentially resumed the radical attacks of the earlier Socialist Education Movement.[16] Throughout the nation's capital, and on campuses across the country, activist students, political instructors, and party members imitated Nie Yuanzi's group and made similar attacks on their school leaders.

Critics besieged party committees in universities throughout Beijing; many of them organized emergency meetings, panicked at the prospect of being dragged into the purges of the Beijing party apparatus. Their fears were justified: within a week the party secretary of Nanjing University was also denounced and removed from his post. He had incurred the wrath of students in his humanities division by sending them to a distant new rural campus to combine study and manual labor, in line with Mao's recent pronouncements about education. But the students and faculty deeply resented the fact that the science and engineering division remained in downtown Nanjing. The president stood firm and tried to silence the critics as anti-Mao, a stance for which he was stripped of his position and denounced as an arch-revisionist.[17]

In a seeming replay of the earlier Socialist Education Movement, work teams were sent into universities and high schools with orders to solicit mass criticisms and orchestrate purges of grassroots party leaders. They would be withdrawn in late July, after Mao returned from a long absence from Beijing to denounce them for "suppressing the masses." Mao blamed Liu Shaoqi and Deng Xiaoping for this "error of line," and the two were further sidelined as a direct result, the first step toward political oblivion as China's leading "revisionists."[18] As the work teams were withdrawn, they were charged by their opponents, and by some of Mao's radical followers, for attempting to blunt mass mobilization and thereby protect power holders in the party apparatus. Closer examination of the actual impact of work teams has shown that they in fact facilitated attacks by students and others that devastated most party organizations, splitting school authorities and student bodies, pitting them against one another, inadvertently laying the foundations for subsequent divisions that would plague the Red Guard movement.[19]

When work teams entered a university, they faced several choices. The first was to leave the party leadership intact and let them conduct purges of lesser figures. If the work team rejected this approach and forced the entire party leadership to stand aside, they faced a further choice: should they selectively purge some while affirming the loyalty of others, or should they adopt a radical stance and denounce the entire party organization as rotten to the core? Work teams initially hesitated, but most of them rapidly shifted to more radical approaches.[20] Each approach, however, generated opposition and created divisions among students, party members, and cadres. If the work team left the party leadership intact, those who criticized the top leaders in imitation of Nie Yuanzi would suffer retribution. If the work team designated some leaders as reliable and others as targets of the purge, this split party organizations and alienated large percentages of the party apparatus and their supporters among students and instructors. If the work team denounced the entire party apparatus, this alienated large numbers of party members and student activists who were tainted by association. Under virtually all of these scenarios, vocal minorities began to resent work teams and demand that they be removed or replaced.

Work teams that permitted unrestricted accusations against party authorities also faced another problem: by permitting unrestricted criticism of anyone, work teams inadvertently encouraged students to take matters violently into their own hands. This raised questions about who was in charge, and many work teams worried about losing control of the forces that they had unleashed. When work teams responded to violence by attempting to control student activists, they bred antagonism among some of the more militant students, who resented attempts to "suppress" them.

These problems were illustrated by events at Peking University on June 18, less than three weeks after the work team arrived. The work team absorbed Nie Yuanzi's group of dissidents and proceeded with a purge of the entire party organization. They targeted prominent administrators and faculty for impure class origins, foreign connections, and anyone who sided with the former university president in earlier political battles. By early July only one of the twenty party general branch secretaries was spared from the purge—Nie Yuanzi herself. Fewer than 8 percent of the school's cadres were found to be free of political error; two-thirds were found to have committed errors serious enough to be removed from their posts.[21]

The work team soon found it difficult to control the students. The unfolding of the campaign at Peking University was a shocking contrast to the brief Hundred Flowers period less than a decade before. In 1957 students mobilized to put up critical wall posters, but their intentions were very different. They protested the imposition of authoritarian party rule and the unthinking dogmatism inspired by Stalinist doctrine, and they demanded greater freedom of thought and expression. Some of them even criticized the personality cult formed around Mao Zedong. In line with its liberal tradition going back to the May Fourth Movement of 1919, Peking University students were at the forefront of a growing campaign to have China follow the liberalizing tendencies in the Soviet bloc.

What a difference a decade had made. Now the school's student activists—like their counterparts on campuses across the country—vied with one another to demonstrate their mettle as militant and dogmatically unthinking enforcers of proletarian dictatorship. They went after faculty with foreign educations or with liberal reputations, many of whom were earlier the targets of the thought reform and antirightist campaigns. They also went after party officials who in their view facilitated the influence of these "alien class elements."

Even more striking than this narrow-minded dogmatism was the propensity of student activists to engage in harsh and extreme denunciation coupled with personal cruelty and physical violence. During proliferating struggle sessions, which consciously imitated the ritualized humiliations meted out to landlords and other class enemies during revolutionary land reform and other political campaigns, student activists made the accused wear tall hats and hung heavy placards around their necks. Their targets were subjected to screaming accusations and insults, shoved about violently, their hair pulled, and their arms extended painfully behind them while kneeling in the "jet plane" position. In some cases they were beaten severely. At Peking University, which was by no means unusual in this regard, the work team recorded 178 cadres, teachers, and students who were treated in this manner by mid-June, leading to a series of suicides.

The work team finally took a stand against unrestricted violence on June 18, when a series of violent struggle sessions broke out across the campus. Close to seventy cadres and faculty members were dragged onto makeshift platforms, faces smeared with black ink, and were beaten, kicked, and subjected to shouted accusations. Particularly disturbing were reports that two female officials had their clothes partially stripped off and were humiliated by a young man who groped their genitals. Most of the victims were members of the school's party committee or were lower-ranking general branch and branch secretaries. The work team sent members across the campus to halt the violence and give the victims first aid.[22]

The work team denounced the violence and sent a report to the Party Secretariat (still functioning under Liu Shaoqi and Deng Xiaoping) condemning this "June 18 incident." The report was transmitted to party committees nationwide two days later as a Central Committee document, with the comment that the work team's actions were "correct and timely." Armed with this new directive, work teams throughout the country cracked down on students who refused to conform. Students who persisted in violent activities in defiance of work teams were singled out, criticized, and detained. Those who resisted the authority of work teams were warned to desist and threatened with punishment. Those who called for the withdrawal of the work team, or who demanded that students and faculty should themselves be responsible for their own Cultural Revolution, might be subjected to criticism sessions and accused of antiparty activity. During the brief campaign to reassert work team authority, a significant minority of work team opponents in virtually every school were criticized, sometimes given stigmatizing political labels, and had their names recorded by work teams, who kept records on troublemakers.[23]

It was this document and the campaign to consolidate work team authority that gave Mao the pretext to return to Beijing in mid-July and angrily denounce the work teams—and Liu Shaoqi and Deng Xiaoping—for "suppressing the student movement" and instituting "dictatorship" on college campuses. Mao ignored the fact that most work teams had prosecuted his campaign against campus revisionism with extraordinary thoroughness, and he showed no concern whatsoever for the widespread violence that served as the cause of the work teams' backlash against selected campus militants. Mao ordered all work teams to be withdrawn at the end of July; henceforth campuses would conduct the campaign on their own.[24]

Mao presumably intended that with the work teams properly denounced and withdrawn, student militants would unite in a common assault on school officials. This did not happen, because the student movement was deeply divided from the very start. Mao had failed to consider the fact that most work teams permitted virtually unfettered attacks on school party organizations. This appealed to the majority of student militants on campuses, who formed close relationships with their radical work teams and who supported the backlash against the minority of activists who challenged work team authority. When work teams withdrew, the students who had cooperated with work teams, a solid majority, assumed control of campuses and proceeded to organize elections for campus Cultural Revolution committees, which they naturally ended up dominating.

This laid the foundations for deep and enduring splits. Students who had clashed with work teams—many of them punished as a result—demanded that the campaign shift its focus from school authorities to the work teams. They charged that the students who cooperated with work teams were complicit with an attempt to suppress rebellion, and therefore had no right to lead their school's cultural revolution. They demanded that work team members return to campus for struggle sessions and confess to their crimes of trying to suppress "revolutionary masses."

The majority of student activists, however, saw these charges as a scarcely veiled accusation against them. They felt justified in claiming that they had cooperated with purges coordinated by radical work teams, that the disgruntled minority was exaggerating the errors of work teams and distorting their record. The disgruntled minority implied that the majority of students were revisionist, or "conservative," while the majority implied that the minority deserved the treatment they received, and were only interested in clearing their records. During the month of August, universities were roiled with vociferous debates between students in these two camps, which sometimes degenerated into brawls. As Red Guard organizations formed, these two groups generated splits on almost all campuses into majority and minority factions.[25]

Majority factions took control of their campuses and, to demonstrate their militant credentials, organized struggle sessions and herded the accused into makeshift cells and "labor reform brigades" that dug ditches or cleaned latrines. Minority factions, instead, wanted to keep the focus on the errors of the work team and challenged the validity of elections that brought majority factions to power. If Mao and the CCRG had intended to inspire a huge upsurge of student activism that would carry on the rebellion against revisionism, they were sorely disappointed. From the very outset, the university Red Guards were at cross-purposes, preoccupied with fighting one another.

The High School Red Guards

The student rebels in the high schools were initially much more prominent than their university counterparts and received fulsome public praise from Mao. The first student organization to adopt the name Red

Guard *(hongweibing)* was reportedly founded at Tsinghua University High School near the end of May 1966. The students in that organization struggled with the school's authorities over their right to form the organization, and later struggled with the school's work team over the same issue. They put up wall posters challenging the work team and drafted several essays expressing their spirit of rebellion. A parallel struggle was under way at Peking University High School, where another progenitor of the Red Guard movement, which called itself Red Flag Battle Group, challenged the work team sent to their school.

Shortly after work teams were withdrawn, Mao and the CCRG went out of their way to draw attention to these two student organizations and lavish them with praise. At forums held with high school leaders, Jiang Qing and other officials praised these groups and welcomed their leaders to share the stage and microphone. Mao read the students' essays and responded enthusiastically. He wrote to them on August 1, affirming that their wall posters were "revolutionary," and he applauded their militant stand. He ordered that two of their posters, along with his letter, be reprinted and circulated to all participants at the party's Eleventh Plenum, which began in early August. Mao also took the opportunity to express his support for Peking University High School Red Flag. Mao's public message read, in part, "Your two wall posters . . . express anger and condemnation toward the oppression of workers, peasants, revolutionary intellectuals, and revolutionary parties and groups by landlords, capitalists, imperialists, revisionists, and their running dogs. This shows that it is right to rebel against reactionaries, and I express to you my enthusiastic support."[26]

In the wake of this praise, Mao invited some 1,500 students onto the reviewing stands for the gigantic Red Guard rally on Tiananmen Square on August 18. More than twenty members of the Tsinghua High School Red Guards received invitations. When they met Mao and identified themselves, Mao responded, "I resolutely support you!" The encounter was described a few days later in the *People's Daily.* At that rally, Mao was presented with a Red Guard armband by a student leader from Beijing Normal Girls' High School who had penned the "first wall poster" at her school. A famous photograph of her on the Tiananmen rostrum fitting the armband onto a smiling Mao Zedong was carried on the front page of newspapers nationwide. In the days to come, the national media published excerpts from the speeches and wall posters of these high school militants.[27]

These student rebels, in line with the denunciation of revisionists in the party leadership, took a militant stance on the party's "class line" in education. This involved a marked emphasis on political indoctrination, an emphasis on class origin and political activism in school admissions, and a criticism of an overly narrow focus on academic excellence and performance on examinations. This message was highly congenial to the first wave of high school Red Guards, most of whom came from households of party members and revolutionary cadres. The early stars of the Red Guard movement from Peking University High School, Tsinghua High School, and Beijing Normal Girls' High School were all from official families that carried the "revolutionary" designation, and they were proud of their backgrounds. Trouble began, however, with the circulation of a derogatory rhyme, a couplet *(duilian)* that praised students of revolutionary parentage and denigrated those from "bad" family origins. This led to the first major divisions among high school Red Guards.

The offending couplet declared that "the son of a hero is a real man; the son of a reactionary is a bastard." The authors defended it as an expression of the party's class line, but many students found it offensive because it suggested that the children of revolutionaries were a hereditary political aristocracy, assumed to be "red" by birth, and that others were damned at birth, regardless of their actual loyalties. The couplet also offended those from proletarian and peasant backgrounds whose parents were not revolutionary heroes. Not surprisingly, many students began to criticize the couplet as immature and self-defeating. Arguments over the issue escalated into violence among Red Guards at neighborhood rallies in early August, when students fought over control of a microphone, leading to beatings and a stabbing.[28]

Members of the CCRG worried that arguments over the couplet would divide and weaken the student movement just as it was getting started. Several members of the group urged students to set the issue aside. Figures like Jiang Qing and Kang Sheng offered less offensive versions of the couplet and tried without success to clarify the question of how class analysis could justify inherited political status, and how to weigh actual political loyalty against family background.[29] These efforts to explain finer distinctions of party doctrine regarding political labels did little to quell the controversy.

A more serious issue, and one that led to the first clear factional split in the high school movement, was the problem of student violence. A wave of violence swept through high schools and city neighborhoods as soon as the work teams were withdrawn. High school students seized party secretaries, principals, teachers, and classmates on their campuses and subjected them to violent beatings, leading to a number of murders and suicides.[30] High school militants also poured off their campuses to attack individuals in targeted categories. In public parks and historic sites they held struggle sessions against officials in educational and youth league offices, prominent novelists, playwrights, and Beijing Opera performers, beating them severely with fists and belts. Red Guards roamed the city's residential streets, terrorizing members of "reactionary" households, invading their homes, and subjecting the occupants to violent struggle sessions. During this period, Red Guards issued handbills that ordered "black class" households to turn over their property to the Public Security Bureau and leave the city immediately.

Members of these households assembled on high school grounds and in neighborhood parks for struggle sessions and beatings. Processions of victims being driven through the streets in the backs of trucks were a common sight. In the month following the first Tiananmen rally on August 18, 114,000 homes in Beijing were searched, and 44.8 million yuan of foreign currency, gold, and other valuables were confiscated, along with more than 2.3 million books and 3.3 million paintings, art objects, and pieces of furniture. In the Western District, the books, paintings, scrolls, and other items confiscated from 1,061 homes were set ablaze and burned for eight days and nights. During this period, 77,000 people were expelled from their homes in Beijing. The violence crested during the last week of August, when an average of more than 200 people were dying every day. The official Beijing death toll for the four weeks after mid-August is 1,772.[31]

The first public objection to these trends came from the Tsinghua High School Red Guards, the group credited with founding the Red Guard movement and praised by Mao in early August. They expressed alarm about the wave of violence that swept over the city and issued an "Urgent Appeal" that denounced "bastards and incompetents" who in the name of the Red Guard movement were "going around everywhere beating people up . . . carrying on like gangsters." The appeal demanded that "genuine leftist organizations" be formed in schools to control "gangster-like behavior." Those who committed such acts should be expelled from Red Guard organizations.[32]

The appeal fell on deaf ears—unlike the earlier wall posters, this document was not publicized in the mass media—and the wave of violence and terror crested in late August. The Tsinghua High School Red Guards later issued an "assessment" of the Red Guard movement that lamented the "utter disregard for human life" of so many students, and argued that this was the behavior that one expected from "fascists," not the behavior of "genuine red guards from the five-red classes."[33]

Mao, unfortunately, did not agree. Student calls to curtail violence ran directly counter to his view, shared by key figures in the CCRG, that violence was an inevitable feature of rebellion, and the suffering of victims was acceptable collateral damage. Top officials were privately informed of the violent course of the movement, but they essentially reacted with a shrug.[34]

From the outset of the student movement, Jiang Qing clearly signaled to student activists that violence against victims would not be considered a serious transgression. In one of her first speeches to the high school Red Guards on July 28, she said:

> We don't fear chaos. Chaos and order are inseparable. . . . We don't advocate beating people, but beating people is no big deal. . . . You can't beat someone's mistaken thoughts out of them, but for beatings to occur during a revolutionary outburst is not a bad thing. Chairman Mao has said, "If good people beat bad people, it serves them right; if bad people beat good people, the good people achieve glory; if good people beat good people, it's a misunderstanding; without beatings you don't get acquainted and then won't need to beat them anymore."

The Red Guard "Urgent Appeal" about violence was issued one week later. Jiang Qing did not initially object to it, but her attitude soon changed. She became convinced that more moderate figures in the leadership were too enthusiastic about its message, seeing it as a pretext for quelling the student rebellion. Mao shared this view. He had been completely indifferent to the work teams' role in restraining student violence, and he was unwilling to let the same considerations place any restrictions on student rebellion. Near the height of violence on August 23, at a meeting with members of the Politburo Standing Committee, he expressed his impatience over the issue: "I don't think Beijing is all that chaotic. . . . Beijing is too civilized, hooligans are only a minority, now is not the time to interfere . . . rushing to make decisions, getting all worked up. Rushing to struggle against leftists . . . rushing to issue urgent appeals." Xie Fuzhi, minister of public security, mirrored Mao's attitude. At the late August meeting where he directed neighborhood police stations to assist Red Guards in identifying "reactionary" households,

Xie said, "I don't approve of the masses killing people, but the masses' bitter hatred toward bad people cannot be discouraged, and it's unavoidable." This attitude was translated into official directives on August 21 and 22, relayed nationwide: local army units and bureaus of public security were strictly prohibited from taking any action to restrict Red Guards.

Given Mao's attitude, restrictions on Red Guard violence would have to be self-imposed.[35] The effort to organize self-policing bred a deep split among high school Red Guards and fed into broader divisions in the Red Guard movement. Here is one of the first of many instances when Zhou Enlai tried to limit damage from the campaign. In late August a group called the Western District Picket Corps announced its formation. One of the founders of the group was the son of one of Zhou Enlai's subordinates in his State Council office. While there is no direct evidence that Zhou instigated the group's formation, the connection seems more than coincidental, given the group's stance and the organized support that Zhou quickly provided for it. This was the first cross-campus alliance of Red Guard organizations.

The Picket Corps dictated a set of ground rules that insisted on "nonviolent struggle": "In the Cultural Revolution from this point forward it is absolutely forbidden to beat people, absolutely forbidden to physically abuse them either openly or in a disguised manner; absolutely forbidden to humiliate people, absolutely forbidden to extract forced confessions"—a prohibition that applied "without exception," even to people who had already been determined to be counterrevolutionaries. They provided explicit detail about what they meant by physical abuse: "kneeling, lying flat, bending at the waist, carrying a heavy weight, standing for long periods, keeping hands raised for long periods, keeping heads bowed for long period, etc., all are open or disguised forms of physical abuse and are not methods of struggle that we should use." The forbidden forms of humiliation included "hanging signboards [from the neck], wearing a tall hat, being made to sing chants, shaving heads, etc." What did they mean by "forced confessions"? "Failing to stress investigation and research, failing to stress facts and evidence, readily believing confessions, having blind faith in confessions, using a combination of violence and threats to force a confession, and then believing the confession."

Because he was unable to use regular police forces, the Picket Corps became Zhou's primary instrument of control. He established a direct line of communication with the Red Guard pickets through the Office of the State Council, and he assigned members of his own State Council office staff to communicate with the groups. Zhou invited members of the Picket Corps onto the rostrum during subsequent rallies at Tiananmen Square. He met with their leaders and had his assistants provide them with office space, funds, uniforms, means of transportation, and printing facilities. Their handbills were professionally printed in large runs at the State Council's printing plant.

The Picket Corps would not last long. In carrying out their duties, they collided with a new campaign by minority faction rebels from the universities, who invaded government offices to capture the leaders of their schools' work teams and subject them to struggle sessions. This drew the Picket Corps into an implicit alliance with the university majority factions, and led to strong countermeasures by the CCRG to realign and redirect the Red Guard movement. It also put these students on a collision course with the CCRG.

The Rise of the Rebels

Minority factions in the universities were on the defensive everywhere in August and September. Unable to control the debate on their campuses, they took their cause off campus. The pioneers of this tactic were the minority factions of two important schools: Aeronautics Institute Red Flag, which staged a daring and prolonged sit-in strike at the gates of the Ministry of Defense, and Geology Institute East Is Red, which demonstrated repeatedly at the offices of the Ministry of Geology, eventually invading the building and occupying it.[36]

Aeronautics Institute Red Flag began their sit-in at the Ministry of Defense on August 26 in an effort to get the head of their school's work team to return to the university to face their accusations. For obvious reasons the official balked at being taken into custody, and the sit-in continued through mid-September, when Zhou Enlai tried unsuccessfully to resolve the standoff. Geology Institute East Is Red took parallel action beginning on August 23 when it sent roughly a thousand of its members to the Ministry of Geology to get their work team head, a ranking official in the ministry, to accompany them back for a denunciation meeting. The official understandably refused their invitation, and the group sent demonstrators to the ministry on two subsequent occasions, eventually invading and occupying the ministry offices on September 19.

These actions attracted the attention of the CCRG, which saw them as a way to break out of the impasse created by the majority-minority split. It now seemed possible to propel university Red Guards into attacks on government ministries to "drag out" the officials who staffed work teams and, inevitably, higher-ranking "revisionist" officials who had sent them. Up to this point the CCRG had tried, without success, to get the university Red Guards to unite and carry on with the Cultural Revolution, but in viewing these new developments they reformulated their strategy and openly supported the minority faction against their opponents.

Here is where the newly formed high school Picket Corps blundered into the middle of the split in the university movement, becoming a stumbling block to the designs of the CCRG.[37] The Picket Corps idolized the People's Liberation Army, whose legendary discipline was their model for restrained Red Guard behavior. They were outraged by protests outside the PLA headquarters at the Ministry of Defense. They were also opposed to the violence that would undoubtedly be meted out in the struggle sessions to which the minority faction rebels intended to subject work team officials. In their first public act on August 31, only six days after their founding statement, a detachment of the Western District Picket Corps showed up at the Aeronautics Institute Red Flag sit-in at the ministry gates, now in its second week. They tried to forcibly dislodge the protesters, but were repelled.

An even more dramatic confrontation occurred at the Ministry of Geology on September 7, where the Geology Institute East Is Red was in the third day of their most recent protest at the ministry offices. When they arrived and demanded the surrender of the work team head on September 5, the Western District Pickets were called in. They surrounded the university students and waded into their sit-in, whipping them with belts and throwing bricks. They seized several protesters and roughed them up; afterward they issued handbills denouncing their attack on the ministry.

It was now evident that the Red Guard movement was hopelessly split, and the progress of the CCRG's rebellion was being blocked. The minority factions, whose new forays the CCRG heartily approved, already had to deal with more powerful opponents on their campuses. Now, it appeared, they were being confronted by the first organized cross-school alliance of high school Red Guards, who were standing in the way of these new assaults on the party-state bureaucracy. To make matters worse, the Red Guard pickets had obvious support from Zhou Enlai and others in the party leadership who were appalled at Red Guard violence, and they were quickly becoming a formidable force, circumventing the prohibition against action by police and army units.

Under Mao's direction, the CCRG initiated a series of countermoves that reshaped and redirected the student movement, openly taking sides in the student splits.[38] If the insurgency was to succeed, it needed a cross-campus alliance and the clear backing of the CCRG. It had both by the end of September, and by mid-October it was routing its opponents. Their alliance, founded September 6, became known as the Third Headquarters. Up to this point, the CCRG had expressed evenhanded support for the Red Guard movement and had repeatedly called for warring students to unite. They now abandoned this stance and took a direct hand in shaping the movement's direction with a wholehearted endorsement of the minority factions, signaled in meetings with Red Guards.

After these meetings, Mao decided to openly favor the minority camp. On September 21, the day after the meetings concluded, the CCRG met with leaders of Aeronautics Institute Red Flag and expressed support for their protest at the Ministry of Defense. They ordered the work team head to surrender to the students. That same week the Geology Institute East Is Red protesters surged through the doors of the Ministry of Geology and raided the offices where the work team's files were kept. They broke open the cabinets and carted off the files compiled on the student opposition. They returned to the Geology Institute to seize power from the majority faction on September 23. A massive brawl over control of the campus broadcasting system left more than 100 injured. News of CCRG support for the minority faction spread quickly, and minority factions across the city seized control of their campus broadcasting systems. The tide was turning.

The shift in CCRG support for the new rebel coalition was publicized by a mass rally of the Third Headquarters on September 26. Zhou Enlai spoke, affirming Mao's support for the minority faction's struggle, and calling for the rehabilitation of all those in the minority faction who had been labeled antiparty. Addressing one of their core concerns (and no doubt trying to lessen their incentive to further attack ministries in searches for their work team leaders), he announced that all "black materials" collected on these individuals would be removed from their files.

The shift in direction was signaled by the rise of a new group of Red Guard leaders. Most striking was the sudden elevation of Tsinghua University's Kuai Dafu, who was a minor figure in his school's large minority faction. Kuai's claim to fame was that he had earlier clashed publicly with party vice chairman Bo Yibo and had lodged accusations against Liu Shaoqi's wife, Wang Guangmei, who took part in Tsinghua's work team.[39] Despite his notoriety, Kuai remained a minor figure in Tsinghua's minority faction, whose leaders considered him too mercurial and reckless to be taken seriously.

Reckless and mercurial, however, was exactly what the CCRG wanted. Kuai's clashes with Bo Yibo and Wang Guangmei motivated him to attack top leaders, and he had shown a willingness to confront virtually anyone. The CCRG intended to steer the student movement into attacks on Liu Shaoqi, and Kuai was clearly the man for the job. Zhang Chunqiao invited Kuai for an individual session on September 23, encouraging him to start a new rebel organization and assuring him of CCRG support. The next day Kuai announced the establishment of his new rebel organization, and he and his group began a rapid ascent to the top of the rebel movement.

The October Turning Point

The decisive shift in support for the Third Headquarters was expressed in an authoritative commentary published in *Red Flag* on October 3. The editorial laid out a new definition of the immediate aims of the Cultural Revolution and pronounced a new verdict on the events of the previous four months. The work teams' errors were part of a "bourgeois reactionary line" that was manipulated from above by officials who opposed Mao and tried to obstruct the Cultural Revolution. "The two-line struggle has by no means concluded," the editorial intoned, and it followed that there were even higher officials in the state hierarchy who had masterminded the conspiracy.[40]

To ensure that officials nationwide understood the new line, Mao convened a Central Party Work Conference during the last three weeks of October. One of the highlights of the conference was a report by Chen Boda—revised repeatedly by Mao beforehand—that summarized the movement's progress. Chen described a "two-line struggle" over the Cultural Revolution. He charged that officials and certain Red Guards tried to impede the campaign and divert its course. Refuting criticisms of Red Guard violence, he denied that they were acting "recklessly" and that they were "opportunists joining up with careerists, thugs, brutal savages." Chen also attacked Red Guards who had defended their work teams, insinuating that their reactionary stance was due to arrogance about their revolutionary cadre parentage.[41] Liu Shaoqi and Deng Xiaoping were blamed for this reactionary line. They were further demoted in the party hierarchy.[42]

Now the student movement was directed to criticize officials who had engaged in this bourgeois reactionary line—anyone who had tried to divert, moderate, or suppress student activism in any form. It was obvious from Chen Boda's speech that this included any effort to restrict Red Guard actions on the pretext of preventing violence. It was also obvious that Red Guards who had collaborated with work teams and who defended them afterward, and Red Guards who had organized to prevent beatings and murders, were complicit in this reactionary line. They were at minimum conservative and arguably reactionary. In one stroke, student activists who were at the vanguard of the movement in August were shunted aside and stigmatized.

Majority factions who had up to this point defended their positions became demoralized and lost influence within their schools. Their efforts to form cross-campus alliances collapsed. In Beijing and across China, the term "Red Guard," while never completely disappearing, seemed increasingly tied to the bourgeois reactionary line. The term "rebel" *(zaofan pai)* became more popular as a name for student organizations, indicating a break with the first Red Guards who had run afoul of the CCRG. Mao and the party center had now spoken: these earlier Red Guards had collaborated with the bourgeois reactionary line, and they had better align themselves with the new direction of the rebel movement. In Beijing the reaction was immediate: the city quickly experienced a massive wave of invasions of government ministries as minority factions attacked in search of work team leaders and files. Liaison stations of minority factions in other major cities transmitted the new direction to local Red Guard organizations, encouraging attacks on officials at the provincial and city level.

The high school Picket Corps also fell into disarray. Now that their stance was clearly repudiated by Mao, Zhou Enlai backed away from them, and their support from the Office of the State Council. Given the obvious indifference and seemingly tacit approval of Mao and other leaders to the beating and murder of victims, some of the former members broke off into small groups that committed such acts themselves. As a coordinated citywide organization, the Picket Corps ceased to exist, but campus-level groups maintained their cohesion and identity for many weeks to come. Some, including many of the early stars of the Red Guard movement, would mount a last-ditch effort to resist, an effort that led to a daring and ill-fated confrontation with the CCRG.

Now that the CCRG had intervened to create a new alliance and rescue the minority faction from oblivion, they inevitably created a rebel movement that depended heavily on their patronage and took orders from above. The ties between the CCRG and the rebels became more explicit and formally organized. Student leaders in the new rebel alliance were granted the funds and resources they needed to conduct the movement, and they were integrated more firmly into the growing CCRG networks. CCRG members visited campuses and attended rallies to make speeches and instruct student leaders and activists. Liaison personnel relayed CCRG instructions and outright orders to favored student leaders and, if necessary, backed them up with threats. In the coming months, rebel leaders looked to these encounters for validation of their course of action and guidance about what to do next.[43]

The Red Guard Backlash and Its Suppression

Former leaders of the now-disgraced majority faction and the high school students who had tried to contain Red Guard violence now found themselves labeled as dupes of a bourgeois reactionary line. Some of them began to fight back, and they crafted a campaign through wall posters, handbills, and in some cases new cross-campus alliances that imitated the minority faction's earlier campaign against the work teams. They turned the campaign against the bourgeois reactionary line against the CCRG itself, charging it with manipulating the student movement, suppressing points of view with which they disagreed, and suppressing those who dared criticize them. Their campaign roiled several college campuses, leading to emotional debates, wall posters attacking the CCRG, and increasingly brazen challenges to CCRG authority. Adherents of the newly anointed rebel faction expressed outrage at the temerity of the dissidents in challenging the sacrosanct authority of the CCRG. The dissident campaign began in mid-November and grew bolder by the week, leading to a CCRG crackdown on dissent that signaled the end of the Red Guard movement as an independent political force.

One center of the campaign was at the Beijing Aeronautics Institute, whose majority-faction Red Guards complained that the CCRG ignored them and brushed them aside as "revisionist."[44] They likened their treatment to that of the minority faction under the work teams and portrayed the CCRG as disdainful of mass opinions, bureaucratic, and manipulative, a suppression of mass activism characteristic of the bourgeois reactionary line. As one of their wall posters put it, "It seems as if those who constantly say they want to criticize the bourgeois reactionary line still haven't recognized what was reactionary about it. . . . The likes of Guan Feng and Qi Benyu, full of bureaucratic airs, simply cannot represent Chairman Mao." As the campaign escalated, the dissident students challenged the actions of the CCRG itself, pointing out that its activities looked suspiciously like an underground party faction that was engaged in a conspiracy to throw the country and party into disorder. Their most incendiary wall poster, appearing in mid-December, essentially accused the CCRG of posing as leftists in order to engineer a coup.

Majority faction leaders echoed these challenges to the CCRG on other campuses. One former Red Guard leader at the Forestry Institute circulated a wall poster titled "Kick Aside the CCRG and Make Revolution on Your Own," employing the same slogan that the minority faction had earlier used against work teams. He pointed out that the CCRG had no standing in the party or state constitution, and that no one had ever stated that they would be exempt from criticism. As he put it, "Members of the CCRG just sit at the upper levels, acting like bureaucrats and overlords. . . . [They] fly about like imperial envoys, spewing all kinds of verbiage, making all kinds of confused statements. Leaders' speeches are cherished like life itself, treated like precious treasures. . . . China can be led only by Chairman Mao. Anything else you can doubt, doubt everything."

These sentiments also appeared in wall posters and debates on high school campuses. More noteworthy, however, was the attempt by some of the original Red Guards at Peking University High School and Tsinghua High School to form an organization to coordinate resistance, calling it United Action *(liandong)*. Among its founders were the same students who had issued the "Urgent Appeal" against Red Guard violence back in August, many of whom had appeared on the rostrum with Mao at the first Red Guard rally on August 18. These students now openly expressed their opposition to the CCRG. They first met to pull together a cross-school alliance of like-minded students from high schools in the Haidian district on November 27, and issued their founding declaration on December 5.[45]

This campaign had particular resonance at Peking University, where Nie Yuanzi still claimed absolute authority over the movement in her school, buttressed by Mao's praise of her "revolutionary wall poster." Nie considered herself politically untouchable, and in many ways she was. The campaign against the bourgeois reactionary line, however, had unsettling implications for Nie and her followers. Nie and her group had cooperated actively with her university's work team, and they had never led a resistance movement to drive it away, as did minority factions on other campuses. Nie had tried to exercise absolute control over her school's Red Guard movement as it emerged in August and September. She issued orders as if her authority was unchallengeable, leading to resistance by Red Guard militants who demanded autonomy. Displaying a pronounced authoritarian streak, she accused rebellious students of political crimes—to oppose her, she claimed, was to oppose the CCRG. This alienated large percentages of Red Guards at her school, driving many of her original supporters—including most of the coauthors of the famous wall poster—into the opposition. Alienated rebels at Peking University echoed attacks on the CCRG as a weapon in their rebellion against Nie.[46]

The attempt to manipulate the student movement had touched off an intense backlash. The effort to mold the student rebellion into an obedient instrument of elite Maoists was being openly challenged, and Mao's trusted representatives were now openly mocked. Rebellion against the CCRG, however, was not to be tolerated. By mid-December the CCRG ordered a counterattack. It began with the publication of an editorial in the December 13 issue of *Red Flag*, which charged that the dissident campaign was "an attack on the genuine left instigated by a small group of capitalist roaders."[47] The editorial called for exercising proletarian dictatorship over class enemies.

This ushered in the ironic transformation of the new rebel faction, born as a protest movement against the dictatorial practices of the work teams, into enthusiastic proponents of "proletarian dictatorship." On December 14, the CCRG met with rebel leaders who peppered them with questions about how to handle the dissident challenge. Kang Sheng told them, "We must carry out severe suppression of counterrevolutionaries, this is the greatest form of democracy. . . . We must carry out dictatorship over counterrevolutionary elements. . . . Only revolutionaries have freedom of speech."

An even more dramatic demonstration of the CCRG backlash was a December 16 mass meeting of high school activists, where Jiang Qing's speech set the tone for a new campaign against the high school Picket Corps. "These so-called picket corps had a small group of little kids carrying out the bourgeois reactionary line. . . . Their aristocratic arrogance, thinking that their bloodline is so noble, treating others so rudely— what nonsense!" Jiang then made a remarkable charge, openly denouncing the officials who worked under Zhou Enlai to organize and supply the Picket Corps. Jiang Qing charged that the Picket Corps were themselves responsible for the cruelty and violence of the Red Guard movement: "We must resolutely carry out dictatorship over this small group of criminals who murder, beat people, sabotage the revolution." In Jiang's distortion of recent history, the Picket Corps was a violent gang of reactionary murderers who received backstage support from officials who were pursing their bourgeois reactionary line to block Mao's Cultural Revolution. The students did so, she claimed, because they had "aristocratic" backgrounds due to their parents' revolutionary heritage, and their violence was a desperate attempt to protect their privileges.

The rebels now understood what was expected and a wave of repression followed. Rebel students seized dissident Red Guards on their campuses and turned them over to public security agencies. In January 1967, Minister of Public Security Xie Fuzhi claimed that the Cultural Revolution had entered a new stage, and those currently being arrested under newly tightened public security regulations were counterrevolutionaries. Public security officers fanned out across the city to arrest dissident students, putting the captives in handcuffs, and then paraded them through the city streets on the back of a truck like convicted criminals, accompanied by throngs of students from the rebel faction who chanted slogans as the procession worked its way downtown.

The CCRG felt compelled to build an elaborate public justification for their actions. Their denunciation campaign completely ignored the dissidents' criticisms, focusing instead on the allegedly violent and reactionary nature of the Picket Corps and United Action. Both were singled out as neofascist organizations that sought to defend the restoration of capitalism. They were part of an alleged conspiracy orchestrated by the State Council officials who had assisted the Picket Corps, and through them in unspecified ways were linked to Liu Shaoqi and Deng Xiaoping. Zhou Enlai, who actually directed these efforts and was directly implicated, escaped untouched.

The shrillness of the campaign was undoubtedly due to two inconvenient facts: many of the leaders of the Picket Corps and United Action were once nationally celebrated Red Guards, and they were the only students ever to have taken a public stand against Red Guard violence—a stand rejected by Mao and the CCRG. The campaign diverted attention from the CCRG's responsibility for violence by permitting them to pose as champions of nonviolence. The tone of the denunciation campaign, which was publicized nationwide, was reflected in official pamphlets: "It is not at all surprising that 'United Action' elements furiously carried out the bourgeois reactionary line. 'United Action' is now behaving crudely, like mad dogs. Whoever is revolutionary, they oppose. Whoever is reactionary, they support. They crave nothing more than chaos nationwide. Although they receive enthusiastic applause and secret overtures from clowns in Moscow and Washington, they have long ago been spurned by the broad masses."

The crackdown on dissident Red Guards marked the death of the student movement as an independent political force. Little noticed at the time, but characteristic of this development, was the fate of Zhu Chengzhao, leader of Geology Institute East Is Red and one of the architects of the Third Headquarters rebel alliance. In mid-December he had begun to express doubts about the direction of the movement. He argued that the rebels had already achieved their main objectives: the rehabilitation of the students targeted by work teams, the destruction of "black materials" in their files, control over their schools, and the clear support of the CCRG. In meetings with colleagues, he complained that the Cultural Revolution had lost the character of a mass movement. Zhu argued that the CCRG was not mobilizing a mass movement but was inciting the masses to struggle with one another, or, as he put it, the Cultural Revolution was "not a mass movement, but manipulation of the masses." He also complained that the persecution of teenage Red Guards and groups like United Action was far too extreme. This talk alarmed other members of his group, one of whom denounced him to the CCRG. Zhu was stripped of leadership and taken into custody. Several months later the CCRG exposed "the crimes of the Zhu Chengzhao counterrevolutionary clique" and organized a denunciation meeting at the school. Zhu was described as a "counterrevolutionary rightist, traitor to East is Red." His "counter-revolutionary clique" had "viciously attacked our great leader Chairman Mao, bombarded the proletarian headquarters headed by Chairman Mao, engaged in planning for a counterrevolutionary coup, betrayed the nation and went over to the enemy, and committed unforgivable crimes." Zhu Chengzhao would spend more than a decade in China's labor camps.[48]

The Final Collapse of Rebel Unity

The Beijing Red Guard movement had presented its sponsors with a series of headaches. First were the emotional divisions over the question of class origins, which tied the CCRG in knots trying to explain the implications of the party's ambiguous and contradictory policies about class origin. Next was the series of declarations by early celebrities of the Red Guard movement that poured contempt on violent Red Guards as "fascists." Then there was the split between the majority and minority factions in universities, which stalemated the movement and once again turned student radicals against one another. Then there was the formation of the Picket Corps, which evaded Mao's prohibitions against reining in violent students, and which soon ended up in a tacit alliance with the majority faction. After that came the concerted effort to redirect the entire student movement by organizing and promoting a new rebel alliance and a new set of student leaders. Finally, there was the remarkably aggressive resistance movement by dissident Red Guards that openly challenged the CCRG, forcing them to drop their ban on suppressing student radicals and crush dissent with public security forces.

In the course of all of this, Mao was understandably losing confidence in the radical student movement as an instrument of his aims. They had one last chance to prove their worth. After the crackdown on dissident students in Beijing, it would seem that the strengthened and disciplined rebel movement was finally poised to carry out the task for which they ultimately had been created: seizing power from the municipal party and government of Beijing. This turned into a fiasco.[49]

In mid-January, CCRG figures instructed rebel leaders to seize power from the city authorities. Nie Yuanzi and Kuai Dafu announced plans to create a Beijing Commune, a new form of government based on a representative assembly of Mao loyalists and rebel leaders. The effort was doomed from the outset. Previously, rebel leaders had been united in their common struggle against their opponents in the majority faction, and later against the dissident backlash. Now, however, they were competitors in the race to seize power in party and government offices. The effort to coordinate their actions quickly broke down, and confusion reigned. "Power seizure groups" from different universities arrived at office buildings at the same time and argued over which of them had precedence. In other cases, rebels from one university seized power, only to confront rebels from another university several days later that declared their own power seizure. The confusion was compounded by the fact that most government and party agencies already had active rebel groups made up of members of their own staff, and they were invariably split into factions. When student rebels arrived to seize power they had to sort out claims and counterclaims by the two sides, and they came to different conclusions about which side to support.

Rebel leaders had succeeded by exhibiting harsh intolerance toward their opponents; they equated compromise and moderation with revisionism. This undermined their efforts to unite behind power seizures. By the end of January student rebels from different universities engaged in physical confrontations for control over ministries, bureaus, and newspapers. New animosities grew among the leaders of the recently victorious rebel coalition. Rebels from the Geology Institute and Beijing Normal University gravitated into an alliance, increasingly in open opposition to Nie Yuanzi at Peking University, Kuai Dafu at Tsinghua, and rebels from Beijing Aeronautics Institute. To make matters worse, the rebels from the Geology Institute and Beijing Normal University supported the large rebel factions that opposed Nie Yuanzi and Kuai Dafu on their campuses.

In early February the plan was abandoned. The CCRG informed the disorganized Beijing rebels that their power seizure was being called off. There would be no mass power seizure in the nation's capital. Instead, a new revolutionary committee for the nation's capital would be formed by administrative fiat, with the Ministry of Public Security and the Beijing Garrison Command playing a major role.[50] The student rebels had missed their chance. They would not be the leading force in the broadening movement to seize power across China.

1. Mao Zedong in Yan'an, 1937–1938, when "Mao Zedong Thought" was developed as part of the Stalinization of the Chinese Communist Party (UIG via Getty Images).

2. Early manifestation of the Mao cult. Parade celebrating the establishment of the People's Republic of China, Beijing, 1949 (Associated Press).

3. Land reform, 1952. Farmer sentenced to death as a "despotic landlord" for owning two-thirds of an acre of land, Fukang County, Guangdong (© Bettmann/CORBIS).

4. Land reform, 1952. Execution of a "despotic landlord" immediately after sentencing, Fukang County, Guangdong (© Bettmann/CORBIS).

5. Mao and Nikita Khrushchev, Beijing, 1958. The two leaders would soon split over the direction of world communism, a development that led to the Cultural Revolution (AFP / Getty Images).

6. Socialist Education Movement, May 12, 1965. A "rich peasant" is denounced in Acheng County, Heilongjiang; he was sentenced to two years of hard labor (© Li Zhensheng / Contact Press Images, from *Red-Color News Soldier*, Phaidon, 2003).

7. Wall posters at Peking University, summer 1966, at the beginning of the Cultural Revolution (*China Pictorial*, November 1967).

8. Chairman Mao greets Red Guards on the rostrum of Tiananmen, August 18, 1966 (ChinaFotoPress via Getty Images).

9. Chairman Mao reviews Red Guards on Tiananmen Square, August 31, 1966, with Lin Biao on the right (Mondadori via Getty Images).

10. Zhou Enlai (left) and other officials who directed the course of the Cultural Revolution, July 1967. To the right of Zhou are Jiang Qing, Chen Boda, Kang Sheng, and Zhang Chunqiao (Gamma-Keystone via Getty Images).

11. First party secretary of Harbin, face smeared with ink, is denounced at a struggle session, August 26, 1966 (© Li Zhensheng / Contact Press Images, from *Red-Color News Soldier*, Phaidon, 2003).

12. Wife of the Heilongjiang provincial governor during a struggle session, August 29, 1966, Harbin (© Li Zhensheng / Contact Press Images, from *Red-Color News Soldier*, Phaidon, 2003).

13. Cleansing of the Class Ranks Campaign, outskirts of Harbin, April 5, 1968. Two individuals sentenced to death as members of a "counterrevolutionary clique" are prepared for execution (© Li Zhensheng / Contact Press Images, from *Red-Color News Soldier,* Phaidon, 2003).

14. Cleansing of the Class Ranks Campaign, outskirts of Harbin, April 5, 1968. Execution of a group condemned for political crimes (© Li Zhensheng / Contact Press Images, from *Red-Color News Soldier,* Phaidon, 2003).

15. Burning buildings in Nanning, Guangxi, during the
military campaign to seize control of the city from armed
fighters of the April 22 faction, July 18, 1968 (New
Century Press, Hong Kong).

16. Mass surrender of April 22 fighters in Nanning, August 5, 1968 (New
Century Press, Hong Kong).

17. Summary executions of April 22 fighters on the streets of Nanning after their surrender, early August 1968 (New Century Press, Hong Kong).

18. Tiananmen Square, April 4, 1976. Citizens surround wreaths commemorating Zhou Enlai piled up around the Revolutionary Martyrs' Monument in Tiananmen Square, in defiance of official prohibitions (ChinaFotoPress via Getty Images).

19. Tiananmen Square, April 4, 1976. Speeches and poems critical of Maoist radicals are read out on the square during protests known as the Tiananmen Incident (ChinaFotoPress via Getty Images).

11

Collapse and Division

THE REPEATED HEADACHES created by the Red Guards eroded Mao's confidence in the students. He and the Central Cultural Revolution Group (CCRG) had to intervene repeatedly to keep them relatively unified and on message, but each time they solved one problem, another took its place. University students, after all, were a very small elite. There were fewer than 675,000 college students in a nation of 740 million. They were too small a group, and too divided, to have the desired impact on the national party hierarchy. These considerations spurred Mao and the CCRG to turn to the mobilization of industrial workers.

Well into November 1966, urban workers were still officially discouraged from organizing their own rebel groups. On November 10, *People's Daily* admonished them to remain at their production posts and not leave their factories to engage in "exchange of revolutionary experiences." Zhou Enlai, in scores of meetings with "representatives of the masses," desperately tried to insulate the economy from the Cultural Revolution, just as he had tried to limit the violence perpetrated by the students. In their much more numerous meetings with Red Guards and worker activists, however, members of the CCRG were more cavalier about this prohibition, and they asserted repeatedly that revolutionary consciousness would have a positive impact on production.[1]

Worker Rebels

In early November the CCRG was already encouraging the formation of a worker-based insurgency behind the scenes. On November 6, the Shanghai Liaison Station of the Beijing student rebels met with politically active workers from seventeen state factories in the city. Encouraged by the students, who spoke on behalf of the CCRG, the workers formed an organization called the Shanghai Workers' Revolutionary Rebel General Headquarters, and named a thirty-two-year-old factory security officer and party member named Wang Hongwen as their commander. Wang had authored the first wall poster that appeared at Shanghai's No. 17 Cotton Mill back in mid-June, and had a record of conflict with the work team sent to his factory.[2]

The group demanded recognition from the Shanghai Municipal Party Committee, which understandably refused to permit the formation of what looked like an independent trade union. More than 2,000 members of the Workers' General Headquarters commandeered a Beijing-bound train to petition for official support. Zhou Enlai ordered the train halted in the Shanghai suburbs. The workers then blocked the rail lines connecting Shanghai with Nanjing and northern China. The action completely disrupted rail traffic. The CCRG's Zhang Chunqiao, himself a ranking Shanghai official, was sent to negotiate. In return for a pledge to halt the blockade and return to Shanghai, Zhang agreed to all of their demands—official recognition of their organization and blaming the incident on the Shanghai Party Committee.[3]

Zhang Chunqiao's unilateral action surprised several of his CCRG colleagues, who initially objected, but Mao quickly signaled his approval. It was still unclear whether the Shanghai agreement marked a fundamental shift in national policy. Zhou Enlai called meetings of industrial ministers and representatives of regional party committees to solicit their views. They fiercely opposed the formation of worker rebel organizations, arguing that the resulting chaos would bring production to a halt. Zhou presented their views to Mao on November 22, who rejected them. On December 9, Beijing finally issued a document affirming the right of workers to set up their own "revolutionary organizations"—but insisted that they participate in politics only in their spare time. A companion document extended the policy to collective farms.[4]

This was a momentous decision, radically expanding the scale and scope of the nationwide insurgency. There were 52 million workers and staff in state and collective enterprises in 1966—seventy-five times larger than the university student population.[5] Essentially, the Maoist authorities gave the green light to the mobilization of the entire industrial workforce. The impact was immediate and explosive. In early December 1966 the insurgency spread throughout the country, pushing the student movement to the sidelines.

If Mao and the CCRG believed that a workers' insurgency would be more pliable and unified than the troublesome student movement, they quickly learned otherwise. Two problems immediately became evident. First, there was nothing to stop workers from concluding that grievances related to pay and living standards were due to "revisionist" managers who were concerned with production targets at the expense of worker welfare. The industrial system China inherited from the Soviet Union mandated low wages, consumer austerity, and housing shortages, and this was the first opportunity since 1957 for industrial workers to openly raise issues of pay and living standards. Second, unlike the universities and high schools, whose party organizations were devastated by work teams and immobilized during June and July, party organizations in factories throughout China were still active and largely intact. There was nothing to prevent networks of party activists from organizing their own rebel groups among workers to oppose disruptive rebel insurgencies. And there was nothing to prevent rivals within the party leadership of factories to organize rebel groups that expressed preexisting antagonisms within the organization. These conditions ensured that the workers' insurgency would grow rapidly and be just as divided as the student movement. Given the much larger scale of the workers' insurgency, the problems it presented were even more severe.

The Collapse of Local Governments

After factory workforces split into factions, it was impossible to maintain the prohibition against political activities during work hours. Factories were disrupted by internal conflicts, and factions linked up with allies in other enterprises to engage in battles off site. Attacks on factory officials by nascent rebel groups, and street actions that disrupted transportation and services, provoked immediate countermobilization led by workers who were party and union activists.[6] Factory officials and municipal authorities did little to discourage such countermobilization. Once it became clear that Mao authorized independent worker organizations, local authorities quickly recognized that mass mobilization by loyal worker groups was in their interest. They learned to provide tacit and in some cases direct support for this kind of rebel group.

Relying on factory party organizations and trade unions, which already had well-established ties with the workforce and considerable resources, these loyalist organizations grew with astonishing rapidity and presented a major challenge to nascent rebel movements. In Shanghai, shortly after the official recognition of the Workers' General Headquarters in mid-November, an opposed workers' alliance known as the Scarlet Guards quickly appeared, and soon was able to mobilize hundreds of thousands of rank-and-file workers into the streets.[7] Whereas rebel organizations grew slowly and built independent organizations through a long period of struggle, loyalist organizations relied on existing party and union networks to generate huge memberships in very short order.

At the factory level, conflict and divisions within the workforce often mirrored divisions within the party leadership. The Yangzi River Machine Works, described earlier as an example of the divisive impact of the Socialist Education Movement, was one such case. Recall that the 1964 campaign split the factory's leadership into factions that had the backing, respectively, of the Fourth Machine Building Ministry and the Nanjing Party Committee. When the Cultural Revolution spread to factories, the party faction earlier backed by the Nanjing authorities mobilized the workers loyal to them into an insurgency aimed at overthrowing the officials aligned with the ministry. The ministry-backed factory officials, in turn, mobilized their loyalists to defend against these attacks. As the workers' insurgency developed during November and December 1966, the dissident worker faction sought and received the backing of the Nanjing party authorities, and subsequently fought to defend them in a broader citywide rebel coalition. The faction mobilized by ministry-backed officials joined the coalition that sought to overthrow the Nanjing authorities.[8]

A second consequence was the rapid escalation of economic demands. Workers' demands would have required greater expenditures on wages and living standards at the expense of investment, undermining a core feature of China's Soviet-inspired industrialization model. In Shanghai, as the conflict between the Workers' General Headquarters and the Scarlet Guards grew, hundreds of new organizations sprang up to pursue livelihood complaints. The primary demands were for higher wages and welfare subsidies, granting of permanent urban household registration, allocation of new apartments, and new job assignments or classifications. Temporary and contract workers formed rebel groups to demand permanent state sector jobs; permanent workers whose wages had been frozen for years demanded immediate wage hikes; workers relocated to the countryside during the post–Great Leap recession demanded a return to the city and their former jobs; poorly paid apprentices demanded promotions and raises; workers in small and marginal collective and cooperative firms demanded the medical and fringe benefits that were provided only for those with state sector jobs.

Workers held factory and government officials hostage until they agreed to these demands. In many cases they were pressured to authorize lump sum payments for "travel expenses." The demands escalated rapidly during December, spreading from small and isolated groups formed around specific grievances to members of larger branches of rebel organizations affiliated with both the Workers' General Headquarters and the Scarlet Guards.[9] These escalating demands, which expressed dissatisfactions bred by China's planned economy, were wholly unanticipated and unwanted by Mao and the CCRG. They did, however, bear out the predictions of industrial officials who were adamantly opposed to independent worker organizations.

An equally crippling blow was the rapid emergence of rebel groups among the white-collar staff of government and party organs. If industrial workers were permitted to rebel, there was nothing to restrain employees in civil administration and the organs of state power. Office staff, even in the headquarters of party and government, formed their own rebel organizations, making accusations against top officials in their units, disrupting normal operations, vying with competing rebel groups within the same office, and linking up with outside rebel groups. As the insurgency spread, party officials could not even be confident that their own office staff would heed their authority.[10]

By the end of 1966, China's large cities were rapidly becoming ungovernable. Workers left their jobs to engage in protests against local party organs, and they often found themselves in pitched battles against other workers who pledged loyalty to the party apparatus. Railway and ferry services were disrupted; ships were unable to load or unload freight in the harbors; and factories shut down. The army and security services had been prohibited from intervening in rebel activities since late August—a prohibition still in place despite the CCRG's suppression of dissident Red Guards in Beijing—so local party organs were unable to call on them. Having lost control over the streets, and increasingly having lost control over their own office staff, party officials reported to Beijing that their offices were "paralyzed." Many local leaders by this point were in fact under detention by rebels, and were carted back and forth for mass meetings and "struggle sessions."[11] If the Cultural Revolution were to accomplish something more than a general collapse of China's economy and civil order, something had to be done.

Shanghai's January Revolution

Shanghai suffered from all of these problems in pronounced form. Clashes between the Workers' General Headquarters and the Scarlet Guards escalated during December, paralyzing the city. The situation became critical when the Scarlet Guards, finally recognizing that their efforts to defend the Shanghai party authorities were futile, withdrew their allegiance and went on the attack. On December 23 they mobilized some 300,000 workers for a rally at the city center to "criticize the reactionary line of the Shanghai Party Committee." They demanded recognition of their organization by Shanghai's mayor, who immediately granted it. But the mayor was forced to repudiate the agreement the next day by the Workers' General Headquarters. After his change of mind was broadcast over the radio, 20,000 to 30,000 Scarlet Guards surrounded the Shanghai Party Committee offices to demand a confrontation with the mayor.

The next day, December 29, the Workers' General Headquarters mobilized a force of almost 100,000 to surround the protesters. A violent battle ensued, and the outnumbered Scarlet Guards were badly battered. On December 31 a force of some 20,000 Scarlet Guards marched along the railway lines to Beijing to protest their treatment. When they reached the outskirts of Shanghai, regiments from the Workers' General Headquarters attacked them. The fighting halted rail traffic in and out of Shanghai once again. Factories, transport hubs, and dockyards in Shanghai were paralyzed as members of both factions either left workplaces for street protests or engaged in battles at work. Rebel workers demanded cash from besieged factory officials, who had little choice but to comply. The bank accounts of state units were drained, and the beneficiaries of the cash windfall swarmed to retail outlets, quickly exhausting supplies of scarce consumer items. Food shortages occurred, and citizens rushed to withdraw their savings from banks, while public transportation was paralyzed.[12]

The response was a contrived "power seizure," designed to restore civil order and industrial production while at the same time replacing the Shanghai party leadership with officials loyal to the Maoist cause. On January 4, CCRG members Zhang Chunqiao and Yao Wenyuan flew to Shanghai. Coordinating their actions with the Workers' General Headquarters, they authorized the takeover of major media outlets by rebels and ordered them to publish editorials demanding the restoration of order. The editorials asserted that the Shanghai authorities plotted to obstruct the Cultural Revolution by instigating factionalism and luring workers into making economic demands—yet another manifestation of the bourgeois reactionary line.[13] Zhang ordered the Workers' General Headquarters to organize a mass rally on January 6 to "overthrow the Shanghai Party Committee." During the rally, attended by 100,000, the first party secretary, mayor, and other leading officials on the Shanghai Party Committee were denounced on the stage, heads bowed.[14]

This move effectively dissolved the Shanghai Party Committee. In short order, forty-five out of fifty-six members were stripped of their positions; the mayor and all seven deputy mayors were deposed. On January 9 local papers published an "Urgent Notice" in the name of the Workers' General Headquarters and other rebel groups, spelling out a series of steps to restore stability. Economic demands were condemned and denounced as a plot by revisionists. Mao told members of the CCRG that the actions of the Shanghai rebels were correct, and that the entire country should "learn from the experience of Shanghai, and take concrete action." A congratulatory telegram was published nationwide on January 12. It expressed approval for the Shanghai power seizure and encouraged similar actions elsewhere. The Scarlet Guards responded by issuing a statement titled "Begging Forgiveness from Chairman Mao," apologizing for their previous opposition to the Workers' General Headquarters.[15]

Zhang Chunqiao announced on January 19 that the new organ of municipal power would be known as the Shanghai People's Commune. Mao, however, perhaps in response to the bungled effort by student rebels to create a Beijing Commune, informed Zhang in mid-February that the name should be changed to Revolutionary Committee. Zhang did so dutifully, and on February 23 the name change was announced: Zhang was the head of the Revolutionary Committee, Yao Wenyuan first vice head, and Wang Hongwen, the leader of the Workers' General Headquarters, was their principal deputy.[16]

Zhang made clear that power was now in the hands of "genuine revolutionaries" and further challenges to authority were forbidden. Zhang ordered rebels to return to work and withdraw from the streets. For the first time since the August prohibition he deployed the military to keep order and prevent further attacks on organs of power. He deployed troops from the Nanjing Military Region, and he had worker militias from loyal factions march through the streets and keep order.[17]

Zhang's power seizure sparked opposition from both student and worker rebels. The first challenge came from the large student alliance known as the Red Revolutionaries. Their leaders viewed the power seizure with suspicion. Backed by the armed forces, it looked suspiciously like the suppression of the mass movement—a crackdown masked with empty rhetoric about "revolution." Zhang, after all, was a senior member of the Shanghai Party Committee. Moreover, he had pushed aside students who were the first to attack the Shanghai Party Committee, working instead with the Workers' General Headquarters. At a meeting with Zhang and Yao Wenyuan on January 27, the Red Revolutionaries held the two for six hours, attempting to force an apology for using troops to suppress rebels. Zhang and Yao were freed without making any concessions, but the next day student radicals kidnapped one of Zhang's top deputies and held him on the Fudan University campus. Zhang dispatched troops to free the aide. The students responded by distributing handbills and wall posters attacking Zhang for suppressing the student movement. In response, Zhang mobilized workers to patrol public spaces to prevent further expressions of dissent. The CCRG issued a public telegram calling the attacks on Zhang "completely mistaken," and warning of dire consequences for those who persisted. The student rebels quickly abandoned their offensive.[18]

Zhang faced similar challenges from rebel groups allied with the Workers' General Headquarters. Several of them objected to the planned Shanghai Commune, which was negotiated without their participation. They balked at an order to dissolve and merge with the Workers' General Headquarters. Geng Jinzhang, the leader of the massive Second Regiment, mobilized a large alliance of workers to openly challenge Wang Hongwen, and they announced the formation of a rival commune. In late February, public security forces arrested Geng Jinzhang and dissolved the independent regiments. From that time on Shanghai did not experience street fighting between large factional alliances. Factional strife persisted but was contained within individual factories.[19] Mao's unwavering support permitted the deployment of public security forces and local militia to make Shanghai an oasis of relative stability as public order collapsed in most of China.

Regional Power Seizures

Shanghai's January Revolution was a model for the rest of the country. It could plausibly claim to be the result of a mass movement. Several large mass organizations supported Zhang Chunqiao, and their leaders were absorbed into new organs of power. Zhang was a trusted radical, a longtime supporter of Mao's initiatives and a member of the CCRG. Finally, Shanghai showed that a power seizure could restore production and civil order after power holders were overthrown. Rebels in provinces throughout the country were urged to seize power in a similar fashion.

While Shanghai was the inspiration, Heilongjiang provided the approved name for the new architecture of power: Revolutionary Committee. Interestingly, the incumbent first party secretary of the province, Pan Fusheng, survived to head a new government that incorporated selected leaders of rebel organizations alongside revolutionary cadres and military officers. Pan Fusheng was a newcomer to the province, having been transferred to the post from elsewhere in October 1965. He therefore did not have strong ties with other local leaders, nor did he have to answer for the actions of provincial leaders in the past. Pan openly welcomed the student rebellion from the very beginning, distancing himself from his longer-serving colleagues and acting as if he was himself the sponsor of the local Red Guards. He presided over massive Red Guard rallies in Harbin in mid-August, during which he imitated Mao's role in Tiananmen Square. When students made accusations against top officials in the province, he readily agreed to them, and even presided over struggle sessions against other top provincial officials. When rebel groups clamored to seize power in late January, Pan openly welcomed them, and with the approval of the CCRG, on January 31 he formed a new power structure with himself at the head. Several large rebel organizations opposed the action, but Pan dispatched the army to suppress them. The CCRG officially approved the new regional government on February 2.[20] Mao came to prefer this name to "commune"—perhaps influenced by the bungled efforts by student rebels to form the Beijing Commune and the stubborn opposition to the Shanghai Commune.

Power seizures appealed even more strongly to figures eager to curb the destructive thrust of the Cultural Revolution. Zhou Enlai, who had initially opposed the inclusion of workers for that reason, became an enthusiastic supporter of power seizures in January 1967. He saw them as the only way to bring order out of chaos and began to encourage them in other parts of the country. Zhou, for example, directly phoned hesitant rebel leaders in Nanjing and urged them to seize power from the Jiangsu Provincial Party Committee.[21] His moves, however, earned the suspicion of members of the CCRG, who saw Zhou's sudden leftist enthusiasm as an unprincipled and expedient effort simply to restore order. The CCRG worried that a Zhou-engineered power seizure might be a cover for a restoration of the status quo. The tension between these two objectives, and between these two political tendencies, would prolong the struggle to create new organs of power well into 1968, ensuring that the greatest disorders for China's provinces, and the highest levels of violence, were still in the future.

The Shanghai model, if replicated nationwide, would obviously allow Mao and the CCRG to claim that the Cultural Revolution had been brought to a victorious conclusion. This seems to have been their hope early in 1967. Initially, they followed the Shanghai and Heilongjiang script with some success: they identified a senior official who demonstrated unswerving loyalty to Mao's line and who was able to earn the support of a significant portion of local rebel forces, and placed that person in charge of the power seizure. Three more provincial power seizures of this kind were approved by mid-February: Guizhou, Shandong, and Shanxi. In each case Beijing officials were able to identify a sufficiently senior local official who had demonstrated loyalty to the CCRG's agenda and who had the support of a large segment of the rebel insurgency. In each case their power seizures stimulated rebel opposition of the variety experienced in Shanghai. And in each case the new leaders, with the backing of Mao, Zhou, and the CCRG, deployed the armed forces to shut down opposition.[22]

After this, the power seizure movement stalled. No further revolutionary committees were approved until August, and only one other for the rest of the year. Efforts to orchestrate power seizures in other regions foundered on the inability of the CCRG to identify a trusted senior cadre to take the lead, or by rebel movements that were so evenly divided that any effort to declare a power seizure would require the massive application of brute force against one of the two sides. The armed forces were called in to maintain order while the political situations in the remaining provinces were sorted out. Without approved power seizures at the provincial level, there could be no approved power seizures at lower levels of government, which meant that these issues remained unresolved down to the grass roots.

Jiangsu Province illustrates the problem: there the effort was plagued by a sharp difference in attitude between Zhou Enlai, who was at the center of negotiations to approve power seizures, and the radical members of the CCRG. In early January, with most of the top leadership of the province held captive by rebel forces, and with the transportation hubs and the port completely paralyzed by street battles, Zhou placed calls to local rebel forces to urge them to seize power. After failing over several days to negotiate relative roles in the new power structure, one group of rebel leaders decided to move ahead without the others. With the support of the local armed forces and the prior approval of both Zhou Enlai and the CCRG, they declared a power seizure on January 25. The rebels who were left behind immediately protested and invaded the offices of the local party newspaper to prevent publication of the announcement. The rebels who seized power waited expectantly for Beijing's approval of their action, but it never came. Instead, Zhou Enlai ordered them to Beijing for negotiations to work out unity in the rebel camp. Large delegations of leaders from each side traveled to Beijing and entered into contentious negotiations with Zhou and other top officials, and could not agree on a senior official to serve as the government's new head. In the end, the negotiations ended in a stalemate, and Jiangsu was placed under military control in early March, essentially a holding strategy. The commander of the Nanjing Military Region, Xu Shiyou, was entrusted to keep order while the situation was sorted out.[23]

Guangdong Province had a similar experience, although the power seizure there took a different form. As in Jiangsu, the city's large rebel movement was unable to negotiate an agreement about seizing power. When one group of rebels went ahead without the consent of the others, they alienated the rebel groups left behind. Their power seizure, however, took a unique form. The Guangdong party secretary, Zhao Ziyang, perhaps trying to imitate Pan Fusheng in Heilongjiang, welcomed the rebels when they arrived to seize power. Zhao agreed to hand over power and pledged that his leading group and their staff would continue to work under supervisors appointed by the rebels. This would ensure that the power seizure was successful and that order could be maintained. The rebels agreed, and the arrangement obviously appealed to Zhou Enlai, who was arguing in Beijing that this was the preferred format for future power seizures. The excluded rebels, however, instantly opposed these arrangements as a "fake power seizure," because it left the province's top officials in place. This charge resonated with the CCRG, who bought the argument and supported the claims of the excluded rebels. Zhou fruitlessly tried to negotiate a settlement and was forced to put Guangdong under military control.[24]

The Consequences of Military Intervention

Because of the unfailing tendency of rebel forces to split, the support of the armed forces was essential in stabilizing new organs of power. It had proved crucial for the first group of province-level revolutionary committees, and rebels who claimed to have seized power eagerly sought military support. In the last week of January Mao sent a note to Lin Biao calling for military support for "the broad masses of the left." There followed a directive that stated, "When genuine proletarian Leftists ask the army for help, the army should send troops actively to support them." Subsequent requests for clarification about how to implement this order led to a January 28 order that forbade mass organizations from attacking military installations, and authorized local commanders to suppress "rightists" and "counterrevolutionary groups."[25]

This fateful order reversed the August 1966 prohibition against PLA interference in the rebel movement. Military control altered the relationship between military units and rebels who claimed to have seized power. Once military control was declared, troops assumed greater authority. In the absence of a revolutionary committee approved by Beijing, military officers had no local civilian authorities to guide their actions (unlike Shanghai or Heilongjiang), and they were forced to exercise their own judgment about how to sort out competing rebel claims, and how to respond when local rebel groups resisted military control. In these circumstances, which characterized most of China, instead of hastening the formation of revolutionary committees, military control inadvertently drew the armed forces into local factional conflicts. This intensified and prolonged the divisions, further delaying the formation of revolutionary committees.

After the late January 1967 order for the PLA to "support the left," there followed a two-month period during which the foundations for deepening factional violence were laid. It was inevitable that clashes between rebel groups and armed forces would occur. When the PLA implemented military control, it confronted rebel groups that had occupied offices and other public installations. Although these power seizures had yet to receive the imprimatur of Mao and the CCRG, the rebels considered their power seizures as legitimate and frequently tried to defend them. When military units took over strategic sites, they weakened the influence of rebel groups that had seized power, and inadvertently strengthened the hand of rival rebels who had been left out of the power seizure. This upset the balance of power in local rivalries. For this reason, military units frequently met with strong resistance from rebels in possession of strategic sites.[26]

These clashes had consequences. Rebel groups forced to yield control frequently interpreted the army's actions as an illegitimate suppression of the mass movement. They understood that losing control of strategic sites weakened their claims to have seized power, and they feared that this would weaken them in their rivalry with other rebels. When the confrontations turned violent, arrests followed, and the seeds of deep antagonism were sown.

Rebels who suffered in these initial encounters frequently mobilized their forces to surround military compounds in protest, orchestrating campaigns of resistance to the army. These confrontations could be dangerous, primarily for the rebels. They resulted in a massacre of 169 rebels outside a military compound in Qinghai in late February, and in shootings that resulted in civilian casualties in Xinjiang, Inner Mongolia, and Henan. More commonly they resulted in mass arrests of rebel groups that organized resistance. In Sichuan, tens of thousands were arrested after a rebel siege of the Chengdu military headquarters. Less dramatic confrontations in Guangzhou and Nanjing resulted in arrests that focused on the factions that claimed to have seized power.[27] Rebel groups that persisted in violent resistance were branded as counterrevolutionary, their leaders and activists incarcerated, their organizations banned.

Mao and the CCRG were not bothered by military suppression in support of approved revolutionary committees. The actions of the military to defend approved new organs of power in Shanghai, Heilongjiang, and elsewhere were deemed entirely legitimate, even essential. Organized resistance under these circumstances was deemed illegitimate; the army's actions were a defense of a local victory for the Cultural Revolution. However, when the army actively suppressed rebels where Beijing had yet to sort out rival rebel claims, they threatened to upset the local balance of power. To Mao and many on the CCRG, the army appeared to be suppressing a mass movement that had been cultivated and encouraged for many months. Mao became concerned that military units with unclear political sympathies were forcing their own solution on regional conflicts, bringing them—and the Cultural Revolution—to a premature end. These concerns were heightened after some of China's most senior military officials angrily confronted members of the CCRG about the disruptions caused by the Cultural Revolution during mid-February 1967 meetings of the remaining party leadership.[28] Lin Biao may have been Mao's most loyal lieutenant, but other military officers, especially regional commanders, seemed to be far from enthusiastic about the rebellion.

By mid-March Mao concluded that the military had gone too far, and that their actions had weakened rebels to an unacceptable degree. He ordered the arrest of several local commanders and purged problematic local commands. On April 6 Lin Biao responded to Mao's concerns by issuing a new directive to the army that reversed the emphasis of the January orders. It ordered army units never to fire on mass organizations and to halt mass arrests. The army was forbidden to ban mass organizations or label them as counterrevolutionary, and such bans were to be lifted and labels removed. Only civilian officials in Beijing could approve such bans and labels in the future. Opposition to the PLA could no longer be the criterion for deciding whether a mass organization was genuinely leftist.[29]

These orders forced the army to curtail its aggressive enforcement of military control and led to the revival of rebel organizations that suffered in February and March. There were unintended consequences as well, because the situation on the ground had changed. When rebel leaders and their followers were released from jail, their organizations were restored and their reactionary labels removed. It was not possible to pretend that the events of the past two months had not occurred. Now they harbored deep grievances against the local military commanders at whose hands they had suffered. More importantly, when their organizations were suppressed, their claims as leaders of a power seizure were undermined. The April 6 directive removed the hand of military suppression, but the liberated rebels now had an urgent new political objective: to regain the influence and prestige that had declined at the hands of the military and to roll back military control.

There was also a more subtle change that would have equally profound implications. The actions of the armed forces inadvertently inserted them into the middle of factional conflicts. Power seizures almost always generated opposition by rival rebels who were marginalized or excluded. This is what happened in Shanghai, when the Second Regiment and Red Revolutionaries both opposed the power seizure orchestrated by the Workers' General Headquarters. The new Shanghai authorities, with clear backing from Mao, confidently deployed the armed forces to stamp out opposition. Something very different happened elsewhere in China, where rebels seized power but waited in vain for Beijing's approval. In these circumstances, dissident rebels who had objected to local power seizures welcomed the military's actions against their opponents. These rebels found military control to be very congenial, because the armed forces refused to recognize their rivals' claims. When rebel factions suppressed by the military reemerged in April to pursue their grievances against the army and regain their former power and status, their rivals felt compelled to defend the army, whose actions had indirectly aided their cause. The foundations for new factional divisions were laid: between rebel groups that opposed, and defended, the actions of the army.

The Foundations for Factional Violence

Efforts to enforce military control inadvertently created the violent summer of 1967. In Nanjing, the armed forces implemented military control in March after the city's rebel movement had split in two—one side supported the power seizure (the Pro faction), and the other side opposed it (the Anti faction).[30] During the failed February negotiations in Beijing between the two sides, the CCRG favored the claims of the Anti faction rebels. That faction contained some of the most prominent rebel commanders in Nanjing, figures well known to the CCRG from the fall campaign against the Jiangsu Party Committee. When the armed forces imposed military control over strategic sites in

Nanjing, they clashed with units of the Pro faction. Arrests followed, and the Pro faction began to protest their treatment by the military. The Anti faction, on the other hand, saw no problem with the army's actions.

After the early April directive that called for the armed forces to pull back from the suppression of rebels, the axis of conflict began to shift. To the earlier antagonism between the Pro and Anti factions over the power seizure was now added a fundamental disagreement about the role of the army. When Pro faction leaders were released from prison, they began a campaign against the army for its "errors of line." The Anti faction, for its part, defended the armed forces. The two sides were now more evenly balanced, and the Anti faction enjoyed close ties with the army. The intensified antagonisms between the two rebel alliances—over the power seizure and military control—escalated in the late spring into renewed fighting over control of schools, offices, and other sites. Street battles became more common, and the Pro faction accused the army of aiding the Anti faction behind the scenes. Because the April directive ordered the armed forces to back off, they did little to intervene in street battles between the two sides.

At this point the CCRG shifted its support from the Anti to the Pro faction. They had originally supported the famous rebels in the Anti faction, but the CCRG was now worried that the armed forces were stamping out the forces of rebellion, and the Pro faction's attacks on the Nanjing Military Region were aligned with their shifting political agenda, while the Anti faction now supported the army. The CCRG began to work with Pro faction forces to promote resistance to the army, which now found itself in the middle of the unfolding factional struggle in Jiangsu. In the wake of the new April directive the army no longer had the authority to curtail street battles between the two sides. The scene was set for large-scale violence.

Essentially the same pattern occurred in Guangzhou. Local rebel forces split over the late January power seizure for the same reasons as in Nanjing.[31] The rebels excluded from the power seizure charged that it was fake because it protected officials who were earlier behind the bourgeois reactionary line. This argument resonated with the CCRG, especially because Zhou Enlai promoted the Guangzhou power seizure as a model. The CCRG favored the Anti faction in February negotiations in Beijing. When the negotiations reached an impasse, military control was imposed in late February. The same sequence of events observed in

Nanjing unfolded in Guangzhou. The rebels who had seized power resisted military control, suffered arrests, and had their organizations banned. The rival rebels approved the military's actions. When the new April directive to the army liberated the arrested rebels, they mobilized to attack the armed forces. This won them the approval of the CCRG, which had previously supported the other rebel faction. Clashes between the two rebel alliances, now more evenly matched, escalated throughout the province. Rebels who opposed the army became known as Red Flag, while their rivals who supported the army's actions became known as East Wind.[32]

Wuhan experienced the same initial splits among rebel forces over their January power seizure, but events subsequently took a very different turn, and in ways that would have huge national repercussions. The province experienced the familiar splits between rebels over representation in the power seizure, and the group that went ahead with the power seizure clashed with the local military, and was denounced and suppressed in return.[33] However, in late March Chen Zaidao, the commander of the Wuhan Military Region, met in Beijing with Zhou Enlai and members of the CCRG, and they agreed that the actions of the dominant rebel faction had been incorrect and that their attacks on the military were not to be tolerated. Drawing confidence from these instructions, Chen returned to Wuhan and conducted an unusually aggressive campaign against the rebel faction that had resisted, imprisoning its leaders and large numbers of followers, crushing the organization and denouncing many of its members as counterrevolutionary.

The rival rebels supported the army's actions, and they cooperated with the army by informing on and denouncing their opponents. However, they also quickly fell afoul of the army. In early March they published an editorial in *Hubei Daily*, a newspaper that they still controlled, warning that the army's crackdown on their rivals should not mislead conservatives into thinking that the status quo would be restored. The rebels were surprised to find that the army interpreted this editorial as an attack on them. The army seized control of the newspaper and forced their leaders to make a self-criticism. Now seemingly out of favor, their organization declined as well.

The army proceeded to stabilize public order and restore production. They set up teams to "promote production" in factories, relying on party and trade union organizations that were severely undermined in previous months. New rebel organizations appeared that in membership and orientation resembled the defunct Scarlet Guards of Shanghai, which had mobilized to defend the Shanghai Party Committee. These organizations firmly supported the army's efforts to restore order in Wuhan.[34]

The actions of the Wuhan military were exactly the type that was prohibited in the April 6 directive that reined in the military. The new directive strengthened the resolve of both wings of the formerly divided rebel movement, who joined together once again in a campaign to attack General Chen Zaidao. The banned rebel organizations re-formed and declared their rebirth, staged marches in the city, raided the offices of the two major daily newspapers, and staged a large hunger strike to demand the release of prisoners.[35]

Unlike those in Nanjing, Guangzhou, and Hangzhou, the factions that developed in Wuhan during May and June 1967 were not two rival wings of the earlier rebel movement. The rebels reunited in opposition to the military, while a completely new alliance, adopting the name Million Heroes, defended the military and had close ties to party, security organs, and militia. Resurgent Wuhan rebels began an offensive against the Wuhan Military Region, staging hunger strikes across the city to demand the release of imprisoned comrades and the recognition of their banned organizations. Small clashes occurred with security forces in early May. The army released some of the imprisoned rebels, but stubbornly insisted that their verdict on the banned rebel organizations was correct. During May and June the rebels expanded and rebuilt their organizations, while the Million Heroes organization grew and strongly supported the local military.[36]

With the two factions gaining strength and the armed forces now prohibited from using armed force, there was no way to restrain escalating factional violence. Large-scale violence did not begin until late May, when the first death was recorded. At this point each faction began to arm itself, primarily with clubs and spears, and occupy buildings, offices, and factories, reinforcing them against attacks by its rivals. The Million Heroes had a distinct advantage, organizing themselves into disciplined units staffed by army veterans, and they took over most of the factories in several city districts as well as the city's party headquarters. The Wuhan military issued repeated calls to end the street violence, but without the ability to use force their appeals fell on deaf ears.

Wuhan became a battleground, with street fighting throughout the city. According to figures compiled by the rebels, during May and June there were 174 violent clashes, involving 70,000 fighters, resulting in 158 deaths and more than a thousand serious injuries. The Million Heroes launched a major offensive against rebel forces in June, systematically taking over districts in rebel hands. Dozens of deaths and even more injuries were reported, and the rebel forces were in disarray. On June 23, units from the Million Heroes captured the headquarters of the main rebel organization, killing twenty-five in the process. The Wuhan rebels were on the verge of total defeat.[37]

The CCRG, monitoring these events, became alarmed at the rebels' plight. On June 26 they sent an urgent telegram to the Wuhan Military Region ordering Chen Zaidao to prevent further attacks. The order criticized the Million Heroes and warned that those responsible for the killings would be punished. The two sides were to be invited to Beijing for negotiations. Street fighting abated as the Million Heroes refrained from further attacks, and each side prepared to present their case in Beijing.[38]

The Wuhan Incident

The venue for the negotiations soon shifted to Wuhan, because Mao Zedong was beginning an unannounced inspection tour of southern provinces and Wuhan would be his first stop. Mao arrived secretly on July 13, bringing CCRG member Wang Li and Minister of Public Security Xie Fuzhi along with him, later joined by Zhou Enlai. Wang and Xie visited rebels at a local university and news of their presence in the city spread.[39] Mao dictated his resolution of the crisis on July 15 and 16. The suppressed rebel organizations must be reinstated and treated equally; the Million Heroes should not be disbanded, but it was a conservative organization; and the Wuhan military leaders must make a self-criticism for their errors. Xie Fuzhi and Wang Li relayed the gist of these instructions to military commanders and mass organizations over the next several days. As the news spread throughout the city, the rebels emphasized the criticisms of the Million Heroes and the errors of the military, and Wang Li reinforced the impression that the decision was tilted against the Million Heroes in an undiplomatic speech to military officers. This appeared to represent a complete defeat for the Million Heroes, whose leaders and activists were outraged, many of whom refused to believe that the verdict was final. Many of them blamed Wang Li for the decision, believing that he was responsible, and soldiers sympathetic to the Million Heroes shared this view.[40]

The dramatic events of the evening of July 20 became known as the Wuhan Incident. That evening a contingent of disgruntled soldiers sympathetic to the Million Heroes broke into the compound where Xie Fuzhi and Wang Li were staying, roughed them up, and kidnapped Wang Li, holding him hostage. Mao was staying in a nearby villa in the same compound and the incursion by hostile soldiers raised alarms about his security. Mao was hustled out of Wuhan and took a plane to Shanghai. Rumors spread that Wang Li's instructions were repudiated by the CCRG and that Mao had rejected his verdict. Million Heroes forces staged celebratory demonstrations throughout the city and posted slogans denouncing Wang Li. Wang was eventually transferred to the custody of military units and released on July 22. Nursing a broken leg and other injuries, he flew back to Beijing for a staged welcome as a returning hero.[41]

Beijing's reaction to Wang Li's return came as a shock to the jubilant Million Heroes. The events of July 20 were called a "counterrevolutionary rebellion," and huge demonstrations were held across China to repudiate "Wuhan reactionaries." Beijing issued an open letter on July 27 calling on the people of Wuhan to struggle against the "evil leaders" of the Wuhan Military Region and the Million Heroes. Chen Zaidao and his subordinates were escorted to the capital and blasted with charges that they had attempted a military coup. The Million Heroes were loudly and repeatedly condemned. The organization quickly disintegrated and disappeared from the political scene. The resurgent rebel forces resumed attacks on members of the Million Heroes; in Wuhan alone more than 600 were killed and some 66,000 suffered permanent injuries in the rebels' violent retaliation in the coming months.[42] Their common enemy vanquished, the rebel forces once again split over their respective places in local organs of power. Unable to compromise, and with the new military authorities adopting a hands-off stance, the two rebel alliances expanded enormously and resumed their violent rivalry.[43]

The Violent Summer of 1967

The Wuhan Incident provoked a radical shift in policy toward the armed forces. On July 31, *People's Daily* and *Red Flag* jointly published an editorial that called for "dragging out a handful of capitalist roaders in the army." The editorial signaled strong support for rebel forces that had challenged local military commanders. Throughout the country, military forces found themselves under renewed attack. Factions that had clashed with the army used the campaign to gain the upper hand in their struggle with rival rebels. In Wuhan and elsewhere, rebels immediately began a campaign to capture military armaments. Army units, prevented from firing on mass organizations, were unable to halt spontaneous arms seizures. During this period Mao himself called for "arming the left" in its fight against its enemies, and some local military units began to supply arms and ammunition to rebel factions that they favored.[44]

These developments had an explosive impact across China. August and September 1967 were the climax of armed battles between rebel factions and of rebel attacks on the military. In Chongqing, one battle fought with military weapons involved an estimated 10,000 fighters and resulted in close to 1,000 casualties. In another fought with tanks and artillery, one harbor district in that city was razed to the ground. Yangzi River shipping was interrupted for more than six weeks.[45] The Yangzi River port city of Luzhou became the scene of an enormous battle in the first few days of September. More than 30,000 fighters took part, armed with military weapons, leading to more than 2,000 deaths. Large sections of the city, especially the dockyards in the port area, were leveled.[46]

In Jiangsu, military forces under General Xu Shiyou had been on the defensive since April. Armed battles escalated between Pro and Anti faction forces during June, and the Pro faction staged a series of raids against Public Security Bureau offices that were under the military authorities. After the Wuhan Incident, local representatives of the CCRG encouraged Pro faction rebels to attack Xu Shiyou directly. They charged that Xu was the "Chen Zaidao of Jiangsu" and said that he needed to be "dragged out." Xu Shiyou, understanding the danger, retreated with trusted subordinates to a secret military site in the neighboring province of Anhui. The anti-Xu forces acted as if they expected soon to overthrow the local military leadership and form a revolutionary committee. The Jiangsu military stayed in their barracks as factional fighting spun out of control.[47]

In Guangzhou, the Red Flag faction, emboldened by the Wuhan Incident, stepped up their offensive against their East Wind opponents and the Guangzhou Military Region. Large street battles fought with military arms broke out in and around Guangzhou, including a four-hour gun battle at a trade union building in mid-August and two large battles at a shipyard and river warehouse complex fought with guns, bombs, and grenades. In one such battle, the Taigu Sugar Refinery warehouses burned, destroying all of the refined sugar.[48] In Zhejiang, battles between the two rebel alliances escalated. Both sides obtained weapons from raids on arms depots and from sympathetic military units. In the coastal port city of Wenzhou, an offensive burned a large swath of the city's central business district to the ground. Atrocities occurred as fighters captured in battle were tortured and executed. Military forces, unable to use force, could not bring the province under control.[49]

Due to the strong support shown by the CCRG for attacks on local military commanders, the armed forces began to show signs of deep internal divisions. Xu Shiyou in Nanjing faced challenges from air force units and other officers under his command, and army units in other parts of Jiangsu openly sided with rebel groups that were leading the attacks on him.[50] The same splits became evident in Zhejiang, with different military units supporting different sides in local factional battles. In Hangzhou, air force units and selected ground troops pledged support to the United Headquarters in their attacks on the leadership of the Zhejiang Military District and Military Control Committee.[51]

Throughout the month of August, Mao, still resident in Shanghai after his hurried retreat from Wuhan, monitored events in the provinces, seemingly undecided about how to respond. His agents on the CCRG encouraged attacks on the military, and they relayed his orders to distribute arms to mass organizations that represented the left. Instead of redressing the balance of forces in regional factional struggles, the arming of rebel groups only led to an increase in destruction and death. Worse, there were growing signs of severe political divisions within regional military commands, and active involvement of local military units on different sides of factional battles, threatening a disintegration of the army itself. Some of the revolutionary committees established early in 1967 began to experience renewed challenges by previously suppressed rebels. Mao's utterances during August seemed intended to relay an air of blithe unconcern, as if all of this were going according to a grand plan known only to him. In fact, Mao was already backtracking on his recent decisions, having concluded that they only created new problems.

Forging a New Order

In late August, Mao reversed course yet again. He expressed doubts about the slogan "drag out a handful of capitalist roaders in the army," and on August 30 ordered the arrest and public disgrace of several CCRG radicals implicated in the attacks on the armed forces, including Wang Li of Wuhan Incident fame, along with several staff members who had worked to support antiarmy insurgencies.[52] These figures became scapegoats for Mao's decision to arm rebels and sanction attacks on the military. Seeing the clear shift in Mao's views, other prominent CCRG members, in particular Zhang Chunqiao and Jiang Qing, quickly backpedaled and withdrew their support for provincial rebels' campaigns against military commanders.[53] Mao ordered army units to stop distributing weapons and to retrieve those in rebel hands. They were told that they had the "right to shoot in self-defense" if any rebels resisted these orders with force.[54]

The impact in provinces like Jiangsu was dramatic and immediate. On August 16, Mao, still in Shanghai, ordered Zhang Chunqiao to fly to Anhui, where General Xu was in hiding, and personally escort him safely to Shanghai. The next day Mao met with General Xu and promised him that neither he nor the Nanjing Military Region would be overthrown. Zhang Chunqiao quickly ordered his rebel allies in Nanjing to halt their attacks on him. Zhou Enlai capitalized on the shift in Mao's attitude to emphasize in his many meetings with regional rebels that attacks on the PLA were now off. Zhou Enlai ordered the Nanjing rebels in no uncertain terms to end their campaign. They did so, but the two rebel factions remained at odds.[55]

Figure 11.1 illustrates the nationwide impact of calls to arm rebels and to encourage attacks on local armed forces. The number of armed battles between rebel factions and attacks on government offices or army installations spiked in August 1967, and rapidly returned to previous levels during September, when Mao reversed himself and leaned heavily toward support for local military commanders. The impact of the distribution of military armaments to rebel forces was even more dramatic. Figure 11.2 shows how much more deadly the factional conflicts became after military weapons were distributed to the combatants. While the number of reported armed conflicts increased by a little more than twofold from July to August 1967, the number of deaths due to these conflicts increased more than fivefold. The difficulty in retrieving these arms

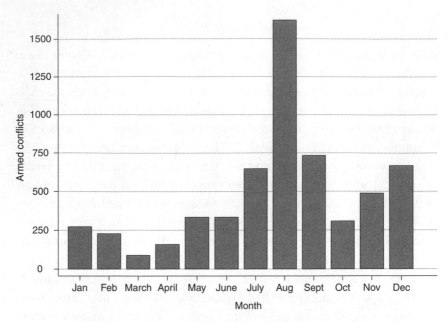

Figure 11.1. Number of reported violent events, by month, 1967.
Source: Tabulations from data in Walder (2014).

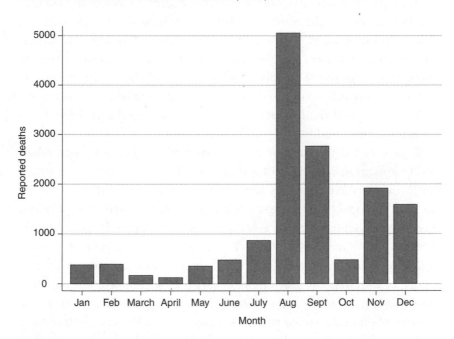

Figure 11.2. Number of reported campaign deaths, by month, 1967.
Source: Tabulations from data in Walder (2014).

from rebel forces meant that the monthly death toll after August remained much higher than it had been beforehand.

Mao had finally abandoned the idea that there was anything more to be gained from trying to manipulate the outcome of regional conflicts among rebel groups and the armed forces. By September 1967 he had concluded that the only way to enforce order was to rely heavily on the armed forces. The Shanghai model was dead and buried. As revolutionary committees were formed, military commanders were almost always placed in the top posts, and military officers would dominate crucial offices that handled security and propaganda. These outcomes would sorely disappoint rebel leaders, who expected to occupy important posts like rebel leaders in Shanghai. The violent battles that raged across China for much of 1967, however, made it almost impossible to place leaders of either rebel faction in positions of real authority. Rebel leaders who had spearheaded attacks on the armed forces were left increasingly at the mercy of their enemies.

The rebuilding of political order in the many provinces under military control was prolonged and contentious. To create a revolutionary committee took six steps. First, a cease-fire between warring mass factions and their military supporters had to be concluded. Second, delegations of representatives would travel to Beijing and, under the supervision of Beijing authorities, engage in self-criticisms and discussions designed to settle the issues that divided them. The third step was to forge an agreement about the leadership of the new revolutionary committee—or, more accurately, force the delegations to accept the candidate ultimately decided upon by Mao, Zhou Enlai, and the CCRG. The fourth step was to criticize and remove factional leaders who proved unwilling to compromise, and who did not understand that the time for fighting was over. The fifth step was to create a new power structure and ban mass organizations that coordinated activity across workplaces and schools. The sixth and final step was for the new authorities to replicate the process in cities, prefectures, and counties, and conduct criticism campaigns within schools and work organizations designed to break down factional ties, create new leadership bodies, and enforce the authority of the army.

Jiangsu Province illustrates the course of these negotiations.[56] On September 4, shortly after Mao halted attacks on General Xu Shiyou, Zhou Enlai pushed the two rebel alliances to sign a cease-fire agreement, and ordered Jiangsu's Military Control Committee to assemble delegations to send to Beijing. More than 180 delegates were chosen from rival factions in Nanjing and key cities elsewhere in Jiangsu. Military officers who had been active in attacks on General Xu and who had supported him formed separate delegations.

The negotiations began with "study classes" where each side was ordered to make self-criticisms for their factional behavior over previous months, but the meetings repeatedly broke down into acrimonious arguments. The negotiations inadvertently rekindled street battles in Nanjing and other cities in Jiangsu, as each rebel faction sought to improve its position on the ground in order to strengthen its hand at the bargaining table. The anti–Xu Shiyou factions refused to drop their accusations against him. Acrimonious meetings continued well into December, testing the patience of officials like Zhou Enlai and Kang Sheng, who angrily reprimanded stubborn delegation leaders on several occasions. As it became apparent in December that the negotiations were deadlocked, violent battles resumed along the rail lines connecting Shanghai with Nanjing, blocking rail traffic once again for several days, and drawing different military units into opposite sides in support of their rebel allies.

After four months of acrimonious and unproductive negotiations, Mao laid down the law. The opponents of Xu Shiyou within the armed forces, along with the leaders of the rebel groups that supported the army, were arrested and denounced as "black hands" that instigated factional fighting. Huge public rallies were held in Nanjing during which they were denounced and roughly handled on the stage. The local media conducted a shrill denunciation campaign against them and their followers. "Inciting attacks against the army" was now a crime and would be punished. Delegates and their local followers were threatened that further pursuit of factional ends was forbidden. The central military command disciplined and transferred officers and military units that were involved in the fighting against Xu Shiyou. This final crackdown put an end to the arguments in Beijing and put a blanket on factional passions back in Jiangsu. With this authoritarian turn, the four-month-long negotiations ended in January 1968.

In February 1968 new delegations, purged of the militant rebels and military officers opposed to Xu Shiyou, met in Beijing to select members of the Jiangsu Revolutionary Committee. At this point there was not much for the delegates to negotiate. Mao had already decided that

Xu Shiyou would head the Jiangsu Revolutionary Committee, and the only real question was which of Jiangsu's former top party officials would be included in the new leadership body. After brief haggling, the new lineup, negotiated by Zhou Enlai in consultation with Xu Shiyou, was presented to the delegation, which dutifully and unanimously approved it on March 20. Although on paper, a majority of the 165 members of the new revolutionary committee were "mass representatives," rebel membership was largely ceremonial. The revolutionary committee as a whole would rarely meet. Its "standing committee" did meet regularly to make key decisions, but military officers completely controlled it. Army officers held fewer than one-fifth of the positions on the revolutionary committee but they monopolized all of the key posts. Xu Shiyou was the head, and all four vice heads except veteran party secretary Peng Chong were army officers. The heads of the key staff offices in charge of politics, production, and security were all military officers. Not a single rebel leader was appointed vice head. One prominent leader from each of the rebel factions was appointed to the thirty-nine-member standing committee, but neither held positions of authority. Xu Shiyou and the troops under his command proceeded to place the province under firm military control.

Jiangsu's revolutionary committee was the seventeenth of twenty-nine provincial revolutionary committees to be established. One of the last, in August 1968, was in Guangxi, a province bordering Vietnam where severe and prolonged fighting had not responded to efforts to negotiate a ccase-fire. Guangxi's Beijing negotiations were themselves marred by violence: Wei Guoqing, the military commander of the Guangxi forces, was attacked and beaten in his hotel by rebels who had traveled from Guangxi to confront him. Guangxi's rebel factions had coalesced around two province-wide alliances. One, called April 22, opposed Wei Guoqing but had the support of main-force PLA units stationed in the capital of Nanning that took orders directly from Beijing. United Command supported Wei Guoqing and had the support of his military units. With military support for each large rebel alliance, the Beijing negotiations were stalemated.

Mao's patience was at an end. On July 3 a strongly worded document ordered the harsh suppression of any group in Guangxi that resisted the imposition of military control, and the main-force PLA unit that supported the April 22 alliance was transferred out of the region. Wei Guoqing launched an offensive against the rebels who still controlled

Nanning. His forces bombarded the city in mid-July and large districts of the city were destroyed. The battle against April 22 continued in Nanning for two weeks, leaving 50,000 homeless and taking more than 10,000 prisoners, more than 2,300 of whom were later executed.[57]

The offensive was waged by regular PLA units and heavily armed United Command fighters across the province. As the fighting extended deep into the rural interior, it touched off massacres in small towns and villages that appear at times to have been only tangentially connected to the major rebel rivalries in the province.[58] In Binyang County, every commune experienced mass killings between July 26 and August 6: 3,681 people were killed. Of the 3,951 killed during the entire Cultural Revolution in Binyang, 93 percent were killed during these eleven days.[59] In Donglan County, the leaders of the United Command faction and their military allies mobilized 3,000 fighters to cleanse the county of their opponents. They arrested over 10,000 and executed 1,016.[60]

Guangxi was the final shocking spasm of violence that crushed rebel opposition and placed most of China under a harsh military regime. PLA generals headed twenty of the twenty-nine provincial-level jurisdictions. In Guangdong, Liaoning, Shanxi, Yunnan, and Hubei, army officers headed between 81 and 98 percent of all revolutionary committees at the county level and above.[61] In Jiangsu, army officers headed every prefecture and sixty out of sixty-eight counties.[62] The PLA had effectively replaced China's civilian party-state. Rebels who had fought against military control were now completely at their mercy.

The Bitter End in Beijing

During the many months that Beijing authorities tried to forge "great alliances" in the provinces, the capital's own student rebels exhibited the same factional tendencies. The university rebels were divided into two large alliances, labeled Heaven and Earth. The main axis of conflict centered on the two largest campuses: Peking and Tsinghua universities. The rebels on these two campuses were split over the controversial leadership of Nie Yuanzi (Peking) and Kuai Dafu (Tsinghua). Large rebel factions at the Geology Institute and Beijing Normal University were the backbone of the Earth faction, and they staunchly supported the opponents of Nie and Kuai, leaders of the Heaven faction, who held out on their campuses.[63]

The split between Heaven and Earth had been a headache for the CCRG since early 1967. Despite their nationwide celebrity as paragons of the capital's rebel movement in late 1966, Nie Yuanzi and Kuai Dafu had become political liabilities. Both behaved in ways that split the large rebel movements on their campuses. The citywide deadlock between Heaven and Earth factions gradually degenerated into violent campus battles. Efforts to enlist cadres for their planned revolutionary committees led each faction to intensify their attacks on the cadres enlisted by the other side. Rebel factions began to take prisoners, and they established torture chambers to extract confessions. They reinforced campus buildings under their control, and proceeded to fight over campus territory. By the spring of 1968 the Peking and Tsinghua university campuses were in a state of civil war, without any recognized campus authority to mediate violent clashes.[64]

The conflict at Peking University came to a head in March 1968, when a large force of rebels from the Earth faction marched onto the campus demanding that Nie Yuanzi be dragged out. Nie organized her fighters to resist, and violent battles followed over the next several days, as thousands of reinforcements from Earth and Heaven factions joined in the fray.[65] Skirmishing between the two sides continued and mutual accusations became more bellicose and threatening. In April, Nie's forces gained the upper hand. Her rivals dug in behind defensive barriers, and she appeared to be on the verge of complete victory. Her opponents tried to hold out behind defense works and stopped issuing their newspaper. Skirmishes broke out when they tried to restore utilities and food deliveries to their buildings. Nie's forces seized and interrogated any opponents that they could capture, and subjected them to public struggle sessions. Several of them were tortured to death. At the end of April Nie held a series of public trials of captured opposition leaders. She established a prison that held more than 200 cadres and faculty, who were regularly beaten and tortured to confess.

Nie brooked no compromise and demanded complete surrender. Near the end of July she prepared for the final battle. Her forces cut off water and electricity to the buildings still controlled by her opponents, touching off a battle fought with roof tiles, spears, and bricks that spread onto adjacent streets. After Nie heard that a large force of workers and soldiers was surrounding the adjacent Tsinghua campus on July 27, she called an emergency meeting to coordinate defenses. They stockpiled

Molotov cocktails and other weapons and posted lookouts. Instead, Nie was summoned to an emergency meeting at the Great Hall of the People at 3 a.m. on July 28.

This summons was a response to events that day at Tsinghua. The struggle between Kuai Dafu and his opponents had long since deteriorated into violent armed conflict. Since early May the large campus was a patchwork of fortified buildings and ill-defined front lines, with Kuai consistently on the offensive. Initially the students were armed with clubs, spears, daggers, bricks, and stones launched from slingshots. Injuries mounted. The first death was recorded near the end of April. In early May members of the opposition carried the corpse of their slain comrade in a protest march to Tiananmen Square, where they held a protest rally. There followed a series of campus skirmishes resulting in casualties and two more deaths, with prisoners captured and brutally beaten. After one of their leaders was killed, the opposition staged another protest march in late May, carrying the corpse to Tiananmen Square in protest.

A turning point was reached on May 30. In a large assault on a building controlled by the opposition, the two sides used spears, knives, Molotov cocktails, gas grenades, and even a makeshift tank. Kuai's forces set the building on fire and captured opposition fighters as they tried to escape. At the end of an eleven-hour battle, three students were dead and more than 300 were wounded. Kuai's forces obtained rifles and set up snipers at the campus gates and outside the buildings where the opposition was barricaded, and began to pick off people who tried to leave or enter. Skirmishes continued, increasingly with grenades, firebombs, improvised explosive devices, and makeshift tanks that were designed and built by engineering students. Desperate, Kuai's opponents appealed repeatedly to the Beijing Revolutionary Committee to put the campus under martial law. On July 7 they marched to Tiananmen Square with the corpse of another slain comrade to dramatize their demand. Fighting continued, and on July 9 a large new building on campus was set on fire and virtually destroyed. By the end of July, twelve people had been killed and several hundred seriously wounded. Most of the campus community had fled, and an estimated force of fewer than 400 diehard fighters remained on campus.

Mao had reached the end of his patience with Kuai and the Beijing student rebels, who had been his favorites back in 1966. He ordered officers from the elite army unit assigned to safeguard national leaders to assemble thousands of workers from more than sixty nearby factories, along with a leadership core of soldiers. They mobilized a force of close to 30,000 to converge on the Tsinghua campus the next morning, armed only with books of Mao's quotations. Mao did not want armed soldiers to enter the campus and use deadly force to suppress the rebels. Instead, this "propaganda team" was to swarm through the gates in overwhelming numbers while chanting slogans from Mao's works, separate the two sides, and clear away barriers and fortifications.

Kuai Dafu saw this as an attempt to steal his victory and declared that there were black hands in the party leadership who had sent the workers. He ordered his followers to resist. During a twelve-hour clash the unarmed workers and soldiers were assaulted as they attempted to enter buildings and convince Kuai's fighters to disarm. Eventually Kuai's forces surrendered, but not until they had killed five members of the propaganda team and wounded more than 700.

Just as the Tsinghua hostilities were winding down, Kuai Dafu, Nie Yuanzi, and three other prominent Red Guard leaders on both sides of the Heaven-Earth divide were summoned to an urgent meeting in the Great Hall of the People. When they arrived in the early morning hours of July 28, they faced a phalanx of top officials headed by Mao himself. Joining him were Lin Biao, Zhou Enlai, Chen Boda, Kang Sheng, Jiang Qing, and several others—literally the entire top ranks of a party leadership badly depleted by purges. The meeting began at 3:30 a.m. and lasted five hours.

Edited transcripts of the meeting were later issued as a printed pamphlet. In them, Mao is by turns solicitous, sarcastic, threatening, and angry.[66] The urgent meeting was obviously a reaction to the Tsinghua events, and Mao began by expressing strong displeasure with Kuai Dafu. Kuai was late in arriving, and Mao asked why he was not there. Mao immediately made clear the reason for the meeting: "Kuai Dafu wants to grab the black hand, so many workers suppressing the red guards—who is the black hand? Now you can't drag him out—the black hand is me!" The central message, despite Mao's characteristic ramblings, was clear: the Red Guard movement was over. Mao was deeply disappointed by their behavior. The universities were to be put under military control.

The key points of the message were issued as a "supreme directive" from Chairman Mao in the name of the five Red Guard leaders. Mao was quoted as saying, "Now we have come to the point where you little generals are committing errors. . . . I don't want you split into Heaven faction and Earth faction. Form one faction and that's the end of it." The key mistake, Mao made clear, was the persistence of violent factional conflict:

> The Cultural Revolution has gone on for two years now! . . . Now the workers, peasants, soldiers and residents are all unhappy, and the great majority of students are unhappy, and even some of the people who support your faction are unhappy. You've become divorced from the workers, divorced from the peasants, divorced from the army, divorced from the residents, and you're divorced from the vast majority of students.

Mao made very clear that his patience was at an end:

> I say you're divorced from the masses; the masses can't accept civil war. . . . Well now we're issuing a nationwide directive, and whoever violates it, striking at the army, sabotaging transportation, killing people, setting fires, is committing a crime. If there's a minority who won't listen to persuasion and refuses to change, then they're bandits, Nationalists. We'll surround them, and if they're stubborn, we'll wipe them out.

Red Guards were told to return to campus and await the arrival of Mao Zedong Thought Propaganda Teams. By the end of August the Beijing Revolutionary Committee and Garrison Command sent more than 10,000 soldiers and 17,000 workers to Beijing's universities. When these units arrived, students found that the Cultural Revolution had come full circle. These were new work teams, ones that would brook no opposition or criticism, unlike the work teams for which Liu Shaoqi was denounced in 1966. In virtually every case army officers led them, and they established their authority in no uncertain terms.

12

Military Rule

Aᶠᵗᵉʳ ᵗʰᵉ ᵛⁱᵒˡᵉⁿᵗ upheavals of 1967 and 1968, it is tempting to think of military control and revolutionary committees as "the restoration of order." Nothing could be farther from the truth. This new period brought radical and wrenching social changes and new persecution campaigns of unprecedented scope and ferocity. Huge numbers of students and bureaucrats were transferred from city to countryside to engage in manual labor. Universities were closed and government offices were emptied of their staffs. The Mao cult escalated to the point where it resembled organized religious worship. Millions were imprisoned, interrogated, tortured, or executed in campaigns that searched for participants in imaginary political conspiracies, or committed suicide. The toll of these campaigns far exceeded the damage wrought by rampaging Red Guards and factional warfare among rebel alliances.

Eliminating Rebel Organizations

Red Guard and rebel leaders were in for a rude awakening after military-led propaganda teams arrived to enforce "proletarian dictatorship" in their organizations. These teams, composed of factory workers and military officers, and backed by military control committees, were not there to declare winners and losers, and they had no intention of permitting movement activists to run the show. Their attitude was that the rebels failed to unite, that both sides had committed severe political errors, and that they had to undergo reeducation and confession in coercive "study classes." The slogan for this reeducation process was "struggle, criticize, transform." Military control committees worked systematically to neutralize the leaders of rebel groups, cut off their communication with allies in other schools and workplaces, and steadily break up factional affiliations within schools, factories, and offices.

"Struggle, criticize, transform" was a coercive process of mutual criticism and thought reform through which the factional divisions of recent years were to be obliterated. In compulsory Mao Zedong Thought Study Classes, faction leaders at all levels were compelled to write self-criticisms that confessed to errors committed during the mass movement. Their confessions were evaluated by the class directors and were criticized by other participants. The mutual criticisms often revealed new errors to which the individuals had yet to confess. Those who refused to acknowledge guilt were subjected to struggle sessions and mass denunciation meetings organized by army officers. The idealized end point was to transform the organization into a unified and disciplined corps of obedient servants of Chairman Mao who had overcome the counterproductive factionalism that had so divided the rebels.

Nationally celebrated rebel leaders were not exempt. Typical of this turn of events was the humiliating demise of Peking University's Nie Yuanzi, the famous author of the "first Marxist-Leninist wall poster" that won Mao's extravagant praise, and a member of the Beijing Revolutionary Committee.[1] After the July 1968 meeting with Mao that signaled the end of the Red Guard movement, Nie returned to her campus, and her faction's newspaper published an editorial to "warmly welcome" the Mao Zedong Thought Propaganda Team. Things changed drastically after the propaganda team entered the campus in mid-August. Her faction's newspaper was immediately shut down. The propaganda team demanded the surrender of all arms and the dismantling of defense works. It took control of all broadcasting equipment, secured the release of all prisoners held in private jails, and demanded an end to mutual recriminations. Nie was immediately informed that she should reflect on how her attempts to forcibly suppress critics created and sustained violent splits.

The leaders of both factions were placed in study classes to confess the errors they had committed during the movement. Nie Yuanzi refused to acknowledge serious errors and continued to make accusations against her rivals. In October the propaganda team held a mass denunciation meeting attended by more than 3,000 people to criticize her for resisting the propaganda team. In late November she was subjected to another denunciation meeting where she was criticized for her "bourgeois stand-point" and "decadent, hypocritical ways."

When Peking University's revolutionary committee was finally established in September 1969, a military officer was the head, and of the six vice heads, three were soldiers and one was a worker on the propaganda team. Only two vice heads were from the university, one of whom was Nie Yuanzi. This was completely for show—the iconic author of Mao's beloved wall poster could not be publicly disgraced. Nie was isolated for reeducation for over a year and was paroled briefly only for a token appearance as a delegate to the Ninth Party Congress in April 1969, at which, remarkably, despite her political troubles, she was elected as an alternate member of the Central Committee. Two months after the school's revolutionary committee was established, she was sent to a state farm for labor reform. Her name quietly disappeared from all leadership lists at the city and national level within two years.

Kuai Dafu, Tsinghua University's famous Red Guard commander, did not fare any better.[2] The propaganda team assigned to Tsinghua disarmed both factions in early August and released all prisoners. When the school's revolutionary committee was established in January 1969, its head was the commanding officer of the army regiment in charge of the propaganda team. The team remained in charge of Tsinghua for most of the next decade.[3] Kuai Dafu was shipped off to a military factory in the remote Ningxia Muslim Autonomous Region. He was briefly returned to Tsinghua in 1970, placed in isolation, and interrogated as a suspected member of an underground organization of ultraleftists. He eventually returned to Beijing to work in a factory "under supervision."

Beijing's other famous rebel leaders all suffered a similar fate. Beijing Normal University's Tan Houlan was assigned to perform manual labor under a military regiment near Beijing in October 1968. In mid-1970 she was returned to her former campus to be interrogated about an alleged conspiracy of ultraleftists. After this ordeal, she worked in a Beijing factory under supervision until the mid-1970s. The Aeronautics Institute's Han Aijing was similarly isolated for investigation at the end of 1968. He was sent to a factory in Hunan in late 1969 to labor under supervision. The Geology Institute's Wang Dabin was assigned to a factory in Sichuan in January 1969. The famous leaders of Beijing's student movement would play no role in the newly established organs of power.

Consolidating Revolutionary Committees

The experience of the famous Beijing rebels captures in microcosm the overall strategy of military commanders in shutting down factions. In Jiangsu, the provincial revolutionary committee was established in Nanjing in April 1968, with General Xu Shiyou in the top post.[4] Whatever influence the rebel leaders had was eliminated through the step-by-step dismantling of their former organizations. The first step was to organize students, workers, and peasants into separate "congresses" at the city level. This effectively prohibited political activities across schools and work units. This did not immediately end factional conflict, but it served to bottle it up inside individual schools and factories. The next step was to organize study classes for faction leaders and conduct the "struggle, criticize, transform" campaign to degrade factional ties. When the leaders of local factions resisted, they became the primary targets of the campaign. Subsequent campaigns against various political conspiracies further cowed active members of rebel factions and landed many of them in prison. Through this step-by-step process, the Jiangsu military steadily tightened their grip over the province without the massive application of armed force.[5]

Rebel leaders on revolutionary committees soon realized that their positions were largely honorary. Their dissatisfaction was heightened after they sent a delegation to visit nearby Shanghai in May 1968 to learn from their model experience. Former rebels from both factions openly praised Shanghai when they returned home. Unlike themselves, Shanghai's former rebels (most notably Wang Hongwen) held positions of real influence. Members from the faction that had led the attacks on Xu Shiyou were upset because they bore the brunt of the "struggle, criticism, transform" campaign.

The process was far from smooth, and resistance occasionally bred violent clashes. From April to July 1968 there were five major skirmishes in Nanjing. Because cross-occupation organization had been eliminated, the factional clashes were within work units, unlike the large street battles of the past. The first such confrontation was in the Nanjing Radio Academy on April 23, a stronghold of anti–Xu Shiyou sentiment. A brawl broke out between members of the two factions. Troops sent to arrest the culprits met resistance, activists from nearby units rushed to the school to reinforce their allies, and a furious battle broke out. A similar clash occurred on May 4 at a military-run manufacturing plant, leading to the dispatch of troops to the scene. This, in turn, led the anti-Xu activists to stage a demonstration at the revolutionary committee headquarters. Similar incidents broke out into early July, one of which resulted in the death of a student.

This chronic low-grade conflict frustrated military authorities, who could only organize more study classes. In August 1968 Xu Shiyou lamented the fact that more than 1.5 million such study classes had been held throughout Jiangsu, without quelling factional quarrels. Although the street battles had ended and the large rebel alliances were broken up, the revolutionary committee's authority at the grass roots was still tenuous.

In July 1968, the same month that Mao called in Beijing's Red Guard leaders to reprimand them, the central authorities issued two strongly worded directives authorizing stern measures against continuing factional warfare in Guangxi and Shaanxi provinces. Xu Shiyou seized this opportunity to adopt harsher measures. Nanjing's rebel leaders were isolated in study classes where the leaders who still resisted were denounced in no uncertain terms. Propaganda teams were sent into schools and factories, where they carried out campaigns that targeted rebel groups who resisted. The authorities' cause was aided further by the emptying out of the schools. In late 1968 university students were assigned jobs and left Nanjing altogether, and most of the high school students were shipped off to the countryside. University rebels in the anti-Xu camp were assigned to jobs far from Nanjing. The students and faculty left behind were soon sent to factories, mines, or the countryside for manual labor, and would not return until 1970.

The events in Jiangsu conformed to the national pattern. Figure 12.1 illustrates the impact of military control and the formation of revolutionary committees. The figure shows the effects of the final push to demobilize mass factions during the summer of 1968. The number of armed battles between rebel factions and the number of attacks on government offices and military installations dropped rapidly. By September 1968 this tumultuous phase of the Cultural Revolution was over.

Closing the Universities

In the tumult of the preceding years, no new students were admitted to universities, no classes were held, and no one graduated with degrees. The national entrance examinations were cancelled in June 1966 and

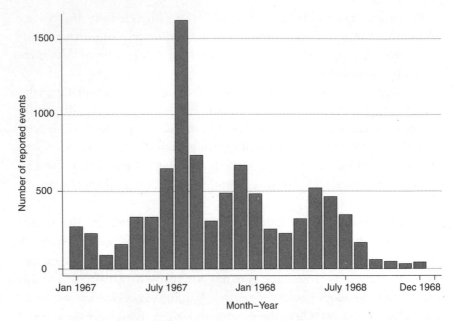

Figure 12.1. Number of reported violent events, by month, 1967–1968.
Source: Tabulations from data in Walder (2014).

were not reinstated. Students who were on university campuses in the spring semester of 1966 remained for the next two years, although many fled in the later stages when campus conflicts became dangerously violent. By the fall of 1968, China's entire population of university and high school students had neither continued their education nor embarked on careers. Three entering classes—1966, 1967, and 1968—had already been skipped. It was now time to decide what to do about the students and the universities.

Initially, the top priority was to ensure military control over warring student factions. Faculty and school officials, who had already been subjected to student attacks for almost two years, underwent further thought reform and ideological remolding. Instead of reopening the universities, admitting a new class of students, and continuing the educations of those whose course work was interrupted in 1966, a radically different option was chosen. The universities were closed indefinitely, and the campuses were emptied of students, faculty, and administrators.

The first step, at the end of 1968, was to declare all students graduated and assign them to jobs. This effectively ended any hope that student rebels would be appointed to positions in new organs of power in their schools, and rebel leaders were usually assigned to jobs in distant locations, typically as manual laborers in factories or as low-level technical staff. The most fortunate students became soldiers—an assignment that favored the politically connected. The political careers of student rebels, in either their schools or local government, were largely ended. The second step, after a harrowing campaign to expose alleged reactionaries and spies, was to send virtually all faculty and administrators to May 7 Cadre Schools, the name for rural facilities set up for the remolding of intellectuals and bureaucrats through manual labor. The faculties of Peking and Tsinghua universities were shipped off together to a single site on the muddy banks of a lake in Jiangxi Province, where they had to build their own shelter and grow much of their own food. The facility was not closed until the early 1970s.[6]

Most universities did not reopen until 1972, after most faculty and administrators returned from their May 7 experience, and the first entering classes made their way to college campuses still under the control of Mao Thought Propaganda Teams. Enrollments were much lower than in 1966 and did not return to previous levels until 1977.[7] The biggest change, however, was in the way that entering students were selected. The meritocratic national examinations had earlier favored students from the former middle classes and households labeled as "reactionary," despite the class label system. These examinations were now abolished. No one would be admitted to university directly from high school. Instead, all college students would be recruited directly from collective farms, factories, or the armed forces. The sole standards would now be an applicant's class label and political activism, and written recommendations based on political assessments submitted by the leaders of local revolutionary committees.[8]

Banishment to the Countryside

The new college admissions process meant that graduates of academic high schools had to abandon immediate college plans to undergo an indefinite period of work in a job that involved manual labor. Students who did not gain admittance to high school, or who completed courses in vocational and technical high schools, were assigned local jobs in factories or other urban work units. The vast majority of academic high school graduates were sent to remote rural villages to work indefinitely as ordinary farmers. The practice had started in the early 1960s on a small scale in large cities like Shanghai, where local jobs could not be found for all graduating seniors who failed the university entrance exams.[9] Now the practice became universal.

This rural sojourn had no time limit. Urban youths were required to make new lives as ordinary farmers. Some obtained party membership and later became cadres in brigades and communes. A lucky few were able to impress their superiors and gain a recommendation for college admission as a "worker-peasant-soldier" student. As might be expected, these youths initially suffered serious problems of adjustment to difficult rural lives, and they found the lower-calorie grain-based rural diet, coupled with hard physical labor, beyond anything they had ever experienced in the cities. Vulnerable young females, living independently far from their families, were subjected to aggressive sexual harassment and even sexual assaults at the hands of rural cadres.[10] Over the next decade more than 18 million urban youths were sent to the countryside. During these years, only 720,000 were able to attend universities as worker-peasant-soldier students.[11]

A separate aspect of the transfer of urban residents to the countryside was the deportation of political outcasts. The banishment of suspect individuals and entire households to the countryside based on class background or other negative political labels began in 1966, but escalated under the revolutionary committees. This was intended to be permanent, but in the waning years of the Mao era these individuals began to protest their plight. In the city of Tianjin, some 15,000 individuals were deported to rural regions, along with more than 25,000 of their family members—roughly 1.3 percent of Tianjin's urban population.[12]

Labor Reform for Bureaucrats

The imperative to force all educated individuals to undergo ideological remolding through manual labor was also applied to the white-collar staffs of bureaucratic agencies. Very few were able to avoid a prolonged period in a rural May 7 Cadre School or as a manual worker in a factory. Offices throughout urban China were almost emptied from 1969 to 1971. Large majorities of administrators and staff spent long periods in manual labor. The emptied offices operated with skeleton staffs, covering only minimal functions. Research virtually ceased, and government services were slashed to a bare minimum. The practice was replicated within large state factories: engineers, accountants, and other technical staff worked at lathes and blast furnaces—or as support staff for cleaning and meal services—as factory offices were emptied out. When these individuals eventually returned to their office jobs, their authority was much reduced.

Initially, this movement to "send down" office workers far outstripped the scale of the transfer of youths to the countryside, but it lasted for a shorter period. In Shanghai, more than 20,000 cadres were sent to work on factory floors, with plans to permanently reduce the staffing of offices at all levels of administration.[13] In Tianjin, more than 70 percent of the office staff in the city's factories were transferred to manual jobs.[14] In Henan, a total of 12,300 cadres working in provincial party and government offices were sent down in three groups to rural camps for manual labor near the end of 1969.[15] In Hubei, more than 8,000 cadres from the provincial government were sent to a converted military camp for their stint of rural labor.[16] Guangdong Province built a total of 313 May 7 facilities, and sent 164,600 cadres from provincial, prefectural, and county and city organs to them. The Guangdong authorities at the time planned to permanently reduce the number of government personnel by more than 150,000.[17] Not until 1971 did the practice begin to wane, and not until 1972 were the rural camps closed.

Cleansing the Class Ranks

As military control committees consolidated their authority, the criticism campaign known as "struggle, criticize, transform" was expanded into a much larger and more draconian hunt for traitors and counterrevolutionaries: the Cleansing of the Class Ranks *(qingli jieji duiwu)*. The national network of newly established revolutionary committees mobilized for a purge campaign of enormous scope. It began shortly after revolutionary committees were formed and continued well into 1969.

The cleansing campaign was initiated through two distinct channels. The first was a series of investigations in Beijing by the Central Case Examination Group formed in 1966 to build cases against national officials who had fallen in the purges of the Cultural Revolution. Close to 1 million cadres were caught up in the nationwide investigations coordinated by this group.[18] Recently deposed high officials were accused of antiparty conspiracies; but conspiracies must have followers, and these followers must be hidden in regions where these officials had formerly worked. Investigators in Beijing ordered local authorities to look into people possibly implicated in a higher-level case. The request was not one that a local revolutionary committee could ignore, and this touched off auxiliary investigations of cases nationwide.

The campaign to uproot the Inner Mongolian People's Party was initiated in this fashion. It began as an investigation of Ulanfu, Inner Mongolia's top official, who was purged at the outset of the Cultural Revolution. In the spring of 1968 the cleansing campaign unfolded as a drive to uproot and eliminate Ulanfu's influence. As the revolutionary committee built a conspiracy case against him, they charged that he headed a nonexistent "New Inner Mongolian People's Party," an alleged conspiracy of ethnic Mongol separatists with links to Mongolia and the Soviet Union. The campaign proceeded via the arrest and torture of suspects, primarily ethnic Mongols, who frequently confessed and were then tortured further to name coconspirators. By March 1969, when Beijing finally intervened to halt the campaign, 790,000 individuals had been targeted and interrogated: 120,000 suffered permanent physical disabilities as a result of beatings or torture, and 22,900 were killed or executed, or committed suicide.[19]

Most of the victims of the cleansing campaigns were not implicated in cases originally fabricated by the Central Case Examination Group. More commonly, the campaign unfolded through local investigations initiated independently in schools and work units. The national campaign began after activities in several model units in Beijing were described in central policy documents distributed nationwide, with a personal endorsement by Mao. The tone was set by a *People's Daily* editorial on New Year's Day 1968: it called for the cleansing of a wide variety of enemies and traitors from the revolutionary ranks as the victory of proletarian power was being consolidated. In late May 1968 the campaign conducted in Beijing's New China Printing Plant was recounted in the first of these central documents. It was carried out by the plant's military control committee, which was composed of officers from the army unit that served as the Politburo's security detail. The factory was an old one, and the campaign was motivated by the premise that employees left over from the old society, who had worked under the Nationalists and the Japanese, had been behind "extremely complex, acute, and violent" class struggles in the factory. Mass meetings were held to expose traitors, unmasking a number of counterrevolutionaries. The suspects were subjected to struggle sessions and forced to write confessions, and told that leniency would be granted only to those who confessed fully.[20]

To conduct the campaign, local governments, offices, factories, and schools formed case groups that were charged with gathering evidence about the alleged crimes of targeted individuals. Political dossiers of suspects were scoured for evidence of prior malfeasance, and former superiors and associates would be contacted for incriminating information. As it unfolded across China the campaign operated through accusation, interrogation, and confession. The first step was an accusation, often supported by nothing more than suspicion based on personal history or associations. The accusations could arrive in the form of a letter transmitted from higher authorities, letters or delegates from other units or localities investigating cases of their own, or from an accusation made by members of "the masses" in meetings or privately.

After the campaign claimed its first victims, the primary source of new accusations was the interrogation rooms themselves. Under the best of circumstances, the interrogations were threatening and bullying. The accused were assumed to be guilty and were coerced by threats of dire punishment if they did not confess. Despite instructions from Beijing that interrogators use "principled" methods, physical abuse was commonly employed, including, according to a number of post-Mao retrospective reports, sadistic torture. Once an unfortunate suspect confessed, the interrogations were not over. Conspiracies by definition involved others. The next step was to name coconspirators. If the suspect refused to name others, the ordeal would continue until additional names were extracted. Those named, in turn, were hauled in for similar interrogations, similar confessions, similar naming of coconspirators. In this manner, the campaign frequently escalated to claim large numbers of victims. Because the charges to which they confessed amounted to counterrevolution, executions often followed—although many in this campaign died under torture in the interrogation rooms or found the means to commit suicide. Suicides could become a problem for investigators because they were taken as an admission of guilt, and they halted the process of extracting the names of coconspirators, leading investigations to a dead end. Early in the campaign, figures like Kang Sheng and Minister of Public Security Xie Fuzhi expressed concern about the rash of suicides, complaining that it served to obstruct investigations.[21]

At Peking University the cleansing campaign began one month after the army took over the university, dismantling rebel organizations and detaining their leaders for reeducation. Case groups ignored all that had transpired in the university over the previous two years and initiated investigations of more than 900 suspected cadres and faculty members. The targets were detained on campus. After grueling interrogations, the propaganda team took a little over a month to rule that 542 of these individuals were "enemies of the people." By the end of the year, eighteen had committed suicide. The dead included one of the first senior party officials to publicly side with Nie Yuanzi in her initial rebellion against the school authorities. He was found in the university's swimming pool, an apparent suicide.[22]

The cleansing campaign cast a wide net. A large proportion of its victims were individuals in social categories that were targeted earlier in the Cultural Revolution—those with overseas and Nationalist affiliations or from landlord and capitalist backgrounds. But there were a great many other ways to fall afoul of the campaign. Party members who had served the organization loyally for decades might find themselves accused of membership in an imaginary spy ring. Those who risked their lives in the party underground before 1949 often found their service taken as evidence that they were Nationalist spies. Those who were active in factional struggles earlier in the Cultural Revolution might now find their activities interpreted as a conspiracy against Mao and socialism. Individuals who made stray critical comments about Jiang Qing or who had praised Liu Shaoqi or other leaders during unguarded moments also fell under suspicion. Those who had earlier offended an individual now entrusted with carrying out the campaign, those who made the mistake of speaking out against torture and murder, or who defended fallen party leaders, were also prime suspects.[23] The terror created during this campaign was due not solely to the draconian treatment of suspects but also to the widespread uncertainty created by the campaign's unpredictability.

The campaign had a major impact in Shanghai, even though the city had been spared the widespread factional warfare that affected most regions of China. The city's revolutionary committee had in mind a disciplined campaign in which hidden class enemies were uncovered and paraded publicly before the masses. Beginning in January 1968 and concluding in April 1969, 169,000 individuals were placed under investigation. Of the top twenty party and government officials in Shanghai on the eve of the Cultural Revolution, seventeen were found to be traitors. The former mayor and one vice mayor died in detention. Some 84 percent of the party and government officials in the city, more than 900 in all, were accused and detained, and forty-six of them died in custody. The campaign's overall death toll by the end of 1968 was more than 5,000—a partial count based only on cases under the jurisdiction of the office in charge of the investigations.[24]

In Guangdong, which experienced violent factional warfare that was quelled by military force, the campaign was fueled by still-strong factional animosities, and escalated locally in horrific ways. In Guangdong Province the army favored the East Wind rebels over their opponents, the Red Flag alliance, which had fought stubbornly against army control until the very end. The cleansing campaign followed closely on the heels of the province's political settlement in February 1968, and it began while there was still last-ditch armed resistance to the final imposition of military control. The mass killings that accompanied the pacification of the Guangdong countryside resulted in the deaths of more than 30,000 in this period alone.[25]

Figure 12.2 conveys the impact of the cleansing campaign relative to the earlier phase of the Cultural Revolution. The cleansing campaign and the contemporaneous armed suppression of factional opponents generated a wave of violent death that far outstripped the worst months of the earlier period. The spike in the death toll during August 1967, when military armaments were distributed to mass factions, is insignificant by comparison. From March through September 1968 the death toll was well in excess of the August 1967 figure, and during that period the monthly death toll was roughly four times higher for five consecutive months. The peak in the death toll from the cleansing campaign coincides with the final drop in rebel activity earlier seen in Figure 12.1. It is evident from these figures that the cure for the malady of violent factional warfare was in fact far worse than the disease.

The cleansing campaign had an initial purpose of suppressing deeply rooted factional conflicts by diverting attention onto hidden enemies. But it is hard to avoid the conclusion that it expanded through an unplanned escalation process. Revolutionary committees were composed

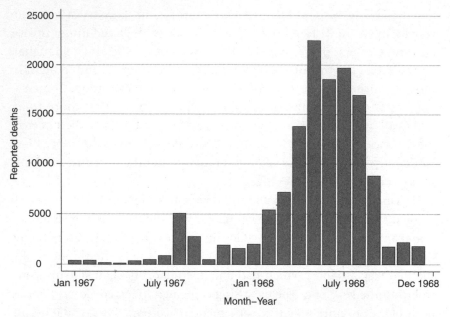

Figure 12.2. Number of reported campaign deaths, by month, 1967–1968.
Source: Tabulations from data in Walder (2014).

of survivors of the struggles of previous years, and they were by no means united in background and orientation. New organs of power were composed of military officers, the dominant group, who were frequently suspicious of leaders from rebel factions. They also included civilian cadres, some of which had been targets of rebels earlier in the Cultural Revolution, but many of which later pledged allegiance out of a sense of self-preservation with a rebel faction that was intent on broadening its base for the anticipated "great alliance." Finally, the new organs of power included selected leaders of rebel factions, sometimes leaders from both sides of bitterly antagonistic struggles. The reality of these new organs of power, and the case groups that they created, was one of insecurity and mutual suspicion, if not barely concealed hostility.

Under these circumstances the cleansing campaign turned into something that resembled inquisitions and witch hunts in other historical settings. Newly established local authorities had every reason to believe that zealous prosecution of the new campaign was a sign of their own loyalty to the new order. Failure to prosecute the campaign with sufficient thoroughness could put one under suspicion. The recent past gave them

every reason to believe that people in positions of authority could themselves become victims if they failed to zealously implement directives
from above.

The insecurity of members of revolutionary committees and special
case groups made it virtually impossible for anyone to speak out to restrain the more zealous or violent inquisitors among them, or to question even the most far-fetched and bizarre accusations. To speak out to
protect those accused, to moderate their treatment during interrogations,
or to restrict the numbers accused and interrogated would risk falling
under suspicion for sympathy with the enemy—perhaps even being oneself a member of an underground conspiracy. Once torture to extract
confessions, both psychological and physical, became common, the process of escalation got under way. Confessions extracted, names named,
meant that others would be pulled in, interrogated and tortured, and
more names named. It would take an act of extraordinary personal
bravery bordering on foolhardiness for an individual to question the validity of confessions, to question the plausibility of gigantic underground
networks of traitors, to demand that something more than suspicion was
needed to subject an individual to the machinery of interrogation, or
that something more substantial than an extracted confession was adequate evidence. To do so would be to express doubts about the leadership, to oppose the Cultural Revolution, to reveal sympathy toward the
enemy.

Like so many other Mao-sponsored campaigns, from the Great Leap
Forward to the Socialist Education Movement to the Red Guard and rebel
movements, the campaign rumbled on, generating outcomes on a scale
that was not originally anticipated. It accelerated like a vehicle without
a brake, ultimately slowing only after Mao himself made comments suggesting that the campaign may have been too severe.[26] By this time it
was too late to prevent the carnage. More than half of the deaths due to
the Cultural Revolution were a result of this campaign—an estimated
600,000 to 800,000.[27]

Mao Worship

It was during the cleansing campaign and its immediate aftermath that
the cult of Mao reached its most extreme forms. Badges, busts, and posters
with Mao's image became ubiquitous. Virtually every home had its

portrait of Chairman Mao on the wall or a bust of the Chairman on full display. Failure to display Mao paraphernalia could put one under political suspicion. In public spaces, large statues of Mao were erected on university campuses, in front of government office buildings, and in city squares. Carefully orchestrated parades with marchers displaying scores of large Mao portraits or mobile floats with statues of the Chairman in a heroic pose were a common event during public holidays.[28] Large stadiums were filled with thousands of performers who engaged in synchronized displays designed to glorify the Chairman and express loyalty. Individuals who inadvertently defaced portraits of the Chairman or who discarded newspapers with his photograph or writings could become targets of harrowing loyalty investigations. Families saved virtually every item with Mao's image because it was politically dangerous to discard them.

The escalation of the Mao cult was part of an organized campaign that originated in the armed forces under Lin Biao and was implemented by military control committees. Known as the "three loyalties and four boundless loves," it promoted loyalty to "Chairman Mao, Mao Zedong Thought, and Chairman Mao's proletarian revolutionary line," and boundless love for "Chairman Mao, the Communist Party, Mao Zedong Thought, and Chairman Mao's proletarian revolutionary line." Popular reverence for Mao had long been encouraged by the regime, but genuine popular respect for China's leader was now transformed into what two leading analysts of the period have termed "a state-sponsored cult complete with carefully orchestrated rituals, the transformation of even the most banal utterances by Mao into holy writ, and coercive mechanisms for dealing with acts of deviance and heresy."[29]

A core element of the campaign was based on the model experience of the Beijing General Knitting Mill. The army officers in charge of the plant invented a method to promote loyalty throughout the working day. At the start of the shift, workers assembled, facing a portrait of Chairman Mao, and "asked for instructions" that would guide their conduct for the day; during the shift, they would read Mao quotations posted on the walls in order to boost their enthusiasm for work; when changing shifts, they exchanged Mao quotes with fellow workers as a way to "show concern and offer help"; and at the end of the working day, they would once again turn to Mao's portrait and "report back," critically reviewing their thought and work performance during that day. The factory leadership submitted a report on their practices to Mao in late 1967, and Mao wrote a marginal comment on the report: "I've read this, and it is very good. Thank you, comrades!"[30] The report was distributed nationwide, and soon millions of people were participating in these organized rituals in their work units.[31]

A core element of the Mao cult was its "living application" in solving seemingly intractable real-life problems, especially those that seemed beyond the capacity of modern science and technology to remedy. Newspapers and radio programs frequently reported on the ways in which diligent study of Chairman Mao's writings inspired ordinary individuals, without scientific training, to redouble their efforts to do the seemingly impossible. A team of surgeons, in one famous case, was able to perform an extraordinarily complicated operation to successfully remove a 100-pound tumor from a patient, despite lacking the necessary experience and without a trained anesthetist. Cancer patients studied Mao Thought diligently as an aid to surviving their ordeal of radiation therapy and its side effects. Untrained orderlies, applying Mao Thought to the rehabilitation of deaf-mutes, enabled them to sing "The East Is Red" and chant "Long Live Chairman Mao." The orderlies were able to accomplish this despite the inability of the hospital's specialized medical personnel to make any progress in the patients' treatment. In other cases, Mao Thought proved similarly efficacious in developing strategies to restore sight to the blind, reattach severed hands, and revive accident victims whose hearts had stopped beating.[32]

These accounts did not directly ascribe magical qualities to Mao Thought. They were intended to demonstrate that Mao Thought Study Classes inspired ordinary individuals to accomplish feats that they would otherwise have thought far beyond their capacity. The subtext for most of these examples was that diligent application of Mao's wisdom by ordinary people brought results superior to those to be attained through the application of modern science and technology, the realm of "bourgeois" experts.[33]

Perhaps the most famous manifestation of the Mao cult was the rapturous celebration touched off by Mao's gift of mangoes to various Beijing schools and factories in early August 1968. Mao received a basket of golden mangoes from the visiting Pakistani foreign minister, and had his aide divide them up and distribute them to various model units in Beijing. Some of them were sent on August 5 to the Mao Zedong Thought

Propaganda Team that had recently been installed at Tsinghua University.[34] On August 7, *People's Daily* reported this act in a large headline on the front page that read, "The greatest concern, the greatest trust, the greatest support, the greatest encouragement; our great leader Chairman Mao's heart is always linked with the hearts of the masses; Chairman Mao gave the precious gifts given by a foreign friend to the Capital Worker and Peasant Mao Zedong Thought Propaganda Team."[35] The accompanying article described the reaction on the campus:

> In the afternoon of the fifth, when the great happy news of Chairman Mao giving mangoes to the Capital Worker and Peasant Mao Zedong Thought Propaganda Team reached the Tsinghua University campus, people immediately gathered around the gift given by the Great Leader Chairman Mao. They cried out enthusiastically and sang with wild abandonment. Tears swelled up in their eyes, and they again and again sincerely wished that our most beloved Great Leader Chairman Mao lived ten thousand years without bounds, ten thousand years without bounds, and ten thousand years without bounds! They all made phone calls to their own work units to spread this great happy news; and they also organized all kinds of celebratory activities all night long, and arrived at [the national leadership compound] Zhongnanhai despite the rain to report the good news, and to express their loyalty to the Great Leader Chairman Mao.

One of the mangoes was sent to the Beijing Textile Factory, whose revolutionary committee organized a large assembly where workers recited Mao quotations and celebrated the gift. The fruit was sealed in wax in order to preserve it, and it was placed on an altar in the auditorium, where workers lined up for a viewing, solemnly bowing as they passed by. After a few days the mango began to rot, and the fruit was peeled and boiled in a pot of water. Once again, the workers filed by and each was given a spoonful of the precious water in which the mango had been boiled. The revolutionary committee made a wax replica of the mango and placed it back on the altar in the auditorium as a centerpiece for future Mao rituals in the factory.

There followed several months of mango fever, as the fruit became a temporary focus of the "boundless loyalty" campaign. More wax replicas were made of the mangoes, some of them encased in glass containers, and the replicas were sent on tours around Beijing and elsewhere in China to work units that organized welcoming parties, celebrations, and viewings. Beijing was besieged with requests from revolutionary committees in outlying provinces for visits from the precious mangoes. Replicas encased in glass cases were manufactured to meet requests that were impossible to fulfill with the rotting originals. They were shipped around China like touring celebrities. An estimated half million people greeted the mango replicas when they arrived in Chengdu, and the mangoes were shuttled to other cities by special train, where they were welcomed with mass demonstrations.[36] Mao badges and wall posters were produced in the millions that contained the mango image. A cigarette factory in Henan began producing a line of mango-brand cigarettes. Some years later a film about class struggle was produced that employed Mao's mangoes as a key to the story line.[37]

Another prominent Mao cult activity was a "loyalty dance" to express veneration and love for the Chairman. It involved a series of steps reputedly inspired by ethnic minority folk dances, accompanied by a standard melody and lyrics that expressed boundless loyalty to the Chairman by a million hearts beating in unison. This dance might be performed anywhere at any time: on trains, public buses, or airplanes, or during political meetings in factories and offices. Once the loyalty dance was invoked in any setting, there was no way to refuse participation, an obvious sign of disloyalty. According to individuals who lived through these years, young women were more willing and competent participants in this ritual, and for some of them the dancing appears to have been a form of entertainment. Elderly individuals, those without a sense of rhythm, and veteran blue-collar workers who found the whole thing embarrassing, were less amused.[38]

In recounting these events, one might be tempted to conclude that they express a kind of collective hysteria driven by actual belief in the magical powers of Mao's thought, or at least by a genuine veneration of Mao as a great political leader. While it is not possible to know what was in the minds of hundreds of millions of individuals when they experienced these activities, we do know a great deal about the political context in which they took place. The Mao cult reached its height during the Cleansing of the Class Ranks Campaign—designed to uncover hidden traitors and enemies of the revolution. The entire exercise had a barely concealed coercive element; an implicit threat that hinted at what might happen to someone who failed to exhibit sufficient enthusiasm. In the words of one perceptive analyst of the Mao cult, "for most Chinese, taking part in public worship became a crucial element of surviving within a completely volatile situation dominated by witch hunts against supposed counterrevolutionaries." Insufficient compliance made one suspect: "Everyone who, intentionally or not, failed to partake in the cult rituals, misspelled Mao quotations, or vilified cult symbols faced being sentenced as an 'active counterrevolutionary.'"[39]

There are many reported cases of individuals imprisoned or executed during this period for remarks seen as disrespectful toward Mao, for inadvertent slips of the tongue, or use of material that contained Mao's words or images as toilet paper.[40] Ordinary individuals need not have witnessed such punishments in order to understand the implicit threat. In the context of an organized campaign to root out hidden traitors, and where it was clear to many that the accusations lodged against unfortunate victims were obviously false, it would have been foolishly dangerous to put yourself and your family at risk by failing to conform with these relatively cost-free outward displays of veneration and loyalty. To feign boundless admiration for the Great Leader was a small price to pay to avoid the attention of case groups during the cleansing campaign.

Given the extraordinarily threatening political context, it seems more plausible to conclude that the entire population felt compelled to behave as if they were gripped by irrational beliefs. In a radically different form, this was the same kind of collective pressure to conform that led to the systematic self-deception observed during the Great Leap Forward, when expressions of belief in the efficacy of the campaign were made into a mark of political loyalty. Compared to the Great Leap famine, the loyalty campaign was relatively harmless. But it was the same species of collective behavior and had the same sources. These activities continued until the loyalty campaign was officially called off in June 1969, after the more embarrassing aspects of Mao worship came under criticism, with Mao's apparent blessing, at the Ninth Party Congress in April of that year.[41]

More Investigation Campaigns

On the heels of the cleansing campaign and the high tide of the Mao cult, two overlapping new campaigns targeted "counterrevolutionary" activities and sought to further consolidate military control and the authority of revolutionary committees. The first of these was the One Strike, Three Anti *(yida sanfan)* campaign, launched in February 1970, and it appears to have been conducted in most of the country by the end of that year. "One Strike" referred to a crackdown on "counterrevolutionary destructive activities." In a number of regions around China, there was still sub-rosa resistance to the imposition of authority, or stubbornly rooted factional conflict. This aspect of the campaign was designed to wipe out any lingering opposition. The document that launched the campaign instructed local authorities as follows:

> Resolutely put down those active counterrevolutionary elements who collude with the enemy and betray the nation, conspire to revolt, gather military intelligence, steal state secrets, commit murder and physical assault, commit arson and poison people, counterattack to settle old scores, viciously slander the party and the socialist system, plunder state property, and disrupt the social order. . . . Resolutely execute those counterrevolutionary elements who are swollen with arrogance after having committed countless heinous crimes and against whom popular indignation is so great that nothing save execution will serve to calm it.[42]

The targets designated by the term "Three Anti" were "graft and embezzlement," "profiteering," and "extravagance and waste." This appears to have been intended to tighten discipline over new authorities at the local level who spent excessively on dinners, gifts, guest houses, and furnishings for offices, or who began to barter goods with other units as a form of "cooperation."

The One Strike, Three Anti campaign had a much narrower scope than the cleansing campaign, even if the criteria for deciding whom to target were still flexible and vague. It did not have anywhere near the impact of the cleansing campaign, but it did leave large numbers of victims in its wake. In urban Beijing, 5,757 "renegades, special agents, counterrevolutionaries, and other bad elements" were identified, and more than 6,200 cases of embezzlement and profiteering were prosecuted. In the rural counties surrounding Shanghai, 64,000 individuals were "dragged out and struggled," resulting in 520 deaths. Nationwide, during the first eight months of the campaign, more than 284,800 individuals were arrested.[43] Estimates from local histories published in the post-Mao era suggest that the campaign investigated in some fashion only one-quarter as many individuals as the cleansing campaign and was far less deadly. The national death toll from the One Strike, Three Anti campaign was less than 10 percent that of the massive cleansing of 1968–1969, mostly executions.[44]

The campaign known colloquially as Anti May 16 Elements *(fan wu yao liu fenzi)* was launched on the heels of the One Strike, Three Anti campaign. It was even more tightly focused and smaller in scope. It ostensibly targeted an underground conspiracy of ultraleftists who were said to have conspired to sabotage the Cultural Revolution through extremist behavior. The term originated much earlier, back in 1967, and became associated with the radical members of the Central Cultural Revolution Group, Wang Li, Guan Feng, and others, who were made scapegoats for the wave of attacks on the army in August 1967.[45] The campaign began in many regions in 1970 and reached a peak in 1971. Local authorities interpreted it as a license to haul in, interrogate, intimidate, and in some cases imprison former leaders of mass factions, especially those who had resisted the imposition of military control. It did not matter if these former rebel leaders had long since abandoned their resistance. Revolutionary committees complied with this campaign by placing former rebel leaders in isolation and interrogating them about their alleged underground ties to this suspected national conspiracy of ultraleftist rebels.

Worker rebels were still close at hand and could be readily identified, placed in isolation, and interrogated. Most student rebels, however, had since been assigned to distant collective farms or factories. In these cases authorities had them brought back to the locality where they had led rebel factions and interrogated them there. Famous Beijing Red Guards, for example, were brought back to their universities from their rural exile in 1970 to undergo prolonged interrogations about their factional activities during the student movement.[46] Former rebel leaders in Wuhan were placed in makeshift cells in their work units and interrogated to reveal their secret affiliations with the May 16 group. A total of 33,659 individuals in the city were labeled May 16 Elements; if they were in leading posts, they lost them. Most of them ended up performing penal labor "under supervision." Initial plans to execute eighty-four prominent ringleaders were later abandoned.[47]

In Jiangsu the campaign was unusually severe. It was the final blow against the faction that had opposed military authorities in the province. Launched in the spring of 1970, it peaked near the end of that year and continued sporadically into 1972. More than 130,000 individuals in Jiangsu were charged as May 16 Elements, and 57,000 confessed to underground factional ties. Published accounts later claimed that more than 6,000 of them died or suffered permanent physical or mental disabilities as a result of their treatment in detention. Individuals who participated in internal reinvestigations of these cases in subsequent years have claimed that the real number was twice as large.[48]

The campaign in Jiangsu removed almost all former rebel leaders from any leadership posts they had gained as part of the "great alliance" in 1968, along with many of the veteran civilian cadres that had managed to earn "revolutionary" labels at the time. It was the final step through which General Xu Shiyou established the army's absolute control over the province. The campaign targeted the vast majority of the standing committee of the Jiangsu Revolutionary Committee—twenty-one of the twenty-eight original members. All nine of the former rebel leaders on the standing committee were purged, and all eight veteran provincial cadres were targeted, though some of them were able to keep their posts. The purges extended into the military ranks: a number of officers who had participated in attacks on Xu Shiyou in the summer of 1967 were isolated for interrogation and removed from their posts. Many of them were imprisoned, and one of the most prominent officers died while in custody. Some of the famous Nanjing rebel leaders were so shattered psychologically by their interrogation and imprisonment that they were unable to function normally after their later release from prison.[49]

The years from 1968 to 1971 were a staggering reversal from the previous two years of mass mobilization and protest, during which authority figures of all kinds could be challenged—and were. What had begun as a rebellion against authority inspired by a party chairman who declared that "rebellion is justified" ended in the suppression and persecution of most of the rebels who took up the Chairman's call. A campaign that began by encouraging students and workers to challenge bureaucratic authority ended in an orgy of repression conducted by a newly militarized bureaucracy. New bureaucratic organs conducted escalating witch hunts that terrorized the urban population. Citizens were compelled to engage in the most servile and infantilized forms of hero worship that treated Mao as an almost supernatural being, and that frequently claimed extraordinary powers for his "thought."

This period would soon come to an end. In September 1971 a Trident jet left Chinese airspace and shortly thereafter fell from the sky and crashed on the steppes of Mongolia, killing everyone on board. This event would push China in a new and uncertain direction. The May 7 camps were closed and cadres and white-collar staff returned to their offices. Military control committees were disbanded and soldiers withdrawn from government administration. Civilian officials purged during the Cultural Revolution began to return to their former posts. Criticisms of the worst excesses of the Cultural Revolution were widely circulated. Eventually, industrial workers, whose living standards had stagnated, became restive. Former Red Guards and rebels who had been shunted aside by the military mobilized to protest their marginalization. The first stirrings of a democracy movement appeared. And just a few months before Mao's death, large protests erupted in Beijing and other major cities that openly expressed criticism of the Cultural Revolution and indirectly of Mao.

Normally an aviation accident would not have such wide repercussions, but this aircraft carried the Chinese Communist Party's vice chairman, Marshal Lin Biao, Mao's designated heir and successor, widely credited as the originator of the Mao cult, the head of an army that had effectively run most of China since 1968. He was said to have fled China after an abortive coup that included a plan to assassinate Mao.

13

Discord and Dissent

BEFORE HIS SPECTACULAR DEMISE, several of Lin Biao's subordinates were in political trouble, a sign that Lin himself might soon face demotion or worse. Unlike other prominent victims of Mao's unpredictable judgments, Lin did not quietly exit the political stage. The sensational story about his death—a plane crash while apparently en route to defect to the Soviet Union—had major political implications. This was especially true because of the way that Lin's demise was explained to the nation: his flight was the result of a failed plot to assassinate Mao in the course of a political coup. According to the official story, after his plot was discovered he tried to escape to the Soviet Union, only to crash en route when his jet ran out of fuel.

Whatever the truth about the Lin Biao incident, his death created shock waves that decisively altered the course of Chinese politics. Lin popularized the "little red book" of Mao's quotations within the army that eventually spread nationwide with the Red Guards, and it was the centerpiece of the Mao cult's "boundless loyalty" campaign. He made sure that the army backed the Cultural Revolution and had been extravagant in his praise of the Chairman at every opportunity. The man who symbolized Mao's political line was now unmasked as a traitor. This called into question Mao's judgment, even his competence. It called into question the entire rationale for the Cultural Revolution.

The Lin Biao affair was a considerable blow to Mao personally. He became depressed and withdrawn for several months, contributing to a serious health crisis in 1972.[1] Mao responded by changing course: he decided to repair his relations with veteran officials he had purged during the Cultural Revolution, and to blame the excesses of the movement on

Lin Biao and his coterie of military loyalists. He initially leaned heavily on Zhou Enlai to rebuild these bridges, pulling back from the more damaging policies of recent years. With Mao's blessing, Zhou conducted a national campaign to "criticize Lin Biao" for the extremism that caused such suffering during the course of the Cultural Revolution. During the next two years, Mao entrusted Zhou with rebuilding China's civilian administration and easing uniformed soldiers out of government administration.

This attempt at damage control inadvertently unleashed new waves of conflict that roiled Chinese politics and society until Mao's death in September 1976. As the armed forces withdrew from government administration, which civilians would replace them? There were two very different claimants. The first were civilian cadres, experienced party administrators and professional experts who had been shunted aside, many of whom were still performing manual labor on shop floors or in rural reeducation camps. The second were former rebels who had led the attack on veteran cadres and professionals several years before. Although some of them survived under military rule in largely ceremonial posts, most had lost positions that they initially held on revolutionary committees, or had fallen in the purge campaigns run by the army from 1968 to 1971. The rivalry between these two very different claimants to positions of authority would rekindle conflicts that had lain dormant under military rule.

The post-Lin effort to correct the errors of previous years raised deeper questions that defined Chinese politics during the final years of the Mao era—questions that were inextricably bound up with the question of who would assume positions of civilian leadership. Which practices and policies were counterproductive excesses of "ultraleftism" and which were defining elements of Mao's political line, deviation from which had to be resisted at all costs? These questions divided political actors from top to bottom of Chinese society. In the national leadership, veteran officials who were sidelined during the Cultural Revolution had a broader view of "excesses" and were willing to restore many of the older practices that were recently condemned. Surviving members of the Central Cultural Revolution Group (CCRG) and their supporters, on the other hand, saw efforts to correct excesses as a cover for rolling back the policies of the Cultural Revolution itself. The same differences in viewpoint divided leaders at all levels, and set veteran cadres and former rebel

leaders on a collision course. Mao resolved these disagreements by in-
tervening at crucial turning points, trying to balance opposed forces in
the national leadership. But his views were obscure and his decisions
unpredictable. He signaled them by shifting his support for one side or
the other in the course of their ongoing disputes. Leaning first one way,
then another, the aging Mao ensured political instability during his final
years.

As these conflicts played out, a new and unanticipated force came
into play: ordinary citizens who were uninvolved in factional conflicts
but who suffered during the Cultural Revolution. They were former activists who felt betrayed, and citizens young and old who had grown
weary of sectarian factional battles, stagnating living standards, and
blocked educational and career opportunities. Expressions of dissent over
radical Maoism appeared early in this period and grew in intensity, culminating in massive street demonstrations in Beijing, Nanjing, and many
other cities shortly before Mao's death. They contained the seeds of a
new political mentality that was later expressed more openly in nascent
democracy movements. More than anything else, these massive demonstrations signaled the loss of popular support for radical initiatives and
the futility of any effort to uphold them after Mao had departed the scene.

The Campaign to Criticize Lin Biao

These conflicts were set in motion by the campaign to criticize Lin Biao,
which began in early 1972. Much of the official story about Lin Biao's
demise was clearly a fabrication, especially its depiction of Lin's character and motives. He did die when his plane crashed in Mongolia. Soviet officials found the crash site and identified his remains and those
of his immediate family members. However, Lin Biao was not the ambitious, power-crazed plotter depicted in the official story. He was in fact
reluctant to play a major political role and long felt insecure as Mao's
successor.[2] There is little evidence that Lin himself was involved in a plot
to overthrow Mao and seize power in a coup, although there are indications that Lin Biao's son, an influential air force colonel, may have
discussed organized resistance to his father's impending fall from power
with other young officers, and that these discussions were leaked.

It is clear that by late 1969 Mao had become deeply concerned about
the enormous power he was forced to grant to army officers in 1968.

Mao's position depended almost entirely on the military apparatus, and this apparatus reported to Lin Biao. Lin's military forces achieved a dominant position when provincial party committees were reestablished in the wake of the Ninth Party Congress. In August 1971, military officers were first party secretaries in twenty-two out of twenty-nine provinces, and were an absolute majority of cadres in provincial party bodies.[3] They had pushed aside civilian Maoists.

Factional divisions between Lin's military commanders on the Politburo and the surviving civilian radicals from the CCRG sharpened during 1970. Chen Boda switched sides, abandoning his erstwhile civilian allies to side with the military officers. As the rivalries in the leadership grew, Mao decided to push back against the military wing. Chen Boda became the first victim. Despite his role as one of the early architects of Mao Zedong Thought and as the standard bearer of radical Maoism throughout his life, Chen, the nominal chair of the CCRG, was denounced as a "fake Marxist," "traitor," and "counterrevolutionary" in January 1971. Mao called for apologetic self-criticisms by Lin's military commanders, but their response did not satisfy him, and he began to make changes in the military hierarchy to ensure personal loyalty to him. It was in this context that Lin's son allegedly began discussions with other officers about moving against the civilian radicals and resisting Mao's moves against his father and the military wing of the party. The family boarded a small passenger jet in what appears to have been great haste, without proper refueling, to avoid imminent arrest. While this is the most plausible of the published accounts, the case remains shrouded in official secrecy.[4]

Whatever the reality, it is the official story and the ensuing denunciation campaign against Lin that altered China's subsequent political course. Lin's top commanders on the Politburo were purged and arrested and the military command was reshuffled. But Lin's demise presented Mao and other leaders with a dilemma: how to explain Lin's death in a way that limited the potential political fallout. The message transmitted to the party and government hierarchy, and to the people of China, had four elements. First, Lin planned a military coup to seize power; second, Lin and his coconspirators despised the civilian radicals that had helped Mao launch the Cultural Revolution; third, Lin and his coconspirators viewed the Cultural Revolution as an unmitigated disaster; and fourth, they had come to hold Mao himself in contempt.

The most intriguing feature of this campaign, and its cornerstone, was an official central party document issued in January 1972, titled "The Struggle to Smash the Lin [Biao]-Chen [Boda] Antiparty Clique's Counterrevolutionary Coup." It was first distributed to the party and army leadership at all levels, then to all party members, and its contents were relayed orally to the population at large. The core of the document was a reprinted set of notes purportedly written by the alleged conspirators. It expressed the rationale for a coup that accounted for the political motives of the conspirators.[5]

Whatever the provenance of the material, the content is stunning. The document expresses vehement and powerful criticisms of both Mao and the Cultural Revolution. Presenting the document as "study materials" seemed motivated by a desire to prove beyond any doubt that Lin indeed was a traitor, something that otherwise would be difficult for many Chinese to accept. But the criticisms surely must have struck many in the party leadership, in the party at large, and ordinary citizens as a damaging indictment of Mao, the Cultural Revolution, and the politicians who helped him launch it. Virtually every one of the strongly stated criticisms had a firm foundation in facts that were surely known to almost everyone who read them.

The first theme of the document is that the conspirators did not view the Cultural Revolution as a glorious victory. It had left Chinese society in a mess: "The political situation has been unstable. . . . The broad masses of the peasantry are oppressed, the economy is stagnant, the actual living standard of the masses, basic-level cadres, and soldiers . . . is falling, and the mood of dissatisfaction is spreading daily—people are angry but dare not speak. . . . The ruling group is corrupt, muddled, and incompetent. . . . The ruling group is internally very unstable; the struggling for power, striving for advantage, scheming and locking horns have almost reached a climax."[6]

The document lists all those who were harmed by the Cultural Revolution and the grievances that they harbored. The livelihood of peasants had been neglected: "Peasants lack food and are short of clothing." The sending of youths to the countryside was "really a disguised form of labor reform." The Red Guards were used and then cynically discarded: "During the early stages the Red Guards were cheated and used, and they served as cannon fodder; during the later stages, they were suppressed and made into scapegoats." The civilian officials who formerly ran China were quietly simmering with resentment: "Cadres who were rejected and attacked are angry but dare not speak."[7]

The document expresses contempt for the civilian radicals who supported Mao in launching the Cultural Revolution—individuals who only five years later would be openly denounced as the Gang of Four. They are portrayed as frauds and hypocrites: "wielding the pen [they] still willfully tamper with [and distort] Marxism-Leninism, making it serve their private interests. They use false revolutionary rhetoric . . . in order to deceive and mislead the thoughts of the Chinese people." In reality, according to the authors, their political doctrines amounted to nothing more than a violent and deadly new form of fascism: "Their socialism is, in essence, social fascism. They have turned China's state machine into a kind of meat grinder for mutual slaughter and strife."[8]

In the wake of the recent extremes of the Mao cult, the document's assessment of the Chairman must have come as something of a shock. Mao is portrayed as manipulative, ruthless, and duplicitous: "Today he uses this force to attack that force; tomorrow he uses that force to attack this force. Today he uses sweet words and honeyed talk to those whom he entices, and tomorrow he puts them to death for some fabricated crimes." The document points out Mao's record of purging loyal comrades and those who did his bidding: "[Do you see] anyone whom he has supported initially who has not finally been handed a political death sentence? . . . Is there a single political force which he has been able to work with from beginning to end? . . . His few close comrades-in-arms or trusted aides have also been sent to prison by him."[9]

The authors viewed Mao as anything but the godlike figure of the Mao cult. They saw him as an arbitrary tyrant and political fraud, no better than some of the worst emperors in Chinese history: "He abuses the trust and status given him by the Chinese people. In an historical sense he is going backward. . . . He has become a contemporary Ch'in Shih-huang. . . . He is not a true Marxist-Leninist. . . . He is the biggest feudal despot in Chinese history."[10]

We can only speculate about the reasoning behind the decision to circulate such a critical portrayal of Mao and the Cultural Revolution. It could not have been circulated without Mao's approval, which only deepens the puzzle.[11] But we need not speculate about its impact. This document did to Mao what Khrushchev's 1956 speech did to Stalin: denounced him as an arbitrary and vicious tyrant and stripped him of all ideological posturing. Citizens of China did not need to be told how they had suffered in recent years. They did not need to be told that their living standards were still low and in fact had worsened. But they had not been exposed so widely to unvarnished criticisms that stripped these sufferings of any pretense that they were a necessary part of a higher, noble cause. The civilian radicals were self-serving frauds, ideological deviants who had invented a violent new form of "social fascism." Mao himself was a dangerously duplicitous tyrant, no better than the first Qin emperor, who was renowned for a violent rule that led quickly to the collapse of China's first united empire.

To be sure, many of the remaining true believers who were exposed to this document may have taken it as a shocking revelation of the twisted logic of the worst kind of traitors. This was probably the reaction that they were expected to have. But many others surely found in this document thoughts that they had inwardly harbored but dared not express. This reaction must surely have been common among the many who were abused, purged, or otherwise suffered during the Cultural Revolution, including many of those who had idealistically responded to the early call for rebellion and who were harshly repressed afterward. This document exposed to masses of Chinese an alternate interpretation of reality that sharply contradicted official propaganda. It also provided a language and a rationale with which to criticize the Cultural Revolution, civilian radicals in the leadership, and Mao himself. The impact of the document would soon become apparent. The same language and sentiments later appeared in wall posters on city streets and in underground writings that represented the first stirrings of open dissent in 1970s China. The same language and sentiments would be on display in the large protests in Tiananmen Square and elsewhere in China in late March and early April 1976, just six months before Mao's death.

Restoring Civilian Government, 1972–1973

The campaign to criticize Lin Biao launched an effort to rebuild China's party organization and bring civilian officials back into their former posts. Lin Biao was portrayed as an ultraleftist who distorted Mao's intentions during the Cultural Revolution and drove it to excess. The damage wrought by the Cultural Revolution was now portrayed as part of a plot:

the ludicrous exaggeration of the Mao cult, the enormous toll of the Cleansing of the Class Ranks campaign, the disbanding of organs of civilian administration and the rural labor camps for officials were all "ultraleft" cover for a plan to seize military power. Millions of photographs of Mao with Lin Biao and copies of the "little red book" and other materials that contained epigraphs or quotations from Lin were recalled and destroyed.[12]

With this campaign as political cover, Mao relied on Zhou Enlai to repair the damage and restore civilian administration. Mao went into seclusion, in very poor health for some of this period, and Zhou proceeded on this course until late in 1973.[13] The public rituals of the Mao cult ended. The May 7 Cadre Schools, where millions of officials and other educated staff underwent reform through labor, were closed, and their occupants returned to the cities and their former workplaces. Universities began to admit small numbers of "worker-peasant-soldier" students for short courses of basic-level study. Party committees at all levels, which had ceased to operate in 1966, began to be rebuilt, and after they began to operate, political authority flowed back toward them and away from the revolutionary committees created by the Cultural Revolution.

The primary focus of Zhou's work during his brief period in charge was cadre rehabilitation—the return of disgraced officials to important posts. In March 1972 Zhou prepared a list of more than 400 senior officials who had been vetted and found satisfactory, and submitted the list to Mao, who approved it. The process continued at successively lower levels of government as party committees were restored. This work culminated in the Tenth Party Congress, held in August 1973. Membership in the party's Central Committee reflected a major change from the Ninth Party Congress of April 1969. The number of serving army officers declined sharply, and they were replaced by civilian officials who had spent recent years in disgrace. The most important and most surprising of these returnees was Deng Xiaoping, who in 1967 had been denounced as China's "number two capitalist roader" (Liu Shaoqi, the "number one capitalist roader," died in prison after being denied medical care in 1969). With Mao's approval, Deng returned to Beijing from exile in Jiangxi in February 1973, and shortly afterward was restored to the Central Committee and the post of vice premier.[14]

Deng's rapid elevation, which culminated when he took over Zhou Enlai's duties in December 1973, was Mao's idea. Mao viewed Deng as a more palatable alternative to Zhou Enlai, who fell badly out of favor during the last half of 1973.[15] Politburo radicals mistrusted Zhou and viewed his activities with deep suspicion. They had long viewed him as a compromiser who had consistently tried to blunt the destructive aspects of the Cultural Revolution and who was all too willing to sacrifice Maoist principles for administrative expediency. Throughout 1972 and 1973 they objected repeatedly to the strident critique of ultraleftism and the rehabilitation of veteran cadres at the expense of rebels in the provinces.[16] They seized on his handling of negotiations with the United States to denounce him for selling out China's national interests, and were able to bring Mao around to their point of view. Zhou was removed from his pivotal position at the apex of China's government.[17]

This had two consequences for domestic politics. The first was to place Deng Xiaoping in charge of the unfinished effort to rebuild civilian administration and repair the damage of the Cultural Revolution. The second was a shift in political line from denouncing the excesses of the Cultural Revolution to guarding against the restoration of the pre–Cultural Revolution status quo. This was signaled by a change in the national campaign to criticize Lin Biao. In January 1974 it was converted into a movement to "criticize Lin Biao and Confucius." This signaled a bizarre reversal of the interpretation of Lin's misdeeds: he was now portrayed as someone who actually opposed everything about the Cultural Revolution and plotted to restore the pre–Cultural Revolution status quo, a reactionary stance analogous to that of Confucius. Confucius was portrayed as a character that sought compromise and mediation, stability and harmony, values that expressed the interests of reactionary social classes who opposed revolution. These were also qualities of Zhou Enlai, who was the scarcely concealed target of the campaign.[18] This signaled to those who opposed the rollback of Cultural Revolution policies that it was now time to push back against the trend of restoration.

The "Second Cultural Revolution," 1974

The "Criticize Lin Biao and Confucius Campaign" had two objectives. The first, part of the original campaign to repudiate Lin Biao, was to finally eliminate the army's control over the levers of government. The earlier campaign against the "Lin Biao clique" had drastically reduced the army's power in the national leadership and in many provinces, but army officers who had not been implicated in Lin's alleged plot still held key posts in many regions, and civilian control had yet to be fully restored. At the end of 1973 military commanders in each of China's major military regions were transferred to new regional commands. Local strongmen were removed from the bases they built up after 1968, and they moved to new commands where they lacked personal networks and local allies. The second objective was to slow the ongoing rollback of policies associated with the Cultural Revolution itself. Zhou Enlai had employed the earlier criticism of an ultraleft Lin Biao to push for more effective civilian administration, and this meant the restoration of veteran cadres and party officials to their former positions. The 1974 campaign was a Mao-sanctioned effort to slow the rise of veteran cadres and halt the reversal of the economic and educational policies cherished by the Maoist camp.[19]

Initiated in January 1974, the campaign openly encouraged criticism of leaders who allegedly opposed the aims of the Cultural Revolution and sought to restore the status quo ante. This could include either regional military authorities or veteran civilian cadres. In many regions, an array of local forces mobilized to use the obscure language of central directives to their advantage. One group who seized this opportunity were former rebel leaders who had risen briefly to positions of prominence during the Cultural Revolution, only to be marginalized and thrust aside by military officers and then ignored during the restoration of cadres to their former posts. Former rebels used the campaign to reclaim their influence and assert claims to leadership positions in their sharpening rivalry with veteran party cadres now returning to their posts after years in political limbo. For this reason the campaign encouraged popular mobilization and street protests and was referred to as "a second Cultural Revolution," and in some places a "second power seizure."[20] While the campaign bred unrest along these lines throughout China, it also sparked a countermovement of protest against the Cultural Revolution itself.

Events in Hangzhou in 1974 were what many meant by the term "second Cultural Revolution." During the campaign against Lin Biao, many veteran cadres were reappointed to leading posts, often at the expense of individuals who were associated with the earlier rebel movement.[21] During the last half of 1973 they began to mobilize their forces to criticize the veteran cadres who headed the province and to demand party membership and appointment to leading posts in provincial and municipal governments and factories. A struggle for control of rebuilding trade union organizations pitted young former rebels against veteran officials.[22] In late 1973 delegations of aggrieved rebels who had been denied party membership and leading posts assembled throughout the province, planning to travel to Beijing to complain about their treatment. Wall posters challenging the provincial leadership appeared on the streets of Hangzhou. Near the end of the year a procession of aggrieved rebels marched on the provincial party headquarters and besieged the top leaders, detaining and harassing them, and demanding more appointments. Rebel leaders prepared for broader attacks on the provincial leadership, and began to make the rounds of major factories in the region to encourage workers to rebel against "the wrong political line."[23]

The Criticize Lin Biao and Confucius Campaign signaled that efforts to defend the Cultural Revolution had backing at the highest levels. Provincial leaders were soon under concerted attack, as rebels organized gigantic mass rallies declaring that it was "right to rebel against reactionaries" and called for a fight against "the bourgeois counter-attack to settle old scores and to restore its influence."[24] The rebels presented a series of demands to the provincial leadership, the most important of which was the appointment of hundreds of their followers to leading posts. On the defensive, the local authorities admitted 8,000 new party members and promoted 3,000 of them to leading posts.[25] A second demand was the establishment of workers' militias, which were soon organized throughout the province. Armed primarily with iron clubs, the militias became feared in Hangzhou and other cities, and they engaged in sporadic attacks against soldiers who guarded factories and other facilities. Hangzhou's top rebel leader declared that the militias were prepared to seize military control from the army.[26] Militias obtained more lethal arms, and violent clashes occurred that were reminiscent of the battles of 1967. The conflicts spread to large state factories in Hangzhou and disrupted the railway system. The authorities were powerless to stem the rising tide of conflict.[27]

In Nanjing, however, the campaign took a very different turn, and bred sustained large-scale protests by ordinary citizens who had been victimized by recent political campaigns. In Nanjing veteran provincial cadres used the campaign to finally move the military out of civilian posts in Jiangsu Province. Rebel leaders in Jiangsu played only a supporting role in this effort: they had been so completely crushed by the army's earlier suppression campaigns that they were not a major force in Nanjing politics. Civilian cadres presented themselves as champions of these former rebels, denouncing the military for the repressions meted out to them in the Anti May 16 Elements Campaign of 1971. There were popular protests in Nanjing, but they were spearheaded by those who were victimized by the Cultural Revolution—primarily the tens of thousands who were given political labels and expelled from the cities.[28]

General Xu Shiyou had ruled Nanjing with an iron hand since 1968, and he had dragged his feet in restoring civilians to key posts as party committees were rebuilt in Jiangsu Province. By the end of 1973, more than 2,000 army officers still held party and government posts. All of the first party secretaries at the prefecture level were still army officers, as were thirty-nine of the sixty-eight first party secretaries at the county level.[29] Xu Shiyou was transferred out of the Nanjing Military Region to Guangzhou at the end of 1973, permitting the civilian cadres to move against the remaining military officials.

The veteran cadres in Nanjing conducted a campaign to criticize the armed forces for their suppression campaigns, in particular the campaign against former rebel leaders. But in doing so, they inadvertently mobilized thousands of ordinary citizens into the streets to protest their own suppression at the hands of the military authorities. The torrent of criticism against the army's actions in previous years encouraged urban residents who were expelled from the cities to attempt to return to their homes and former jobs. More than 350,000 urban residents were relocated to villages involuntarily during the first years of military control, 130,000 of them from Nanjing alone. Many of them were from households with "exploiting class" labels or suspect political histories. In late January 1974, several thousand of these expelled residents returned to Nanjing to petition the authorities to restore their urban registrations and jobs. For almost three months, the petitioners demonstrated at the provincial and municipal party headquarters, put up wall posters detailing their plight, and engaged in periodic street marches. Their activities attracted large numbers of onlookers, tying up traffic in the downtown area. The stalemate lasted until late April when the petitioners became agitated and rushed the train station en masse, attempting to force their way onto Beijing-bound trains to petition in the capital. After train crews refused to let them board, they sat down on the tracks and tied up rail traffic to Beijing and Shanghai for several days.

The Nanjing authorities negotiated an agreement with the protesters and restored traffic on the rail lines. In promising to find places for the protesters in their former work units, however, they inadvertently created an even larger problem. As word spread that the petitioners' demands had been met, another 50,000 swarmed into Nanjing from the surrounding countryside, seeking the same deal. The authorities would not negotiate with so many new petitioners and, when this became clear, they clogged the downtown streets to protest, or rushed to take their pleas to Beijing. The rail lines were disrupted again, and some of the petitioners hijacked buses and trucks along the highway. Cadres sent to intercept the protesters were roughed up, some of them wounded. It took months to clear the streets of petitioners after the end of the campaign.

The campaign in Guangzhou saw the emergence of yet another countercurrent against the Cultural Revolution: a self-conscious campaign of political criticism of the Cultural Revolution by former rebel activists. In Guangzhou, politically conscious former rebels took to the streets to protest their harsh suppression at the hands of military authorities. But they went further and developed a critique of the Cultural Revolution that contained the seeds of a different political consciousness. These ideas were expressed in a long essay posted on city streets and widely discussed and reprinted, which is widely viewed as the precursor of China's late 1970s democracy movement. It called for a thorough reform of the Chinese political system by strengthening democracy and the rule of law.[30]

When rebel forces were suppressed in the Guangzhou Military Region in 1968, the Red Flag faction, which had opposed military control, was hit particularly hard. In October 1972 former rebel leaders from Red Flag gained their release from prison. A group of around thirty of them, along with some purged veteran cadres, held discussions about the why the Cultural Revolution had failed, and their critique focused on the actions of the local military. This led some of them to develop a critique of the "Lin Biao system" and circulate drafts of essays in late 1973. When the Criticize Lin Biao and Confucius Campaign began in February 1974, the authors began to post their essays as wall posters under the collective pen name Li Yizhe.[31] The most famous of the essays, "On Socialist Democracy and the Legal System," was put up in a prominent location in Guangzhou in November 1974. It was one of a series of wall posters designed to pressure officials to release more imprisoned members of the former Red Flag faction.

The group coordinated a series of mass meetings and street marches that made common cause with other aggrieved groups: demobilized soldiers who demanded a pay increase, young factory workers unhappy about pay and living conditions, youth sent down to the countryside, and former Red Guards who demanded punishment for army officers responsible for the massacres they perpetrated at the end of the 1960s.[32] The group's activities were treated sympathetically by newly appointed provincial party secretary Zhao Ziyang, who himself was purged during the Cultural Revolution and who was interested in rolling back military control. Several of the former Red Guard leaders who spearheaded the campaign against military misconduct were placed in charge of the Criticize Lin Biao and Confucius Campaign in their workplaces, and one of them was appointed to investigate army abuses for the local party newspaper. These positions afforded them the opportunity to publicize their underground essays and present petitions to provincial leaders.[33]

While the essay "On Socialist Democracy" expressed allegiance to Mao and the aims of the Cultural Revolution, it expressed a fundamentally different political mentality. The primary target was the "Lin Biao system," whose characteristics were very similar to the highly critical description of the Cultural Revolution contained in the documents circulated during the earlier campaign against the "Lin-Chen antiparty clique." The authors ridiculed the "boundless loyalty" campaign of the late 1960s as quasi-religious rituals more appropriate to feudal emperor worship than to modern socialism.[34] They lambasted the arbitrary persecutions of the Cleansing of the Class Ranks and One Strike, Three Anti campaigns against vaguely defined "counterrevolutionary elements." They warned against officials who wanted to return to the days of suppression, beatings, and torture in searches for imagined traitors and class enemies. All of these abuses, they charged, were signs that a new ruling class was forming in China, one that used coercion and emperor worship to solidify their dictatorship and deny China the possibility of socialist democracy. What made these abuses possible was the lack of genuine democracy and legal restraints on official power. Without safeguards to defend the rights of the people against abuse, and restrictions on arbitrary power in the form of legal rules, socialism would degenerate into the kind of "social fascism" recently observed during the three years of the "Lin Biao system"—that is, during the Cultural Revolution.[35]

The essay's primary purpose was to oppose the political turn represented by the Criticize Lin Biao and Confucius Campaign of 1974. The authors argued that the new campaign was actually an effort to return to the social fascism of the Cultural Revolution. What was really needed, they argued, was not a campaign to "oppose restoration" of the pre–Cultural Revolution status quo, but to build a new set of institutions that would protect the democratic rights of the people, restrain arbitrary persecutions, and curtail the special privileges currently enjoyed by those who held political power.[36] This was a new political mentality, and the authors of the essay and others in their group became major actors in the post-Mao democracy campaigns of 1978 and 1979.[37]

Political figures in Beijing were alarmed by the essay's criticism of single-party rule. Most vociferous were the reactions of Politburo radicals, especially Jiang Qing, who denounced the essay as "the most reactionary article yet since Liberation." In early 1975 a citywide denunciation campaign against the essay was organized in Guangzhou, with several struggle sessions against the authors and additional mass meetings to condemn the essay held in schools and factories throughout the city. The authors were banished to the countryside, and an investigation targeted hundreds of individuals who had expressed approval of the authors' ideas.[38]

While the character of local protests varied widely, the rise of civil disorder in many Chinese regions was creating serious economic problems by the middle of 1974. In factories, railway depots, and dockyards, rebel leaders challenged veteran cadres who had tried to reassert their authority and enforce work discipline. In addition to the widespread disruptions in Hangzhou and Nanjing described above, workers on the Shanghai docks halted work to protest the reinstitution of piece rates, and factional fighting in the railway system, especially in the pivotal region of Xuzhou, disrupted China's transport system. When steel, coal, and other crucial supplies piled up at the point of production due to shipping delays, supply shortages slowed production. Industrial output declined during the first three quarters of 1974, reversing the modest upward trend of recent years.

In October these problems finally caught Mao's attention, and he weighed in to call for "unity and stability." While Mao clearly wanted rebel forces to push back against the hasty restoration of pre–Cultural

Revolution practices, he did not want a return to the kind of disorder that had prompted him to lean heavily on a military solution back in 1968. Near the end of the year Mao finally instructed Beijing officials to act decisively to boost the national economy, and he put Deng Xiaoping in charge of the effort, which began in earnest in early 1975.[39]

Restoring Order, Stabilizing the Economy, 1975

With Mao's approval, Deng Xiaoping moved decisively to finish the re-building of party organizations, completely remove the armed forces from civilian administration, and halt the disruptive conflicts that crippled the economy in 1974. He was able to accomplish far more during 1975 than Zhou Enlai during his earlier stint, in large part by moving more decisively than the cautious premier had dared.[40] Deng's initiatives, however, were cut short by the end of the year. He had Mao's support to re-build the party and curtail factional conflicts, creating "unity and sta-bility" and thereby, in Mao's view, consolidating the accomplishments of the Cultural Revolution. However, Deng overstepped his mandate when he moved to create conditions for the modernization of China's industry, a stronger scientific establishment, and a restored system of higher education. These initiatives in fact challenged cherished "accom-plishments" of the Cultural Revolution itself and, like Zhou Enlai be-fore him, Deng soon found himself sidelined and criticized.

Before he was sidelined Deng accomplished a great deal. He was able to remove the armed forces completely from civilian administration. In a series of speeches and directives to military leaders, he criticized the armed forces as bloated and soft, having created comfortable government positions for themselves with civilian perquisites and special privileges. He called on the People's Liberation Army to refocus on military affairs and withdraw from involvement in civil administration, which ham-pered military readiness and weakened discipline. He ordered a renewed focus on upgrading weapons systems, and initiated a campaign to ex-tinguish factionalism within the armed forces. In August 1975 he or-dered the withdrawal of all military personnel from civilian posts.[41]

Deng also reenergized the campaign to rebuild the national party or-ganization. He reasserted the authority of party secretaries and continued the rehabilitation of formerly disgraced officials and professional experts. He made clear that party leadership was supreme, and that rebellion against party authority would no longer be tolerated. He also ordered the reexamination of the new party members admitted after 1968, making clear that their qualifications and sense of discipline should be verified before their party membership was confirmed. Those who "lacked qualifications" or who retained factional allegiances should be expelled. Newer members who clamored for elevation into leading posts, or who had already attained them, should remain in low-level positions to gain the necessary experience that comes with seniority.[42]

Deng directed a vigorous campaign to suppress factionalism, focusing first on the national railway system and then extending it to the key industrial sectors of coal and steel. The showcase for this effort was the rectification campaign that he ordered in the Xuzhou Railway Bureau—a key railway junction in northern Jiangsu Province where persistent and deeply entrenched factional conflict had created bottlenecks that disrupted the delivery of industrial supplies in much of eastern and northern China. In February 1975 he transferred authority over the Railway System from separate provincial governments to the Ministry of Railways, and issued a central document that labeled factional resistance to ministry authority as "bourgeois" and damage to railway property "counterrevolutionary." He ordered a work team into the Xuzhou Railway Bureau, headed by the minister of railways, and had the head of the bureau, a former rebel leader, arrested. When his followers resisted, they were arrested also. The work team conducted a series of mass denunciation meetings to criticize factional disruption, pushed very hard for a reduction in accident rates and the fulfillment of quotas for freight tonnage, and transferred large numbers of activists to different posts, breaking up local factional networks. The Xuzhou experience was promoted as a national model, and its methods were applied to problematic railway bureaus that had created bottlenecks elsewhere in China.[43] The methods employed in the railway system were quickly applied to major coal and steel centers, which were similarly disrupted.[44]

Rebels in Zhejiang Province who had formed workers' militias to advance their cause during the 1974 "second Cultural Revolution" resisted these readjustment policies, and Deng dispatched a high-powered work team to Hangzhou to sort out the problems. The rebels were put under heavy pressure, and in a predawn raid on the faction's headquarters, the top rebel leader, Weng Senhe, was arrested. PLA troops were sent to major factories in and around Hangzhou to avert further unrest. Other rebel leaders were punished, while the workers' militias were disbanded, and the provincial leadership was reshuffled to strengthen the readjustment program.[45]

The Last Radical Backlash

Deng's decisive actions to restore order and rebuild party authority were entirely within his working mandate. Mao had long been clear that he wanted the military removed completely from civilian administration, and Deng completed the task. Mao was clear that he wanted the party organization to be rebuilt and disgraced officials returned to useful service, and Deng energetically pushed this agenda forward. Mao was also clear that while he wanted to preserve the "positive accomplishments" of the Cultural Revolution, chronic factional conflict that disrupted production and social order was not one of them. Mao wanted order, discipline, and stability, which he saw as consolidating the gains of the Cultural Revolution. The methods that Deng employed to accomplish these objectives were primarily political—reasserting party authority in unambiguous terms, and demanding discipline and unity. None of this overstepped the limits of what Mao had asked Deng to do.

Deng, however, also went beyond these purely political measures to create the foundations for a modern economy. It appears that these initiatives, as modest as they seem in retrospect, may have caused Mao to lose confidence in Deng's fidelity to the Cultural Revolution. Given Deng's subsequent embrace of market-oriented reforms after Mao's death, Mao's intuition can hardly be faulted. Deng initiated several measures that went beyond reinforcing order and stability. He authorized the drafting of an ambitious plan for reviving Chinese industry and boosting economic growth, advocating the importation of advanced foreign technology, the adoption of international trade practices that involved foreign credits, and the strengthening of work incentives and industrial discipline by implementing the principle of payment according to work. A second plan called for the strengthening of science and technology, and in particular the rebuilding of the Chinese Academy of Sciences. The plan advocated the revival of professional journals, the withdrawal of military officers and propaganda teams, greater access to research materials and equipment including foreign publications, the final return of all former scientific personnel who still remained in the countryside, and the targeting of high-technology fields like computers, lasers, and remote sensing, as well as basic research in nuclear energy and particle physics. The plan also called for the revival of social science research and the creation of a separate Chinese Academy of Social Sciences. A third initiative addressed higher education: it reaffirmed the value of faculty trained as specialists before the Cultural Revolution, the admission of students directly from high school instead of from factories and farms based on political recommendations, the reduction or elimination of compulsory factory work as part of university education, and the restoration of longer courses of specialized training with much higher academic standards.[46] The subtext for all of these initiatives was that Chinese industry and science had fallen badly behind those of other countries, and that its system of higher education was inadequate. The prescribed new policies clearly implied that the Cultural Revolution had intensified China's backwardness.

Mao developed severe misgivings at the end of 1975. There arc different views about what triggered his rapid loss of confidence in Deng, but his attitude began to shift decisively in September and by November had reached the point where Mao authorized severe criticism of Deng for policy errors.[47] In retrospect it is hard to fault Mao's perception that Deng was interested less in consolidating the gains of the Cultural Revolution than in rolling back its counterproductive initiatives and rebuilding much of what it had destroyed. In January 1976 Deng stopped appearing in public and was stripped of his leadership responsibilities. After the death of Zhou Enlai that month, Hua Guofeng was named acting premier and was promoted to first vice premier, effectively replacing Deng Xiaoping.[48] At the same time, a shrill denunciation campaign against revisionism and "restorationism" began, focusing first on officials who had headed Deng's initiatives in industry, science and technology, and higher education. These officials were subjected to criticism in the mass media, wall poster accusations, and mass meetings where they were loudly denounced and repudiated in a style reminiscent of the late 1960s. One official collapsed during a struggle session and died of a heart attack shortly thereafter.[49] These officials were denounced for following the designs of an unnamed "unrepentant capitalist roader," a scarcely veiled reference to the as-yet-unnamed Deng Xiaoping.

The Qingming Protests of 1976

The death of Zhou Enlai, the demotion of Deng Xiaoping, and the harsh campaign to denounce restorationism, all occurring in mid-January

1976, marked a shift in China's political atmosphere. Rebel leaders in the provinces who were suppressed during Deng's recent campaign against factionalism saw this as a sign that they could make a comeback. In provincial capitals like Nanjing, Hangzhou, and Wuhan they mobilized to attack local veteran cadres for the same errors committed by Deng Xiaoping. In these cities rebel leaders once again challenged veteran cadres, sought to unseat recently appointed officials, put up wall posters, and held demonstrations in front of government offices.[50] To them, it looked as if the tide had turned once again, and they were ready to seize their chance at a comeback.

This new offensive incited, for the first time, public resistance by ordinary citizens. The period after the death of Lin Biao had been one of quiet ferment, with underground study groups reexamining Marxism-Leninism, former Red Guards reflecting on the defeat of their movement, and ordinary citizens writing anonymous handbills and petitions that denounced the Cultural Revolution, Jiang Qing, and even Mao himself.[51] During the first stages of this new campaign to criticize restorationism, obviously targeting Deng and by implication Zhou, similar sentiments surfaced in the form of handbills and wall posters.[52]

These underground stirrings became public in a dramatic fashion in the early spring of 1976. They appeared to reflect a much larger slice of the population than the dissident rebels in the provinces, and represented a reaction diametrically opposed to the January shift in political atmosphere. The catalyst was the handling of Zhou Enlai's state funeral, and more importantly Beijing's subsequent efforts to discourage local commemorations of the veteran revolutionary. Zhou was given a full and proper official state funeral on January 15, but the amount of publicity devoted to it fell below what many citizens expected. Only a few scenes from the funeral were shown on television, and Deng Xiaoping, who gave the eulogy, was not mentioned in the media accounts. Shortly after the funeral, the Central Committee issued a directive banning local commemorative meetings for Premier Zhou. Instead, citizens were instructed to pour their energies into the criticism of the "right deviationist wind"— an obvious reference to Deng Xiaoping, but seemingly an indirect swipe at Zhou Enlai, who was closely associated in the popular mind with the kinds of policies that Deng pushed. This stance offended public opinion and served as a trigger for massive street demonstrations that represented a challenge to the Politburo radicals and indirectly to Mao himself.

The earliest and best-known protests were in Nanjing, and began at Nanjing University, the cradle of the city's Red Guard and rebel movements. Mourning for Zhou Enlai began spontaneously on the campus and in other organizations around Nanjing shortly after his January death was announced.[53] A few days afterward, however, the Central Committee issued a directive banning commemorative meetings, and many workplaces and schools canceled their planned activities. Nanjing University nonetheless went forward with theirs. Local citizens were offended by the low level of publicity surrounding the state funeral, and by the launching of a campaign to criticize the policies identified with Zhou. The propaganda campaign met with little enthusiasm. Local rebels who saw themselves as loyal followers of Mao's line attacked Nanjing's party leaders for their lack of enthusiasm, and accused them of complicity with Deng's revisionism.

Public reaction did not surface, however, until a March 25 article in the Shanghai newspaper *Wenhui bao* pointedly referred to an "unrepentant capitalist roader who helped an unrepentant capitalist roader come back to the political stage."[54] Whether intended or not, this was widely interpreted to refer to Zhou Enlai, and the reaction in Nanjing was immediate. The next day, wall posters went up all over the Nanjing University campus, emotionally repudiating the *Wenhui bao* article and challenging those who dared to attack Premier Zhou. The posters were openly critical of the Politburo radicals, whose political base was in Shanghai. Jiang Qing was insulted in a wall poster that claimed that the author "missed Yang Kaihui," one of Mao's earlier wives, who was executed by the Nationalists. Students marched to Nanjing's train and bus stations to paste slogans on departing vehicles, informing those in other cities of the Nanjing movement to defend the memory of Zhou Enlai.

Two weeks before the April 4 Qingming festival to commemorate the dead, wreaths dedicated to Zhou began to appear around the city, and wall posters declared "We will forever remember Premier Zhou." Large numbers of wreaths appeared on a hill south of the city used by the Nationalists as an execution ground, which had been a traditional place for residents to lay wreaths after 1949. There were physical confrontations at the entrance to the park when a delegation of 400 students was barred from entering. Instead, the students marched through the city center, displaying their wreaths on March 28. This drew large crowds onto the city streets. Even more pointedly worded wall posters defended

Zhou and attacked Politburo radicals. One prominent wall poster warned of "Khrushchev-like conspirators who want to usurp power" and another named Zhang Chunqiao a "careerist and double-dealer." Alarmed by these reports, on April 1 the Central Committee ordered the suppression of street gatherings and the removal of wreaths and wall posters.

On April 2 Beijing's ban on commemorations was distributed in Nanjing, and cadres and workers were ordered to cover up the offending wall posters and slogans.[55] These actions, however, failed to stem the rising tide of protest against the rebel resurgence. Even larger protests broke out on April 3, which were instigated by the directive banning wall posters and wreaths. Protestors put up wall posters and chanted slogans that were even more confrontational and aggressive: "Commemorating Premier Zhou is not counterrevolution" and "We are resolved to fight a fierce battle against careerists who raise the white flag and oppose Premier Zhou." An estimated 140,000 marched to a park south of Nanjing on April 3. The crowds grew to a remarkable 600,000 in the streets of Nanjing in succeeding days, reaching a peak on April 4.[56] The Nanjing events sparked similar outpourings in other cities and county seats in southern Jiangsu.[57]

Similar events occurred on a smaller scale in Hangzhou. The attacks on Deng Xiaoping spurred a group of party cadres in one of the city offices to put up a wall poster refuting the charge that cadres had degenerated into capitalist roaders. The *Wenhui bao* article that seemed to attack Zhou as an "unrepentant capitalist roader" spurred wall posters that attacked Shanghai's party secretary, a protégé of the Politburo radicals. Party members from a steel mill placed a large commemorative wreath in memory of Zhou at the labor bureau on April 1, on a flagpole at the top of the building, where it could be seen for several blocks. Other factories and work units in Hangzhou followed suit, as did individuals at Zhejiang University. Wall posters in the city declared, "Whoever opposes Premier Zhou opposes revolution" and "Be strictly on guard against Lin Biao–type bourgeois careerists and plotters seizing party and state power." Excitement about these political expressions was focused on the main downtown department store, the gates of the university, and several major squares. As in Nanjing, slogans were painted on trains that were scheduled to depart for Beijing and other cities.[58]

These provincial events may have helped to catalyze the much larger and more momentous Beijing demonstrations on April 4 and 5. The slogans placed on trains bound for the capital had their intended effect: one of the first banners posted in Tiananmen Square reportedly declared, "We are determined to support the Nanjing people in their revolutionary struggles."[59] In Beijing, commemorative wreaths appeared in Tiananmen Square as early as March 19. These were quickly removed, and the Public Security Bureau was ordered to compile lists of everyone who laid wreaths at the square. On March 30 and 31, as news of the Nanjing movement reached the capital, wreaths became more numerous, and antiradical poems and statements were posted on the square, as the number of visitors increased rapidly. In the few days before April 4, more than 1 million people are estimated to have visited the square. The Public Security Bureau set up a joint command post at one corner of the square that was staffed also by members of the workers' militia and troops from the Beijing Garrison. It broadcast statements that the Qingming festival was a feudal custom, that work units should not send delegations with wreaths, and that the Nanjing events were a "reactionary incident." They did not move against the crowds, however, and only made a few arrests and removed some of the wreaths.[60]

On the day of the festival, April 4, the crowd on the square grew to an estimated 2 million. Many more wreaths were carried to the square, along with poems, handbills, wall posters, and spontaneous speeches and shouting of slogans. The atmosphere grew increasingly tense as the day went on, with sporadic fistfights and injuries of public security officers who intervened. Most statements were emotional eulogies for Premier Zhou, but as in Nanjing, some were sharply critical of Politburo radicals, alluding especially to Jiang Qing and Zhang Chunqiao. More noteworthy was the defiance exhibited toward Mao himself. The demonstrations were obviously in opposition to Mao's new criticism campaign, and more fundamentally against the Cultural Revolution. While not being named directly, Mao was attacked in some of the posters and speeches. One poem posted on the square that day referred to the Politburo radicals thus:

> Despicable are the demons who, overrating themselves,
> Once gain attempt to stir up evil winds and bloody rains,
> Talking glibly and carrying their mistress' train
> —what a ridiculous lot they are, a bunch of monkeys
> Trying to crown themselves!
> . . . Look around, you despicable lot:

Flowers blanket Tiananmen Square like snow
And tears fall in showers around the monument.
We cherish the memory of Premier Zhou; but you do not.
We offer our libation; but you do not.
China is no longer the China of the past,
And the people are no longer wrapped in utter ignorance,
Gone for good is Qin Shi Huang's feudal society,
. . . To hell with scholars who emasculate Marxism-Leninism![61]

The obvious challenge to both the Politburo radicals and Mao could not be tolerated, and the party leaders decided in a late-night meeting to clear the square of all wreaths; the few remaining people who lingered on the square late at night were detained. There was no public explanation for the removal of the wreaths, but word spread rapidly and by 8 a.m. on April 5 roughly 10,000 agitated people had already gathered in the square, and the crowd grew several-fold into the afternoon. The crowd was angry and confrontational: they massed on the steps of the Great Hall of the People and demanded the return of the wreaths. A police van that broadcast messages denouncing "class enemies" was overturned, and the joint command post of the Public Security Bureau was overrun by protesters and set on fire. The police and militia did not move against the crowd until after dark, when the lights were turned out and a recorded speech by Beijing's mayor denounced "bad elements" who "deceived people" and asked that everyone return home. After the speech was played a number of times, at 11 p.m. the police and militia finally moved in with clubs to beat and cart off the remaining stragglers on the square, which was then cordoned off. Rumors of massive casualties appear to be unfounded, and the authorities were apparently able to restore control over the square with relatively little violence. The mood the next day was calm: several thousand people came to pay their respects, and one wreath was laid down and left undisturbed.

The Aftermath of Tiananmen and Mao's Final Days

For obvious reasons, Politburo radicals and their supporters were alarmed by the Tiananmen protests. Mao's nephew, Mao Yuanxin, reported to him on April 7 that "the counterrevolutionary political incident . . . publicly unfurled and embraced the banner of Deng Xiaoping [and] furiously pointed its spearhead at the great leader Chairman Mao."[62] Some of the Politburo radicals charged that Deng Xiaoping had fomented the protests as part of an antiparty plot, and that he had actually been on the square to direct events. Mao was unconvinced, but he understood clearly that the protests indicated a large popular following for a reversal of Cultural Revolution policies, and that figures like Deng and Zhou were becoming a rallying point. He ordered Deng removed from his leadership posts and officially named Hua Guofeng as Zhou's successor as premier (he had been acting premier since February). Hua was also appointed first vice chairman, which suggested that he was Mao's choice as his successor. Deng Xiaoping was publicly denounced, and the four-month campaign against the unnamed "unrepentant capitalist roader" became a "criticize Deng" campaign.[63] This turned out to be Mao's last decisive intervention in Chinese politics.

In the ensuing months, Politburo radicals and their supporters in the capital and the provinces continued to push their criticism of earlier rectification efforts. A nationwide hunt for individuals who sympathized with the Tiananmen protests, or who had expressed similar sympathies, led to the investigation of hundreds of thousands and the arrest of roughly 10,000 people. Mass rallies and parades were organized to celebrate the "smashing of the counterrevolutionary countercurrent."[64] Resistance to veteran cadres revived in the provinces, especially among those who had been punished during Deng Xiaoping's 1975 campaigns to quell factionalism. In cities like Hangzhou and Nanjing, former rebel leaders resumed their push to overthrow veteran cadres who had cooperated with Deng's campaign to quell factionalism at their expense.[65] Hua Guofeng and other leaders who tried to continue the policies of stabilization and revive the economy within the boundaries set by Mao found that they were hemmed in by harsh criticism from more radical officials who seemingly dogged every effort, no matter how limited, to repair the damage of the Cultural Revolution.

In this unsettled situation Mao's health deteriorated rapidly. He had a heart attack on May 11 and remained conscious but was bedridden. He suffered another heart attack on June 26, another on September 2, and died on September 9. Hua Guofeng became acting chairman. The armed forces were placed on alert throughout the country to guard against the recurrence of public protests. Daily memorial services were held in the Great Hall of the People from September 11 to 17. On September 18 a massive memorial meeting was held on Tiananmen Square, with an estimated 1 million in attendance. Hua Guofeng gave the memorial speech, praising Mao as the "greatest Marxist-Leninist of the contemporary era." People stood in silence throughout the country at the appointed time, while the whistles of all factories and locomotives blew a three-minute tribute. Deng Xiaoping and his close associates, all of whom had recently been removed from their posts, were not permitted to attend.[66]

The official account of the events leading to the arrest of the Politburo radicals in early October portrays them as a Gang of Four who plotted to usurp party power. This appears to have the same flimsy relationship to historical reality as the allegations about Lin Biao's plot to seize power. The officials who engineered the arrests—essentially a political coup—most certainly understood that these radical figures would be a thorn in their side, and probably feared that they eventually would attempt to promote one of their own to the top leadership. There is, however, little evidence that Politburo radicals coordinated any effort to usurp the party leadership in the weeks after Mao's death.[67]

To the contrary, the plotting appears to have been almost entirely on the other side, and began barely a week after Mao's death when Hua Guofeng met with other senior officials to discuss how to resolve the "Gang of Four problem." Several senior officials had private and furtive discussions about how to remove them from the leadership, but Hua Guofeng took the initiative. He met with other Politburo members in late September to discuss the issue, stating that he saw conflict with the radicals as unavoidable. They considered calling a Politburo vote to remove them, but saw this as too risky, providing an opportunity for countermobilization by regional rebels.[68] Planning accelerated and drew more officials into the conspiracy. A list of the radicals' prominent supporters in Beijing, also designated for arrest, was drawn up. At the appropriate time, the Beijing Garrison would be ordered to secure the New China News Agency, People's Radio, *People's Daily,* the airport, and other strategic sites in the capital.

The scheme was set into motion by inviting key radicals to a Politburo meeting on the morning of October 6. Zhang Chunqiao, Wang Hongwen, and Yao Wenyuan were arrested as they arrived for the ostensible meeting; Jiang Qing and Mao's nephew Mao Yuanxin were arrested at their homes shortly afterward. The Beijing Garrison moved in to secure strategic sites and the operation was completed in less than an hour.[69] Over the next week, officials from the provinces and military regions were summoned to Beijing for briefings about what had transpired. Around thirty of the radicals' prominent allies in the capital were also arrested. Party leaders in Shanghai, the radicals' primary power base, were puzzled by their inability to contact their allies in Beijing, and suspected that "revisionists" had seized power. They held an emergency meeting on October 8 and decided to mobilize the militia to resist. On October 12 some Shanghai officials made plans to issue a message to the entire nation supporting the rebel cause, and stage strikes, organize demonstrations, and blow up bridges and resist in the manner of the Paris Commune. The plan was never implemented. Shanghai officials were pressured to go to Beijing for consultations, and after their return they were tight-lipped about what they were told. When the arrest of the Gang of Four was publicized nationally on October 14, Shanghai residents were puzzled. As the names of those arrested became known the next day, popular enthusiasm for the coup became evident, and all plans for organized resistance were dropped.[70]

In the waning weeks of his life, Mao appeared to realize that the game might be lost. In a famous statement to Hua Guofeng during the summer of 1976, he reflected on the future of his "last revolution":

> I have accomplished two things in my life. First, I fought Chiang Kai-shek for a few decades and drove him to a few islands. After eight years of war against the Japanese, they were sent home. We fought our way to Beijing, at last entering the Forbidden City. There are not many people who do not recognize these achievements. . . . The other matter you all know about. It was to launch the Cultural Revolution. On this matter few support it, many oppose it. But it is not finished, and its legacy must be handed down to the next generation. How to do this? If not in peace, then in turmoil. If it is not done well, then there will be bloodshed. Only heaven knows how you are going to handle it.[71]

If Mao thought that Hua would balance a strongly divided leadership, helping his radical loyalists to survive, he once again miscalculated. Barely one month after his death, his wife and nephew were in prison along with their political allies. In the years to come, Mao's reputation as a founding father would be preserved, but the legacy of his final years would be rejected. The party's subsequent campaign to "thoroughly repudiate the Cultural Revolution" would so vilify the radical officials who loyally did Mao's bidding that it sometimes appeared to imply that they, not Mao, were really responsible for the "decade of turmoil." But the party's official verdict, issued only five years after his death in the 1981 "Resolution on Party History," could not avoid stating the obvious: "The 'cultural revolution,' which lasted from May 1966 to October 1976, was responsible for the most severe setback and the heaviest losses suffered by the Party, the state and the people since the founding of the People's Republic. It was initiated and led by Comrade Mao Zedong."[72]

14

The Mao Era in Retrospect

A T THE TIME of his death Mao had accomplished very little of what he hoped to achieve after the mid-1950s. His two major accomplishments—the establishment of a unified Chinese state and the installation of a socialist economy modeled after that of the Soviet Union—were still basically intact. But both were severely damaged. Mao left China with a divided party organization riven by factional discord and a government that had yet to recover from the sustained assault of the past decade. The industrialization drive had stalled. Rural poverty was still widespread. Urban living standards had stagnated and in some respects had deteriorated. The university system was backward, and science and technology were decades behind world standards. Due to Mao's initiatives, China had fallen increasingly behind other nations in its quest for development. Mao left a country that was backward and weak, having fulfilled few of the aspirations of the early 1950s.

Unwanted Outcomes, Frustrated Ambitions

Almost every one of Mao's interventions after 1956 put his initial accomplishments in jeopardy, generating outcomes that were both unanticipated and unwanted. The first such instance was the Hundred Flowers. Mao tried to position himself as a champion of post-Stalin liberalization in a stable and secure new socialist regime, calling for public criticism of party cadres, against strong opposition from other party leaders. The crescendo of surprisingly harsh criticism and organized protest by students, a wave of strikes by industrial workers, the rollback of collective farms, and occasional rural rebellions all showed that China's citizens were far less accepting of the new party-state than Mao had imagined. The subsequent crackdown during the Antirightist Campaign was in many ways a humiliating retreat for Mao, and it set him on a course back toward his original Stalinist instincts that did not bode well for the future.

An even more spectacular defeat was the disastrous Great Leap Forward. Mao was convinced that socialism could be built much more rapidly than Stalin and other Chinese leaders thought possible, and he pushed for the rapid socialist transformation of the economy, completing the process in 1957, years ahead of schedule. This gave him confidence that the new socialist institutions, driven forward by political cadres who mobilized the population in ways reminiscent of the final stages of the civil war, would generate a quantum leap in China's economic development. Mao was right to be confident about the ability of his party organization to mobilize China's population. The outpouring of energy and nationwide activity was in many ways astonishing, and few modern states could have contemplated such a campaign. The result, however, was precisely the opposite of what Mao had intended. Quite apart from the staggering death toll of the devastating famine, the campaign damaged both agriculture and industry for many years to come. Mao's failure on this occasion was so total that he subsequently abandoned his early preoccupation with rapid economic growth, embarking instead on a political offensive designed to cope with the political fallout from the disaster he had brought upon his own people. He continued that struggle, with little success, until the end of this life.

On its own terms, the accomplishments of the Cultural Revolution were mixed at best. Ultimately it failed in the end, inflicting enormous damage in the process. From one perspective, though, it was remarkably successful. Mao was able in short order to mobilize an extraordinarily large insurgency against the party-state, which was effectively demolished by 1967. Relying on the armed forces, he was able to destroy the old party and government structures without leading to the complete disintegration of the nation-state. He subsequently put into place a new set of governmental institutions in the form of revolutionary committees that replaced the old parallel structures of party and government.

These were, however, hollow victories. Mao and his radical associates were able to instigate nationwide rebellions, but their efforts to direct and shape the course of conflict were constantly frustrated. Mao had to shift course and change tactics repeatedly after his initial strategies failed. The student movement was divided from the outset and resisted repeated efforts to get student rebels to unite. After the Central Cultural Revolution Group (CCRG) intervened to favor one faction, abandoning the students who had helped them launched the movement, they became the target of the faction they had cast aside. These dissident Red Guards were suppressed, leaving the field to student rebels loyal to the CCRG. But these rebels, in turn, divided into two new factions that fought one another to the very end.

After Mao's disappointing experience with students, he shifted to the mobilization of the working class. Initially this strategy looked promising. Large coalitions of worker rebels quickly overwhelmed local party authorities, but the workers also developed unwanted tendencies. Many of them demanded improvement in wages and living standards, and large numbers mobilized to defend local party leaders and battle with other workers, quickly paralyzing industry and transport. Shanghai's January power seizure appeared initially to be a solution—a coalition of worker rebels and loyal Maoist officials took over from the party authorities, suppressed economic demands, and put down opposition. A few provinces followed suit, but the effort soon fell apart. Similar power seizures failed almost everywhere else early in 1967, forcing Mao to impose military control. This had the unanticipated effect of injecting local armed forces into conflicts with rebel groups, which in turn deepened and prolonged the splits in rebel forces, drawing local army units into factional struggles.

As large-scale armed battles between rebel forces broke out across China in spring and summer of 1967, Mao tried to tip the scales toward a favorable outcome. He called for distributing military arms to "the Left" and sanctioned rebel attacks on army units that were taking the wrong side in local struggles. This served only to escalate armed warfare and the death toll from factional conflicts, now fought with military armaments. Entire districts of several regional cities were destroyed in the battles, and provinces where an initially tenuous order had been created were once again destabilized. Realizing that his initiative to strengthen rebel forces and resolve regional conflicts had badly backfired, Mao shifted sharply toward full support for the armed forces, purging scapegoats in the CCRG who had loyally carried out his recent directives, and called for mass factions to be disarmed. After a year of difficult and protracted negotiations to unite warring factions, Mao leaned increasingly toward a harsh authoritarian solution and instituted a virtual military dictatorship in which his once-treasured rebel leaders were subjected to harsh suppression and replaced by more pliable "mass representatives." Most of those who managed to survive did so as mere figureheads.

Throughout this confused period Mao tried to leave the impression that these twists and turns were all unfolding in ways that were favorable for his ultimate plans. The new revolutionary committees installed across most of China by late 1968 were celebrated as a great victory. Indeed, they did represent a new form of government built on the rubble of the old. But they did not operate as advertised, and they did not last very long. Except for Shanghai and Beijing, almost all provincial revolutionary committees were completely dominated by army officers, and most were a thinly disguised form of military dictatorship. These networks of revolutionary committees, which extended down to the grass roots, soon unleashed a massive cleansing campaign, one of the largest and deadliest traitor hunts in the history of the People's Republic. By 1969 it dawned on Mao that that the enormous power he had been forced to hand over to military officers made him excessively dependent on them. His moves to reduce their power led to the crisis of the Lin Biao affair.

The death of Lin Biao undermined the entire political rationale for the Cultural Revolution and signaled the end of China's brief period of military rule. Mao spent the rest of his life in an erratic and ultimately unsuccessful effort to preserve something of value from the earlier upheaval. He gave Zhou Enlai the task of rebuilding the party organization and removing the army from civilian administration, and had him lead a campaign that blamed Cultural Revolution atrocities on an "ultraleftist" Lin Biao. He then cast Zhou aside and turned to a "second Cultural Revolution" to defend the legacy of the Cultural Revolution while continuing to withdraw the army from civilian rule. When that campaign destabilized large parts of China, paralyzing industry and transport, Mao turned to Deng Xiaoping to reestablish discipline and order, stabilize the economy, and resume the task of rebuilding the civilian party-state. After Deng showed little regard for Cultural Revolution dogma, Mao cast him aside as well, a final turn that ignited large street demonstrations in Nanjing, Beijing, and other cities that expressed disdain for Maoist radicals and for the Cultural Revolution. Mao put the centrist official Hua Guofeng in charge, hoping that he could maintain a balance between Maoist radicals and establishment officials in the party leadership. Instead, Hua arrested and denounced the remaining Maoist radicals only one month after Mao's death, an act that was the first step on the path toward a very different post-Mao China.

It is hard to avoid the conclusion that Mao's contributions to China after 1956 were unsuccessful by his own standards and destructive in ways that he surely did not imagine. During both the Great Leap Forward and the Cultural Revolution, the destructive aspects of Mao's initiatives far outweighed any outcomes that could be construed as positive. The Cultural Revolution succeeded in its agenda of destroying the structure of China's party-state, and in sidelining the many officials who might have harbored inner doubts about Mao's vision, but it created nothing lasting in its place. During the Cultural Revolution Mao tried repeatedly to put a positive face on each unexpected and unwanted development, asserting that out of disorder a greater order would eventually be born. But the public celebrations of the "great victories" of the Cultural Revolution, accompanied by the escalating intensity of the cult of Mao, all turned out to be as hollow as Mao's earlier insistence that the accomplishments of the Great Leap were "nine fingers" and the shortcomings "one finger." As Mao's health failed during his final two years, he appeared to resign himself to the fact that his legacy was far from assured, and that powerful forces in the leadership and in society at large were arrayed against it.

After his death, Mao's surviving colleagues had a similar view of his legacy. Chen Yun, an official who had long been sidelined by Mao for his insistence that China's development had to be balanced and steady, expressed this common view with a certain restraint near the end of 1978: "Had Chairman Mao died in 1956, there would have been no doubt that he was a great leader of the Chinese people, a respected, loved and outstanding great man in the proletarian revolutionary movement of the world. Had he died in 1966, his meritorious achievements would have been somewhat tarnished but still very good. Since he actually died in 1976, there is nothing we can do about it."[1]

China's National Trajectory under Mao

The Mao era should not be judged exclusively through the lens of Mao's intentions and their outcomes. Even more important is the overall record of China's progress as a nation under the new state and economic system that the party installed during the 1950s. When China's new leaders consolidated state power and chose to adopt a Soviet-inspired model of economic development, they chose a model that promised rapid industrialization. Mao pushed to put it into place more rapidly than many of his colleagues thought wise, and after it was in place he pushed even further to speed up its operations through political mobilization. The model had already proven itself adept at rapid wartime mobilization and the creation of an impressive heavy industrial base in the Soviet Union. Shortly after China put its version of the Soviet model in place, Khrushchev had turned to improving the livelihoods of Soviet citizens, and was boasting that the Soviet Union would soon reach levels of development and prosperity that rivaled those of the United States. These predictions seem foolhardy in retrospect, but at the time they were made they did not seem so farfetched, and they inspired Mao to follow suit.

In the Great Leap Forward, Mao pushed this development model to the limit. Denigrating the expertise of technical specialists, he urged party organizations nationwide to mobilize labor to speed up and work longer hours, accelerating the pace of economic development. The result was a severe industrial depression and a famine of historic proportions. Shortly after the economy recovered in the mid-1960s, Mao attacked the economic bureaucracy once again during his Cultural Revolution, placing officials and experts at all levels under political attack, banishing most of them for several years of manual labor. After the retrenchment that followed the Lin Biao affair, the economy became a political battleground, as leaders at all levels were paralyzed by a struggle over the role of technical experts, methods of enterprise management, work incentives, and the workers' livelihood.

As the Mao era drew to a close, the heavy costs of Maoism were impossible to ignore. In some respects, China exhibited the hallmarks of successful economic development. Measures of public health improved steadily. The crude death rate, 25.8 per thousand in 1953, had shrunk to 7.8 per thousand in 1976. Infant mortality, which was 175 per thousand births in 1953, was 45 per thousand in 1976. Life expectancy at birth, which was only 40 years in 1953, had risen to 64 years, a level usually attained only at much higher levels of economic development.[2] These indicators were a testament to a government infrastructure that had the capacity to improve public health and deliver basic medical care to the vast majority of the population. This is the same government infrastructure that conducted the remarkably effective campaigns against organized crime, the drug and sex trades, and urban and rural gangs during the 1950s.

In addition to these genuine accomplishments, which survived to the end of the Mao era, aggregate measures of China's gross domestic product (GDP) were also impressive. Gross output of China's industry and agriculture grew in nominal terms almost tenfold during the Mao era; industrial output grew twice as fast.[3] From this perspective, it appeared that the Maoist version of the Soviet economic system performed in much the way that had been originally anticipated.

But beneath the surface, severe problems were apparent. The first obvious problem was that China's population was growing as fast as the economy: it had almost doubled after 1952, growing from 584 to 932 million. Population pressures prevented aggregate growth rates from translating into improved living standards. This also was due to wrongheaded political intervention. In the wake of the Great Leap, Mao ordered the repudiation of population experts who counseled fertility control, condemning such views as anti-Marxist, bourgeois Malthusian ideas that blamed the poor for their own poverty. Moreover, he reasoned, population control made little economic sense, because human labor is the source of all value, and therefore the more labor power, the more prosperous the economy.

The booming population, coupled with a development strategy premised on high levels of investment, meant that an increasingly large population would be condemned indefinitely to living standards barely above subsistence level. By the end of Mao's life there were unmistakable signs that both agriculture and industry were in serious trouble, and that the problems were worsening. China's overall trend of economic growth, as measured by per capita GDP, was still on an upward trajectory after 1952, despite the Great Leap depression of 1961–1962 and the Cultural Revolution downturn of 1967–1968. The cumulative rate of economic growth in real GDP per capita from 1950 to 1973, however, was only 2.9 percent per year. This placed China somewhere near the middle of Asian nations during the same period, somewhat above the rates of growth in the Philippines and Indonesia and twice India's growth rate, but far behind the six best performers in the region, including Thailand (Table 14.1).

Table 14.1. Growth of per capita GDP, Asian nations, 1950–1973

Country	Annual Growth (%)
Japan	8.1
Taiwan	6.7
South Korea	5.8
Hong Kong	5.2
Singapore	4.4
Thailand	3.7
China	2.9
Philippines	2.7
Indonesia	2.6
Malaysia	2.2
Sri Lanka	1.9
Pakistan	1.7
India	1.4
Bangladesh	−0.4

Source: Maddison (2006, 143).
Note: Growth rate is annual average compound growth, GDP per capita.

The pattern of economic growth was highly unstable, as Figure 14.1 makes clear. Growth rates fluctuated erratically throughout the Mao era, and not only due to the Great Leap Forward and early Cultural Revolution. While generally positive except for those two periods, the economy never exhibited the steady growth pattern associated with a Soviet system that was designed to eliminate the boom-and-bust cycles of market capitalism. Most revealing is the fact that the economy did not revive after the worst years of the Cultural Revolution, and in fact appeared to be settling into a period of stagnation. After 1970, when the army was withdrawn from civilian administration and white-collar experts were returned to their posts, growth averaged only 2.4 percent. The economy registered almost no growth in 1974, a year of political upheaval, and it fell into a recession in 1976, the year of Mao's death, shrinking by 3.4 percent.[4]

Economic growth slowed because of problems in both agriculture and industry. Collective farms struggled to increase output per acre of cultivated land, and increases in output barely kept pace with China's rapidly growing population. Procurement of grain to feed the cities stagnated in the 1970s, and without rapid increases in agricultural productivity a food supply crisis loomed in the near future. Industry was the primary cause of looming economic stagnation, in particular the heavy indus-

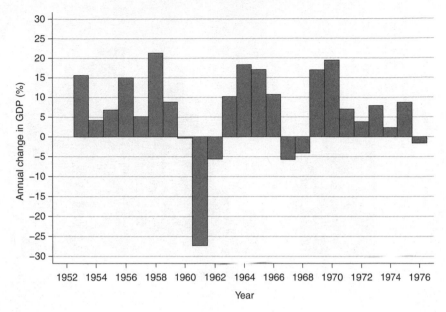

Figure 14.1. Annual change in gross domestic product, constant prices, 1952–1976. *Source:* Calculated from State Statistical Bureau (1983, 22 and 103).

trial sector, which by design absorbed the lion's share of investment at the expense of consumer goods, services, and housing. China plowed ever-greater resources into heavy industry, despite its inefficiency. The sector absorbed 52 percent of national investment in 1953; by the Great Leap Forward it absorbed 87 percent, and remained well above 80 percent almost every year until the end of the Mao era.[5]

Lavished with resources, heavy industry used them inefficiently, a problem that became most pronounced after 1970. Figure 14.2 illustrates trends in multifactor productivity. A figure above 1.0 means that industry is producing more in output than it is receiving as inputs; a figure below 1.0 means that the products are less valuable than the resources expended in producing them. The higher this figure is above 1.0, the greater is industry's efficiency in the use of resources. The lower the figure is below 1.0, the greater is the waste of national economic resources and their diversion from other uses. Figure 14.2 makes clear that Chinese industry was relatively inefficient until the 1970s—and catastrophically inefficient in the wake of the Great Leap Forward. Not until the early 1970s did factor productivity rise to levels associated with rapid and sustainable

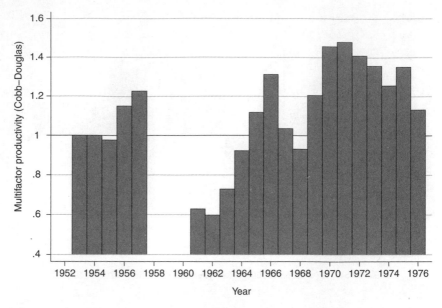

Figure 14.2. Productivity trends in industry, 1953–1976. *Source:* Kuan et al. (1988, 583).

economic growth. Immediately afterward, however, industrial efficiency began a steady decline, dropping every year except one through 1976.

These unmistakable signs of stagnation signaled flaws at the very heart of an economic system that was designed as a growth machine. Inefficiencies in the performance of China's economic institutions, particularly industry, were draining resources away from other urgent uses, while showing very modest results. A wasteful industrial system was literally sucking resources away from infrastructure, housing, wages, and consumer goods production that would raise China's standard of living. China's population was sacrificing for a heavy industrial system whose politically induced inefficiencies were condemning China to backwardness.

China could barely afford economic stagnation. In 1976, after twenty-seven years of fitful socialist development, its per capita GDP was equivalent to only $163, virtually the same as a still-impoverished India ($164).[6] While somewhat higher than Bangladesh ($140), a country that had by this point in time become a symbol of severe economic misery, China's level of development in 1976 was far behind agrarian Indonesia ($286). China already lagged very far behind South Korea ($824), a nation devastated by the war of 1950–1953 and whose level of development in 1953 was not much different from China's. Hong Kong, a seedy port that could not compare with vastly more prosperous Shanghai before 1950, now boasted a GDP per capita of $2,849. Japan, approaching the middle years of its rapid postwar economic ascent, was already at $5,111. The underperformance of China's Maoist economy is even more evident if we compare its position in 1976 with China's subsequent record of growth. By 1990, after a decade of modest market reforms, China's per capita GDP was $314. By 2000, it was $949; by 2010, $4,433.

The extent to which China was falling behind other comparable economies is evident in Figure 14.3, which tracks per capita GDP in constant prices, employing the "purchasing power parity" method that adjusts for differences in price structures across countries that would otherwise distort the comparison. China's long-standing aspiration to catch up with more advanced economies, or even with more developed state socialist economies, clearly was in danger of becoming permanently beyond reach. China's progress is barely discernible when plotted against the trajectory of Taiwan, South Korea, Japan, the Soviet Union, and Eastern Europe, and the gap between them became progressively larger over the years. Figure 14.4 provides a somewhat different perspective on these

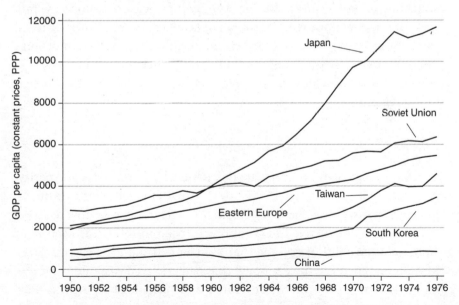

Figure 14.3. Economic growth trends, selected countries, 1950–1976.
Source: Maddison (2006, 304 and 479).

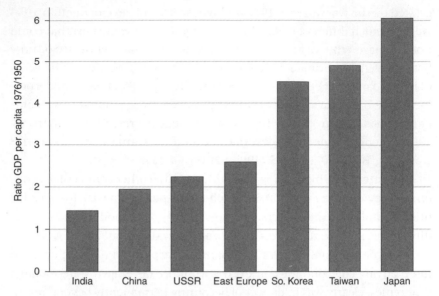

Figure 14.4. Economic expansion, selected countries, 1950–1976.
Source: Maddison (2006, 304 and 479).

trends. It displays net changes in per capita GDP over this period (not adjusting for purchasing power parity). By this measure China's overall growth was superior to that of India but lagged behind the other ("revisionist") socialist states, and far behind neighboring East Asian economies. China clearly was being left far behind its neighbors and was stuck at a low level of development that placed it among the poorest countries in the region.

Incomes and Living Standards

Spartan living conditions and the postponement of material prosperity were inherent in the design of the Soviet growth model. Overinvestment in heavy industry was the mechanism by which rapid growth was to be ensured. The destructive interventions by Mao in the Great Leap Forward, and the political crusade that Mao launched during the Cultural Revolution, however, took a model that had achieved sustained and dynamic growth earlier in Soviet history and turned it into an unstable model that created stagnation even at low levels of industrial development. Mao's effort to forge a path of development that would permit

China to rival Soviet economic accomplishments had clearly failed. By keeping the core of the Soviet model intact, and by elevating the role of party officials and political activists and denigrating the expertise of educated managers and engineers, Mao's interventions had done little more than exacerbate the inherent inefficiencies of the system.

Although they were strongly favored relative to residents of collective farms, urban residents themselves suffered from stagnating incomes and poor supply of consumer goods, housing, and services. Industrial wages were effectively frozen after the last national round of wage readjustments in 1963, during which roughly 40 percent of the workforce received promotions in grade and raises. There were no subsequent wage readjustments until two years after Mao's death. Bonuses linked to productivity were banned on political grounds after 1966. Work units tried to remedy the hardship of frozen wages by finding reasons to provide small money supplements or deliver goods and services in kind, but these were stopgap measures. As new generations of workers were added to the labor force at the lowest pay grades—and as they remained there—the average wage for urban workers dropped steadily. Figure 14.5 shows the long downward trend in urban wages that began with the nationalization

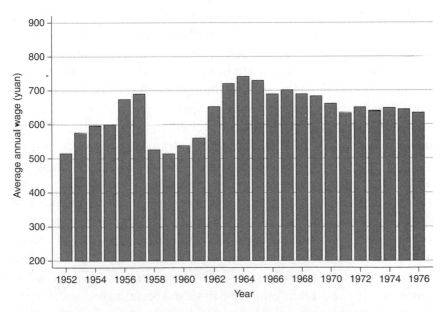

Figure 14.5. Average wages in Chinese state industry, 1952–1976. *Source:* State Statistical Bureau (1983, 490).

of industry in 1956 and continued over the next two decades. The only break in the gradual pattern of decline was the sharp drop during the Great Leap Forward, when millions of new workers were hired at the lowest wage levels and then rapidly laid off as the economy collapsed. The average annual wage was just under 700 yuan in 1957; by 1976 it had dropped to a little more than 630 yuan.[7]

Increasingly tight household budgets were matched by a supply of consumer goods that fell far short of meeting demand for either volume or quality. The rationing system for industrial products was still in force and would not be abandoned for more than a decade. The most valued commodities were primitive by the standards of nearby market economics. Any urban resident in the period could recite a standard list of the most sought-after household durables: sewing machine, wristwatch, radio, and certain name-brand bicycles. The sewing machines were foot-powered models that were copied from a 1950s Soviet design that was in turn a copy of a 1920s model marketed by Singer in the United States. The sewing machines were needed to make most efficient use of the annual ration of cloth. The radios used vacuum tubes. The bicycles were durable one-speed models that served as a primary means of urban transportation.

The rationing system eliminated queues for major industrial goods, but rationing did not solve the problem of shortages. Specific items were always hard to find: shoes and premade clothing in the right sizes and styles, furniture, toilet paper, kitchen knives that would remain sharp with use, and pots and pans that would not crack when heat was applied. Dissatisfaction with availability, quality, and size was rife. State stores were periodically unable to meet demand for fresh fruit, vegetables, fish, and pork, and when they were able to do so the products were often wilted, bruised, or malodorous. Vigilant shopping was required, and the scarcity of consumer goods of the right size or quality fueled a thriving culture of mutual help and cooperation among friends and others to whom one developed mutually supportive "connections." Foreign visitors to China in the early post-Mao years, expecting to find an austere and egalitarian society unaffected by the rampant consumerism of the West, found themselves pressed by urgent requests from acquaintances to purchase items on their behalf in special stores reserved for foreigners. They were often surprised by the intense focus on procuring scarce consumer items and the aggressive urban culture of trading favors for mutual advantage.[8]

The most visible manifestation of deteriorating urban living standards was the housing stock. Housing was already overcrowded in the 1950s and became progressively more so over the next twenty years. Housing comprised 12.5 percent of national expenditures on capital construction in 1953 and declined steadily thereafter as investment in producers' goods industries rose. In the decade after 1966, housing fluctuated between 2.6 and 6.5 percent of national construction expenditures.[9] This translated into long waits for apartments for newly married couples, and even longer waits for young families that needed larger quarters. It also translated into deferred maintenance of existing buildings, which deteriorated badly over the years. In 1956 each urban resident occupied an average of 4.3 square meters of housing space; by 1976 this number had shrunk to 3.6 square meters. By official standards, 50 percent was officially considered to be in "poor repair," and 10 percent "dangerously" so.[10]

By the mid-1970s it was not uncommon for a family of four to occupy a single room. A desk would be used for family meals, cleared for study after dinner, and made up as a bed at night. Lack of space was only one dimension of the problem. Urban apartments lacked basic infrastructure. Very few apartments had private toilets and bathing facilities. Toilets were in the hallways of apartment blocks, in courtyards, or on the street in older neighborhoods. Some apartments had running water, but most families used communal sinks in their apartment buildings. Few apartments had private kitchens; cooking areas were typically shared. Coal-fired stoves were the most common form of indoor heating, and the same coal briquettes were also the most common source of heat for cooking. Inadequate ventilation could result in death by carbon monoxide poisoning. Electric fans were still rare; air conditioning was unknown. Private telephone lines were basically unavailable to anyone but ranking cadres. In urban neighborhoods, telephone calls were typically made at public telephones located in or near the residents' committee office. Individuals who received calls had to be summoned to the telephone by the individuals—often retirees—who worked as neighborhood volunteers. International service was unheard of, and well after the Mao era one still had to book a long-distance call at the municipal headquarters of the State Post and Telecommunications Bureau, and wait in line.

A final aspect of the neglect of citizens' livelihood was the extraordinarily limited scope of the urban service sector. Before the elimination of the private sector in the mid-1950s, Chinese cities were crowded with small family service establishments: food stalls and restaurants, guest houses, teahouses, bars, small retail outlets of all varieties, barber shops, repair shops, dentists, knife sharpeners, practitioners of traditional medicine, bathhouses, and so forth. By the early 1960s these had virtually all disappeared. They had either been shut down in attacks on the private economy, or they had been merged into a small number of collective or state service establishments. The service sector never recovered. The government-run restaurants were few in number, large in size, badly overcrowded, and famous for poor quality and rude service. Work units tried to compensate by providing many of these vanishing services for their employees. This is the main reason why so many work units provided meal services and shower and bathing facilities for their employees. Work units tried to internalize many of the functions formerly filled by the private sector, but they could never fully compensate for the loss of so many services, and those who were unfortunate enough to work for poorly provisioned work units missed out.

Equality and Inequality

It is tempting to think that these depressed living standards were the hallmark of an economic system that valued equality more than prosperity. As economic inequality skyrocketed in post-Mao China, one heard frequent references to the Mao era as having one of the world's most egalitarian distributions of income. Although income inequality in China today is vastly greater than it was in 1976, this egalitarian image of Mao's China is only partially accurate.

The most common measure of income inequality is the Gini index, which ranges from 0 to 1, with a higher value indicating a higher level of inequality. By this measure, the world's most egalitarian income distributions in the 1970s were to be found in the industrialized socialist economies (see Table 14.2). Several of them had Gini indexes of .20 or .21, far below China's 1979 figure of .33. Even the Soviet Union, much reviled by Maoist ideologues in China as a revisionist bastion of capitalist restoration, had levels of income inequality that were significantly lower than China. China was the world's most unequal socialist economy.

On the other hand, China's income distribution was at the low end among economies in Asia. It was considerably more equal than those of Indonesia and the Philippines, and somewhat more equal than India's. However, China's level of income inequality was basically the same as

Table 14.2. Comparative national measures of income inequality (Gini index), 1970s

Socialist	Gini	Asia	Gini	Industrialized	Gini
East Germany	.20	Taiwan	.28	China	.33
Bulgaria	.21	China	.33	United Kingdom	.34
Czechoslovakia	.21	Pakistan	.33	Canada	.39
Yugoslavia	.21	Sri Lanka	.33	Sweden	.39
Poland	.22	India	.38	West Germany	.39
Hungary	.25	Thailand	.42	Italy	.40
Soviet Union	.27	Indonesia	.44	United States	.40
China	.33	Philippines	.47	Japan	.42

Sources: For socialist and industrialized countries, Kornai (1992, 318) and Jain (1975, 41, 107); for Asia, World Bank (1983, vol. 1, 94) and Jain (1975, 108). The figure for China is for 1979; all others are for various years in the early 1970s.

those of Sri Lanka and Pakistan. Taiwan's distribution of income was significantly more equal than China's. China's rank relative to the industrialized market economies was similar. It was considerably more equal than the United States and Japan, somewhat more equal than Canada and West Germany, but not much different than the United Kingdom.

These figures would surprise visitors to urban China at the end of the Mao era. Chinese cities exhibited almost no signs of conspicuous wealth. Living standards seemed highly equal—and very modest. Clothing styles and modes of transportation (bicycle) appeared highly uniform. The rationing system appeared to have a remarkable equalizing effect. Wage differences in state enterprises were modest. And these impressions would not be misleading. The distribution of income in urban China was by far the most equal in the world. The Gini index for urban Chinese incomes in 1981 was a remarkable .16. In Asian economies the comparable figures ranged from Pakistan's .36 to Malaysia's .52 during the 1970s.[11] How could urban China have such a remarkably equal distribution of income, yet still have a nationwide income distribution that was high for a socialist country but unremarkable compared to market economies in Asia and the industrialized world?

The answer is that China had an unusually large gap between the incomes of urban and rural regions, and between prosperous and poor rural regions. There were two major reasons for this. The Soviet development model, as we have seen, was designed to extract maximum amounts of grain from collective farms and keep prices low, and to keep rural incomes and even rural consumption of staple foods at much lower levels than in cities. The second reason, which exacerbated the first, was the very strict controls exercised by the household registration and grain rationing systems. Farmers could not migrate to urban areas in search of more highly compensated wage labor—even temporarily—and they could not move from the most impoverished rural regions to more prosperous ones.[12] The much higher levels of inequality in other Asian cities were due to the migration of the landless poor to urban slums. This did not happen in Mao-era China.

Household registration and grain rations kept China's poorest citizens out of cities and permanently anchored in the most remote rural regions, where grinding poverty was still widespread. In market economies labor migrates to cities or to other regions with stronger economies, a migration that tends to equalize income levels between country and city, as the rural poor move to cities. This also means that poverty is much more visible in cities, where the poor congregate in slums that blight many cities in developing countries. This created the impression that inequality and poverty was much worse in countries like India and Indonesia than in China. The impression would not be incorrect, but it would be limited to cities, and it reflected the effectiveness of China's household registration system in keeping the poor bottled up in isolated rural regions, not the more egalitarian structure of the Chinese economy overall, or its allegedly superior ability to eliminate poverty.

Rural Poverty

The failure to eliminate the most abject forms of rural poverty was perhaps the most surprising fact revealed in the late 1970s, and it represented one of the most damning failures of Maoism. One would have expected that the extraordinary organizational capacity of the new state could deliver basic subsistence to the rural population, regardless of where it was located. A regime that could mobilize hundreds of millions to work around the clock during the Great Leap Forward, or millions of Red Guards and rebels to attack revisionists in the party leadership, could surely ensure at least that its poorest citizens had enough food to eat. Such was not the case. By the end of the Mao era, large percentages of the rural population were still mired in desperate poverty.

Surveys conducted in the late 1970s yielded a sobering picture of rural living standards. One-fifth of China's rural population had diets that were below the level of daily calorie consumption defined by the Chinese government at the time as permitting individuals a bare subsistence. And the Chinese government's standard for subsistence was below the standard set by international agencies. Average total daily calorie consumption in 1976 was at the average for poor countries in the region—higher than Bangladesh, slightly above India, and lower than Pakistan and Indonesia.[13] The quality of the average rural diet for the residents of collective farms was low. Collective agriculture forced rural Chinese into grain-centered subsistence agriculture, resulting in a steady decline in the consumption of vegetable oils, meat, and other proteins. The percentage of calories supplied by staple grains in the rural Chinese diet was high by international standards. When the post-Mao government surveyed rural living standards, it found that in 1978, 30 percent of the rural population, or 237 million people, were living on incomes below official poverty levels as defined by the Chinese government—a level significantly below that set by international agencies.[14] It is hard to avoid the observation that the Mao era was a long and tumultuous struggle over many years that succeeded in producing outcomes that were far from revolutionary. The nonrevolutionary approach to land reforms conducted in Taiwan, Japan, and South Korea during the 1950s created the foundation for a prosperous rural market economy based on widespread smallholding agriculture, leading to rising living standards and rapid economic growth—without the bloodshed of China's violent land revolution. Levels of rural poverty were reduced drastically in China after 1978, as collective agriculture was abandoned—an indication that the failures of the Maoist era were self-induced.

The Human Costs of Maoism

These modest accomplishments were offset by enormous human costs. The largest of such costs was the death through starvation of 30 million people in the famine created by the Great Leap Forward. Recent studies suggest that a significant portion of this number were in fact executed or beaten to death during regional campaigns against "rightism" or the "hiding" of grain, or punitively denied food supplies in the midst of famine. The enormous death toll generated by the Great Leap Forward can only be gauged against the more horrific episodes in China's long history. The total number of Chinese civilian and military deaths during the war against Japan from 1937 to 1945 is generally estimated to be as high as 12 million—a figure that includes 2 million battlefield deaths and an estimated 4 million dead in the Henan famine of 1943.[15] The one modern event that is directly analogous to China's Great Leap famine is the starvation caused by forced collectivization in Russia, Ukraine, and Kazakhstan from 1932 to 1933. The estimates for that episode range from 5.7 to 8.5 million deaths, which represents roughly the same percentage of the total Soviet population as China's famine.[16]

The human cost of the Great Leap Forward far outstrips the magnitude of the death toll from the deliberate episodes of bloodletting in post-1949 China. The famine was vastly more costly than the wave of executions that accompanied revolutionary land reform and the campaign to suppress counterrevolution in the early 1950s, generally estimated to have resulted in 1 to 2 million deaths. It also dwarfs the death toll directly attributable to the conflicts and political campaigns associated with the Cultural Revolution. A conservative statistical procedure based on data included in accounts from a near-complete set of published local histories yields an estimate of 1.1 to 1.6 million dead during the five years from 1966 to 1971. These same sources suggest that three-fourths of these deaths were generated by the actions of revolutionary committees or the armed forces, primarily after the first months of 1968, and well over half—at least 600,000—were generated by the Cleansing of the Class Ranks alone. This was triple the number of estimated deaths generated by the activities of rebels, almost all of which were due to armed battles between mass factions.[17] A significant proportion of these battlefield deaths were attributable to Mao's misguided order to distribute military arms to mass factions in the summer of 1967. It is sobering to realize that the draconian campaign to restore order after a nationwide insurgency that Mao himself had fomented generated far greater numbers of dead and other kinds of victims than the upheaval itself. As in the Great Leap Forward, these lives were sacrificed for a cause that was badly misconceived and accomplished nothing of lasting value.[18]

The Limits of Maoism

In many quarters, both in China and abroad, Mao Zedong earned a reputation as a daring and creative thinker who expanded the limits of

Marxism-Leninism, departed from Soviet doctrine, and proposed striking solutions to the seemingly inevitable tendency of communist revolutions to evolve into rigid bureaucratic autocracies ruled by self-perpetuating elites. Mao in power could surely be described as daring—indeed reckless. The rebellion he fostered against his own party-state during the 1960s was certainly a stunning departure from Soviet doctrines and practices, and seemed to signal a flexibility and creativity of thought that placed him well outside the mainstream of Soviet-inspired communism.

It would be wrong, however, to view Mao's actions and their outcomes as the product of a creative and daringly innovative politician. To the contrary, this account emphasizes the narrow limits of Mao's thinking, the rigidity and dogmatism with which he clung to old and outmoded ideas, and his unwillingness to learn and adapt to changes in the world socialist movement. His core commitments were inspired by a relatively simple set of ideas that he adopted in the 1930s, while still in Yan'an. The most important of these were found in the Stalinist party history, the *Short Course*, which crystallized Mao's understanding of class struggle and the building of socialism. These doctrines fit well with Mao's earlier views, expressed in the 1920s, about the essential role of violent struggle in generating revolutionary social change, and the necessity for a unified and armed party to lead the masses. These commitments were reinforced in the crucible of the civil war, during the all-out mobilization in the late 1940s that achieved a seemingly impossible victory over the Nationalists.

Mao was never willing to deviate from these commitments for the rest of his life, and his actions during his last twenty years were essentially a struggle against communists at home and abroad who had long shown a willingness to depart from Mao's core understandings, which to many seemed increasingly outdated, anachronistic, and counterproductive. From this perspective, Mao was in many ways a reactionary who clung to Stalinist doctrines long after their time.

Narratives designed to explain the course of events in the Mao era inevitably focus on a series of decisions and interventions made by Mao at crucial turning points, and our account has been no different. However, when we consider Mao's core commitments, which were formed before the communist victory in 1949, we are pointing to a deeper set of causes that drove most of the developments that we have described. These were decisions about the party's objectives and means for achieving them that were not subsequently revisited. The course of the Chinese revolution after 1949 was driven by Mao's unwillingness to alter these earlier decisions, and indeed by his increasingly strong reaction to what he perceived as the possibility that other leaders wanted to revise them.

What were these core ideas that had such a decisive impact on China after 1949? The first was perhaps the oldest: Mao's conviction that only violent conflict could bring about genuine social change and liberate the oppressed. These ideas were already clearly formed in Mao's mind in the 1920s and were fully articulated in his essays on the peasant movement. In these writings the young Mao insisted that violence in the course of rebellion was an inevitable by-product of social change, and that it should never be considered as deplorable "excesses." Violence and humiliation of elites is necessary for a decisive break from the old to the new. Mao not only made a strong case for the functions of violence in the course of genuine social change, he also condemned those who recoiled from violence of the kind reflected in the peasant movement he described. In his view, they forfeited any claim to be part of the revolution and became reactionary themselves.

These beliefs were reflected through the subsequent history of the Chinese Communist Party, from the struggle sessions staged by party cadres during rural land reform, to the use of public struggle sessions in consolidating control over China's cities in the 1950s, to the ritualized humiliation and beating of party cadres and intellectual elites during the Cultural Revolution. They are at the core of Mao's conception of the Cultural Revolution as a mass movement against an entrenched elite. There is no way to conceive of the specific form that this movement took without reference to this bedrock belief. These beliefs were also displayed in Mao's open disregard for the victims of Red Guard murders in Beijing in the summer of 1966, or in his cavalier attitude toward the death toll generated by the armed battles of the summer of 1967. They were also evident in his disdain for party officials who viewed the Red Guard violence as appalling, reflecting their own reactionary nature. Mao called on officials to applaud and support the Red Guards—it was a test of their revolutionary mettle, much as attitudes toward the "excesses" of the peasant movement in 1927 were a litmus test of the revolutionary or reactionary nature of Nationalists and Communists alike. Mao's consistent attitude, from the beginning of his revolutionary career to the end of his life, was that the violence of class struggle is unavoidable and even essential in accomplishing genuine revolutionary change, and one should never shrink in the face of inevitable collateral damage.

The second idea was that class struggle exists under socialism; that it becomes more intense as the final push to socialism approaches; and that different ideas about economic policy and the pace of socialist transformation are expressions of class conflict. This was an idea that Mao absorbed from the Soviet *Short Course* and it was the core Stalinist idea to which he held dogmatically even after Stalin came to ignore it in his later years, and after Stalin's successors roundly rejected it as erroneous and destructive. It was the inspiration for the destructive hunt for traitors within the party during the 1943 rectification campaign in Yan'an. It was of course the core idea that justified Mao's purges of officials who were critical of the "rash advance" toward socialism, or who had the temerity to challenge the accomplishments of the Great Leap. It shaped Mao's interpretation of the disastrous outcome of the Great Leap Forward—that the lower reaches of the CCP in rural areas had been taken over by remnants of the Nationalists and exploiting classes who were sabotaging Mao's great revolution. Only class enemies, he reasoned, could show such inhuman cruelty toward starving peasants. It was the animating idea behind the Socialist Education Movement, an erratic and incoherent campaign that Liu Shaoqi pushed with enthusiasm before it was ultimately dropped. The USSR's rejection of this dogma was one of the main reasons that Mao condemned the Soviet Union as revisionist, on the road back to capitalism. Without this core idea, the Cultural Revolution would have been unthinkable.[19]

The third idea is that the only way to achieve revolution and the construction of socialism is through a hierarchically organized communist party that is highly disciplined and unified in thought and action. Moreover, both of these characteristics are strengthened by a cultivated faith in the correctness and ultimate infallibility of the party leadership and especially of the supreme leader. What the post-Stalin Soviets condemned as a "leadership cult," Mao viewed as highly functional in generating the discipline and faith in the party rank and file that made it possible first to defeat the Nationalists and then to transform China and build socialism. The essential tenet of this doctrine is that the great leader alone has the ability to define the correct course, to decide which policies are revolutionary and which are reactionary. And because class struggle becomes more intense as the victory of socialism approaches, the great leader must be vigilant in rooting out bourgeois tendencies in the leadership and the party at large. Mao, like Stalin, saw ironclad faith in a single leader as essential to maintain the unity and discipline of the party as a fighting force—otherwise it degenerates into a mess of competing factions. What was distinctive about Mao's belief was that these features of the revolutionary party must be maintained far longer than others felt was necessary or desirable. Revolution did not end with the seizure of power, nor did it end with the liquidation of class enemies and the transformation of the system of ownership. Revolution had to continue for an indefinite period, which required inspired revolutionary leadership.

The fourth idea is that the form of socialism created in the Soviet Union in the 1930s in both agriculture and industry—specifically one that rejected private enterprise, market mechanisms, and profit incentives—was the definition of socialism. Moreover, this economic model could and must be created rapidly, by revolution from above, in the same way that it had been created in the 1930s under Stalin. Despite the fact that Stalin himself counseled China to take a more measured pace toward socialism, and that in his later years he began to credit new ideas about "objective economic laws" that applied to both socialism and capitalism, Mao held tightly to the older faith. Mao ultimately rejected any reconsideration of the role of political mobilization in pushing the pace of economic change and development, and he ultimately rejected the claim that modern science and technology and highly trained experts and professional administrators were an essential part of socialist development. Mao was even more adamantly opposed to the idea that the well-known inefficiencies of the Soviet model could be alleviated by partial reliance on economic mechanisms borrowed from capitalism—price mechanisms, competition, and the calculation of profit for the sake of improved efficiency. For Mao, these were completely beyond the pale, ensuring that socialism would be replaced by capitalism. And those who flirted with such ideas, Mao asserted, were expressing the interests of the capitalist class, domestically and internationally, to overturn socialism.

As Mao refused to budge from this narrow set of ideas, the socialist world was changing around him. The moderation of Soviet doctrines began after World War II, even before Stalin's death, and accelerated in the Soviet Union after 1953. By the time of Khrushchev's 1956 speech, many of Mao's core commitments were openly under attack. The new doctrine did not deny the core Marxist idea that class struggle is the motivating force of human history, but once a socialist economy is put in place, the foundation for classes and class struggle no longer exists, and the task is to develop the economy and improve the lives of citizens. The "dictatorship of the proletariat" and its mass repressions must be relaxed. Class struggle does not exist under socialism—this was roundly denounced as Stalin's most erroneous innovation, having little foundation in Marxism. The glorification of the great leader that became so extreme under Stalin was even more regrettable, an absurd fantasy that served as a cover for Stalin's cowardly and fanatical persecutions of his enemies, perceived and real. These were not core tenets of revolutionary Marxism-Leninism—they were deviations, distortions, and, in Khrushchev's terms, historic crimes against the party and people. No "great leader" should ever be allowed to determine by fiat which policies were revolutionary and which were reactionary.

Mao resisted these ideas from the outset. He refused to accept the idea that China's socialist transformation had to be slow and gradual, that economic development subsequently would be steady and balanced, that the era of large campaigns and class struggles was over. He resisted the "excessive" denigration of Stalin. Briefly in 1956 and 1957, he tried to pose as a post-Stalin liberalizer, but after the Hundred Flowers backfired on him, he lurched back toward class struggle in antirightist campaigns and crash mobilization for economic development in the Great Leap Forward. After the Leap disaster, Mao doubled down on the core Stalinist tenet of class struggle, and orchestrated an antiparty conspiracy and mass movement to tear down the bureaucratic party system and replace it with new "revolutionary" institutions. Mao's actions appeared to be those of an innovative and unorthodox revolutionary, but his underlying motives were based on core ideas that in the rest of the communist world, and indeed by some in his own party, were viewed as essentially conservative, if not reactionary.

Mao is often said to have been uniquely concerned with the bureaucratization of communist regimes, and their tendency to generate self-perpetuating elites that seize privileges for themselves and create new forms of class oppression. That Mao took this problem seriously is evident from the fact that the Cultural Revolution sought not only to remove officials who lacked loyalty to Mao's vision, but also to mobilize the entire population to smash the party-state machine and put something new in its place.

Here too, however, the remarkably narrow limits of Mao's thinking are evident. He refused to contemplate a radically different, yet painfully obvious diagnosis of the problem: that the problems were inherent in bureaucratic socialism—in the placement of all means of production in the hands of a state bureaucracy dominated by appointees of a single, dictatorial party. Mao was dealing with the consequences of a bureaucratic monopoly over both property and power, and a privileged stratum that was an inevitable consequence of a system of career mobility based on political loyalty. Mao refused to rethink the Soviet economic model, in particular its denial of any role for market competition, material incentives, and the calculation of profit, and he especially refused to reconsider the Stalinist notion that there was only one right answer—the top leader's—and that disagreements about practical matters were expressions of class struggle.

Mao's diagnosis of the Soviet Union's reversion to "capitalism" was in fact extremely odd—it was the Soviet leaders' reliance on bureaucratic experts and on piece rates and monetary incentives that made Soviet socialism capitalist. Yet virtually none of the defining features of capitalism existed in the USSR: there was no private ownership of means of production, no market competition among firms, no use of price mechanisms to regulate supply and demand. The Soviet Union still had essentially the same bureaucratic system as the one that China had copied in the 1950s, with a few minor adjustments in the way that it operated.

Despite his reputation, Mao was not much of an antibureaucratic thinker. He was not actually opposed to bureaucratic hierarchy—he simply preferred one type of bureaucracy to another. Mao refused to cede authority to individuals with professional expertise and scientific training. He wanted party bureaucrats who were absolutely loyal to him and his vision, individuals selected and promoted according to political loyalty. Mao's favored bureaucracy was operated by committed ideologues or, less flatteringly, dogmatic party hacks. His only answer, when the party's monopoly of power and privilege inevitably solidified into a stable and oppressive bureaucratic hierarchy, was to smash the machine and begin again, replacing party hacks with new party loyalists with presumably more pure motivations. This, however, simply reproduced the original circumstances that led to the problem in the first place: monopoly by a formally organized hierarchy staffed by party loyalists, who had a monopoly over property, power, and the allocation of career opportunities and privileges. Moreover, by threatening his apparatus of party loyalists with the charge of treachery and class conspiracy, he drove his loyal agents into repeated bouts of destructive overconformity. This was at the core of the disastrous Great Leap, when party cadres pledged huge increases, lied about accomplishments, and then extracted grain from starving villages—all under threat of a harsh campaign against "rightism." This was also at the core of the 1968 cleansing campaign, as Mao's new agents at the local level responded zealously to calls to search for traitors, unable and unwilling to restrain the wildly escalating persecutions.

Mao's diagnosis was fundamentally wrong: the problem was not the resurgence of capitalism but the tenacity of bureaucratic hierarchies. The problems that he decried were an inevitable outcome of the system that he insisted was the only correct one, one not to be altered, but only revitalized back into its original form. Mao's diagnosis led to a prescribed remedy that promised only continuing cycles of conflict and destruction, with his country mired increasingly in backwardness. This was, for China, a tragic failure of vision by a rigidly dogmatic leader with extremely narrow and outdated ideas. Only after the aging dictator's death could China's leaders break out of the circular logic of Maoist doctrine and consider organizational and economic alternatives that genuinely departed from Soviet models. Given the spectacular collapse of the Soviet Union and its empire a decade later, it appears that this was a timely decision.

The Road Ahead

Mao Zedong left China in a quiet crisis, an unsettled state and society very much in flux. After the arrest of the officials on whom Mao depended to launch the Cultural Revolution and fight to preserve its legacy, there was little doubt that the Cultural Revolution, and the core ideas that had inspired it, would be repudiated. There was obvious popular yearning for social and political stability and a rise in living standards. In many ways, the devastation that Mao left in his wake gave his successors the opportunity for a new start. So much of the Soviet-inherited institutions had been smashed and had yet to be rebuilt. There was great uncertainty about the direction that China should take. Mao

inadvertently gave his successors an opportunity to make choices that
fell far outside the narrow limits of Maoist doctrine, and more orthodox
varieties of Marxism-Leninism as well.

Post-Mao China was in some ways back to square one, looking once
again for models that would hasten it along the path to prosperity and
national strength. In the late 1940s, the Soviet Union presented a plausible choice, and indeed that system continued to work well into the
1960s. But the world had changed drastically since the late 1940s, when
China's leaders last faced a fundamental choice. By the late 1970s the
Soviet Union was no longer the attractive development model that it had
been thirty years earlier. Growth rates in the Soviet Union and its satellite states had long since slowed, and they had entered the years of stagnation that would soon lead to their demise. Hungary had become an
oasis of prosperity in the Soviet bloc through limited market reforms
and concessions to the small-scale private sector. Unreformed Poland
was experiencing fiscal problems that would soon lead to price hikes
that touched off the Solidarity movement and the near collapse of the
regime.

Enviable growth models were now on China's doorstep: most star-
tlingly Japan, but also South Korea, Taiwan, Hong Kong, and Singapore.
Unlike the situation in the 1940s, it was now clear that market capitalism
was not going to collapse, and it did not again experience the kind of
destabilizing depressions that occurred in the 1930s. Of these increasingly prosperous regions, only Japan was constitutionally a multiparty
system, and even then it had been under virtual single-party control for
decades. Singapore had a more rigid form of single-party rule. South
Korea and Taiwan were harsh dictatorships, and Hong Kong a colonial
possession ruled from London. Yet all of these regions were integrated
into the world economy, with considerable state direction of private economic activity, thriving on export-led growth. It therefore dawned on
China's post-Mao leaders that it would be possible to greatly accelerate
China's development by adopting market mechanisms, opening to the
outside world, and yet maintain their party's dictatorship.

Mao's designated successor, Hua Guofeng, began this process, well
before Deng Xiaoping's return to power at the end of 1978.[20] The list of
new policy departures that violated Mao's core commitments grew
slowly, but within a few years there was a breathtaking reversal. The
new leadership expressed unreserved support for the adoption of modern

science and technology; they made their peace with scientific and technical experts; they revived China's scientific infrastructure, rebuilt the university system, and reestablished social scientific fields; they pushed to increase China's research capacities through educational and research exchanges with advanced capitalist economies; they sent tens of thousands of students abroad; they abandoned collective agriculture in favor of household farming; they removed restrictions on small private and family enterprises, especially in the service sector; they loosened restrictions on emigration; invited foreign experts to advise them; they took out foreign loans and accepted foreign aid; they began to experiment with price and profit mechanisms in an effort to reform a woefully inadequate state industrial sector; and in "special economic zones" they began tentatively to welcome capital investment by foreign private enterprises.

It would be tempting to say "and the rest is history." Not quite: China was still badly shattered; it was still deeply divided. Youths were alienated, and many repudiated not only the Mao era but also the Communist Party itself, which suffered a terrible loss of trust. In 2009 the CCP, ever self-congratulatory, celebrated thirty years of successful "reform and opening." But it is often forgotten that the first decade, from 1979 to 1989, was tumultuous, marked by leadership divisions over the extent and pace of both political and economic reform. There were, in addition, repeated popular campaigns for more democracy: the "democracy wall" campaign of 1978–1979, student mobilization for democratic elections to local people's congresses in 1980, a nationwide student movement to demand political reform and greater democracy at the end of 1986, and eventually the student democracy movement in the spring of 1989, which spread into a nationwide upheaval that shook the regime to its very foundations, leading to the massacre of activists and bystanders in the nation's capital, and to martial law that lasted for almost a year.[21] It would take a long time to work out the problems that had accumulated during Mao's reign, and the regime would have to weather a major political crisis in 1989, the year that saw the unraveling of communism in Eastern Europe and the beginning of the end of the Soviet Union.

Today, half a century after the launch of the Cultural Revolution, Mao has been reduced to a benign cultural icon. His image is displayed on China's national currency, replacing the workers, peasants, tractors, and steam shovels of the Mao era. His face adorns the ubiquitous badges, posters, and other artifacts produced in the hundreds of millions during the era of the Mao cult, now marketed everywhere to tourists. Theme restaurants with Cultural Revolution–era decor entertain diners with songs and dances from the Red Guards and "loyalty to Mao" era. "New left" intellectuals, dissatisfied with the corruption and inequality spawned by China's turn toward market-oriented state capitalism, hark back to the Mao era for its positive accomplishments; ordinary citizens reflect with nostalgia on the Mao era as a simpler, less money conscious, more egalitarian, and less corrupt time. The party leadership celebrated the 110th anniversary of Mao's birth by emphasizing the positive accomplishments of his reign, seeking to solidify the party's legitimacy, celebrate its history, and reinforce national pride. These views of Mao, and of the Mao era, are very different from the ones that prevailed in the late 1970s, as China began the long process of recovering from the damage of his misrule. They are based on highly selective historical memory and a great deal of forgetting.

NOTES

REFERENCES

INDEX

Notes

1. Funeral

1. Nathan (1983), Wilbur (1983).
2. Kuhn (1980), Rowe (2009, 149–296).
3. Kuhn (1978), Platt (2012), Spence (1996).
4. Esherick (1987), Silbey (2012).
5. A superb synthesis is in Rowe (2009, 149–296).
6. Young (1983, 217–228).
7. Ch'i (1976), Nathan (1976), Gasster (1980).
8. Isaacs (1961), Wilbur (1983).
9. Mitter (2013, 5–6).

2. From Movement to Regime

1. Wilbur (1983, 620–672) describes the protracted course of the split and purge, which also divided the Nationalist Party itself. The cited party membership figures are from Lee (1991, 16–17).
2. Ch'en (1986, 204–216; troop estimates, 198), Dreyer (1995, 185–200; troop estimates, 186–187 and 199).
3. Apter and Saich (1994, 190–194) describe the region in vivid detail.
4. See Stinchcombe (1965, 169–180) and Tilly (1978, 189–222).
5. An early statement of this view is in Schwartz (1951).
6. The earliest version of this argument is in Taylor (1940), later elaborated by Johnson (1962).
7. Selden (1971) was an influential early advocate of this interpretation.
8. This is consistent with broader explanations for revolution in China and Vietnam as expressions of class conflict, for example, Moore (1966) and Paige (1975).
9. Thaxton (1983) and Marks (1984), following Scott's (1976) ideas about the "moral economy" of rebellion.

10. Hofheinz (1969, 1977). Benton's (1992) detailed account of the activities of Communist forces left behind in South China after the evacuation of the Jiangxi Soviet reinforces this point.
11. Van Slyke (1986, 651–652).
12. Ibid., 674–676.
13. Westad (2003, 61).
14. Dreyer (1995, 317–318), Van Slyke (1986, 621).
15. Taylor (2011, 142).
16. These events are known as the Xi'an Incident (Ch'en 1986, 226–229).
17. Taylor (2011, 150).
18. Ch'i (1982, 42–43), Mitter (2013, 98–108), Yang Tianshi (2011). Harmsen (2013) is a dramatic book-length account of the Nationalists' ill-fated defense of Shanghai in 1937.
19. Mitter (2013, 124–144).
20. Taylor (2011, 168–169); also MacKinnon (2011).
21. Van Slyke (1986, 613), Benton (1999), Pantsov and Levine (2012, 290).
22. Van Slyke (1986, 613–614).
23. Ibid., 631.
24. The advocates of more aggressive military resistance included Zhou Enlai, Wang Ming, Peng Dehuai, and Zhu De (Apter and Saich 1994, 58–59; Pantsov and Levine 2012, 313–314).
25. Van Slyke (1986, 672–673).
26. Ibid., 676–681; also Yang Kuisong (2011). Friedman, Pickowicz, and Selden (1991, 44–51) describe the destruction of the resistance movement in one county in central Hebei during this period.
27. Taylor (2011, 168–169).
28. Ch'i (1982, 68–81), Van Slyke (1986, 705–709), Wang (2011).
29. Ch'i (1982, 81).
30. Eastman (1984, 156).
31. van de Ven (2011) analyzes this bias and its sources.
32. Eastman (1984, 130); see also Drea and van de Ven (2011).
33. Eastman (1984, 136).
34. Taylor (2011, 297–298).
35. Lüthi (2008, 25–26).
36. Wilbur (1983, 719–720).
37. Ch'i (1982, 23).
38. Ibid., 37.
39. Ibid., 40–82.
40. Ibid., 3.
41. Eastman (1984, 130).
42. Kirby (1984, 157–158).
43. Ch'i (1982, 235).
44. Liu Shaoqi ([1939] 1984, 136–137).

45. Taylor (2011, 157).
46. Eastman (1984, 207–208).
47. Dickson (1993), Eastman (1981), Taylor (2011, 191–196, 212–217).
48. Averill (1995, 96–99; 2006, 389–391), Guillermaz (1972, 216–217).
49. Averill (2006, 390); see also Pantsov and Levine (2012, 239–245).
50. Rowe (2007, 310–316, at 313).
51. Ibid., 313–315; Benton (1992, 313–314).
52. Benton (1992, 239–240, 264, 282–283, 316–317, 337–339). Apter and Saich (1994, 49–54) describe these purges as conflicts between local guerrilla forces and the central party command. See also Saich (1996, 530–550).
53. The text was the "first major document" studied by senior cadres during the campaign (Apter and Saich 1994, 275, 277).
54. Teiwes and Sun (1995, 341–342), Van Slyke (1986, 616).
55. Benton (1975, 341–342); see also Apter and Saich (1994, 54–59).
56. Lüthi (2008, 26–29), Pantsov and Levine (2012, 317–318), Teiwes and Sun (1995).
57. Leese (2011, 8–12).
58. Wylie (1980, 10–12).
59. Commission of the Central Committee of the Communist Party of the Soviet Union (1939), Hua-Yu Li (2006, 91–101).
60. Hua-Yu Li (2006, 101–102).
61. Tucker (1977), Walder (1991).
62. Hua-Yu Li (2010), Pantsov and Levine (2012, 335), Wylie (1980).
63. Teiwes (1976, 20–32).
64. Of the 800,000 party members at the time, 90 percent had recently joined (Apter and Saich 1994, 267).
65. Ibid., 279–281.
66. These criticisms are described in Apter and Saich (1994, 59–64), Cheek (1984, 30–37), Goldman (1967, 19–32), and Dai (1994, 3–30).
67. The campaign against the critics and their treatment is described in Cheek (1984, 37–44), Goldman (1967, 32–50), and Dai (1994, 31–75). Translations of Wang Shiwei's essays, and those of like-minded critics, are in Benton and Hunter (1995, 69–83), and Dai (1994), which also includes translations of critical accusations against Wang.
68. MacFarquhar (1997, 290–292).
69. Apter and Saich (1994, 289–292), Teiwes and Sun (1995, 370–375).
70. Seybolt (1986, 57–65).
71. Teiwes and Sun (1995, 364–365, 370–375).
72. Seybolt (1986, 66).
73. Ibid., 67.
74. Teiwes and Sun (1995, 373–375), Walder (2009, 15–16).
75. Seybolt (1986, 40).
76. Pantsov and Levine (2012, 348).

77. Westad (2003, 122–123).
78. Ibid., 148.
79. Pepper (1999, 7–41), Westad (2003, 69).
80. Eastman (1984, 80–81).
81. Ibid., 86–87; see also Pepper (1999, 118–131).
82. Pantsov and Levine (2012, 348).
83. Westad (2003, 152).
84. Levine (1987, 224–226).
85. Dikötter (2013, 64–74), Westad (2003, 134).
86. Levine (1987, 229). Thaxton's (2008, 83–88) account of a village in North China also emphasizes the transformative effect of mobilization during the civil war on the Communist Party, which intensified a coercive stance toward the rural population.
87. Westad (2003, 168–172).
88. Pantsov and Levine (2012, 350).
89. Westad (2003, 175–178).
90. Ibid., 181–211; Pepper (1999, 42–93, 132–195).
91. Westad (2003, 197).
92. Ibid., 198–199.
93. Ibid., 199–208.
94. Dikötter (2013, 3–8, 20–22).
95. Yick (1995).
96. Dikötter (2013, 22–32), Westad (2003, 221–255).
97. Brook (2010, map on 41).
98. Rowe (2009, 71–78).
99. Rossabi (2005, 30–31).
100. Chen (2001, 27).
101. Chen (2007, 131–32), Westad (2003, 118–119).
102. Chen (2007, 132–133), Westad (2003, 234–235). This shift in position mirrored a similar one in the Soviet Union that took place after World War II—the role of Russia in bringing "culture, enlightenment and order to its borderlands" was emphasized by Stalin for the first time (Service 2004, 496–497).
103. Gao (2007).
104. Goldstein (1989, 58–66).
105. Ibid., 522–610; Westad (2003, 92–94).
106. Goldstein (1989, 619–690).
107. Ibid., 690–736; Westad (2003, 92–94).
108. Chen (2007, 157–159).
109. Levine (1987, 93–101), Westad (2003, 172–178).
110. Teiwes and Sun (1999, 13).
111. Levine (1987, 247–248).

3. Rural Revolution

1. Skocpol (1979).
2. Another early advocate was the Guangdong party activist Peng Pai, who created the first rural Soviet in eastern Guangdong Province in 1927 and was executed by the Nationalists in 1929 (Galbiati 1985).
3. Pantsov and Levine (2012, 156–157).
4. Mao (1926a).
5. Mao (1926b).
6. Mao (1926e).
7. Mao (1926d).
8. Wilbur (1983, 591–594).
9. Brandt (1958, 88–90), Taylor (2011, 61–62), Wilbur (1983, 606–608).
10. Mao (1927b).
11. Mao (1926c).
12. Mao (1927a, 430).
13. Ibid., 446.
14. Ibid., 434–435.
15. Ibid., 467.
16. Ibid., 433.
17. Schram (1995, 36); see also Pantsov and Levine (2012, 196).
18. Wilbur (1983, 673–681, 690–696).
19. Hinton (1966, 110–117).
20. Ibid., 132–138.
21. Ibid., 139–146.
22. Ibid., 222–240.
23. Ibid., 275–311.
24. Ibid., 332–366. Friedman, Pickowicz, and Selden (1991, 92–110) describe a similar sequence of violent events in another North China village during this period; an initially terroristic land reform via manufactured class struggle and then two waves of work teams to correct the errors of the previous campaigns.
25. Thaxton (2008, 70–83) provides another account of the revolutionary process in a village not far from Hinton's, one that changed hands more than once during the civil war. The fierce contest between the Nationalists and Communists was marked by violent retribution against collaborators each time the region changed hands. This had the effect of elevating the most ruthlessly violent militia leaders into top positions in the new village governments.
26. Ch'ü (1962), Rowe (2009, 48–62), Siu (1989, 41–87).
27. Barkan (1990), Duara (1990), Watson (1990).
28. Yang (1959, 103, 106). See also Siu (1989, 88–115) for a parallel description of a nearby county.
29. Yang (1959, 109–110).

30. Yang (1945, 143–156 and 173–189) describes a similar village in the northern province of Shandong.
31. Yang (1959, 146–166).
32. Ibid., 167–175.
33. Ibid., 169, 174. See also Huaiyin Li (2009, 5) and Siu (1989, 116–142).
34. Riskin (1987, 51).
35. Friedman, Pickowicz, and Selden (1991, 84, 86, 105) and Huaiyin Li (2009, 11–19) detail this transformation of landholding at the village level.
36. Wang (1999, 324–328), Tien (1989, 23–24).
37. Bernstein (1968).
38. Ibid.
39. Brown (2007). Dikötter (2013, 76–80) documents widespread collective resistance and isolated rebellions in a range of locations in the southern half of China.
40. Strauss (2006).
41. Dikötter (2013, 83).
42. Schoenhals (2008b, 72). This number includes both urban and rural regions but excludes deaths during land reform. Schoenhals (2008b, 68–73) provides a critical review of various estimates. Strauss (2006, 91) notes the range of estimates, which have run as high as 5 million executions.
43. Friedman, Pickowicz, and Selden (1991, 111–122), Lardy (1987b).
44. Oi (1989, 43–44), Shue (1980, 214–245).
45. Cheng and Selden (1994, 660).
46. Bernstein (1967).
47. Oi (1989, 13–42), Siu (1989, 143–167).
48. Tucker (1990, 69–145).
49. According to Service (2004, 566), "Stupendous hypocrisy was on display here. If ever there had been an attempt to transform an economy through sheer will and violence, it had been at the end of the 1920s under Stalin's leadership."
50. Mao (1977).
51. Hua-Yu Li (2006, 61–94).
52. Teiwes and Sun (1999, 20–52, 70–77).
53. Riskin (1987, 86).
54. Bernstein (1967), Conquest (1986).
55. Bernstein (1967), Dikötter (2013, 208–225). Friedman, Pickowicz, and Selden (1991, 122–198), Huaiyin Li (2006; 2007; 2009, 23–49), and Thaxton (2008, 89–117) trace the halting course of change from household farms to collectives. All of them detail the serious problems encountered at each stage, and the subtle and open resistance by many farm households— most pronounced in the later stages. Bernstein (1967) and Liu and Wang (2006) analyze the political pressures on local cadres that accelerated collectivization faster than originally planned.
56. Oi (1989, 132–145).

57. Ibid., 5.
58. Ibid., 43–65.
59. Ash (2006), Oi (1989, 55).
60. Oi (1989, 135–137), Walder (1986, 54–56).
61. Burns (1981), Oi (1989, 138–141).
62. Huaiyin Li (2009, 44–47).
63. Ibid., 5.

4. Urban Revolution

1. Pepper (1999, 332).
2. Gao (2004, 14–16), Pepper (1999, 376–380).
3. Pepper (1999, 386–390), Wakeman (2007).
4. Strauss (2006) also mentions a fourth type of campaign, designed to mobilize the population to complete community-oriented tasks, like planting trees, eradicating rats and mosquitoes, or cleaning up health hazards in urban neighborhoods.
5. Gao (2004, 69–79), Vogel (1969, 46–51).
6. Gao (2004, 47–51), Vogel (1969, 51–55).
7. Brown (2012, 16–22), Gao (2004, 51–64), Vogel (1969, 55–60), Wakeman (2007).
8. Wakeman (2007, 23–25).
9. Ibid., 43.
10. Dikötter (2013, 50–51, 53–55), Wakeman (2007, 52–58).
11. Dikötter (2013, 104–120, 124–127), Hooper (1986).
12. Lieberthal (1980, 53–77), Strauss (2002). Dikötter (2013, 83–99) provides a vivid description of the campaign, based primarily on party archives.
13. Gao (2004, 140–146), Vogel (1969, 62–65), Yang (2008).
14. Gao (2004, 144).
15. Schoenhals (2008b, 72); also Gao (2004, 140), Strauss (2002, 87–89; 2006, 901). Dikötter (2013, 99–100) finds a figure of 2 million executions in both urban and rural regions a more credible estimate based on archival materials.
16. Yang (2008, 109).
17. Dikötter (2013, 89–92), Strauss (2002, 89–92), Yang (2008, 110).
18. Yang (2008, 112–120).
19. Dikötter (2003).
20. Ibid.; Dikötter (2013, 243–254).
21. Hung (2010, 400).
22. Ibid., 401–403; Lieberthal (1973, 243–244; 1980, 14–16).
23. Hung (2010, 403–404).
24. Ibid., 404–417; Lieberthal (1980, 108–119). Dikötter (2013, 196–206) surveys the broader assault on Buddhism, Taoism, Christianity, and Islam during the 1950s.

25. Lieberthal (1973, 245–250; 1980, 22–25), Hershatter (1986, 120–131).
26. Martin (1996, 79–189), Wang (1967).
27. Lieberthal (1973, 250–255; 1980, 60–77).
28. Lieberthal (1973, 261–264).
29. Dikötter (2013, 51–53).
30. Henriot (1995), also Hershatter (1997).
31. Henriot (1995).
32. Hershatter (1986, 210–240), Perry (1993, 109–237).
33. Perry (2007).
34. Ibid.
35. Andreas (2009, 20–22).
36. Chen (1960, 33).
37. Ibid., 31–33.
38. Gao (2004, 146–151).
39. Dikötter (2013, 180–187).
40. Chen (1960, 2).
41. Ibid., 45. See Chen (1960, 38–50) for an account of some of the other famous educators and scholars who were targeted for this kind of denunciation.
42. Ibid., 2.
43. Ibid.
44. Ibid., 62–63.
45. Ibid., 63–64.
46. Joravsky (1970, 40–54).
47. The Soviet scientist Medvedev (1969, 134) described Lysenko's scientific findings, published in his own journal, as "fraudulent" and lamented that "these illiterate, shameful articles were advertised as achievements of progressive science" with "mythical transformations" that were supported primarily with reference to Stalin's authority.
48. Quoted in Medvedev (1969, 134).
49. Joravsky (1970), Medvedev (1969). The Chinese leadership eventually realized that Michurin was wrong and that Lysenko was a charlatan, and in 1956, with Zhou Enlai's encouragement, Chinese scientists debunked his theories (Lüthi 2008, 52–53).
50. See the China memoir of the Soviet scientist Klochko (1964, 10–33, 64–65, 82–88).
51. So (2002, 694).
52. Ibid., 698.
53. Dikötter (2013, 157–163), Gao (2004, 159–163), Sheng (2006).
54. Sheng (2006, 72–79).
55. Dikötter (2013, 163), Sheng (2006, 76).
56. Dikötter (2013, 163–173), Dillon (2007), Gao (2004, 160–179), Gardner (1969), Lieberthal (1980, 125–152).
57. State Statistical Bureau (1983, 214).

58. Dillon (2007).
59. Cheng and Selden (1994, 644).
60. Brown (2012, 29–47), Cheng and Selden (1994, 652–653).
61. Cheng and Selden (1994, 655).
62. Ibid., 655–657.
63. Cheng and Selden (1997, 32–46).
64. Whyte and Parish (1984, 22–23).
65. Ibid., 18–22.
66. State Statistical Bureau (1983, 214).
67. Whyte and Parish (1984, 37–42), Walder (1986, 68–74).
68. Davis-Friedmann (1991, 102–116), Walder (1986, 44–45), Whyte and Parish (1984, 71–76).
69. Henderson and Cohen (1984, 10–46), Whyte and Parish (1984).

5. The Socialist Economy

1. Kirby (2006, 881–882).
2. Commission of the Central Committee of the Communist Party of the Soviet Union (1939), Hua-Yu Li (2010).
3. Hua-Yu Li (2006, 1, 170).
4. Kirby (2006, 882), Lüthi (2008, 39–40).
5. Dittmer (1992, 17–25).
6. Kaple (1994).
7. Gatrell and Harrison (1993).
8. Calculated from the downloadable database that accompanies Maddison (2006).
9. Ibid., 478, and calculations from the downloadable database.
10. Calculated from ibid., 279.
11. Halpern (1993, 110).
12. These features of the growth model are outlined in Kornai (1992, 160–202); its origins and evolution in the Soviet Union are examined in Zaleski (1980).
13. See Baran and Sweezy (1966) for an extended example of this kind of critique.
14. Kornai (1992, 131–159).
15. The following paragraphs are based on my transcripts of interviews in Hong Kong during 1979 and 1980 with retired factory managers who had recently emigrated from China, as part of a study of authority in Chinese industry (Walder 1986, 270–272, informants number 5, 23, 55, and 65). Kornai (1992, 110–130) provides a structural overview of the planning process and how it operated in practice.
16. Kornai (1992, 228–261) provides an overview of the impact of hoarding from a macroeconomic perspective. This is a condensation of his classic work on the subject (Kornai 1980).

17. Kornai (1979).
18. See, for example, Berliner (1957), whose work was based on interviews with émigré Soviet managers in postwar Europe.
19. Walder (1992).
20. Calculated from data in Kornai (1992, 175). The figures cover eight socialist and seven capitalist countries over two separate periods, 1965–1973 and 1973–1983. The socialist countries ranged from a low of 34 percent in Hungary to a high of 54 percent in China. The capitalist countries ranged from a low of 16 percent in Denmark to a high of 32 percent in the United Kingdom. According to Gregory (2004, 122–123), "comparative appraisals reveal that the command economies produced economic outcomes quite different from market economies. The USSR and Eastern Europe consistently produced more heavy industry and defense goods, fewer services, less foreign trade, higher investment rates, and lower urbanization than market economies at a similar level of economic development."
21. Calculated from data in Kornai (1992, 187). The study compared Czechoslovakia, Poland, and the Soviet Union with France, Japan, and the United Kingdom.
22. Henderson and Cohen (1984), Walder (1986).
23. Other socialist economies permitted greater labor turnover; China's draconian limits on job changes were due to the necessity to curb migration from countryside to city and its oversupply of urban labor (Walder 1986, 68–75).
24. Ibid., 40–43; Whyte and Parish (1984, 71–76).
25. This figure refers to the city of Tianjin and comes from the survey data cited in Walder (1992). The same survey found that 44 percent of the population lived in public housing provided by the local government, and 18 percent lived in privately owned housing that was primarily a family legacy from before 1949.
26. Walder (1986, 59–67).
27. Walder (1992, 532).
28. Ibid.
29. The dossier system is described by Lee (1991, 329–342) and Walder (1986, 91–93).
30. Whyte and Parish (1984, 25–26).
31. Zaleski (1980, 465–481).
32. Huenemann (1966), Whyte and Parish (1984, 85–100).
33. Walder (1986, 210–212).
34. Kornai (1959), Lewin (1974).
35. Baylis (1974).
36. The earliest discussions predated the postwar period. See Dunayevskaya (1944). The best-known postwar economists who forwarded these ideas were Kornai (1959), Lange (Lange and Taylor 1964), Liberman (1971), and Šik (1966; 1967; 1972).

37. Fung (1982), Lin (1981).
38. Mao (1977) laid out his objections to late Stalinist economics in his unpublished reading notes on Stalin's last work, *The Economic Problems of Socialism,* and a 1950s Soviet textbook on political economy. Service (2004, 566–567) describes the key themes of these late Stalin-era views of socialist economics and how they revised earlier doctrines from the prewar period.

6. The Evolving Party System

1. Vogel (1967) was one of the first to analyze these implications.
2. Lee (1991, 16), Van Slyke (1986, 621).
3. Lee (1991, 16).
4. See Kraus (1981). A third designation applied to those who were the offspring of someone who died after sacrificing for the cause: "revolutionary martyr." Barnett (1966) and Vogel (1967) describe further status distinctions among the revolutionary generation.
5. Oksenberg (1968, 92) put it less charitably: "The Party, representing the best avenue for upward mobility, attracted opportunists."
6. Organization Department, Central Communist Party Office for Research on Party History, and Central Party Archives (2000, vol. 12, 1227).
7. Ibid., vol. 9, 40–48.
8. Ibid., vol. 12, 1227.
9. Ibid., vol. 12, 1229.
10. See Lee (1991, 56–57).
11. These figures are calculated from the survey data analyzed in Walder, Li, and Treiman (2000).
12. The same pattern was observed in the Soviet Union: Hough (1977).
13. Vogel (1965) was the first to write about the variations in political pressures across social settings; Whyte (1974) analyzed these differences in a more systematic fashion.
14. Schoenhals (2013, 17–26, 30–46). Schoenhals based his account on internal ministry documents, training manuals, and professional publications.
15. Ibid., 63–64.
16. Ibid., 5.
17. Ibid., 58–82.
18. Ibid., 93.
19. The three types of agents are described in ibid., 85–109.
20. The prescribed recruitment strategies are described in ibid., 138–169.
21. Ibid., 170–204.
22. Lewis (1963, 106–107).
23. This paragraph is based on Li and Walder (2001).
24. Oksenberg (1968, 64–65) was perhaps the first to describe the choices facing young Chinese as they navigated career opportunities presented

by this system, and the way that opportunities narrowed by early middle age.

25. The figures in this paragraph and the next come from Walder, Li, and Treiman (2000). These figures are not percentages, as in earlier paragraphs, but are odds ratios estimated in event-history models. They represent an estimate of how the net odds of subsequently joining the party are affected by the given individual characteristic. Similar estimates are reported in Li and Walder (2001, 1385).

26. Walder, Li, and Treiman (2000).

27. Fitzpatrick (1993).

28. Fitzpatrick (1979).

29. Fitzpatrick (1978), Tucker (1977).

30. Fitzpatrick (2005, 24, 37–49).

31. Ibid., 14–18.

32. Walder and Hu (2009).

33. See, for example, Brown (2015), Leese (2015), and Yang (2015).

34. Croll (1984), Unger (1984).

35. Stacey (1983).

36. This paragraph is based on Walder and Hu (2009, 1413); similar estimates are reported in Li and Walder (2001).

37. This paragraph is based on figures in China Education Yearbook (1984, 965–966, 969, 971, 1001, 1023).

38. Rosen (1982, 12–66), Unger (1982, 11–47, 83–109).

39. Lang (1946).

40. Andreas (2009, 23–32) vividly documents the operations of the party's control over the allocation of political credentials and opportunity at an elite university.

41. Shirk (1982), Unger (1982).

42. Walder (2009, 23).

43. Walder (1995). Long before the availability of data from life history surveys, Oksenberg (1968, 67) made essentially the same observation: "Once someone had opted for goals found outside the political system, he could not decide at a later date to pursue the goals offered by the system."

44. This paragraph and the one that follows is based on Walder, Li, and Treiman (2000, 200). Parallel findings from a different set of survey data are reported in Bian, Shu, and Logan (2001).

45. Li and Walder (2001, 1398, 1402).

46. Organization Department (2000, vol. 14, 1224–1231).

47. Schoenhals (1985).

48. Oksenberg (1976) analyzed the implications for leaders who reached the apex of the political system, but he noted earlier that the lack of the exit option applied to all careers within the bureaucracy (Oksenberg 1968, 66–67).

7. Thaw and Backlash

1. Baring (1972, 3–49), Bruce (2003, 159–165).
2. Kramer (1999, 13).
3. Ibid., 15.
4. Ibid., 15–17.
5. Ibid., 17–22; Ostermann (2001, 113–142).
6. Baring (1972, 51–113), Bruce (2003, 165–199), Kramer (1999, 40–45, 48–50, 52–54), Ostermann (2001, xxxi–xxxvi, 1–21).
7. Brown (2009, 234), Kecskemeti (1961, 40–46), Knight (1993, 194–200, 203–224), Taubman (2003, 250–263).
8. Nagy (1957) wrote a book-length defense of these more moderate post-Stalin policies in 1955–1956, making him the standard bearer of Hungarian de-Stalinization.
9. Applebaum (2012, 437), Kramer (1999, 5–6), Taubman (2003, 275–277).
10. Brown (2009, 203–209), Johnson (1972, 65–121), Rusinow (1977, 32–70).
11. Brown (2009, 272–276), Milenkovitch (1971, 54–120).
12. Brown (2009, 236–243).
13. Ibid., 240–243; Taubman (2003, 270–271).
14. Khrushchev (1962, S20–S21).
15. Taubman (2003, 271–273). A full English-language text of the speech is Khrushchev (1962).
16. Taubman (2003, 274).
17. Lüthi (2008, 48–49), Taubman (2003, 277–282).
18. Taubman (2003, 290).
19. According to one account, an Israeli intelligence officer in Warsaw obtained a copy and passed it to the U.S. Central Intelligence Agency, which soon relayed it to the *Times* through the U.S. State Department (Taubman 2003, 284). In another, the first secretary of the Polish party recalled that he had personally given copies to correspondents of foreign newspapers (Leese 2011, 29–30).
20. Leese (2011, 30).
21. Chen (2015, 108–114).
22. Machcewicz (2009, 35–86).
23. Kramer (1998, 168–174), Machcewicz (2009, 97–124).
24. Machcewicz (2009, 125–157).
25. Kramer (1998, 168–174), Machcewicz (2009, 158–189, 241–252), Taubman (2003, 291–294).
26. Kecskemeti (1961, 17–39, 71–82).
27. Ibid., 47–70. The Petöfi Circle was named after the national poet who had helped inspire the Hungarian revolution of 1848. Many of its members were young party members and youth league activists who were in favor of a new reform-oriented course (Applebaum 2012, 448–455; Brown 2009, 279–280).

28. Kecskemeti (1961, 47–82), Taubman (2003, 290). Sebestyen (2006) recounts these events and adds a detailed and dramatic description of the street fighting in Budapest and its subsequent suppression.
29. Brown (2009, 278–288), Kramer (1998, 175–210), Taubman (2003, 294–299). See also Ekiert (1996, 49–98).
30. Goldman (1967, 58–66, 119–122, 129–139).
31. Lin (2009, 484–495).
32. Ibid., 523–525.
33. Chen (1960, 88–90), Dikötter (2013, 187–189), Goldman (1967, 129–157), Lin (2009, 501–521).
34. Lin (2009, 520–521).
35. Ibid., 558; Vogel (1969, 136–138).
36. Leese (2011, 30–36), Lüthi (2008, 49–50), MacFarquhar (1974, 43–48).
37. Lüthi (2008, 50–53), MacFarquhar (1974, 43–48; 1989, 6–7).
38. MacFarquhar (1974, 78–85).
39. Ibid., 100–102.
40. Shen (2008, 322–323).
41. MacFarquhar (1974, 148, 165), Organization Department (2000, vol. 9, 36, 40–41).
42. Leese (2011, 38–46).
43. MacFarquhar (1974, 120–121).
44. Ibid., 178–183, 189–199; Shen (2008, 491–501).
45. MacFarquhar (1974, 177–178); Shen (2008, 501–522).
46. Leese (2011, 51–54), Lüthi (2008, 63, 70), MacFarquhar (1989, 9).
47. Mao (1957), Shen (2008, 470–476). See also Goldman (1967, 187–191).
48. Leese (2011, 57–60).
49. MacFarquhar (1974, 184–199).
50. See the series of ten speeches translated in MacFarquhar, Cheek, and Wu (1989, 191–362); Shen (2008, 476–490).
51. Cheek (1997, 174–175), Goldman (1967, 179–186), MacFarquhar (1974, 178–180). The short story by a twenty-two-year-old writer, Wang Meng, "A Young Man Arrives at the Organization Department," was published in *People's Literature* in September 1956. It is translated in Nieh (1981b, 473–511).
52. Cheek (1997, 175–182), MacFarquhar (1974, 192–194).
53. MacFarquhar (1974, 200–207).
54. Shen (2008, 523–551).
55. MacFarquhar (1960, 51–53).
56. Ibid., 59–76.
57. Ibid., 117–120; similar complaints are described in Andreas (2009, 34–38), Chen (1960, 152–170), and Shen (2008, 579–581).
58. Nieh (1981b, 323–324). The author was Xu Mouyong, in an essay titled "Random Notes from Chanzaoju." Goldman (1967, 191–202) surveys the range of criticism offered by novelists and poets, and Nieh (1981a) provides

translations of essays that criticize the party's doctrines regarding literature and poetry.

59. MacFarquhar (1960, 88–89).

60. Ibid., 106–107.

61. Ibid., 49. Other harsh criticisms along these lines are described in Zhu (2005, 195–201).

62. MacFarquhar (1960, 73). The speaker was Ge Yang, a veteran communist and journalist. Similar calls for fundamental change are detailed in Shen (2008, 573–579).

63. Wang et al. (1998, 515–516).

64. Leese (2011, 61).

65. Goldman (1962), MacFarquhar (1960, 130–141).

66. According to Moody (1977, 189–192), Lin Xiling was the pen name of Cheng Haiguo, a People's Liberation Army veteran discharged in 1953 who later enrolled at Chinese People's University.

67. Doolin (1964, 23–25).

68. Ibid., 27.

69. Ibid., 27–28.

70. Ibid., 31.

71. Ibid., 32–33.

72. Ibid., 38, 41–42.

73. Ibid., 16.

74. Ibid., 45–46.

75. Ibid., 60.

76. Ibid., 61–62.

77. Ibid., 65–66. This writer was echoing the criticism of China's top leaders made by Wang Shiwei during the Yan'an rectification movement, described in Chapter 2.

78. Shen's (2008, 584–596) description of student and worker agitation is based primarily on these internal bulletins.

79. MacFarquhar (1974, 221), Wang et al. (1998, 517).

80. Shen (2008, 587–590), Zhu (2005, 218–222).

81. Shen (2008, 590–591).

82. MacFarquhar (1960, 143–164), Shen (2008, 591).

83. Perry (1994), Shen (2008, 591–593).

84. Huaiyin Li (2009, 57).

85. Ibid., 55–76; Huaiyin Li (2007).

86. Shen (2008, 593–594).

87. Wang (2015).

88. MacFarquhar (1974, 218–219, 225–240, 248–249, 261–269), Shen (2008, 597–608).

89. Chen (1960, 171–201), Shen (2008, 637–673). It was not only those with strong grievances who criticized the party during the Hundred Flowers.

U (2012) analyzes the motives that drove privileged regime loyalists to offer criticisms of the party, despite the potential risks.
90. See, for example, Friedman, Pickowicz, and Selden (1991, 209–213).
91. MacFarquhar (1974, 266–269). Schoenhals (1986) analyzes these changes in detail. A translation of the original version is Mao (1957).
92. Leese (2011, 65–66), Shen (2008, 673–680).
93. Shen (2008, 662). The devastating impact on prominent literary figures is detailed in Goldman (1967, 202–242).
94. Hoffmann (1974, 146–147), MacFarquhar (1974, 224).
95. MacFarquhar (1974, 283–289).
96. Ibid., 289–310; Leese (2011, 63–64) disputes this interpretation, viewing Mao as more firmly in control.
97. Taubman (2003, 310–324).
98. Lüthi (2008, 71–74).

8. Great Leap

1. Bernstein (1969), Teiwes and Sun (1993; 1997; 1999, 20–52).
2. Teiwes and Sun (1999, 67–69).
3. MacFarquhar (1983, 16). "Important products" included iron ore, pig iron, steel, coal, petroleum, electric power, cement, and selected consumer items like sugar, woolen textiles, and leather footwear.
4. Ibid., 17; Teiwes and Sun (1999, 70–71).
5. MacFarquhar (1983, 17).
6. Lardy (1987a, 360).
7. Ibid., 362.
8. Lieberthal (1987, 300). Chen Yun's writings on China's development strategy during this period are translated in Lardy and Lieberthal (1983).
9. In Lardy's (1987a, 363) view, "The Great Leap Forward was predicated on Mao's misunderstanding of the constraints facing Chinese agriculture."
10. MacFarquhar (1983, 52–63), Teiwes and Sun (1999, 73–77).
11. Dikötter (2010, 15–24), Teiwes and Sun (1999, 85–86).
12. Teiwes and Sun (1999, 90–93).
13. Lieberthal (1987, 301).
14. Teiwes and Sun (1999, 96–97).
15. MacFarquhar (1983, 88–90), Teiwes and Sun (1999, 100–105).
16. Lardy (1987a, 367).
17. Ibid., 366.
18. Ibid., 363–365; Yang (2012, 163–167).
19. Dikötter (2010, 47–55), MacFarquhar (1983, 103–106), Yang (2012, 167–170).
20. Yang (2012, 168–169).
21. Dikötter (2010, 56–63), Yang (2012, 77–78). Friedman, Pickowicz, and Selden (1991, 216–240) and Thaxton (2008, 118–156) document the prac-

tices associated with the Great Leap in two villages in Hebei Province. Huaiyin Li (2009, 82–102) chronicles the campaign in a Jiangsu village and Siu (1989, 170–188) in the Pearl River delta in Guangdong.

22. Yang (2012, 168–169).
23. Oi (1989, 59–62).
24. For these and other examples, see Yang (2012, 274–275).
25. Dikötter (2010, 166–173).
26. Ibid., 174–188. Zhou (2012, 72–90) translates internal party documents that described this kind of destruction after the fact.
27. These are quotations from local interviews conducted by Yang (2012, 32).
28. Ibid., 52.
29. Ibid., 52–56.
30. Xue Muqiao, quoted in ibid., 257.
31. Xue Muqiao, quoted in ibid., 258.
32. Yang (2012, 258).
33. Bernstein (2006), Dikötter (2010, 67–72), Zhou (2012, 4–16).
34. Mao's speech to the Second Zhengzhou Conference, February 27, 1959, as translated in Yang (2012, 438–439).
35. Dikötter (2010, 86–87).
36. Bernstein (1984).
37. Li and Yang (2005, 845–846) compare the initially reported output with the subsequent figures adjusted in the years after the Leap.
38. Dikötter (2010, 85).
39. Ibid., 85–86, and the document translated in Zhou (2012, 23–25, at 25).
40. Quoted in Yang (2012, 49).
41. Yang (2012, 335–336). In this commune, more than 1,000 local leaders were dismissed from their posts, and 173 people were beaten to death.
42. For extensive documentation of this surprisingly little-known campaign, see Yang (2012, 28–37, 224–229, 335–338), and Zhou (2012, 18–19, 25–36).
43. An internal report submitted in Sichuan Province in 1961 reported that local officials set up private jails and labor camps to which peasants were summarily consigned, and used methods of torture that included "hanging people up, beating them, forcing them to kneel on burning charcoal, piercing their mouths, clipping off their fingers, stitching their lips, pushing needles into their nipples, force-feeding them feces, stuffing dried beans down their throats, and so on" (Zhou 2012, 21). An internal report submitted to Henan Province in 1961 listed additional tortures: tearing out hair, cutting off ears, driving bamboo strips into the palms of the hand, driving pine needles into the gums, forcing burning embers into the mouth, tearing out pubic hair, piercing genitals, burying alive, and a torture known as "lighting the celestial candle"—stripping people naked, hanging them up, dousing them with oil, and lighting them on fire (Yang 2012, 30–31).
44. Thaxton (2008, 188–198) provides a village-level view of these events.

45. There are many accounts of the events at the Lushan Plenum: see Dikötter (2010, 90–99), Lüthi (2008, 126–135), MacFarquhar (1983, 193–251), Teiwes and Sun (1999, 202–212). The specific claims in this paragraph are from Yang (2012, 350–393).

46. By "Stalin in his later years," these officials almost certainly did not mean the massive purges and executions of 1937–1938, for which there was no parallel in China at this point in time. Instead, they appear to be referring to Stalin's capricious and bullying behavior toward members of the Politburo in the last few years of his life, something that was complained about loudly by Khrushchev and other top Soviet officials immediately after Stalin's death in 1953 (Service 2004, 531–540).

47. Bernstein (2006) traces the evolution of Mao's shifting and erratic response to bad news during the Leap and the reasons for his defensive reaction at the Lushan Plenum.

48. Bernstein (2006), Yang (2012, 384–385).

49. This included Liu Shaoqi and Zhou Enlai: Yang (2012, 367–383).

50. Ibid., 385–386.

51. Ibid., 387.

52. Ibid.

53. Ibid., 388.

54. Ibid., 390, 392. Thaxton (2008, 143–156) details the pressures placed on village leaders during this period to enforce party directives with enthusiasm and the punishments applied to those who failed.

55. Yang (2012, 445).

56. Ibid., 60–61.

57. Ibid., 62.

58. Speech by Second Secretary of the Central South Bureau of the CCP Wang Renzhong, December 6, 1960, translated in Yang (2012, 63).

59. Ibid., 61.

60. Ibid., 61–64.

61. Ibid., 406–407.

62. Aird (1982, 278), Coale (1981, 89).

63. Professional demographers have generated definitive estimates of famine deaths, based on the analysis of population age structures in successive national censuses. Ashton and colleagues (1984, 614, 619) estimated excess mortality of 29.5 million, Banister (1987) 28.9 million, and Coale (1984) 30.7 million with substantially the same data. Yang (2012, 421–425, 428–430) reviews various estimates based on alternate estimation methods from noncensus data by Chinese scholars and finds 36 million to be the most plausible number. Others (e.g., Dikötter 2010, 324–334) believe that archival records could actually support numbers as high 50 million. Such numbers cannot be reconciled with age-specific population data. For larger estimates to be plausible, the national censuses would have to underreport population figures in the early census and overreport population figures

in the later censuses in exactly the right age groups—an unlikely proposition. Coale (1984, 64–74) explains the life-table methodology.

64. The official story also minimizes the number of famine deaths, setting the death toll at 17 million, calculated according to an undisclosed "optimization" method that attributes huge percentages of excess mortality to "natural causes." Yang Jisheng (2012, 421–425) critically reviews the range of estimates by Chinese authors.
65. Peng (1987, 651).
66. Li and Yang (2005, 843). Kung and Lin (2003, 66–67) reached similar conclusions about the contribution of weather to regional death rates.
67. Lardy (1987a, 369–370).
68. Li and Yang (2005, 845).
69. Ashton et al. (1984, 626).
70. Brown (2011; 2012, 53–75).
71. MacFarquhar (1997, 3).
72. Ashton et al. (1984, 630 632). Frequent reports of famine issued by anti-communist sources were generally dismissed as biased.
73. Dikötter (2010, 72–83), Lüthi (2008, 109–111, 153–154).
74. See MacFarquhar (1997, 23–31).
75. Ashton et al. (1984, 622).
76. Dikötter (2010, 269–273).
77. Ibid., 145–154.
78. MacFarquhar (1997, 33–36).
79. State Statistical Bureau (1983, 126).
80. Ibid., 103; Brown (2012, 77–107).
81. State Statistical Bureau (1983, 213).
82. Estimates for the Soviet famine range from 5.7 to 8.5 million (Davies and Wheatcroft 2004, 414–415). As percentages of the population, the two famines were of roughly equal severity.
83. Lardy (1987a, 395).

9. Toward the Cultural Revolution

1. MacFarquhar (1997, 13–19).
2. Ibid., 12–13; excerpts from the "Twelve Points on Agriculture" are translated in Yang (2012, 437). These measures were extended and formalized in the "Sixty Articles on Agriculture" in 1961 (MacFarquhar 1997, 45–48, 63–65).
3. Yang (2012, 437–438), Central Documents Research Office (1996, 364–367).
4. The political secretaries included Tian Jiaying, Hu Qiaomu, and Chen Boda (Yang 2012, 61, 436).
5. MacFarquhar (1997, 39–43, 48–63).
6. Ibid., 61–120.

7. Ibid., 137–145.
8. Ibid., 145–152.
9. Ibid., 152–158.
10. Yang (2012, 502).
11. Lieberthal (1987, 325–331), MacFarquhar (1997, 158–168), Yang (2012, 502–503).
12. Yang (2012, 505).
13. Ibid., 508.
14. MacFarquhar (1997, 209–233).
15. The conversation was reported in a biography of Liu Shaoqi written by his wife and son, as translated in Yang (2012, 506–507). See also Dikötter (2010, 337). The "Three Red Banners" is a slogan that stood for the General Line, the Great Leap Forward, and the people's communes. It embodied Mao's emphasis on pushing forward the pace of economic development as fast as possible (Yang 2012, 87).
16. Goldman (1987, 432–444).
17. Ibid., 436; MacFarquhar (1997, 244–248).
18. MacFarquhar (1997, 234–235).
19. Goldman (1969, 59–60).
20. Goldman (1987, 437–438).
21. Goldman (1969, 62–63).
22. Fung (1982, 82–110).
23. Goldman (1969, 61–63).
24. Ibid., 69–73.
25. MacFarquhar (1997, 155–157).
26. Cheek (1997, 176–187).
27. Goldman (1969, 79–83; 1987, 442–447), MacFarquhar (1997, 250–252).
28. MacFarquhar (1997, 254–256).
29. Goldman (1969, 74).
30. Goldman (1981, 32–36), MacFarquhar (1997, 252–253).
31. Lieberthal (1987, 331–335), MacFarquhar (1997, 274–281).
32. Yang (2012, 510–511).
33. MacFarquhar (1997, 283–286).
34. Yang (2012, 512).
35. Guo and Lin (2005, 9–29).
36. Ibid., 30–99; MacFarquhar (1997, 334–348).
37. Brown (2012, 111–136), Chan, Madsen, and Unger (1984, 37–73), Guo and Lin (2005, 99–156), MacFarquhar (1997, 403–407).
38. Guo and Lin (2005, 156–187, 204–252).
39. MacFarquhar (1997, 410–415).
40. Lüthi (2008, 285–301).
41. Brown (2009, 264–265), MacFarquhar (1997, 416–417), Taubman (2003, 3–17, 614–619).
42. Guo and Lin (2005, 253–274).

43. MacFarquhar (1997, 419–425), Yang (2012, 516–517).

44. Guo and Lin (2005, 274–296), MacFarquhar (1997, 425–428).

45. MacFarquhar (1997, 409–410).

46. This account is based on Dong and Walder (2011a, 18–19).

47. The account in these paragraphs is based on Walder (2006, 1025–1027). See also Guo and Lin (2005, 187–203).

48. This was a general pattern across the country—cleavages opened up during the later phases of the Socialist Education Movement folded directly into grassroots conflicts in the early stages of the Cultural Revolution (Guo and Lin 2005, 296–349).

49. Lüthi (2008, 236–245).

50. Ibid.; MacFarquhar (1997, 353–354).

51. Lüthi (2008, 260–272), MacFarquhar (1997, 349–350).

52. MacFarquhar (1997, 360–362).

53. Ibid., 363.

54. Ibid., 363–364.

55. MacFarquhar and Schoenhals (2006, 15–17).

56. Leese (2011, 122–124), MacFarquhar (1997, 382–384, 439–440).

57. Leese (2011, 94–107). A full account of the compilation, printing, and distribution of the little red book is in Leese (2011, 108–122).

58. MacFarquhar (1974, 148, 165).

59. MacFarquhar (1997, 439–440), Walder (2009, 15–16).

60. See Chapter 2; and Walder (2009, 16).

61. MacFarquhar (1997, 434–435).

62. Ibid., 447–448; MacFarquhar and Schoenhals (2006, 19–20, 36–37).

63. MacFarquhar (1997, 448–450), MacFarquhar and Schoenhals (2006, 20–27).

64. MacFarquhar (1974, 180–184, 195–196, 202–207, 270–273).

65. MacFarquhar (1997, 445–447), MacFarquhar and Schoenhals (2006, 17–18).

66. MacFarquhar and Schoenhals (2006, 34–35).

67. Ibid., 38–44.

68. Ibid., 48–51.

10. Fractured Rebellion

1. MacFarquhar and Schoenhals (2006, 156–160).

2. Ibid., 43–44.

3. The same fate befell the CCP's International Liaison Department (handling relations with other communist parties) and Central Investigation Department (which directed the intelligence community) (ibid., 95–98).

4. Kang Sheng and Chen Boda, the two highest-ranking figures, were alternate members of the Politburo in May 1966.

5. For more biographical detail on these individuals, and more detail on the evolution of the CCRG, see Walder (2009, 14–18).

6. MacFarquhar and Schoenhals (2006, 100–101).

7. Ibid., 98–99.

8. This paragraph and the next are based on MacFarquhar and Schoenhals (2006, 277, 281–284) and Schoenhals (1996).

9. Schoenhals (2008a).

10. MacFarquhar and Schoenhals (2006, 79–81), Walder (2009, 169–170).

11. Walder (2009, 154–171).

12. Leese (2011, 129–134).

13. Walder (2009, 148–150).

14. MacFarquhar and Schoenhals (2006, 56–57).

15. Walder (2006, 1025–1026; 2009, 35–36).

16. Walder (2006, 1027–1028; 2009, 36–37).

17. Dong and Walder (2011a, 11–12).

18. It is plausible to assume that Mao was setting up Liu Shaoqi for a fall; he had a good idea how Liu would attempt to implement his campaign, given his earlier approach to the Socialist Education Movement, and did not object to the sending of work teams and refused to state clearly either his support or opposition to sending them (MacFarquhar and Schoenhals 2006, 63–65, 76–78, 81–85).

19. The evidence for this conclusion is in Walder (2009, 28–58).

20. Ibid., 56–57.

21. Ibid., 37–38; similar figures were reported at a series of other major universities in the capital (ibid., 38–57).

22. This account is based on Walder (2006, 1028–1029; 2009, 61–62).

23. Walder (2009, 62–63, 70–84).

24. MacFarquhar and Schoenhals (2006, 81–84).

25. This summarizes a much longer analysis in Walder (2009, 88–119).

26. Ibid., 129–135; Mao's full statement is at 133–134.

27. MacFarquhar and Schoenhals (2006, 106–110), Walder (2009, 134–135).

28. Chan, Rosen, and Unger (1980), Rosen (1982, 109–118), Walder (2009, 136–138).

29. Walder (2009, 137–142).

30. Based on entries in Wang (2004), who details twenty such cases during this period.

31. This summarizes a longer presentation in Walder (2009, 142–145). In Shanghai during September there were 354 beating deaths and 704 suicides, and high school students beat more than 10,000 people, severely injuring almost 1,000 (Perry and Li 1997, 11–12). See also MacFarquhar and Schoenhals (2006, 117–131) for a longer account of Red Guard activities during this period of "red terror" nationwide.

32. Walder (2009, 145).

33. Ibid., 146.

34. The next several paragraphs are based on ibid., 148–150.
35. The next several paragraphs are based on ibid., 150–153.
36. The following paragraphs are based on ibid., 119–122.
37. The following paragraphs are based on ibid., 156–157.
38. The next few paragraphs are based on ibid., 157–163; also MacFarquhar and Schoenhals (2006, 133–135).
39. Walder (2009, 67–73).
40. MacFarquhar and Schoenhals (2006, 135).
41. Walder (2009, 164–166).
42. MacFarquhar and Schoenhals (2006, 136–140).
43. Walder (2009, 167–171).
44. The next several paragraphs summarize a much longer account in ibid., 174–184.
45. Ibid., 184–186.
46. Walder (2006, 1032–1034; 2009, 106–107).
47. The following paragraphs are based on Walder (2009, 186–200).
48. Ibid., 201–202.
49. This section is based on ibid., 203–217.
50. Ibid., 204–207.

11. Collapse and Division

1. MacFarquhar and Schoenhals (2006, 141).
2. Perry and Li (1997, 31–33, 45–47). Nie Yuanzi of Peking University also spent several weeks in Shanghai beginning in mid-November, during which she encouraged rebellion against the Shanghai party leadership (Walder 2006, 1034; Wang 2001, 754–762).
3. Perry and Li (1997, 32–36).
4. MacFarquhar and Schoenhals (2006, 142–144).
5. State Statistical Bureau (1983, 123).
6. Walder (1996).
7. Perry and Li (1997, 71–85). Similar developments are reported in Hangzhou and Wuhan by Forster (1990, 20–29) and Wang (1995, 90–94).
8. Dong and Walder (2011a, 18–22). Divisions among factory party officials also defined the cleavages that split worker factions in Shanghai, cleavages that were opened up and exacerbated during the Socialist Education Movement (Perry and Li 1997, 30–31, 45–47, 132–136).
9. Perry and Li (1997, 97–111), Walder (1978, 39–46). Forster (1990, 27–28) and Wang (1995, 112–113) allude to similar trends in Hangzhou and Wuhan.
10. For examples, see Dong and Walder (2011b, 428–430), Perry and Li (1997, 17–18, 86), and Walder (2009, 203–207).
11. See Dong and Walder (2010, 679–680), Forster (1990, 24–32), Walder (1978, 35–36).

12. Perry and Li (1997, 86–88, 114–116), Walder (1978, 46–50).
13. MacFarquhar and Schoenhals (2006, 163–164), Walder (1978, 51–57).
14. MacFarquhar and Schoenhals (2006, 164–165), Perry and Li (1997, 89).
15. MacFarquhar and Schoenhals (2006, 165–166).
16. Ibid., 166–169; Perry and Li (1996, 126–127), Walder (1978, 60–63). In 1976, these three leaders, along with Mao's wife Jiang Qing, were purged and labeled the Gang of Four.
17. Walder (1978, 51–63).
18. Perry and Li (1997, 20–21), Walder (1978, 60).
19. Perry and Li (1997, 119–144), Walder (1978, 58–59).
20. Bu (2008, 390–392). MacFarquhar and Schoenhals (2006, 171) report that Pan originally put the leader of a mass organization in the top spot, but this was overruled by Beijing.
21. Dong and Walder (2010, 678–682).
22. Bu (2008, 306–307, 383–390), Central Documents Research Office (1998, 124–125), Wang (2001, 750–753).
23. Dong and Walder (2010).
24. Yan (2014).
25. MacFarquhar and Schoenhals (2006, 175–177).
26. See, for example, Dong and Walder (2011b).
27. Dong and Walder (2011a, 2011b), MacFarquhar and Schoenhals (2006, 177–181), Yan (2014).
28. MacFarquhar and Schoenhals (2006, 191–197).
29. Ibid., 180–182.
30. This account is based on Dong and Walder (2010, 2011b).
31. This account is based on Yan (2014).
32. A parallel split developed in the rebel forces in Hangzhou. The alliance that clashed with the armed forces and subsequently opposed military control was known as the United Headquarters, and the rebels who avoided clashes with the military and later supported their actions became known as Red Storm (Bu 2008, 414–416; Forster 1990, 29–33; Jin 2000, 242–246).
33. Wang (1995, 113–121).
34. Ibid., 121–128.
35. Ibid., 128–132.
36. Ibid., 138–141.
37. Ibid., 144–146, 148.
38. Ibid., 147–148.
39. MacFarquhar and Schoenhals (2006, 206–208), Wang (1995, 149–150).
40. MacFarquhar and Schoenhals (2006, 208–210), Wang (1995, 150–154).
41. MacFarquhar and Schoenhals (2006, 210–212), Wang (1995, 154–157).
42. MacFarquhar and Schoenhals (2006, 212–214), Wang (1995, 165–166).
43. Wang (1995, 170–175).
44. MacFarquhar and Schoenhals (2006, 214–216), Schoenhals (2005, 279–282, 284–289), Wang (1995, 161–163).

45. MacFarquhar and Schoenhals (2006, 217).
46. Schoenhals (2005, 292–293).
47. Dong and Walder (2011b).
48. Guangdong Annals Editorial Committee (2005, 595–597), Hai (1971, 150–175).
49. Forster (1990, 44–50).
50. Dong and Walder (2011b).
51. Forster (1990, 47–48).
52. MacFarquhar and Schoenhals (2006, 229–233), Schoenhals (2005, 296).
53. Dong and Walder (2011b, 437–438).
54. Schoenhals (2005, 297).
55. Dong and Walder (2011b, 438).
56. This account is based on Dong and Walder (2012a).
57. MacFarquhar and Schoenhals (2006, 244–245).
58. Su (2011).
59. Guangxi Cultural Revolution Chronology Editorial Group (1990, 116–117).
60. Ibid., 125.
61. MacFarquhar and Schoenhals (2006, 245–246).
62. Dong and Walder (2012b, 901).
63. Walder (2009, 204–222).
64. Ibid., 223–242.
65. This account of the final battles at Peking and Tsinghua universities is based on ibid., 242–245.
66. This account of Mao's encounter with the Red Guard leaders is based on ibid., 245–247.

12. Military Rule

1. This account is based on Walder (2006, 1044–1045; 2009, 247–248).
2. This account is based on Walder (2009, 248–249). Andreas (2009, 138–142) describes the imposition of propaganda team control at the university.
3. See Andreas (2006) for a description of this period.
4. This account of Jiangsu Province is based on Dong and Walder (2012a, 24–29).
5. Forster (1990, 56–91) describes a similar process in Zhejiang Province and its capital of Hangzhou.
6. This camp is described in Yue and Wakeman (1985, 251–273). For a memoir of an intellectual's experience in a Henan Province camp, see Yang (1984).
7. State Statistical Bureau (1983, 511).
8. Andreas (2009, 188–210).
9. Bernstein (1977a, 36–44), White (1978; 1979).
10. Bernstein (1977a, 121–171; 1977b), Unger (1982).
11. China Education Yearbook (1984, 969).

12. Brown (2012, 137–168) describes the practice and its impact in the city; for deportation figures, see pp. 139 and 144.
13. Contemporary China Editorial Office (1993, 262).
14. Contemporary China Editorial Office (1989, 148).
15. Contemporary China Editorial Office (1990, 607).
16. Contemporary China Editorial Office (1991a, 109).
17. Contemporary China Editorial Office (1991b, 118).
18. Schoenhals (1996, 109).
19. MacFarquhar and Schoenhals (2006, 257–258).
20. Ibid., 254–255.
21. Ibid., 255–256.
22. Walder (2006, 1044–1045), Wang (2006). This period at the university is described in Yue and Wakeman (1985, 233–250).
23. See the range of examples in MacFarquhar and Schoenhals (2006, 256–262).
24. Xu (1990).
25. Contemporary China Editorial Office (1991b, 118).
26. MacFarquhar and Schoenhals (2006, 259–260).
27. Walder (2014).
28. Leese (2011, 210–219).
29. MacFarquhar and Schoenhals (2006, 262).
30. Ibid., 263.
31. Leese (2011, 195–202).
32. Urban (1971, 1–27).
33. Leese (2011, 187–194).
34. Baum (1969), Leese (2011, 219–221).
35. The following account is based on Chau (2010, 257–259).
36. Leese (2011, 221).
37. A book produced in conjunction with a museum exhibition about the mango phenomenon covers the episode in considerable detail, with photographs of mango worship and the entire range of mango-related artifacts (Murck 2013, 113–233). The plot of the 1976 film *Song of the Mangoes* is detailed by Chau (2013).
38. Leese (2011, 204–206), MacFarquhar and Schoenhals (2006, 264).
39. Leese (2011, 174, 206–207).
40. Ibid., 207.
41. Ibid., 226–231.
42. MacFarquhar and Schoenhals (2006, 302).
43. Ibid., 306–307.
44. Walder (2014).
45. MacFarquhar and Schoenhals (2006, 221–233).
46. Walder (2009, 248–249).
47. Wang (1995, 224–225).

48. Dong and Walder (2012b, 900–901).
49. Ibid., 901, 905.

13. Discord and Dissent

1. Teiwes and Sun (2007, 31–32). Mao's collapse during treatment of his lung infection in January 1972 was nearly fatal (MacFarquhar and Schoenhals 2006, 356).
2. Teiwes and Sun (1996) convincingly make the case for this view.
3. MacFarquhar and Schoenhals (2006, 300).
4. See Jin (1999, 163–199), Leese (2011, 231–237), MacFarquhar and Schoenhals (2006, 325–336), Teiwes and Sun (2007, 31–34).
5. MacFarquhar and Schoenhals (2006, 337–339), Teiwes and Sun (2007, 34–35).
6. Kau (1975, 81, 84).
7. Ibid., 84.
8. Ibid., 83.
9. Ibid., 89.
10. Ibid., 83–84. Chin Shi-huang (or Qin Shi Huang) was the founder of the first Chinese dynasty. Widely credited with uniting China for the first time through armed force, he became an arbitrary despot, slaughtering educated officials, and his dynasty soon collapsed.
11. According to Teiwes and Sun (2007, 35), at least one important Politburo member, Ji Dengkui, opposed distributing the material, given the highly unflattering portrait of Mao that it contained. Ever unpredictable, Mao overruled Ji and ordered the material distributed nationwide.
12. Leese (2011, 238–239).
13. MacFarquhar and Schoenhals (2006, 339–347).
14. Ibid., 360–365; Teiwes and Sun (2007, 42–85).
15. MacFarquhar and Schoenhals (2006, 358–360).
16. Forster (1990, 116–118).
17. Teiwes and Sun (2007, 85–109, 132–146), Vogel (2011, 61–79).
18. Forster (1990, 118), Goldman (1975), MacFarquhar and Schoenhals (2006, 366–373).
19. MacFarquhar and Schoenhals (2006, 358–373), Teiwes and Sun (2007, 110–118, 146–171).
20. Teiwes and Sun (2007, 111, 172–178).
21. Forster (1990, 110–114).
22. Ibid., 120–128.
23. Ibid., 133–139.
24. Ibid., 144–145.
25. Ibid., 148–151.
26. Ibid., 152–155, 163–164.

27. Ibid., 155–159, 172.
28. The account of Nanjing in these paragraphs is based on Dong and Walder (2012b).
29. Ibid., 902.
30. Chan, Rosen, and Unger (1985, 9–16, 31–86).
31. Ibid., 2–6. The pen name borrowed one character from the names of each of three coauthors: *Li* Zhengtian, Chen *Yi*yang, and Wang Xi*zhe*.
32. Ibid., 9–12; Rosen (1985, 4–5).
33. Chan, Rosen, and Unger (1985, 6–9).
34. Leese (2011, 243–244).
35. A full translation of the essay is available in Chan, Rosen, and Unger (1985, 32–85).
36. Ibid., 10–13. Moody (1977, 209–216) was one of the first to summarize the essay and provide an analysis.
37. Chan, Rosen, and Unger (1985, 16–28), Rosen (1985).
38. Chan, Rosen, and Unger (1985, 13–28) detail the subsequent careers of the authors, who were arrested and imprisoned shortly after Mao's death, finally to be released from prison and exonerated in 1979.
39. Forster (1990, 164–172), Teiwes and Sun (2007, 197–199).
40. MacFarquhar and Schoenhals (2006, 381–382).
41. Ibid., 388–391; Vogel (2011, 97–98).
42. Vogel (2011, 121).
43. Ibid., 103–109.
44. MacFarquhar and Schoenhals (2006, 382–387), Vogel (2011, 109–114).
45. Forster (1990, 198–219; 1992), MacFarquhar and Schoenhals (2006, 386–387).
46. MacFarquhar and Schoenhals (2006, 400–402), Teiwes and Sun (2007, 324–348), Vogel (2011, 125–133, 137–140).
47. Teiwes and Sun (2007, 363–381, 388–399) trace the shift in Mao's attitude in detail, and see the dispute over higher education at Tsinghua University, one of Mao's favored model units, and the intervention of Mao's nephew Mao Yuanxin, a radical leader in Liaoning Province, as decisive in crystallizing Mao's views. See also MacFarquhar and Schoenhals (2006, 404–412) and Vogel (2011, 140–151).
48. MacFarquhar and Schoenhals (2006, 414–417).
49. Teiwes and Sun (2007, 416–426).
50. Dong and Walder (2014), Forster (1990, 235–242), Wang (1995, 258–265).
51. Heilmann (1993, 1996), MacFarquhar and Schoenhals (2006, 349–352).
52. MacFarquhar and Schoenhals (2006, 420–422).
53. This account of the Nanjing events is based Dong and Walder (2014), Garside (1981, 110–114), and Louie and Louie (1981).
54. Louie and Louie (1981, 339); also Zweig (1978).
55. The account in these two paragraphs is based on Dong and Walder (2014).
56. Wu (2002, 22).

57. Yan and Gao (1996, 492).
58. Forster (1986).
59. Louie and Louie (1981).
60. This account is based on Teiwes and Sun (2004; 2007, 471–475) and Mac-Farquhar and Schoenhals (2006, 422–427). See also Garside (1981, 115–135) and Yan and Gao (1996, 492–501).
61. Garside (1981, 127).
62. Teiwes and Sun (2007, 489).
63. MacFarquhar and Schoenhals (2006, 427–430).
64. Heilmann (1994, 46–53), MacFarquhar and Schoenhals (2006, 431–432).
65. Dong and Walder (2014), Forster (1990), MacFarquhar and Schoenhals (2006, 434).
66. Teiwes and Sun (2007, 551–552), Vogel (2011, 174–175).
67. Teiwes and Sun (2007, 536–568, 572–579).
68. Ibid., 570–571.
69. Ibid., 579–580.
70. Ibid., 584–585. MacFarquhar and Schoenhals (2006, 443–449) offer an account of the planning and the arrest that differs only in details.
71. Quoted in Teiwes and Sun (2007, 595).
72. Quoted in MacFarquhar and Schoenhals (2006, 3).

14. The Mao Era in Retrospect

1. Quoted in Lardy and Lieberthal (1983, xi).
2. Banister (1984, 254), Henderson (1993).
3. State Statistical Bureau (1983, 13).
4. Calculated from data in Figure 14.1.
5. State Statistical Bureau (1983, 339).
6. The data in this paragraph and the next are from http://data.worldbank.org/data-catalog/world-development-indicators.
7. Walder (1986, 195).
8. Ibid., 179–186, 194–205.
9. State Statistical Bureau (1983, 339).
10. Walder (1986, 194–196).
11. Riskin (1987, 249).
12. The Soviet Union and Eastern Europe had long since become predominantly urban economies, and without the enormous rural population of China, they had never exercised similarly strict control over population movements. The freer movement of the population reduced income differences between rural and urban populations.
13. World Bank (1983, 101), adjusting China's 1979 figures for the 19 percent increase over 1977.
14. Oi (2008, 3).
15. Mitter (2013, 5–6).

16. Davies and Wheatcroft (2004, 414–415). Based on an estimated Soviet population of 150 million in 1933, the famine's death toll ranged from 3.8 to 5.7 percent of the population. China's 30 million famine deaths represented 4.6 percent of a population of 653 million. The estimates for the Soviet famine range so widely because, unlike China, the Soviet Union had no census for the period preceding and immediately following the event, forcing historians to rely on extrapolations from incomplete archival records.

17. Walder (2014).

18. The death toll of the Cultural Revolution is roughly of the same magnitude as Stalin's "great terror" of 1937–1938, during which an estimated 800,000 to 1.2 million died. However, due to the large differences in the base populations, the Soviet figures represent a death rate due to political persecution that is at least five times that of China during the Cultural Revolution (ibid.).

19. Walder (1991).

20. Teiwes and Sun (2011; 2013).

21. See Baum (1994).

References

Aird, John S. 1982. "Population Studies and Population Policy in China." *Population and Development Review* 8: 267–297.

Andreas, Joel. 2006. "Institutionalized Rebellion: Governing Tsinghua University during the Late Years of the Chinese Cultural Revolution." *China Journal*, no. 55: 1–28.

———. 2009. *Rise of the Red Engineers: The Cultural Revolution and the Origins of China's New Class.* Stanford, Calif.: Stanford University Press.

Applebaum, Anne. 2012. *Iron Curtain: The Crushing of Eastern Europe, 1944–1956.* New York: Doubleday.

Apter, David E., and Tony Saich. 1994. *Revolutionary Discourse in Mao's Republic.* Cambridge, Mass.: Harvard University Press.

Ash, Robert. 2006. "Squeezing the Peasants: Grain Extraction, Food Consumption and Rural Living Standards in Mao's China." *China Quarterly*, no. 188: 959–998.

Ashton, Basil, Kenneth Hill, Alan Piazza, and Robin Zeitz. 1984. "Famine in China, 1958–61." *Population and Development Review* 10: 613–645.

Averill, Stephen C. 1995. "The Origins of the Futian Incident." In *New Perspectives on the Chinese Communist Revolution,* edited by Tony Saich and Hans van de Ven, 79–115. Armonk, N.Y.: M. E. Sharpe.

———. 2006. *Revolution in the Highlands: China's Jinggangshan Base Area.* Lanham, Md.: Rowman and Littlefield.

Banister, Judith. 1984. "An Analysis of Recent Data on the Population of China." *Population and Development Review* 10: 241–271.

———. 1987. *China's Changing Population.* Stanford, Calif.: Stanford University Press.

Baran, Paul A., and Paul M. Sweezy. 1966. *Monopoly Capital: An Essay on the American Economic and Social Order.* New York: Monthly Review Press.

Baring, Arnulf. 1972. *Uprising in East Germany: June 17, 1953,* translated by Gerald Onn. Ithaca, N.Y.: Cornell University Press.

Barkan, Lenore. 1990. "Patterns of Power: Forty Years of Elite Politics in a Chinese County." In *Chinese Local Elites and Patterns of Dominance,* edited by Joseph W. Esherick and Mary Backus Rankin, 191–215. Berkeley: University of California Press.

Barnett, A. Doak. 1966. "Social Stratification and Aspects of Personnel Management in the Chinese Communist Bureaucracy." *China Quarterly,* no. 28: 8–39.

Baum, Richard. 1969. "China: Year of the Mangoes." *Asian Survey* 9: 1–17.

———. 1994. *Burying Mao: Chinese Politics in the Age of Deng Xiaoping.* Princeton, N.J.: Princeton University Press.

Baylis, Thomas A. 1974. *The Technical Intelligentsia and the East German Elite: Legitimacy and Social Change in Mature Communism.* Berkeley: University of California Press.

Benton, Gregor. 1975. "The 'Second Wang Ming Line' (1935–1938)." *China Quarterly,* no. 61: 61–94.

———. 1992. *Mountain Fires: The Red Army's Three-Year War in South China, 1934–1938.* Berkeley: University of California Press.

———. 1999. *New Fourth Army: Communist Resistance along the Yangtze and the Huai, 1938–1941.* Berkeley: University of California Press.

Benton, Gregor, and Alan Hunter, eds. 1995. *Wild Lily, Prairie Fire: China's Road to Democracy, Yan'an to Tian'anmen, 1942–1989.* Princeton, N.J.: Princeton University Press.

Berliner, Joseph S. 1957. *Factory and Manager in the USSR.* Cambridge, Mass.: Harvard University Press.

Bernstein, Thomas P. 1967. "Leadership and Mass Mobilisation in the Soviet and Chinese Collectivisation Campaigns of 1929–30 and 1955–56: A Comparison." *China Quarterly,* no. 31: 1–47.

———. 1968. "Problems of Village Leadership after Land Reform." *China Quarterly,* no. 36: 1–22.

———. 1969. "Cadre and Peasant Behavior under Conditions of Insecurity and Deprivation: The Grain Supply Crisis of the Spring of 1955." In *Chinese Communist Politics in Action,* edited by A. Doak Barnett, 365–399. Seattle: University of Washington Press.

———. 1977a. *Up to the Mountains and Down to the Villages: The Transfer of Youth from Urban to Rural China.* New Haven, Conn.: Yale University Press.

———. 1977b. "Urban Youth in the Countryside: Problems of Adaptation and Remedies." *China Quarterly,* no. 69: 75–108.

———. 1984. "Stalinism, Famine, and Chinese Peasants: Grain Procurements during the Great Leap Forward." *Theory and Society* 13: 339–377.

———. 2006. "Mao Zedong and the Famine of 1959–1960: A Study in Wilfulness." *China Quarterly,* no. 186: 421–445.

Bian, Yanjie, Xiaoling Shu, and John R. Logan. 2001. "Communist Party Membership and Regime Dynamics in China." *Social Forces* 79: 805–841.

Brandt, Conrad. 1958. *Stalin's Failure in China, 1924–1927.* Cambridge, Mass.: Harvard University Press.

Brook, Timothy. 2010. *The Troubled Empire: China in the Yuan and Ming Dynasties.* Cambridge, Mass.: Belknap Press of Harvard University Press.

Brown, Archie. 2009. *The Rise and Fall of Communism.* New York: Ecco.

Brown, Jeremy. 2007. "From Resisting Communists to Resisting America: Civil War and Korean War in Southwest China, 1950–51." In *Dilemmas of Victory: The Early Years of the People's Republic of China,* edited by Jeremy Brown and Paul G. Pickowicz, 105–129. Cambridge, Mass.: Harvard University Press.

———. 2011. "Great Leap City: Surviving the Famine in Tianjin." In *Eating Bitterness: New Perspectives on China's Great Leap Forward and Famine,* edited by Kimberly Ens Manning and Felix Wemheuer, 226–250. Vancouver: University of British Columbia Press.

———. 2012. *City versus Countryside in Mao's China: Negotiating the Divide.* Cambridge: Cambridge University Press.

———. 2015. "Moving Targets: Changing Class Labels in Rural Hebei and Henan." In *Maoism at the Grass Roots: Everyday Life in China's Era of High Socialism,* edited by Jeremy Brown and Matthew Johnson. Cambridge, Mass.: Harvard University Press.

Bruce, Gary. 2003. *Resistance with the People: Repression and Resistance in Eastern Germany, 1945–1955.* Lanham, Md.: Rowman and Littlefield.

Bu Weihua. 2008. *Zhonghua renmin gongheguo shi: Di 6 juan. "Zalan jiu shijie": Wenhua da geming de dongluan yu haojie, 1966–1968* [History of the People's Republic of China, vol. 6, "Smashing the old world": The catastrophic turmoil of the Cultural Revolution, 1966–1968]. Hong Kong: Zhongwen daxue chubanshe.

Burns, John. 1981. "Rural Guangdong's 'Second Economy,' 1962–1974." *China Quarterly,* no. 88: 629–643.

Central Documents Research Office, ed. 1996. *Jianguo yilai Mao Zedong wengao, di jiuce, 1960.1–1961.12* [Mao Zedong's manuscripts since the founding of the state, vol. 9, January 1960–December 1961]. Beijing: Zhongyang wenxian chubanshe.

———, ed. 1998. *Jianguo yilai Mao Zedong wengao, di shi'er ce, 1966.1–1968.12* [Mao Zedong's manuscripts since the founding of the state, vol. 12, January 1966–December 1968]. Beijing: Zhongyang wenxian chubanshe.

Chan, Anita, Richard Madsen, and Jonathan Unger. 1984. *Chen Village: The Recent History of a Peasant Community in Mao's China.* Berkeley: University of California Press.

Chan, Anita, Stanley Rosen, and Jonathan Unger. 1980. "Students and Class Warfare: The Social Roots of the Red Guard Conflict in Guangzhou (Canton)." *China Quarterly,* no. 83: 397–446.

———, eds. 1985. *On Socialist Democracy and the Chinese Legal System: The Li Yizhe Debates.* Armonk, N.Y.: M. E. Sharpe.

Chau, Adam Yuet. 2010. "Mao's Travelling Mangoes: Food as Relic in Revolutionary China." *Past and Present* 206: 256–275.

———. 2013. "Political Awakening through the Magical Fruit: The Film *Song of the Mango.*" In *Mao's Golden Mangoes and the Cultural Revolution,* edited by Alfreda Murck, 78–95. Zurich: Museum Rietberg Zürich and Verlag Scheidegger and Spiess.

Cheek, Timothy. 1984. "The Fading of Wild Lilies: Wang Shiwei and Mao Zedong's *Yan'an Talks* in the First CPC Rectification Movement." *Australian Journal of Chinese Affairs,* no. 11: 25–58.

———. 1997. *Propaganda and Culture in Mao's China: Deng Tuo and the Intelligentsia.* Oxford: Clarendon Press.

Ch'en, Jerome. 1986. "The Communist Movement 1927–1937." In *The Cambridge History of China,* vol. 13, *Republican China, 1912–1949, Part 2,* edited by John K. Fairbank and Albert Feuerwerker, 168–229. Cambridge: Cambridge University Press.

Chen, Jian. 2001. *Mao's China and the Cold War.* Chapel Hill: University of North Carolina Press.

———. 2007. "The Chinese Communist 'Liberation' of Tibet, 1949–51." In *Dilemmas of Victory: The Early Years of the People's Republic of China,* edited by Jeremy Brown and Paul G. Pickowicz, 130–159. Cambridge, Mass.: Harvard University Press.

———. 2015. "The Beginning of the End: 1956 as a Turning Point in Chinese and Cold War History." *Modern China Studies* 22: 98–125.

Chen, Theodore H. E. 1960. *Thought Reform of the Chinese Intellectuals.* Hong Kong: Hong Kong University Press.

Cheng, Tiejun, and Mark Selden. 1994. "The Origins and Social Consequences of China's *Hukou* System." *China Quarterly,* no. 139: 644–668.

———. 1997. "The Construction of Spatial Hierarchies: China's *Hukou* and *Danwei* Systems." In *New Perspectives on State Socialism in China,* edited by Timothy Cheek and Tony Saich, 23–50. Armonk, N.Y.: M. E. Sharpe.

Ch'i, Hsi-sheng. 1976. *Warlord Politics in China, 1916–1928.* Stanford, Calif.: Stanford University Press.

———. 1982. *Nationalist China at War: Military Defeats and Political Collapse, 1937–45.* Ann Arbor: University of Michigan Press.

China Education Yearbook. 1984. *Zhongguo jiaoyu nianjian 1949–1981* [China education yearbook 1949–1981]. Beijing: Zhongguo dabaike quanshu chubanshe.

Ch'ü, T'ung-tsu. 1962. *Local Government in China under the Ch'ing.* Cambridge, Mass.: Harvard University Press.

Coale, Ansley J. 1981. "Population Trends, Population Policy, and Population Studies in China." *Population and Development Review* 7: 85–97.

———. 1984. *Rapid Population Change in China, 1952–1982.* Washington, D.C.: National Academy Press.

Commission of the Central Committee of the Communist Party of the Soviet
Union. 1939. *History of the Communist Party of the Soviet Union (Bolshevik):
Short Course*. New York: International.

Conquest, Robert. 1986. *Harvest of Sorrow: Soviet Collectivization and the Terror-
Famine*. New York: Oxford University Press.

Contemporary China Editoral Office. 1989. *Dangdai Zhongguo de Tianjin* [Con-
temporary China: Tianjin]. Beijing: Zhongguo shehui kexue chubanshe.

———. 1990. *Dangdai Zhongguo de Henan* [Contemporary China, Henan].
Beijing: Zhongguo shehui kexue chubanshe.

———. 1991a. *Dangdai Zhongguo de Hubei* [Contemporary China, Hubei].
Beijing: Dangdai Zhongguo chubanshe.

———. 1991b. *Dangdai Zhongguo de Guangdong* [Contemporary China, Guang-
dong]. Beijing: Dangdai Zhongguo chubanshe.

———. 1993. *Dangdai Zhongguo de Shanghai* [Contemporary China: Shanghai].
Beijing: Dangdai Zhongguo chubanshe.

Croll, Elisabeth. 1984. "Marriage Choice and Status Groups in Contemporary
China." In *Class and Social Stratification in Post-Revolution China*, edited by
James L. Watson, 175–197. Cambridge: Cambridge University Press.

Dai, Qing. 1994. *Wang Shiwei and "Wild Lilies": Rectification and Purges in the
Chinese Communist Party, 1942–1944*, translated by Nancy Liu and Law-
rence R. Sullivan. Armonk, N.Y.: M. E. Sharpe.

Davies, R. W., and Stephen G. Wheatcroft. 2004. *The Years of Hunger: Soviet
Agriculture, 1931–1933*. New York: Palgrave Macmillan.

Davis-Friedmann, Deborah. 1991. *Long Lives: Chinese Elderly and the Communist
Revolution*, exp. ed. Stanford, Calif.: Stanford University Press.

Dickson, Bruce J. 1993. "The Lessons of Defeat: The Reorganization of the
Kuomintang on Taiwan, 1950–52." *China Quarterly*, no. 133: 56–84.

Dikötter, Frank. 2003. "The Emergence of Labour Camps in Shandong
Province, 1942–1950." *China Quarterly*, no. 175: 803–817.

———. 2010. *Mao's Great Famine: The History of China's Most Devastating Catastrophe, 1958–62*. London: Bloomsbury.

———. 2013. *The Tragedy of Liberation: A History of the Chinese Revolution,
1945–57*. London: Bloomsbury.

Dillon, Nara. 2007. "New Democracy and the Demise of Private Charity in
Shanghai." In *Dilemmas of Victory: The Early Years of the People's Republic of
China*, edited by Jeremy Brown and Paul Pickowicz, 80–102. Cambridge,
Mass.: Harvard University Press.

Dittmer, Lowell. 1992. *Sino-Soviet Normalization and Its International Implications, 1945–1990*. Seattle: University of Washington Press.

Dong, Guoqiang, and Andrew G. Walder. 2010. "Nanjing's Failed 'January
Revolution' of 1967: The Inner Politics of a Provincial Power Seizure."
China Quarterly, no. 203: 675–692.

———. 2011a. "Factions in a Bureaucratic Setting: The Origins of Cultural
Revolution Conflict in Nanjing." *China Journal*, no. 65: 1–25.

———. 2011b. "Local Politics in the Chinese Cultural Revolution: Nanjing under Military Control." *Journal of Asian Studies* 70: 425–447.

———. 2012a. "From Truce to Dictatorship: Creating a Revolutionary Committee in Jiangsu." *China Journal*, no. 68: 1–31.

———. 2012b. "Nanjing's 'Second Cultural Revolution' of 1974." *China Quarterly*, no. 212: 893–918.

———. 2014. "Foreshocks: Local Origins of Nanjing's Qingming Demonstrations of 1976." *China Quarterly*, no. 220: 1092–1110.

Doolin, Dennis J., trans. 1964. *Communist China: The Politics of Student Opposition*. Stanford, Calif.: Hoover Institution.

Drea, Edward J., and Hans van de Ven. 2011. "An Overview of Major Military Campaigns during the Sino-Japanese War, 1937–1945." In *The Battle for China: Essays on the Military History of the Sino-Japanese War of 1937–1945*, edited by Mark Peattie, Edward Drea, and Hans van de Ven, 27–47. Stanford, Calif.: Stanford University Press.

Dreyer, Edward L. 1995. *China at War, 1901–1949*. London: Longman.

Duara, Prasenjit. 1990. "Elites and the Structures of Authority in the Villages of North China, 1900–1949." In *Chinese Local Elites and Patterns of Dominance*, edited by Joseph W. Esherick and Mary Backus Rankin, 261–281. Berkeley: University of California Press.

Dunayevskaya, Raya. 1944. "A New Revision of Marxian Economics." *American Economic Review* 34: 531–537.

Eastman, Lloyd E. 1981. "Who Lost China? Chiang Kai-shek Testifies." *China Quarterly*, no. 88: 658–668.

———. 1984. *Seeds of Destruction: Nationalist China in War and Revolution, 1937–1949*. Stanford, Calif.: Stanford University Press.

Ekiert, Grzegorz. 1996. *The State against Society: Political Crises and Their Aftermath in East Central Europe*. Princeton, N.J.: Princeton University Press.

Esherick, Joseph W. 1987. *The Origins of the Boxer Uprising*. Berkeley: University of California Press.

Fitzpatrick, Sheila. 1978. "Cultural Revolution as Class War." In *Cultural Revolution in Russia, 1928–1931*, edited by Sheila Fitzpatrick, 8–40. Bloomington: Indiana University Press.

———. 1979. *Education and Social Mobility in the Soviet Union, 1921–1934*. Cambridge: Cambridge University Press.

———. 1993. "Ascribing Class: The Construction of Social Identity in Soviet Russia." *Journal of Modern History* 65: 745–770.

———. 2005. *Tear Off the Masks! Identity and Imposture in Twentieth-Century Russia*. Princeton, N.J.: Princeton University Press.

Forster, Keith. 1986. "The 1976 Ch'ing-ming Incident in Hangchow." *Issues and Studies* 22, no. 4: 13–33.

———. 1990. *Rebellion and Factionalism in a Chinese Province: Zhejiang, 1966–1976*. Armonk, N.Y.: M. E. Sharpe.

————. 1992. "Spontaneous and Institutional Rebellion in the Cultural Revolution: The Extraordinary Case of Weng Senhe." *Australian Journal of Chinese Affairs,* no. 27: 39–75.

Friedman, Edward, Paul G. Pickowicz, and Mark Selden. 1991. *Chinese Village, Socialist State.* New Haven, Conn.: Yale University Press.

Fung, K. K., ed. 1982. *Social Needs versus Economic Efficiency in China: Sun Yefang's Critique of Socialist Economics.* Armonk, N.Y.: M. E. Sharpe.

Galbiati, Fernando. 1985. *P'eng P'ai and the Hai-Lu-Feng Soviet.* Stanford, Calif.: Stanford University Press.

Gao, James Z. 2004. *The Communist Takeover of Hangzhou: The Transformation of City and Cadre, 1949–1954.* Honolulu: University of Hawai'i Press.

————. 2007. "The Call of the Oases: The 'Peaceful Liberation' of Xinjiang, 1949–53." In *Dilemmas of Victory: The Early Years of the People's Republic of China,* edited by Jeremy Brown and Paul G. Pickowicz, 184–204. Cambridge, Mass.: Harvard University Press.

Gardner, John. 1969. "The *Wu-fan* Campaign in Shanghai: A Study in the Consolidation of Urban Control." In *Chinese Communist Politics in Action,* edited by A. Doak Barnett, 477–539. Seattle: University of Washington Press.

Garside, Roger. 1981. *Coming Alive: China after Mao.* New York: McGraw-Hill.

Gasster, Michael. 1980. "The Republican Revolutionary Movement." In *The Cambridge History of China,* vol. 11, *Late Ch'ing, 1800–1911, Part 2,* edited by John K. Fairbank and Kwang-ching Liu, 463–534. Cambridge: Cambridge University Press.

Gatrell, Peter, and Mark Harrison. 1993. "The Russian and Soviet Economies in Two World Wars: A Comparative View." *Economic History Review, New Series* 46: 425–452.

Goldman, Merle. 1967. *Literary Dissent in Communist China.* Cambridge, Mass.: Harvard University Press.

————. 1969. "The Unique 'Blooming and Contending' of 1961–62." *China Quarterly,* no. 37: 54–83.

————. 1975. "China's Anti-Confucian Campaign, 1973–74." *China Quarterly,* no. 63: 435–462.

————. 1981. *China's Intellectuals: Advise and Dissent.* Cambridge, Mass.: Harvard University Press.

————. 1987. "The Party and the Intellectuals: Phase Two." In *The Cambridge History of China,* vol. 14, *The People's Republic of China, Part 1: The Emergence of Revolutionary China, 1949–1965,* edited by Roderick MacFarquhar and John K. Fairbank, 432–477. Cambridge: Cambridge University Press.

Goldman, René. 1962. "The Rectification Campaign at Peking University: May–June 1957." *China Quarterly,* no. 12: 138–153.

Goldstein, Melvyn C. 1989. *A History of Modern Tibet, 1913–1951: The Demise of the Lamaist State*. Berkeley: University of California Press.

Gregory, Paul R. 2004. *The Political Economy of Stalinism: Evidence from the Soviet Secret Archives*. Cambridge: Cambridge University Press.

Guangdong Annals Editorial Committee. 2005. *Guangdong sheng zhi, dashiji* [Guangdong province annals, chronology]. Guangzhou: Guangdong renmin chubanshe.

Guangxi Cultural Revolution Chronology Editorial Group. 1990. *Guangxi wen'ge dashi nianbiao* [Chronology of the Cultural Revolution in Guangxi]. Nanning: Guangxi renmin chubanshe.

Guillermaz, Jacques. 1972. *A History of the Chinese Communist Party, 1921–1949,* translated by Anne Destenay. New York: Random House.

Guo Dehong, and Lin Xiaobo. 2005. *Siqing yundong shilu* [An account of the Four Cleans Campaign]. Hangzhou: Zhejiang renmin chubanshe.

Hai Feng. 1971. *Guangzhou diqu wen'ge licheng shulüe* [An account of the Cultural Revolution in the Canton area]. Kowloon: Youlian yanjiusuo.

Halpern, Nina P. 1993. "Creating Socialist Economies: Stalinist Political Economy and the Impact of Ideas." In *Ideas and Foreign Policy: Beliefs, Institutions, and Political Change,* edited by Judith Goldstein and Robert O. Keohane, 87–110. Ithaca, N.Y.: Cornell University Press.

Harmsen, Peter. 2013. *Shanghai 1937: Stalingrad on the Yangtze*. Philadelphia: Casemate.

Heilmann, Sebastian. 1993. "The Social Context of Mobilization in China: Factions, Work Units, and Activists during the 1976 April Fifth Movement." *China Information* 8, no. 3: 1–19.

———. 1994. "The Suppression of the April Fifth Movement and the Persecution of 'Counterrevolutionaries' in 1976." *Issues and Studies* 30, no. 1: 37–64.

———. 1996. *Turning Away from the Cultural Revolution: Political Grass-Roots Activism in the Mid-Seventies*. Stockholm: Center for Pacific Asia Studies, Stockholm University.

Henderson, Gail. 1993. "Public Health in China." In *China Briefing, 1992,* edited by William A. Joseph, 87–110. Boulder, Colo.: Westview.

Henderson, Gail E., and Myron S. Cohen. 1984. *The Chinese Hospital: A Socialist Work Unit*. New Haven, Conn.: Yale University Press.

Henriot, Christian. 1995. " 'La Fermeture': The Abolition of Prostitution in Shanghai, 1949–58." *China Quarterly*, no. 142: 467–486.

Hershatter, Gail. 1986. *The Workers of Tianjin, 1900–1949*. Stanford, Calif.: Stanford University Press.

———. 1997. *Dangerous Pleasures: Prostitution and Modernity in Twentieth-Century Shanghai*. Berkeley: University of California Press.

Hinton, William. 1966. *Fanshen: A Documentary of Revolution in a Chinese Village*. New York: Vintage.

Hoffmann, Charles. 1974. *The Chinese Worker*. Albany: State University of New York Press.

Hofheinz, Roy, Jr. 1969. "The Ecology of Chinese Communist Success: Rural Influence Patterns, 1923–45." In *Chinese Communist Politics in Action*, edited by A. Doak Barnett, 3–77. Seattle: University of Washington Press.

———. 1977. *The Broken Wave: The Chinese Communist Peasant Movement, 1922–1928*. Cambridge, Mass.: Harvard University Press.

Hooper, Beverley. 1986. *China Stands Up: Ending the Western Presence, 1948–1950*. Boston: Allen and Unwin.

Hough, Jerry F. 1977. "Party 'Saturation' in the Soviet Union." In *The Dynamics of Soviet Politics*, edited by Paul Cocks, Robert V. Daniels, and Nancy Whittier Heer, 117–133. Cambridge, Mass.: Harvard University Press.

Huenemann, Ralph W. 1966. "Urban Rationing in Communist China." *China Quarterly*, no. 26: 44–57.

Hung, Chang-tai. 2010. "The Anti-Unity Sect Campaign and Mass Mobilization in the Early People's Republic of China." *China Quarterly*, no. 202: 400–420.

Isaacs, Harold R. 1961. *The Tragedy of the Chinese Revolution*, 2nd rev. ed. Stanford, Calif.: Stanford University Press.

Jain, Shail. 1975. *Size Distribution of Income: A Compilation of Data*. Washington, D.C.: World Bank.

Jin, Qiu. 1999. *The Culture of Power: The Lin Biao Incident in the Cultural Revolution*. Stanford, Calif.: Stanford University Press.

Jin Yanfeng, ed. 2000. *Dangdai Zhejiang jianshi, 1949–1998* [Brief history of contemporary Zhejiang, 1949–1998]. Beijing: Dangdai Zhongguo chubanshe.

Johnson, A. Ross. 1972. *The Transformation of Communist Ideology: The Yugoslav Case, 1945–1953*. Cambridge, Mass.: MIT Press.

Johnson, Chalmers A. 1962. *Peasant Nationalism and Communist Power: The Emergence of Revolutionary China*. Stanford, Calif.: Stanford University Press.

Joravsky, David. 1970. *The Lysenko Affair*. Cambridge, Mass.: Harvard University Press.

Kaple, Deborah A. 1994. *Dream of a Red Factory: The Legacy of High Stalinism in China*. New York: Oxford University Press.

Kau, Michael Y. M. 1975. *The Lin Piao Affair: Power Politics and Military Coup*. White Plains, N.Y.: International Arts and Sciences Press.

Kecskemeti, Paul. 1961. *The Unexpected Revolution: Social Forces in the Hungarian Uprising*. Stanford, Calif.: Stanford University Press.

Khrushchev, Nikita S. 1962. "Crimes of the Stalin Era: Special Report to the 20th Congress of the Communist Party of the Soviet Union, February 24–25, 1956." New York: The New Leader. Internet Archive, https://

archive.org/details/TheCrimesOfTheStalinEraSpecialReportToThe
20thCongressOfThe.

Kirby, William C. 1984. *Germany and Republican China.* Stanford, Calif.:
Stanford University Press.

———. 2006. "China's Internationalization in the Early People's Republic:
Dreams of a Socialist World Economy." *China Quarterly,* no. 188: 870–890.

Klochko, Mikhail A. 1964. *Soviet Scientist in Red China,* translated by Andrew
MacAndrew. New York: Praeger.

Knight, Amy. 1993. *Beria, Stalin's First Lieutenant.* Princeton, N.J.: Princeton
University Press.

Kornai, János. 1959. *Overcentralization in Economic Administration: A Critical
Analysis Based on Experience in Hungarian Light Industry,* translated by John
Knapp. Oxford: Oxford University Press.

———. 1979. "Resource-Constrained versus Demand-Constrained Systems."
Econometrica 47: 801–819.

———. 1980. *Economics of Shortage.* Amsterdam: North-Holland.

———. 1992. *The Socialist System: The Political Economy of Communism.*
Princeton, N.J.: Princeton University Press.

Kramer, Mark. 1998. "The Soviet Union and the 1956 Crises in Hungary and
Poland: Reassessments and New Findings." *Journal of Contemporary History*
33: 163–214.

———. 1999. "The Early Post-Stalin Succession Struggle and Upheavals in
East-Central Europe: Internal-External Linkages in Soviet Policy Making
(Part 1)." *Journal of Cold War Studies* 1, no. 1: 3–55.

Kraus, Richard Curt. 1981. *Class Conflict in Chinese Socialism.* New York:
Columbia University Press.

Kuan, Chen, Hongchang Wang, Yuxin Zheng, Gary H. Jefferson, and Thomas
G. Rawski. 1988. "Productivity Change in Chinese Industry: 1953–1985."
Journal of Comparative Economics 12: 570–591.

Kuhn, Philip A. 1978. "The Taiping Rebellion." In *The Cambridge History of
China,* vol. 10, *Late Ch'ing, 1800–1911, Part 1,* edited by John K. Fairbank,
264–317. Cambridge: Cambridge University Press.

———. 1980. *Rebellion and Its Enemies in Late Imperial China: Militarization and
Social Structure, 1796–1864,* 2nd ed. Cambridge, Mass.: Harvard University
Press.

Kung, James Kai-sing, and Justin Yifu Lin. 2003. "The Causes of China's
Great Leap Famine, 1959–1961." *Economic Development and Cultural Change*
52: 51–73.

Lang, Olga. 1946. *Chinese Family and Society.* New Haven, Conn.: Yale University Press.

Lange, Oskar, and Fred M. Taylor. 1964. *On the Economic Theory of Socialism.*
New York: McGraw-Hill.

Lardy, Nicholas R. 1987a. "The Chinese Economy under Stress, 1958–1965."
In *The Cambridge History of China,* vol. 14, *The People's Republic of China,*

Part 1: The Emergence of Revolutionary China, 1949–1965, edited by Roderick MacFarquhar and John K. Fairbank, 360–397. Cambridge: Cambridge University Press.

———. 1987b. "Economic Recovery and the 1st Five-Year Plan." In *The Cambridge History of China*, vol. 14, *The People's Republic of China, Part 1: The Emergence of Revolutionary China, 1949–1965*, edited by Roderick MacFarquhar and John K. Fairbank, 144–184. Cambridge: Cambridge University Press.

Lardy, Nicholas R., and Kenneth Lieberthal, eds. 1983. *Chen Yun's Strategy for China's Development: A Non-Maoist Alternative*, translated by Mao Tong and Du Anxia. Armonk, N.Y.: M. E. Sharpe.

Lee, Hong Yung. 1991. *From Revolutionary Cadres to Party Technocrats in Socialist China*. Berkeley: University of California Press.

Leese, Daniel. 2011. *Mao Cult: Rhetoric and Ritual in China's Cultural Revolution*. Cambridge: Cambridge University Press.

———. 2015. "Revising Political Verdicts in Post-Mao China: The Case of Beijing's Fengtai District." In *Maoism at the Grass Roots: Everyday Life in China's Era of High Socialism*, edited by Jeremy Brown and Matthew Johnson. Cambridge, Mass.: Harvard University Press.

Levine, Steven I. 1987. *Anvil of Victory: The Communist Revolution in Manchuria, 1945–1948.* New York: Columbia University Press.

Lewin, Moshe. 1974. *Political Undercurrents in Soviet Economic Debates: From Bukharin to the Modern Reformers*. Princeton, N.J.: Princeton University Press.

Lewis, John Wilson. 1963. *Leadership in Communist China*. Ithaca, N.Y.: Cornell University Press.

Li, Bobai, and Andrew G. Walder. 2001. "Career Advancement as Party Patronage: Sponsored Mobility into the Chinese Administrative Elite, 1949–1996." *American Journal of Sociology* 106: 1371–1408.

Li, Huaiyin. 2006. "The First Encounter: Peasant Resistance to State Control of Grain in East China in the Mid-1950s." *China Quarterly*, no. 185: 145–162.

———. 2007. "Confrontation and Conciliation under the Socialist State: Peasant Resistance to Agricultural Collectivization in China in the 1950s." *Twentieth-Century China* 33, no. 2: 73–99.

———. 2009. *Village China under Socialism and Reform: A Micro History, 1948–2008*. Stanford, Calif.: Stanford University Press.

Li, Hua-Yu. 2006. *Mao and the Economic Stalinization of China, 1948–1953*. Lanham, Md.: Rowman and Littlefield.

———. 2010. "Instilling Stalinism in Chinese Party Members: Absorbing Stalin's *Short Course* in the 1950s." In *China Learns from the Soviet Union, 1949–Present*, edited by Thomas P. Bernstein and Hua-Yu Li, 107–130. Lanham, Md.: Lexington.

Li, Wei, and Dennis Tao Yang. 2005. "The Great Leap Forward: Anatomy of a Central Planning Disaster." *Journal of Political Economy* 113: 840–877.

Liberman, E. G. 1971. *Economic Methods and the Effectiveness of Production*. White
    Plains, N.Y.: International Arts and Sciences Press.

Lieberthal, Kenneth. 1973. "The Suppression of Secret Societies in Post-
    Liberation Tientsin." *China Quarterly*, no. 54: 242–266.

———. 1980. *Revolution and Tradition in Tientsin, 1949–1952*. Stanford, Calif.:
    Stanford University Press.

———. 1987. "The Great Leap Forward and the Split in the Yenan Leader-
    ship." In *The Cambridge History of China*, vol. 14, *The People's Republic of
    China, Part 1: The Emergence of Revolutionary China, 1949–1965*, edited by
    Roderick MacFarquhar and John K. Fairbank, 293–359. Cambridge:
    Cambridge University Press.

Lin, Cyril Chihren. 1981. "The Reinstatement of Economics in China Today."
    China Quarterly, no. 85: 1–48.

Lin Yunhui. 2009. *Zhonghua renmin gongheguo shi, di 2 juan. Xiang shehuizhuyi
    guodu: Zhongguo jingji yu shehui de zhuanxing, 1953–1955* [History of the
    People's Republic of China, vol. 2, Moving toward the transition to
    socialism: The transformation of China's economy and society, 1953–1955].
    Hong Kong: Zhongwen daxue chubanshe.

Liu, Jianhui, and Hongxu Wang. 2006. "The Origins of the General Line for
    the Transition Period and of the Acceleration of the Chinese Socialist
    Transformation in Summer 1955." *China Quarterly*, no. 187: 724–731.

Liu Shaoqi. (1939) 1984. "How to Be a Good Communist." In *Selected Works of
    Liu Shaoqi*, vol. 1, 107–168. Beijing: Foreign Languages Press.

Louie, Genny, and Kam Louie. 1981. "The Role of Nanjing University in the
    Nanjing Incident." *China Quarterly*, no. 86: 332–348.

Lüthi, Lorenz M. 2008. *The Sino-Soviet Split: Cold War in the Communist World*.
    Princeton, N.J.: Princeton University Press.

MacFarquhar, Roderick, ed. 1960. *The Hundred Flowers Campaign and the
    Chinese Intellectuals*. New York: Praeger.

———. 1974. *The Origins of the Cultural Revolution 1: Contradictions among the
    People, 1956–1957*. New York: Columbia University Press.

———. 1983. *The Origins of the Cultural Revolution 2: The Great Leap Forward,
    1958–1960*. New York: Columbia University Press.

———. 1989. "The Secret Speeches of Chairman Mao." In *The Secret Speeches of
    Chairman Mao: From the Hundred Flowers to the Great Leap Forward*, edited by
    Roderick MacFarquhar, Timothy Cheek, and Eugene Wu, 3–18. Cam-
    bridge, Mass.: Council on East Asian Studies, Harvard University.

———. 1997. *The Origins of the Cultural Revolution 3: The Coming of the Cataclysm,
    1961–1966*. New York: Columbia University Press.

MacFarquhar, Roderick, Timothy Cheek, and Eugene Wu, eds. 1989. *The Secret
    Speeches of Chairman Mao: From the Hundred Flowers to the Great Leap Forward*.
    Cambridge, Mass.: Council on East Asian Studies, Harvard University.

MacFarquhar, Roderick, and Michael Schoenhals. 2006. *Mao's Last Revolution*.
    Cambridge, Mass.: Belknap Press of Harvard University Press.

Machcewicz, Pawel. 2009. *Rebellious Satellite: Poland, 1956,* translated by Maya Latynski. Washington, D.C.: Woodrow Wilson Center Press.

MacKinnon, Stephen. 2011. "The Defense of the Central Yangtze." In *The Battle for China: Essays on the Military History of the Sino-Japanese War of 1937–1945,* edited by Mark Peattie, Edward Drea, and Hans van de Ven, 181–206. Stanford, Calif.: Stanford University Press.

Maddison, Angus. 2006. *The World Economy, Volume 1: A Millennial Perspective; Volume 2: Historical Statistics.* Paris: OECD.

Mao Zedong. 1926a. "An Analysis of the Various Classes among the Chinese Peasantry and Their Attitudes toward the Revolution" (January). In Schram 1994, 303–309.

———. 1926b. "Resolution Concerning the Peasant Movement: Resolution of the Second National Congress of the Chinese Guomindang" (January 19). In Schram 1994, 358–360.

———. 1926c. "Some Points for Attention in Commemorating the Paris Commune" (March 18). In Schram 1994, 365–368.

———. 1926d. "Resolution on the Problem of *Mintuan*" (October 28). In Schram 1994, 409–410.

———. 1926e. "The National Revolution and the Peasant Problem" (September 1). In Schram 1994, 387–392.

———. 1927a. "Report on the Peasant Movement in Hunan" (February). In Schram 1994, 429–464.

———. 1927b. "Report to the Central Committee on Observations Regarding the Peasant Movement in Hunan" (February 16). In Schram 1994, 425–428.

———. 1957. "On the Correct Handling of Contradictions among the People (Speaking Notes)" (February 27). In MacFarquhar, Cheek, and Wu 1989, 131–189.

———. 1977. *A Critique of Soviet Economics,* translated by Moss Roberts. New York: Monthly Review Press.

Marks, Robert. 1984. *Rural Revolution in South China: Peasants and the Making of History in Haifeng County, 1570–1930.* Madison: University of Wisconsin Press.

Martin, Brian G. 1996. *The Shanghai Green Gang: Politics and Organized Crime, 1919–1937.* Berkeley: University of California Press.

Medvedev, Zhores A. 1969. *The Rise and Fall of T. D. Lysenko,* translated by I. Michael Lerner. New York: Columbia University Press.

Milenkovitch, Deborah D. 1971. *Plan and Market in Yugoslav Economic Thought.* New Haven, Conn.: Yale University Press.

Mitter, Rana. 2013. *Forgotten Ally: China's World War II, 1937–1945.* Boston: Houghton Mifflin Harcourt.

Moody, Peter R. 1977. *Opposition and Dissent in Contemporary China.* Stanford, Calif.: Hoover Institution Press.

Moore, Barrington, Jr. 1966. *Social Origins of Dictatorship and Democracy: Lord and Peasant in the Making of the Modern World.* Boston: Beacon.

Murck, Alfreda, ed. 2013. *Mao's Golden Mangoes and the Cultural Revolution.*
    Zurich: Museum Rietberg Zürich and Verlag Scheidegger and Spiess.
Nagy, Imre. 1957. *On Communism: In Defense of the New Course.* New York:
    Praeger.
Nathan, Andrew J. 1976. *Peking Politics 1918–1923: Factionalism and the Failure of
    Constitutionalism.* Berkeley: University of California Press.
———. 1983. "A Constitutional Republic: The Peking Government, 1916–28."
    In *The Cambridge History of China,* vol. 12, *Republican China, 1912–1949,
    Part 1,* edited by John K. Fairbank, 256–283. Cambridge: Cambridge
    University Press.
Nieh, Hualing, ed. 1981a. *Literature of the Hundred Flowers,* vol. 1, *Criticism and
    Polemics.* New York: Columbia University Press.
———. 1981b. *Literature of the Hundred Flowers,* vol. 2, *Poetry and Fiction.* New
    York: Columbia University Press.
Oi, Jean C. 1989. *State and Peasant in Contemporary China: The Political Economy
    of Village Government.* Berkeley: University of California Press.
———. 2008. "Development Strategies, Welfare Regimes, and Poverty
    Reduction in China." Geneva: United Nations Research Institute for
    Social Development.
Oksenberg, Michel. 1968. "The Institutionalisation of the Chinese Revolution:
    The Ladder of Success on the Eve of the Cultural Revolution." *China
    Quarterly,* no. 36: 61–92.
———. 1976. "The Exit Pattern from Chinese Politics and Its Implications."
    China Quarterly, no. 67: 501–518.
Organization Department, Central Communist Party Office for Research on
    Party History, and Central Party Archives. 2000. *Zhongguo gongchandang
    zuzhishi ziliao* [Materials on the organizational history of the Chinese
    Communist Party], 19 vols. Beijing: Zhonggong dangshi chubanshe.
Ostermann, Christian F., ed. 2001. *Uprising in East Germany 1953: The Cold War,
    the German Question, and the First Major Upheaval behind the Iron Curtain.*
    Budapest: Central European University Press.
Paige, Jeffery M. 1975. *Agrarian Revolution: Social Movements and Export
    Agriculture in the Underdeveloped World.* New York: Free Press.
Pantsov, Alexander V., with Steven I. Levine. 2012. *Mao: The Real Story.* New
    York: Simon and Schuster.
Peng, Xizhe. 1987. "Demographic Consequences of the Great Leap Forward in
    China's Provinces." *Population and Development Review* 13: 639–670.
Pepper, Suzanne. 1999. *Civil War in China: The Political Struggle, 1945–1949,* 2nd
    ed. Lanham, Md.: Rowman and Littlefield.
Perry, Elizabeth J. 1993. *Shanghai on Strike: The Politics of Chinese Labor.*
    Stanford, Calif.: Stanford University Press.
———. 1994. "Shanghai's Strike Wave of 1957." *China Quarterly,* no. 137: 1–27.
———. 2007. "Masters of the Country? Shanghai Workers in the Early
    People's Republic." In *Dilemmas of Victory: The Early Years of the People's*

Republic of China, edited by Jeremy Brown and Paul G. Pickowicz, 59–79. Cambridge, Mass.: Harvard University Press.

Perry, Elizabeth J., and Li Xun. 1997. *Proletarian Power: Shanghai in the Cultural Revolution.* Boulder, Colo.: Westview.

Platt, Stephen R. 2012. *Autumn in the Heavenly Kingdom: China, the West, and the Epic Story of the Taiping Civil War.* New York: Alfred A. Knopf.

Riskin, Carl. 1987. *China's Political Economy: The Quest for Development Since 1949.* Oxford: Oxford University Press.

Rosen, Stanley. 1982. *Red Guard Factionalism and the Cultural Revolution in Guangzhou (Canton).* Boulder, Colo.: Westview.

———. 1985. "Guangzhou's Democracy Movement in Cultural Revolution Perspective." *China Quarterly,* no. 101: 1–31.

Rossabi, Morris. 2005. *Modern Mongolia: From Khans to Commissars to Capitalists.* Berkeley: University of California Press.

Rowe, William T. 2007. *Crimson Rain: Seven Centuries of Violence in a Chinese County.* Stanford, Calif.: Stanford University Press.

———. 2009. *China's Last Empire: The Great Qing.* Cambridge, Mass.: Belknap Press of Harvard University Press.

Rusinow, Dennison. 1977. *The Yugoslav Experiment, 1948–1974.* Berkeley: University of California Press.

Saich, Tony, ed. 1996. *The Rise to Power of the Chinese Communist Party: Documents and Analysis.* Armonk, N.Y.: M. E. Sharpe.

Schoenhals, Michael. 1985. "Elite Information in China." *Problems of Communism* 34, no. 5: 65–71.

———. 1986. "Original Contradictions: On the Unrevised Text of Mao Zedong's 'On the Correct Handling of Contradictions among the People.'" *Australian Journal of Chinese Affairs,* no. 16: 99–112.

———. 1996. "The Central Case Examination Group, 1966–79." *China Quarterly,* no. 145: 87–111.

———. 2005. "'Why Don't We Arm the Left?' Mao's Culpability for the Cultural Revolution's 'Great Chaos' of 1967." *China Quarterly,* no. 182: 277–300.

———. 2008a. "Out-Sourcing the Inquisition: 'Mass Dictatorship' in China's Cultural Revolution." *Totalitarian Movements and Political Religions* 9, no. 1: 3–19.

———. 2008b. "The People's Republic of China, 1949–1976." In *Crimes against Humanity under Communist Regimes: Research Review,* edited by Klas-Göran Karlsson and Michael Schoenhals, 67–87. Stockholm: Forum for Living History.

———. 2013. *Spying for the People: Mao's Secret Agents, 1949–1967.* Cambridge: Cambridge University Press.

Schram, Stuart, ed. 1994. *Mao's Road to Power, Revolutionary Writings 1912–1949.* Vol. 2, *National Revolution and Social Revolution, December 1920–June 1927.* Armonk, N.Y.: M. E. Sharpe.

————, ed. 1995. *Mao's Road to Power, Revolutionary Writings 1912–1949.* Vol. 3, *From the Jinggangshan to the Establishment of the Jiangxi Soviets, July 1927–December 1930.* Armonk, N.Y.: M. E. Sharpe.

Schwartz, Benjamin I. 1951. *Chinese Communism and the Rise of Mao.* Cambridge, Mass.: Harvard University Press.

Scott, James C. 1976. *The Moral Economy of the Peasant: Rebellion and Subsistence in Southeast Asia.* New Haven, Conn.: Yale University Press.

Sebestyen, Victor. 2006. *Twelve Days: The Story of the 1956 Hungarian Revolution.* New York: Pantheon.

Selden, Mark. 1971. *The Yenan Way in Revolutionary China.* Cambridge, Mass.: Harvard University Press.

Service, Robert. 2004. *Stalin: A Biography.* Cambridge, Mass.: Belknap Press of Harvard University Press.

Seybolt, Peter J. 1986. "Terror and Conformity: Counterespionage Campaigns, Rectification, and Mass Movements, 1942–1943." *Modern China* 12: 39–73.

Shen Zhihua. 2008. *Zhonghua renmin gongheguo shi, di 3 juan. Sikao yu xuanze: Cong zhishi fenzi huiyi dao fan youpai yundong, 1956–1957* [History of the People's Republic of China, vol. 3, Reflections and choices: The consciousness of Chinese intellectuals and the Anti-Rightist Campaign, 1956–1957]. Hong Kong: Zhongwen daxue chubanshe.

Sheng, Michael M. 2006. "Mao Zedong and the Three-Anti Campaign (November 1951 to April 1952): A Revisionist Interpretation." *Twentieth-Century China* 32, no. 1: 56–80.

Shirk, Susan L. 1982. *Competitive Comrades: Career Incentives and Student Strategies in China.* Berkeley: University of California Press.

Shue, Vivienne. 1980. *Peasant China in Transition: The Dynamics of Development toward Socialism, 1949–1956.* Berkeley: University of California Press.

Šik, Ota. 1966. *Economic Planning and Management in Czechoslovakia,* 2nd rev. ed., translated by M. I. Parker. Prague: Orbis.

————. 1967. *Plan and Market under Socialism*. White Plains, N.Y.: International Arts and Sciences Press.

————. 1972. *Czechoslovakia: The Bureaucratic Economy.* White Plains, N.Y.: International Arts and Sciences Press.

Silbey, David J. 2012. *The Boxer Rebellion and the Great Game in China.* New York: Hill and Wang.

Siu, Helen F. 1989. *Agents and Victims in South China: Accomplices in Rural Revolution.* New Haven, Conn.: Yale University Press.

Skocpol, Theda. 1979. *States and Social Revolutions: A Comparative Analysis of France, Russia, and China.* Cambridge: Cambridge University Press.

So, Bennis Wai-yip. 2002. "The Policy-Making and Political Economy of the Abolition of Private Ownership in the Early 1950s: Findings from New Materials." *China Quarterly,* no. 171: 682–703.

Spence, Jonathan D. 1996. *God's Chinese Son: The Taiping Heavenly Kingdom of Hong Xiuquan.* New York: Norton.

Stacey, Judith. 1983. *Patriarchy and Socialist Revolution in China.* Berkeley: University of California Press.

State Statistical Bureau. 1983. *Zhongguo tongji nianjian 1983* [China statistical yearbook 1983]. Hong Kong: Xianggang jingji daobaoshe.

Stinchcombe, Arthur L. 1965. "Social Structure and Organizations." In *Handbook of Organizations,* edited by James G. March, 142–193. Chicago: Rand McNally.

Strauss, Julia C. 2002. "Paternalist Terror: The Campaign to Suppress Counterrevolutionaries and Regime Consolidation in the People's Republic of China, 1950–1953." *Comparative Studies in Society and History* 44: 80–105.

———. 2006. "Morality, Coercion and State Building by Campaign in the Early PRC: Regime Consolidation and After, 1949–1956." *China Quarterly,* no. 188: 891–912.

Su, Yang. 2011. *Collective Killings in Rural China during the Cultural Revolution.* Cambridge: Cambridge University Press.

Taubman, William. 2003. *Khrushchev: The Man and His Era.* New York: Norton.

Taylor, George E. 1940. *The Struggle for North China.* New York: International Secretariat, Institute of Pacific Relations.

Taylor, Jay. 2011. *The Generalissimo: Chiang Kai-shek and the Struggle for Modern China,* new ed. Cambridge, Mass.: Belknap Press of Harvard University Press.

Teiwes, Frederick C. 1976. "The Origins of Rectification: Inner-Party Purges and Education before Liberation." *China Quarterly,* no. 65: 15–53.

Teiwes, Frederick C., and Warren Sun, eds. 1993. *The Politics of Agricultural Cooperativization in China: Mao, Deng Zihui, and the "High Tide" of 1955.* Armonk, N.Y.: M. E. Sharpe.

———. 1995. "From a Leninist to a Charismatic Party: The CCP's Changing Leadership, 1937–1945." In *New Perspectives on the Chinese Communist Revolution,* edited by Tony Saich and Hans van de Ven, 339–387. Armonk, N.Y.: M. E. Sharpe.

———. 1996. *The Tragedy of Lin Biao: Riding the Tiger during the Cultural Revolution, 1966–1971.* London: Hurst.

———. 1997. "The Politics of an 'Un-Maoist' Interlude: The Case of Opposing Rash Advance, 1956–1957." In *New Perspectives on State Socialism in China,* edited by Timothy Cheek and Tony Saich, 151–190. Armonk, N.Y.: M. E. Sharpe.

———. 1999. *China's Road to Disaster: Mao, Central Politicians, and Provincial Leaders in the Unfolding of the Great Leap Forward, 1955–1959.* Armonk, N.Y.: M. E. Sharpe.

———. 2004. "The First Tiananmen Incident Revisited: Elite Politics and Crisis Management at the End of the Maoist Era." *Pacific Affairs* 77: 211–235.

———. 2007. *The End of the Maoist Era: Chinese Politics during the Twilight of the Cultural Revolution, 1972–1976.* Armonk, N.Y.: M. E. Sharpe.

———. 2011. "China's New Economic Policy under Hua Guofeng: Party Consensus and Party Myths." *China Journal*, no. 66: 1–24.

———. 2013. "China's Economic Reorientation after the Third Plenum: Conflict Surrounding 'Chen Yun's' Readjustment Program, 1979–80." *China Journal*, no. 70: 163–187.

Thaxton, Ralph A., Jr. 1983. *China Turned Rightside Up: Revolutionary Legitimacy in the Peasant World*. New Haven, Conn.: Yale University Press.

———. 2008. *Catastrophe and Contention in Rural China: Mao's Great Leap Famine and the Origins of Righteous Resistance in Da Fo Village*. Cambridge: Cambridge University Press.

Tien, Hung-mao. 1989. *The Great Transition: Political and Social Change in the Republic of China*. Stanford, Calif.: Hoover Institution Press.

Tilly, Charles. 1978. *From Mobilization to Revolution*. Reading, Mass.: Addison-Wesley.

Tucker, Robert C. 1977. "Stalinism as Revolution from Above." In *Stalinism: Essays in Historical Interpretation*, edited by Robert C. Tucker, 77–108. New York: Norton.

———. 1990. *Stalin in Power: The Revolution from Above, 1928–1941*. New York: Norton.

U, Eddy. 2012. "Dangerous Privilege: The United Front and the Rectification Campaign of the Early Mao Years." *China Journal*, no. 68: 32–57.

Unger, Jonathan. 1982. *Education under Mao: Class and Competition in Canton Schools, 1960–1980*. New York: Columbia University Press.

———. 1984. "The Class System in Rural China: A Case Study." In *Class and Social Stratification in Post-Revolution China*, edited by James L. Watson, 121–141. Cambridge: Cambridge University Press.

Urban, George, ed. 1971. *The "Miracles" of Chairman Mao: A Compendium of Devotional Literature, 1966–1970*. Los Angeles: Nash.

van de Ven, Hans. 2011. "The Sino-Japanese War in History." In *The Battle for China: Essays on the Military History of the Sino-Japanese War of 1937–1945*, edited by Mark Peattie, Edward Drea, and Hans van de Ven, 446–466. Stanford, Calif.: Stanford University Press.

Van Slyke, Lyman. 1986. "The Chinese Communist Movement during the Sino-Japanese War 1937–1945." In *The Cambridge History of China*, vol. 13, *Republican China, 1912–1949, Part 2*, edited by John K. Fairbank and Albert Feuerwerker, 609–722. Cambridge: Cambridge University Press.

Vogel, Ezra F. 1965. "From Friendship to Comradeship: The Change in Personal Relations in Communist China." *China Quarterly*, no. 21: 46–60.

———. 1967. "From Revolutionary to Semi-Bureaucrat: The 'Regularisation' of Cadres." *China Quarterly*, no. 29: 36–60.

———. 1969. *Canton under Communism: Programs and Politics in a Provincial Capital, 1949–1968*. Cambridge, Mass.: Harvard University Press.

———. 2011. *Deng Xiaoping and the Transformation of China*. Cambridge, Mass.: Belknap Press of Harvard University Press.

Wakeman, Frederic, Jr. 2007. " 'Cleanup': The New Order in Shanghai." In *Dilemmas of Victory: The Early Years of the People's Republic of China*, edited by Jeremy Brown and Paul G. Pickowicz, 21–58. Cambridge, Mass.: Harvard University Press.

Walder, Andrew G. 1978. *Chang Ch'un-ch'iao and Shanghai's January Revolution.* Ann Arbor: Center for Chinese Studies, University of Michigan.

———. 1986. *Communist Neo-Traditionalism: Work and Authority in Chinese Industry.* Berkeley: University of California Press.

———. 1991. "Cultural Revolution Radicalism: Variations on a Stalinist Theme." In *New Perspectives on the Cultural Revolution,* edited by William A. Joseph, Christine P. W. Wong, and David Zweig, 41–61. Cambridge, Mass.: Council on East Asian Studies, Harvard University.

———. 1992. "Property Rights and Stratification in Socialist Redistributive Economies." *American Sociological Review* 57: 524–539.

———. 1995. "Career Mobility and the Communist Political Order." *American Sociological Review* 60: 309–328.

———. 1996. "The Chinese Cultural Revolution in the Factories: Party-State Structures and Patterns of Conflict." In *Putting Class in Its Place: Worker Identities in East Asia,* edited by Elizabeth J. Perry, 167–198. Berkeley: Center for Chinese Studies, University of California.

———. 2006. "Factional Conflict at Beijing University, 1966–1968." *China Quarterly,* no. 188: 1023–1047.

———. 2009. *Fractured Rebellion: The Beijing Red Guard Movement.* Cambridge, Mass.: Harvard University Press.

———. 2014. "Rebellion and Repression in China, 1966–1971." *Social Science History* 38, no. 4.

Walder, Andrew G., and Songhua Hu. 2009. "Revolution, Reform, and Status Inheritance: Urban China, 1949–1996." *American Journal of Sociology* 114: 1395–1427.

Walder, Andrew G., Bobai Li, and Donald J. Treiman. 2000. "Politics and Life Chances in a State Socialist Regime: Dual Career Paths into the Urban Chinese Elite, 1949 to 1996." *American Sociological Review* 65: 191–209.

Wang, Haiguang. 2015. "Radical Agricultural Collectivization and Ethnic Rebellion: The Communist Encounter with a 'New Emperor' in Guizhou's Mashan Region, 1956." In *Maoism at the Grass Roots: Everyday Life in China's Era of High Socialism,* edited by Jeremy Brown and Matthew Johnson. Cambridge, Mass.: Harvard University Press.

Wang Li. 2001. *Wang Li fansi lu: Wang Li yigao* [Wang Li's Reflections: Wang Li's Manuscripts]. Hong Kong: Beixing chubanshe.

Wang, Peter Chen-main. 1999. "A Bastion Created, a Regime Transformed, an Economy Reengineered, 1949–1970." In *Taiwan: A New History,* edited by Murray A. Rubinstein, 320–365. Armonk, N.Y.: M. E. Sharpe.

Wang, Qisheng. 2011. "The Battle of Hunan and the Chinese Military's Response to Operation Ichigō." In *The Battle for China: Essays on the Military*

History of the Sino-Japanese War of 1937–1945, edited by Mark Peattie, Edward Drea, and Hans van de Ven, 403–418. Stanford, Calif.: Stanford University Press.

Wang, Shaoguang. 1995. *Failure of Charisma: The Cultural Revolution in Wuhan*. Oxford: Oxford University Press.

Wang Xuezhen, Wang Xiaoting, Huang Wenyi, and Guo Jianrong, eds. 1998. *Beijing daxue jishi (yibajiuba–yijiujiuqi)* [Beijing University chronology (1898–1997)], 2 vols. Beijing: Beijing daxue chubanshe.

Wang, Y. C. 1967. "Tu Yueh-Sheng (1888–1951): A Tentative Political Biography." *Journal of Asian Studies* 26: 433–455.

Wang Youqin. 2004. *Wenge shounanzhe: Guanyu pohai, jianjin yu shalu de xunfang shilu* [Victims of the Cultural Revolution: An investigative account of persecution, imprisonment, and murder]. Hong Kong: Kaifang zuzhi she.

———. 2006. "Liushisan ming shounanzhe he Beijing daxue wen'ge" [Sixty-three victims of the Cultural Revolution at Peking University]. *Ershiyi shiji*, no. 2: 42–55.

Watson, Rubie S. 1990. "Corporate Property and Local Leadership in the Pearl River Delta, 1898–1941." In *Chinese Local Elites and Patterns of Dominance*, edited by Joseph W. Esherick and Mary Backus Rankin, 239–260. Berkeley: University of California Press.

Westad, Odd Arne. 2003. *Decisive Encounters: The Chinese Civil War, 1946–1950*. Stanford, Calif.: Stanford University Press.

White, Lynn T., III. 1978. *Careers in Shanghai: The Social Guidance of Personal Energies in a Developing Chinese City, 1949–1966*. Berkeley: University of California Press.

———. 1979. "The Road to Urumchi: Approved Institutions in Search of Attainable Goals during Pre-1968 Rustication from Shanghai." *China Quarterly*, no. 79: 481–510.

Whyte, Martin K. 1974. *Small Groups and Political Rituals in China*. Berkeley: University of California Press.

Whyte, Martin K., and William L. Parish. 1984. *Urban Life in Contemporary China*. Chicago: University of Chicago Press.

Wilbur, C. Martin. 1983. "The Nationalist Revolution: From Canton to Nanking, 1923–28." In *The Cambridge History of China*, vol. 12, *Republican China, 1912–1949, Part 1*, edited by John K. Fairbank, 527–720. Cambridge: Cambridge University Press.

World Bank. 1983. *China: Socialist Economic Development*. Vol. 1, *The Economy, Statistical System, and Basic Data*. Washington, D.C.: World Bank.

Wu Xueqing. 2002. "1976 nian 'Nanjing shijian' shimo" [The whole story behind the 1976 "Nanjing Incident"]. *Bainian chao*, no. 8: 18–24.

Wylie, Raymond F. 1980. *The Emergence of Maoism: Mao Tse-tung, Ch'en Po-ta, and the Search for Chinese Theory, 1935–1945*. Stanford, Calif.: Stanford University Press.

Xu Jiangang. 1990. " 'Sirenbang' pohai Shanghai ganbu qunzhong de sanchang yundong" [Three campaigns by the "Gang of Four" that persecuted cadres and masses in Shanghai]. *Shanghai dangshi,* no. 12: 18–25.

Yan, Fei. 2014. "Rival Rebels: The Political Origins of Guangzhou's Mass Factions in 1967." *Modern China.* doi: 10.1177/0097700414533633.

Yan, Jiaqi, and Gao Gao. 1996. *Turbulent Decade: A History of the Cultural Revolution,* translated and edited by D. W. Y. Kwok. Honolulu: University of Hawai'i Press.

Yang, C. K. 1959. *A Chinese Village in Early Communist Transition.* Cambridge, Mass.: MIT Press.

Yang, Jiang. 1984. *Six Chapters from My Life "Downunder,"* translated by Howard Goldblatt. Seattle: University of Washington Press.

Yang, Jisheng. 2012. *Tombstone: The Great Chinese Famine, 1958–1962,* translated by Stacy Mosher and Guo Jian. New York: Farrar, Straus and Giroux.

Yang, Kuisong. 2008. "Reconsidering the Campaign to Suppress Counterrevolutionaries." *China Quarterly,* no. 193: 102–121.

———. 2011. "Nationalist and Communist Guerrilla Warfare in North China." In *The Battle for China: Essays on the Military History of the Sino-Japanese War of 1937–1945,* edited by Mark Peattie, Edward Drea, and Hans van de Ven, 308–327. Stanford, Calif.: Stanford University Press.

———. 2015. "How a 'Bad Element' Was Made: The Discovery, Accusation, and Punishment of Zang Qiren." In *Maoism at the Grass Roots: Everyday Life in China's Era of High Socialism,* edited by Jeremy Brown and Matthew Johnson. Cambridge, Mass.: Harvard University Press.

Yang, Martin C. 1945. *A Chinese Village: Taitou, Shantung Province.* New York: Columbia University Press.

Yang, Tianshi. 2011. "Chiang Kai-shek and the Battles of Shanghai and Nanjing." In *The Battle for China: Essays on the Military History of the Sino-Japanese War of 1937–1945,* edited by Mark Peattie, Edward Drea, and Hans van de Ven, 143–158. Stanford, Calif.: Stanford University Press.

Yick, Joseph K. S. 1995. *Making Urban Revolution in China: The CCP-GMD Struggle for Beiping-Tianjin, 1945–1949.* Armonk, N.Y.: M. E. Sharpe.

Young, Ernest P. 1983. "Politics in the Aftermath of Revolution: The Era of Yuan Shih-k'ai, 1912–16." In *The Cambridge History of China,* vol. 12, *Republican China, 1912–1949, Part 1,* edited by John K. Fairbank, 208–255. Cambridge: Cambridge University Press.

Yue, Daiyun, as told to Carolyn Wakeman. 1985. *To the Storm: The Odyssey of a Revolutionary Chinese Woman.* Berkeley: University of California Press.

Zaleski, Eugène. 1980. *Stalinist Planning for Economic Growth, 1933–1952,* translated by Marie-Christine MacAndrew and John H. Moore. Chapel Hill: University of North Carolina Press.

Zhou, Xun, ed. 2012. *The Great Famine in China, 1958–1962: A Documentary History.* New Haven, Conn.: Yale University Press.

Zhu Di. 2005. *Yijiu wuqi nian de Zhongguo* [China in 1957]. Beijing: Huawen chubanshe.

Zweig, David S. 1978. "The Peita Debate on Education and the Fall of Teng Hsiao-p'ing." *China Quarterly,* no. 73: 140–159.

Index

Aeronautics Institute, 219–20, 221, 225, 230, 265

agriculture: and de-Stalinization, 136, 137; diversion of labor from, 158, 160, 174; and export of grain, 173; and grain procurement, 53, 171, 172, 322; and grain production, 154, 157–60, 163–64, 170–74, 332, 333; and grain rationing, 54, 57, 58, 95; and Great Leap, 153, 154–55, 157–61, 170–71, 178, 316; and income inequality, 331–32; and Mao Zedong Thought, 338; methods in, 160–61; private plots in, 182, 184, 188; and retreat from Great Leap, 180, 181, 183, 184; and socialist economy, 86, 321, 322, 332, 333; state control of, 56–60; statistics on, 170–71; subsistence, 8, 14, 58, 333; targets for, 154–55. *See also* collectivization; peasants; rural areas

All-China Federation of Trade Unions, 70

Anhui, 164, 251, 253

anti-Japanese resistance. *See* Japanese invasion

Anti May 16 Elements (*fan wu yao liu fenzi*) campaign, 284, 298

Antirightist Campaign (1957), 9–10, 148–51, 185, 316; and Cultural Revolution, 211; and Great Leap, 152, 153, 156, 160, 175, 178

April 6 directive, 244–45, 246, 248

April 22 faction, 257, 258, *illus.* 15–17

Bangladesh, 333

barter trade, 87, 88–89, 93, 176

Beijing: CCP takeover of, 35; and cleansing campaign, 271–72; and Cultural Revolution, 196–97, 202; and One Strike, Three Anti campaign, 283; and Qingming protests, 308–10; rebel factions in, 258–62; Red Guards in, 206, 223, 229–30, 235; religious sects in, 67

Beijing Commune, 230, 240

Beijing Garrison Command, 230, 312

Beijing General Knitting Mill, 278–79

Beijing Municipal Party Committee, 186, 187, 193, 199

Beijing Normal Girls' High School, 214, 215

Beijing Normal University, 230, 258, 265

Beijing Revolutionary Committee, 230, 259, 260, 262, 264, 318

Beijing Textile Factory, 280

Beria, Lavrentiy, 128

Berlin Wall, 125

bicycles, 85, 93, 96, 118, 328, 331

Bierut, Bolesław, 130, 131

birth control campaigns, 79

black market, 58. *See also* barter trade

Bolsheviks, 25, 26

border regions, 105, 148, 350n102.
    See also minority nationalities

Boxer Uprising (1900), 2–3

Bo Yibo, 222

Buddhism, 67, 353n24

Bukharin, Nikolai, 26, 154

Bulgaria, 125–26, 331

bureaucracy: and barter trade, 88; and CCP, xii, 2, 27, 40, 100, 123; and civil war, 16, 27; and class categories, 108; and Cultural Revolution, 122, 200, 201, 202–5, 285, 320; and de-Stalinization, 121, 127; and economy, 81, 98–99, 123, 340; and employment, 63, 79, 358n48; and Great Leap, 156, 158–69, 174; and labor reform, 263, 270–71; and Mao, 8–9, 81, 121, 340; and Mao Zedong Thought, 335, 339, 340–41; militarized, 39; Nationalist, 80; rural, 56–57, 59, 158–59; self-deception of, 159–62; Soviet model of, 80, 81, 120–21, 123, 174, 201, 340; traditional Chinese, 48, 79, 80; urban, 62, 63, 78–81

factions, 223, 229; and religious sects, 67; in rural areas, 15, 20, 24, 51–53, 52, 61, 100, 103–104, 106, 350n86, 351n25; secret service of, 29; Secretariat of, 193, 203, 211; and Socialist Education Movement, 189–93; and Soviet model, 80–81, 82; Stalinization of, 25, *illus.* 1; student attacks on, 207–13; surveillance by, 104–6; in urban areas, 43, 61–62, 100, 103, 104, 106; and USSR, 6–7, 15–16, 25, 100; and worker rebels, 232, 234, 236; in Yan'an, 6–7, 16, 19, 25, 27–31, 34, 38, 120. *See also* bureaucracy; cadres; Politburo, CCP

Chinese Communist Party, membership in, 15, 100–101, 270, 358n25; and class categories, 107, 108, 110, 112; Deng's review of, 303; and discipline, xi, 24–25, 38–39, 120; and education, 112–13; and elites, 8, 104, 108; and Hundred Flowers, 142, 144; incentives for, 8, 116, 120–21; of peasants, 103, 104; and political activism, 115–16, 117; recruitment for, 106–8, 117; and Second Cultural Revolution, 296, 297

Chongqing, 3, 20, 35, 251

Christianity, 60, 67, 73. *See also* Catholic Church

civil war (1945–1949), 31–35; and CCP, 15, 16–19, 38–39, 100, 123; and class categories, 110; end of, 35–37, 38; vs. Great Leap, 174, 179; hyperinflation in, 32, 34; land reform in, 18, 33; legacies of, 38–39; Lin Biao in, 31–32, 34, 35, 197; and Mao Zedong Thought, 335; mass mobilization in, 16, 31, 33–34, 39, 151, 179, 201, 350n86; Nationalists in, 3–4, 15, 16, 18, 31–35, 38; in rural areas, 18, 32, 33, 38, 53, 351n25

class labels: and Antirightist Campaign, 150–51; categories of, 108–12, 113, 357n4; and CCP membership, 107, 108, 110, 112; and cleansing campaign, 274; and college recruitment, 269; couplet on, 215; in Cultural Revolution, 210, 215–17, 223; and gender, 112; and Great Leap, 169, 181; and Hundred Flowers, 145; inheritance of, 111, 113; and land reform, 47, 49; vs. meritocracy, 113–15; and opportunities, 112–17; and punishment, 270, 298; and Rectification Campaign, 29; and Red Guards, 227, 229; registration of, 63

class struggle: and Antirightist Campaign, 150, 151; and capitalism, 26, 72, 228; and class categories, 109; and Communist victory, 17–18; and de-Stalinization, 127, 137; in East Germany, 125; and Great Leap, 152, 153, 155, 163, 166, 167, 168, 180, 181; and Hundred Flowers, 139, 144; and intellectuals, 185; and land reform,

17, 40–45, 61, 347n8 (ch.2), 351n24; Mao on, 42–43, 188; in Mao Zedong Thought, 335, 336–37, 339, 340, 341; within Party, 26, 188; in post-Stalin USSR, 121; and science, 72, 74–75; and Sino-Soviet split, 194; under socialism, 6, 151, 181, 189, 337; and Socialist Education Movement, 189, 191, 193; and socialist transformation, 148–49

Cleansing of the Class Ranks (*qingli jieji duiwu*), 12, 271–77, 318, *illus.* 13–14; criticism of, 294, 300; death rates in, 275, 276, 277, 334; and Mao cult, 281–82; and Mao Zedong Thought, 341; and One Strike, Three Anti campaign, 283–84

collectivization, 7, 53–60, 86, 123–24; and agricultural cooperatives, 54, 55, 93; bonded labor in, 57; and Great Leap, 153, 154, 156, 157–58, 163, 180, 181; and household registration, 77; and Hundred Flowers, 147–48, 315; and industry, 57–58; and land reform, 53, 56, 123; and living standards, 58–59, 333; of manufacturing, 62, 63; and Mao, 54–55, 188; and Mao Zedong Thought, 338; and organization of communes, 56–57; and peasants, 40, 53, 57, 59; in Poland, 131, 132; and post-Mao reform, 343; rapid completion of, 55–56; resistance to, 9, 56, 352n55; and rural economy, 56–59, 60; of service sector, 62, 63; and social structure, 56–59; Soviet, 129, 178, 334; stages of, 352n55; and state procurement system, 57–60

Communist Youth League, 9, 67, 106, 116, 148

Confucianism, 67

consumer goods, 85, 86, 93, 94–97, 118–19, 324, 327; rationing of, 14, 328. *See also* living standards

corruption, 59, 119, 159; attacks on, 62, 76–77, 80; and Mao's legacy, 344; of Nationalists, 68, 80; and One Strike, Three Anti campaign, 283; and Socialist Education Movement, 189, 190, 191

crime: campaigns against, 53, 62, 321; drug and sex trades, 7, 62, 69–70, 80, 321; Mao on, 41; rural, 60; suppression of, 7, 49, 63–65, 67, 68, 80; and traditional local government, 48; urban, 63–64

criticism/self-criticism: in Cultural Revolution, 193, 198, 247, 249; and Great Leap, 156, 162, 181; and intellectuals, 71–72, 73; and military control, 264, 290; and revolutionary committees, 255, 256. *See also* struggle sessions

Criticize Lin Biao and Confucius campaign, 295–302

Criticize Lin Biao campaign, 288, 289–93, 295, 296